"Roxanne Dunbar-Ortiz, one of our preeminent radical historians, once again delivers a powerful and provocative indictment of settler colonialism and white nationalism, which were foundational in building this country. It could not be more timely."
—BARBARA RANSBY,
author of *Making All Black Lives Matter*

"This is a must-read to finally discard unquestioning settler American liberalism and patriotism."
—HARSHA WALIA,
author of *Border and Rule:*
Global Migration, Capitalism, and the Rise of Racist Nationalism

"Historian Roxanne Dunbar-Ortiz rightly argues that the United States is not 'a nation of immigrants' but, more accurately, a nation of colonizers. A must-read."
—NICK ESTES (LAKOTA),
author of *Our History Is the Future*

"Roxanne Dunbar-Ortiz methodically unravels the pernicious myth of 'a nation of immigrants,' standing in the way of collective well-being on this continent and beyond."
—MANU KARUKA,
author of *Empire's Tracks: Indigenous Nations,*
Chinese Workers, and the Transcontinental Railroad

"Once again, Roxanne Dunbar-Ortiz demonstrates why she is one of the foremost historical scholars we have today, and *Not 'A Nation of Immigrants'* is her most crucial offering yet, opening new insights on this country's sordid history of systemic oppression, exclusion, and erasure."
—TIM Z. HERNANDEZ,
author of *All They Will Call You*

"Simply put, if you read this book and learn its lessons, you will have to change everything you think about the history of the United States and the terms we use to fight for justice."
—WALTER JOHNSON,
author of *The Broken Heart of America:*
St. Louis and the Violent History of the United States

"From being deeply shaken and disturbed, to ultimately feeling exhilarated and optimistic by Dunbar-Ortiz's conclusion and 'call to arms,' this is a paradigm-shifting work." —PATRICK HIGGINS, anti-imperialist historian and activist

"You will never look at US history the same way after reading *Not A Nation of Immigrants*.'" —AVIVA CHOMSKY, author of *Undocumented: How Immigration Became Illegal*

"Roxanne Dunbar-Ortiz's sweeping revisionist history challenges received versions of US origins, arguing convincingly that United States society was the product of settler colonialism and slavery rather than immigration. She demonstrates how the destruction of Indigenous nations was airbrushed out of history, to be replaced by the self-indigenization of both the earliest settlers and waves of later immigrants. Building on her magisterial *Indigenous Peoples' History of the United States*, Dunbar-Ortiz makes a significant contribution to our understanding not only of the United States but of settler colonialism as a mode of domination and elimination of Indigenous peoples and cultures." —RASHID KHALIDI, author of *The Hundred Years' War on Palestine*

"A compelling counter-narrative to America's autobiography as the making of a 'nation of immigrants.' Roxanne Dunbar-Ortiz not only chips away at this settler account but also provides the narrative glue for an emancipatory movement beyond the settler-native dichotomy." —MAHMOOD MAMDANI, author of *Neither Settler nor Native: The Making and Unmaking of Permanent Minorities*

NOT "A NATION OF IMMIGRANTS"

SETTLER COLONIALISM,
WHITE SUPREMACY,
and a HISTORY of
ERASURE and EXCLUSION

ROXANNE DUNBAR-ORTIZ

BEACON PRESS BOSTON

BEACON PRESS
Boston, Massachusetts
www.beacon.org

Beacon Press books
are published under the auspices of
the Unitarian Universalist Association of Congregations.

24 23 22   8 7 6 5 4 3 2

This book is printed on acid-free paper that meets the uncoated paper
ANSI/NISO specifications for permanence as revised in 1992.

Text design and composition by
Wilsted & Taylor Publishing Services

Library of Congress Cataloging-in-Publication Data

Names: Dunbar-Ortiz, Roxanne, author.
Title: Not "a nation of immigrants" : settler colonialism, white supremacy,
and a history of erasure and exclusion / Roxanne Dunbar-Ortiz.
Other titles: Settler colonialism, white supremacy, and a history of
erasure and exclusion
Description: Boston : Beacon Press, [2021] | Includes bibliographical
references and index.
Identifiers: LCCN 2021012712 (print) | LCCN 2021012713 (ebook) | ISBN
9780807036297 (hardcover) | ISBN 9780807036303 (ebook)
Subjects: LCSH: United States—Historiography. | Immigrants—United
States—Historiography. | United States—Emigration and
immigration—Historiography. | Settler colonialism. | Whites—Race
identity—United States—History. | United States—Race
relations—History. | United States—Ethnic relations—History.
Classification: LCC E175 .D86 2021 (print) | LCC E175 (ebook) | DDC
305.800973—dc23
LC record available at https://lccn.loc.gov/2021012712
LC ebook record available at https://lccn.loc.gov/2021012713

In memory of Ramón Casiano

1916–1931

So, if ever built, what will the United States Native American
    Genocide Memorial Museum contain? What will it exhibit?
It will be one room, a fifty-foot square with the same large
    photo filling the walls, ceiling, and floor.
There will only be one visitor allowed at any one time.
There will be no furniture.
That one visitor will have to stand or sit on the floor.
Or lie on the floor if they feel the need.
That visitor must remain in that room for one hour.
There will be no music.
The only soundtrack will be random gunshots from rifles
    used throughout American history.
Reverberation.
What will that one photo be?
It will be an Indian baby, shredded by a Gatling gun, lying
    dead and bloody in the snow.
It is a photo taken by a U.S. Cavalry soldier in the nineteenth
    century.
Very few people have seen that photo.
I have not seen that photo.
But I know it exists.
The Smithsonian keeps such photos locked away from us.
The United States wants all of us to forget the crimes it committed
    against the Indigenous.
The United States wants us to forget.
The United States wants us to forget.
The United States wants us to forget.

—Sherman Alexie, from *You Don't Have to Say You Love Me*

CONTENTS

INTRODUCTION

On George Washington's birthday, 2018, the Trump administration's director of the US Citizenship and Immigration Services, L. Francis Cissna, changed the agency's official mission statement, dropping the language of "a nation of immigrants" to describe the United States. The previous mission statement had said the agency "secures America's promise as a nation of immigrants by providing accurate and useful information to our customers, granting immigration and citizenship benefits, promoting an awareness and understanding of citizenship, and ensuring the integrity of our immigration system."[1] The revised mission statement read: "U.S. Citizenship and Immigration Services administers the nation's lawful immigration system, safeguarding its integrity and promise by efficiently and fairly adjudicating requests for immigration benefits while protecting Americans, securing the homeland, and honoring our values."[2]

The Trump administration's official negation of the US as a nation of immigrants was unlikely to change the liberal rhetoric. During Joe Biden's 2020 bid for the presidency, the campaign issued a statement on his immigration plan, titled "The Biden Plan for Securing Our Values as a Nation of Immigrants," asserting that "unless your ancestors were native to these shores, or forcibly enslaved and brought here as part of our original sin as a nation, most Americans can trace their family history back to a choice—a choice to leave behind everything that was familiar in search of new opportunities and a new life."[3] Unlike the previous "nation of immigrants" statement, the Biden campaign's did acknowledge prior and continuing Native presence, as well as specifying that enslaved Africans were not immigrants. However, the new rhetoric continues to mask the settler-colonial violence that established and maintained the United States and turns immigrants into settlers.

It appears ironic that Donald Trump positioned himself as anti-immigrant, being the son of an immigrant mother (from Scotland) and the grandson of an immigrant paternal grandfather (from Germany), as well as being married to an immigrant (from Slovenia). But Trump was not against European immigrants. In a January 2018 staff meeting on temporary immigration status, Trump asked, "Why do we need more Haitians? Take them out. . . . Why are we having all these people from shithole countries come here? Why do we want all these people from Africa here? They're shithole countries. . . . We should have more people from Norway."[4] The month before, referring again to Haitians, Trump said that they "all have AIDS," and about Nigerians, he said that once they had seen the United States, they would never "go back to their huts" in Africa.[5]

In his quest for the presidency, Trump made immigration the center of his campaign, focusing on the exclusion of Mexicans, promising to build a border wall and militarize the southern border. He claimed, "The U.S. has become a dumping ground for everybody else's problems,"[6] and railed, "When México sends its people, they're not sending their best. They're bringing drugs. They're bringing crime. They're rapists. And some, I assume, are good people, but I speak to border guards."[7]

Democratic Party politicians and liberals in general insisted that Trump and his supporters were un-American in denying the "nation of immigrants" ideology that has been a consensus for more than a half century and remains a basic principle of the Democratic Party. Most people around the world viewed the US as a nation of immigrants, while questioning if the US was backsliding on its promise in electing Trump.

With the Democratic Party back in power in 2021, the nation of immigrants rhetoric appears be firmly back in place, although the exclusionary policies of the US will continue as they did during the Obama administration.

As Osha Gray Davidson, who has collected dozens of examples of how the phrase is used, points out, "nation of immigrants" is generally used to counter xenophobic fears.[8] But the ideology behind the phrase also works to erase the scourge of settler colonialism and the lives of Indigenous peoples. "We in America are immigrants, or the children of immigrants," is the refrain.[9] The theme of Mitt Romney's acceptance speech as the Republican nominee for president in 2012 included "a nation of immigrants": "Optimism is uniquely American. It is what brought us to America. We are a nation of immigrants."[10] Speaking at a Nevada high school to a large audience, President Barack Obama said: "We are a nation of immigrants, and that means we are constantly being replenished with fighters who believed in the American dream, and it gives us a tremendous advantage over other nations."[11] Presidential candidate Hillary Clinton, in 2016, evoked a nation of immigrants, with "the Statue of Liberty reminding us of who we are and where we came from. We are a nation of immigrants, and I am proud of it."[12]

"A nation of immigrants" was a mid-twentieth-century revisionist origin story. The United States emerged from World War II undamaged by bombs and heavy population loss, which was the experience of most of the combatant nations. In fact, the United States became a beefed-up industrial powerhouse exhibiting military might, including the atomic bomb. It was poised to become the economic, military, and moral leader of the "free world." The country that actually defeated the army of the Third Reich, the Soviet Union, was the new adversary. US postwar administrations scrambled to conceal any trace of the United States' colonialist roots, system of slavery, and continued segregation as they developed military and counterinsurgent strategies to quell national liberation movements in former European colonies. The Soviet Union and Communist China, which took power in 1949, denounced Western imperialism and colonialism in Africa, Asia, Latin America, the Pacific, and the Caribbean.

In 1958, then US senator John F. Kennedy, surely informed by liberal historian Arthur Schlesinger Jr., published the influential and best-selling book *A Nation of Immigrants*, which advanced the notion that the United States should be understood or defined through the diversity of the immigrants it had welcomed since independence.[13] This thesis was embraced by US historians and found its way into textbooks and school curriculums. It is neither coincidental nor surprising that Kennedy would introduce this idea as, at the time, he was strategizing how to become the first president born of immigrants—albeit very wealthy ones—and the first Catholic president in a Protestant-dominated culture. Aspiring to the presidency, Kennedy introduced a clear context and narrative in which he could transform this negative into a positive. This founding text of "a nation of immigrants" was published during Kennedy's 1954–1960 first term as US senator from Massachusetts, two years before he was elected president.

Given that in the twenty-first century "immigration" is practically synonymous with the México-US border that was established in 1848, it is striking that Kennedy never mentioned México or Mexicans or the US-México border in the text, nor did he use the terms "Latino" or "Hispanic." Yet, this was 1958, late in the period of the contract labor Bracero Program, which began during World War II. A total of two million Mexican citizens, with the participation of the Mexican government, migrated to the United States, particularly California, as de facto indentured agricultural workers under time-limited contracts. Meanwhile, the burgeoning agribusiness industry in California recruited even more Mexican workers outside the program, without documentation or civil rights, and subject to deportation. More egregious than Kennedy's omission of any mention of México or the border is that the federal program known by its offensive official name "Operation Wetback" began during Kennedy's first year as senator and continued beyond his senatorial career through his presidency. "Operation Wetback" began in 1954 to round up and deport more than a million Mexican migrant workers, mainly in California and Texas, in the process subjecting millions—many who were actually US citizens—to illegal search and detention and deportation, forcing them to forfeit their property. Workers were deported by air and trains and ships far from the border, leaving those who were US citizens stranded and without the documents enabling them to return to their homes in the United States. "Operation Wetback" was a repeat of the Hoover administration's deportation of a million Mexicans in the 1930s, dubbed "Mexican Repatriation."

Regarding the status of Indigenous peoples in Kennedy's nation of immigrants scheme, the then senator wrote, "Another way of indicating the importance of immigration to America is to point out that every American who ever lived, with the exception of one group, was either an immigrant himself or a descendant of immigrants." The exception, Kennedy went on, was "Will Rogers, part Cherokee Indian, [who] said that his ancestors were at the docks to meet the Mayflower." But Kennedy disagreed, claiming that "some anthropologists believe that the Indians themselves were immigrants from another continent who displaced the original Settlers—the aborigines." This is the bogus speculation of US white nationalists who claim that those imagined original aborigines were in fact European, possibly Irish. A few pages on in the text, in the only other mention of Native Americans, Kennedy refers to them as "the first immigrants," while dismissing their presence as "members of scattered tribes."[14]

Equally unsettling, Kennedy includes enslaved Africans as immigrants, although the book contains the infamous drawing of a slave ship, with humans chained down on their backs, scarcely an inch between each, packed like sardines. It is striking to read how profoundly Kennedy whitewashed history by noting that "the immigration experience was not always pleasant" or that "the Japanese and Chinese brought their gentle dreams to the West Coast." He failed to mention the Chinese Exclusion Act of 1882 or its extension a few years later to all Asians.

This idea of the United States as a nation of immigrants was hatched in the late 1950s, and while Kennedy was its ambassador, it came to reflect the US ruling-class response to the challenges of the post–World War II anticolonial national liberation movements, as well as civil and human rights social movements domestically. In the United States, the National Congress of American Indians (NCAI) was founded in 1944 by D'Arcy McNickle, Helen Peterson, and other longtime Indigenous activists. At the same time, African American attorneys and other professionals were developing a legal strategy for desegregating public schools, while in 1951, more radical African Americans, including Paul Robeson and members of the Civil Rights Congress, petitioned the recently established United Nations with the detailed document *We Charge Genocide*, based on the 1948 UN Convention on the Prevention and Punishment of the Crime of Genocide. A mass movement against segregation was emerging. Around the same time, Native American activists were contextualizing the situation of Native nations within the decolonization/national liberation context, and Mexican farmworkers were organizing in the fields, defeating the Bracero Program and forming unions.

These cracks in the racial order of settler colonialism and capitalism constituted a radical departure in a society locked down in patriarchal white domination and obsessed with "real" Americanism. At the end of World War II, the US social, economic, and political order was solidly and confidently a white patriarchal Protestant republic, dominated by corporations with worldwide investments and financial reserves, along with a massive military machine far greater than that of any other country in the world. Unionization movements, primarily made up of white workers, were seduced by home ownership and middle-class status, their unions becoming business oriented with their own profit-making privatized healthcare, while the United Kingdom and Western European states responded to militant union demands to institute universal, public healthcare. Black descendants of enslaved Africans lived under a totalitarian Jim Crow system in the former Confederate states and were ghettoized and discriminated against when they escaped the South in migrations for northern and coastal industrial urban areas that were stalked by urban police forces resembling slave patrols. Native Americans were abandoned on shrunken land bases that could not support life, forcing many to find work in nearby or faraway cities, while Congress began reversing New Deal reforms that had acknowledged the Native land base and governments. This culminated in the congressional termination of Native status and land bases in 1953, an erasure that took the Red Power movement two decades to reverse. On the other hand, Irish and Central, Southern, and Eastern European immigrants, mainly Catholics and Jews, had made gains in being accepted as equal, that is, as white. But on the West Coast, US citizens of Chinese and Mexican descent were discriminated against and subject to deportation, while US citizens of Japanese descent had been incarcerated in wartime concentration camps, stripped of their property and citizenship rights. Want ads for jobs segregated men and women as well as white and Black, with lower wages for women and Black workers. Ivy League universities were overwhelmingly white and for men only, with quotas to limit the number of Jewish men.

The explosion that cracked the white republic was the 1954 US Supreme Court school desegregation decision under Chief Justice Earl Warren, who ironically, as the wartime attorney general of California, had facilitated rounding up Japanese Americans for federal incarceration. Based on decades of organizing for African American desegregation, the order for school desegregation under *Brown v. Board of Education of Topeka*, was a great achievement, but the backlash commenced immediately. White Citizens' Councils organized all over the United States, linking racial integration with communism and labeling it un-American. Within three years of the Supreme Court desegregation decision, the white nationalist John Birch Society was launched by Robert Welch, the heir to the Welch candy fortune in Massachusetts, along with others such as Fred Koch, father of the Koch brothers, who, in the twenty-first century, have funded legislation and movements to end all government benefits and promote the privatization of public goods. The Supreme Court composition was the target of this white nationalist movement, using the Republican Party as the vehicle, and had largely achieved its goals with the Trump administration's appointment of three justices, shifting the court's ideological spectrum to five ultraconservative justices, one moderate conservative, and three liberal ones.[15]

The promise of permanent progress was the context within which the Black civil rights movement grew and contributed momentum to other ongoing movements for liberation, including Puerto Rican independence and Native American self-determination, as well as the Mexican farmworker unionization movement of the 1960s, the women's and LGBTQ rights movements, and the rising student antiimperialist and anti-war movements that grew in opposition to the accelerating US war to overthrow the government of Vietnam. The counterrevolution against these advances brought Richard Nixon, then Ronald Reagan, to the presidency. By 1990, capitalism and militarism were triumphant in dissolving the Eastern European socialist bloc and organized liberation movements that had taken state power in Africa, Asia, and the Caribbean, which became shadows of their former aspirations.

The first highly visible sign of a well-organized counterrevolution inside the United States vying for political power was the evangelical antiabortion mass movement that soared following the *Roe v. Wade* Supreme Court decision to decriminalize abortion, in 1972. And, significantly, the relatively benign, century-old National Rifle Association was taken over by the Second Amendment Foundation, a white nationalist organization that had been founded in 1974 by Harlon Carter, who had been the border chief of the 1950s mass deportation of Mexicans in "Operation Wetback." This is the moment when the Second Amendment became a white nationalist cause, relying on the right-wing ideology of originalism—that is, interpreting the original meaning of the US Constitution. Parallel to postwar liberation movements, the US Central Intelligence Agency ran counterinsurgent operations against national liberation movements before and after they took power in Latin America, the Caribbean, the Pacific, and Africa, while J. Edgar Hoover's Federal Bureau of Investigation (FBI) ran similar operations against domestic movements, including COINTELPRO, a domestic counterintelligence program. Anticommunism was the connective tissue among these organizations until the socialist bloc collapsed in 1990, although anticommunism remained a social and political weapon of control domestically and internationally.

In the mid- and late 1960s and early 1970s, while the US war in Vietnam raged, the then liberal United States ruling class and its brain trust sought ways of responding to social demands while maintaining economic, political, and military domination. They settled on multiculturalism, diversity, affirmative action, and yes, the nation of immigrants ideology in response to demands for decolonization, justice, reparations, social equality, public spending on social welfare, and an end to US imperialism, counterinsurgency, and overthrow of governments. Given attempts to offset an exclusive emphasis on white settler history and the winning of the West as the nationalist triumphal narrative, "a nation of immigrants" fit the multicultural agenda. No longer was the US a "melting pot" of assimilation to whiteness but rather a many-colored quilt. Kennedy's

A Nation of Immigrants had called the United States "a nation of nations." Despite the surging of white nationalism during the twelve-year period of the Reagan-Bush administrations, by the early 1990s, the "waves of immigrants," "nation of immigrants," and Native peoples as "the first immigrants" narrative Kennedy had conceived was a consensus concept as it entered public school textbooks. This neoliberalism also triggered textbook wars over history standards, the right wing pushing for and demanding a return to the original narrative, especially founding fathers iconography to support their constitutional philosophy of "originalism."

During the nearly two centuries of British colonization of the North Atlantic coast and up to US independence, the great majority of European American settlers were Protestant Anglo-Saxon, Scots Irish, and German-speaking (before Germany was a nation-state). From 1619 onward, there was a steadily increasing number of enslaved Africans. When the United States won independence, the founders inscribed in the Constitution the requirement that citizenship could be held by white males only. Despite expressed fears, especially by Alexander Hamilton and the Federalist Party regarding immigration and the Alien and Sedition Acts, no immigration laws or procedures existed, not even during the arrival in the 1840s of 1.5 million Irish famine refugees. In 1875, the US Supreme Court declared that only the federal government, not the states, could create immigration laws and that regulation of immigration was a federal matter, though the federal immigration service was not established until 1891. Tellingly, the first federal immigration law, which created the foundation for US immigration, was the 1882 Chinese Exclusion Act. It is crucial to recognize that when and how "immigration" as such began, it was based on overt, blatant racism and a policy of exclusion, and it has never lost that taint. Although immigrant bashing is not new, and has long targeted Asian and Mexican workers, it has become a more fraught issue as it crystalized in the late twentieth century and accelerated in the early twenty-first century, targeting Mexicans, Asians, and Arab Muslims.

Yet, those who defend immigrants and immigration, mostly metropolitan liberals, often immigrants or children of immigrants themselves, employ the idea of a nation of immigrants naively without acknowledging the settler-colonial history of the United States and the white nationalist ideology it reproduces. Such advocates were caught by surprise and in shock when Mexican hating led to a successful presidential campaign in 2016, and even more surprised by the January 6, 2021, white nationalist violent takeover of the US Capitol.

The elephant in the room of immigration is the US military invasion and annexation of half of Mexican territory that spanned more than two decades, 1821 to 1848. During that same period, the eastern half of the United States was being ethnically cleansed with the forced removal of Native nations. White supremacy and settler-colonial violence are permanently embedded in US topography. The United States has a foundational problem of white nationalism that wasn't new with Nixon or Reagan or Trump.

White nationalism was inscribed in the founding of the United States as a European settler-colonial expansionist entity, the economy of which was grounded in the violent theft of land and in racial slavery, and with settlers armed to the teeth throughout its history, presently numbering over three hundred million people with the same number of firearms in civilian hands. Yet only a third of the population own those guns, an average of eight each, and 3 percent of the population own 50 percent of the guns in civilian hands. A great majority of this minority of gun owners are white men who are descendants of the original settlers, or pretend to be.[16] These descendants are most obvious in the former Confederate and border states but actually are also scattered in clusters and communities in all parts of the United States. They are the latter-day carriers of the United States' national origin myth, a matrix of stories that attempts to justify conquest and settlement, transforming the white frontier settler into an "indigenous people," believing that they are the true natives of the continent, much as the South African Boers regarded themselves as the "true" children of Israel, powered by Calvinism; the Calvinist Scots settlers did in Ulster, Ireland; or Jewish settlers in Palestine—all established by an imaginary God-given covenant making them the chosen peoples.

Given the powerful influence of this cultural, religious, and demographic minority, it is essential to acknowledge its existence in order to understand persistent white supremacy and mistrust of non-European immigrants as well as Indigenous North Americans, descendants of enslaved Africans, and Mexicans. Since the Iranian revolution of 1978–1979, the United States has launched counterinsurgent wars in Afghanistan and Arab countries, accelerating anti-Muslim bigotry in the United States. And although US evangelicals enthusiastically support the settler state of Israel, which matches their religious belief that Jesus will return when Jews return to Jerusalem, there is an underlying anti-Semitism in US white nationalism, mostly centered on a narrative of imagined Jewish domination, which works to transfer responsibility for capitalist exploitation from European and European American ruling classes to a behind-the-scenes Jewish conspiracy and control. The sacred text of US white nationalists, *The Turner Diaries*, first published in 1978, is a fictional illustration of that anti-Semitism. It is mixed with hatred of Black Americans and all people of color, the argument being that Jews use people of color to conceal their devious plan of dominance, and that the Black civil rights movement was controlled by Jews, because white nationalists deem people of color as not fully human and incapable of theory or action on their own.[17]

Those current realities and their history underlie the narrative of this book. The first chapter, "Alexander Hamilton," interrogates the neoliberal celebration of founding father Alexander Hamilton. During the Obama administration, the nation of immigrants chorus actually became a musical, celebrating Hamilton as an immigrant. More than a year after *Hamilton* premiered on Broadway in 2015, writer and director Lin-Manuel Miranda, who is of Puerto Rican heritage, staged a private performance at the White House for President Obama and his family and invitees. Before the show began, President Obama spoke in praise of the work, saying, "In the character of Hamilton—a striving immigrant who escaped poverty, made his way to the New World, climbed to the top by sheer force of will and pluck and determination—Lin-Manuel saw something of his own family, and every immigrant family."[18] Portraying Hamilton as an immigrant, although he was a British colonial settler in New York and virulently suspicious of "aliens," obfuscates while celebrating his role—as a federalist—in structuring the fiscal-military state, a capitalist state created for war. Further, portraying continental-based Puerto Ricans as immigrants obscures the continued US colonization of Puerto Rico.

Chapter 2, "Settler Colonialism," examines the genesis of the first full-fledged settler state in the world, which went beyond its predecessors in 1492 Iberia and British-colonized Ireland with an economy based on land sales and enslaved African labor, an implementation of the fiscal-military state. Both the liberal and the right-wing versions of the national narrative misrepresent the process of European colonization of North America. Both narratives serve the critical function of preserving the "official story" of a mostly benign and benevolent USA as an anticolonial movement that overthrew British colonialism. The pre-US independence settlers were colonial settlers just as they were in Africa and India or like the Spanish in Central and South America. The nation of immigrants myth erases the fact that the United States was founded as a settler state from its inception and spent the next hundred years at war against the Native Nations in conquering the continent. Buried beneath the tons of propaganda—from the landing of the English "pilgrims" (Protestant Christian evangelicals) to James Fenimore Cooper's phenomenally popular *The Last of the Mohicans* claiming settlers' "natural rights" not only to the Indigenous peoples' territories but also to the territories claimed by other European powers—is the fact that the founding of the United States created a division of the Anglo empire, with the US becoming a parallel empire to Great Britain, ultimately overcoming it. From day one, as was specified in the Northwest Ordinance, which preceded the US Constitution, the new "republic for empire," as Thomas Jefferson called the new United States, envisioned the future shape of what is now the forty-eight states of the continental US. The founders drew up rough maps, specifying the first territory to conquer as the "Northwest Territory." That territory was the Ohio Valley and the Great Lakes region, which was already populated with Indigenous villages and farming communities thousands of years old. Even before independence, mostly Scots Irish settlers had seized Indigenous farmlands and hunting grounds in the Appalachians and are revered historically as first settlers and rebels, who in the mid-twentieth century began claiming indigeneity.

Self-indigenizing by various groups of settlers is a recurrent theme in the chapters that follow.

The third chapter, "Arrivants," narrates how enslaved Africans were hauled in chains thousands of miles from their villages and fields, naked and with no belongings, and forcibly denied not only their freedom but also their languages, customs, histories, and nationalities. Not only were they used as forced and unpaid labor, but their very bodies were legally private property to be bought and sold, soon creating a thriving, legal domestic slave market, which by 1840 was of greater monetary value than all other property combined, including all the gold in circulation, all bank reserves, and all real estate.[19] The Cotton Kingdom was the fiscal-military center of US capitalist development with the industrial production of cotton, giving rise to a permanent racial capitalism, even after legalized slavery ended. Plantation owners and managers maintained a military-like counterinsurgency to control the enslaved workers, often calling in the US Army to quell insurrections. During Reconstruction, following the Civil War, Ku Klux Klan terrorism against Black political or economic power was the result of the inadequacy of the US Army occupation of the former Confederate states. Army divisions were being shifted west of the Mississippi to destroy Native nations and seize the rest of continent. With the end of the occupation, Jim Crow segregation laws gave rise to a form of policing that spread in the twentieth century to major urban areas as African Americans fled the South and which continues in the twenty-first century. The Fourteenth Amendment to the US Constitution, ratified after the Civil War, changed all-white citizenship to include those African Americans freed from enslavement (although keeping male only) but continued segregation, discrimination, and police killings, creating a kind of contingency of full citizenship.

Chapter 4, "Continental Imperialism," begins with Anglo settlers seizing the agricultural lands of Indigenous peoples of the Southeast for plantation agribusiness in cotton and importing enslaved people from the original slave states for the grueling labor. One group of US slavers moved into the Mexican province of Texas soon after the Mexican people won their decade-long war for independence from Spain. The two-year US military invasion of México that began in

1846 finally seized México City in 1848. Under US occupation, the Mexican government, through the Treaty of Guadalupe Hidalgo, was forced to relinquish the northern half of its territory. What became the states of California, Arizona, New México, Colorado, Utah, and Texas were then opened to Anglo settlement, and in the process legalizing those Anglo slavers in Texas who had already settled there illegally. The Indigenous nations in the seized territory—the Apache, Navajo, Kiowa, and Comanche—resisted US conquest for decades, as they had resisted the Spanish empire. The small class of Hispano elite in New México had welcomed and collaborated with US occupation, which led to late-twentieth-century Hispano claims of indigeneity while living on lands their ancestors had forcibly taken from the Indigenous Pueblos. This then was another site of the fiscal-military state and racial capitalism taking hold to contribute to US imperial dominance.

Chapter 5, "Irish Settling," traces the history of the English colonization of Ireland that led to the 1840s famine and the first mass migration to the United States. The Irish refugees were mostly Catholic and were despised by the majority US Anglo-Protestants, but they quickly became the nation's second-largest European-national group, a political force to be reckoned with. Many settled in urban slums and had few skills, having been agricultural workers. They took whatever unskilled jobs they could find, the men and boys working on the docks, pushing carts, digging canals, and constructing the railroad, and obtaining work as slave patrollers in the Cotton Kingdom and early urban police forces. Women worked as housekeepers and nannies, in factories, and often in sex work. How subsequent generations of Irish Americans became settlers, even one of their own ascending to the presidency in 1960, is a tragic story.[20] As well, the nearly cultlike formation of twentieth-century urban police forces and the FBI drew on Irish recruits until they became dominant and definitive as police. Racialized urban policing increasingly became a major component of the fiscal-military state.

Chapter 6, "Americanizing Columbus," tells the story of European immigrants, mostly Catholic and Jewish, who were considered not quite white. During the decade 1880–1890 alone, more than five million Central and Eastern Europeans arrived in search of jobs in burgeoning industrial and mining sites in the Northeast, Midwest, and West. Many Jewish immigrants were fleeing pogroms, while other immigrants, particularly German, were driven out by political repression and brought with them strong organizational experience that was socialistically inclined. The immigrant-driven workers' movements forced the reformulation of industrial capitalism, but their status as immigrants made them vulnerable to political deportation in the early twentieth century. During that period, Italian immigrants arrived, mostly from southern Italy. Suffering the stigma of being Catholic and also dark complected, they were subjected to extreme discrimination. Italians and other Catholic immigrants became Americanized and accepted as white through the Roman Catholic Church and a process rooted in the myth of Columbus, especially with the 1882 founding of the Knights of Columbus and the subsequent four-hundred-year anniversary of Columbus's first landing in the Caribbean. This, too, was another self-indigenizing process, with the Catholic Columbus being positioned as the original founding father of the United States. In this chapter, the important role of ideology and identity politics in building the fiscal-military state is demonstrated.

The seventh chapter, "Yellow Peril," interrogates the origins and staying power of the Western panic against Asian immigrants, starting in medieval Europe to the US Chinese Exclusion Act of May 6, 1882, and into the twenty-first century. All European American trade unions were corrupted and weakened by their anti-Chinese bigotry and support for barring Chinese workers, which accelerated the spread of yellow peril racism. In Oakland, California, socialist, union activist, and celebrity writer Jack London was among the loudest voices spewing hatred. Yellow peril suspicions also led to the internment of US citizens of Japanese descent under the liberal Franklin Roosevelt administration. Fear of Asians in general and of the Chinese in particular persists today with the US reaction to China's economic development. This chapter considers immigration from all parts of Asia, focusing on the integral relationship of US wars and immigration, highlighting the 1950–1975 US wars in Southeast Asia.

The final chapter, "The Border," argues that since the early twentieth century, immigrant hating in the United States is primarily about Mexicans (not Latinos in general) and is directly related to the unsettled border established in 1848 when the US annexed half of México. The fact that a third of the continental territory of the United States today was brutally annexed through a war of conquest is inscribed on that international border. The cold war against México has never ended, and the border is an open wound. There is a history of US aggression against México and Mexicans, militarily and economically as well as ideologically, from Walt Whitman to Patrick Buchanan and Donald Trump. This chapter traces the painful history of the recruitment and expulsion of masses of Mexican agricultural workers from the 1920s to the present. US occupations of Nicaragua and the decade-long Contra War ended the Sandinista regime. During the same period, the US government armed and advised murderous regimes in El Salvador and Guatemala. The 2008 US-backed coup in Honduras produced waves of refugees from that country who, along with Salvadorans and Mayans from Guatemala, have been criminalized and their children deported, dispersed, and even lost in the ongoing situation at the US-México border.

The conclusion grapples with the position of immigrants in a settler state. One of the unspoken requirements for immigrants and their descendants to become fully "American" has been to participate in anti-Black racism and to aspire to "whiteness." With the post–World War II work of civil rights, Black Power, and other anti-racist movements, whiteness lost much of its desirability for several generations. This process coincided with and influenced the 1965 immigration reform law that removed restrictions on immigration that had been in effect since the 1924 immigration law, which limited immigration to Western Europeans. Thereby, since the late 1960s, greater numbers of immigrants have come from the "third world," mostly from formerly colonized countries, and many of them refugees from civil wars or US-instigated wars in their countries. The "new" immigrants are more likely than past immigrants to be college graduates or professionals. They often experience racism and "othering" in their daily lives, and for Muslims in particular, virulent hostility, which for some leads to solidarity with anti-racist movements. How they as immigrants experience and react to settler colonialism varies, with some becoming dedicated to solidarity with Native peoples' resistance while most remain indifferent or even negate the demands of Indigenous communities and the reality of settler colonialism. Although immigrants from Asia, Africa, Latin America, and the Caribbean are not pressured to become "white," as immigrants were in the past, they do automatically become settlers unless they resist that default. Anti-racism and diversity are widely accepted, but the problem is the general denial or refusal to acknowledge settler colonialism. As Mahmood Mamdani observes, "The thrust of American struggles has been to deracialize but not to decolonize. A deracialized America still remains a settler society and a settler state."[21]

CHAPTER 1

ALEXANDER HAMILTON

In the waning days of the Obama presidency, the nation of immigrants liberal ideology dynamically soared with the 2015 Broadway musical *Hamilton*.[1] In the musical, Hamilton and the Frenchman Marquis de Lafayette celebrate their actions at the battle at Yorktown by proclaiming, "Immigrants: We get things done!" Of course, the United States did not yet exist in 1781 when the Yorktown engagement took place, and neither of the men were immigrants by any definition. Lafayette was a wealthy Frenchman militarist who threw his lot into the gunplay, then returned home to France without a thought of remaining in North America, while Hamilton was a citizen of Great Britain, as were all the secessionists who created the United States out of the thirteen British colonies. Citizens in Great Britain's overseas colonies, including the thirteen colonies on the Atlantic coast of North America and those in the Caribbean, were free to move wherever they wished.

Alexander Hamilton was born in 1755 in the British Caribbean slave colony of Nevis, one of dozens of British, French, Danish, and Spanish slave colonies, whose primary product was sugar. Hamilton's mother, who was French Huguenot, was from the mixed-European then Danish slave island of St. Croix, today part of the US colony the Virgin Islands. She moved with her sons back there when Hamilton was ten years old. When Hamilton's mother died, a wealthy British merchant adopted him, and he apprenticed for the export-import business of Beekman and Cruger that supplied slavers and occasionally traded slave bodies. Everything in the Caribbean was about slavery. Haitian historian of Caribbean slavery Michel-Rolph Trouillot writes, "The British and French sugar islands . . . were not simply societies that had slaves, they were *slave societies*. Slavery defined their economic, social, and cultural organisation: it was their raison d'étre. The people who lived there, free or not, lived there because there were slaves."[2]

When Hamilton was seventeen, local businessmen funded his further education at King's College (renamed Columbia College after independence) in New York. Certainly, Hamilton was moving to a different locale, but in the same manner as that of a young white man from the South Carolina colony or some other British colony in the Caribbean might move to New York for college. There were no institutions of higher learning in the British Caribbean colonies.

HAMILTON, THE FANTASY

Hamilton is a musical created by Lin-Manuel Miranda, who was born and grew up in New York City. His Puerto Rican father, Luis Miranda, moved to New York City when he was seventeen and met his wife, Luz Towns, there. Lin-Manuel Miranda presents himself and claims identification with Hamilton as an immigrant, obfuscating the reality of Puerto Rico as a US colony whose residents have been US citizens by birth since 1917. The musical is based on a best-selling 2004 novelistic hagiography of "founding father" Alexander Hamilton.[3] It may be surprising to learn that the author, Ron Chernow, was not trained in history. He holds an undergraduate degree in English and is a journalist, but has been well rewarded for his hagiographies of founding fathers and wealthy capitalists, including a biography of George Washington for which he won the 2011 Pulitzer Prize. He is also the recipient of the National Book Award for Nonfiction for his celebration of US capitalism in his book *The House of Morgan: An American Banking Dynasty and the Rise of Modern Finance*. His 1998 biography of John D. Rockefeller and 2004 biography of Alexander Hamilton were both nominated for National Book Critics Circle Awards.[4] It is significant that Miranda chose to stick closely to Chernow's history, and that Chernow was credited as the historical consultant for the Broadway musical.

In both the book and the musical, much is made about Hamilton's age, which is puzzling, since a number of the prominent "founders" were young. In 1776, Hamilton was twenty-one, but Aaron Burr was only twenty; John Marshall and Nathan Hale were twenty-one; James Madison and Henry Knox, twenty-four; John Jay was thirty; Jefferson, thirty-three; Washington, forty-four. Ben Franklin, at seventy, stood out as being twice or more the age of most.

Historian Nancy Isenberg observes that Miranda's revision of the founding era and characterization of Hamilton has more to do with current politics than history, making Hamilton a symbol for the Obama era. Miranda debuted the musical in the White House for the Obamas and their guests, and Hamilton is given Obama-like qualities: "He is superior (a genius), pragmatic (concerned with finance, credit, and banks), stubborn (unrelenting and contentious); his most far-fetched attribute is that of a hip, multicultural pop star. By this calculation, if Hamilton is Obama-esque, then the American Dream is possible."[5]

The reality couldn't be more different: Hamilton was not an immigrant and certainly no friend of immigrants either. The anti-immigrant policy of Hamilton's Federalist Party is absent from the script, allowing Hamilton to be the immigrant-made-good who was an advocate of immigrants. Isenberg notes that "a more accurate musical about the immigrant experience would be named *Gallatin* [for the politician Albert Gallatin]. Here is the story of a Swiss émigré mocked for his French accent and hounded by the Federalists who, with him in mind, crafted a constitutional amendment that aimed to deny immigrants the right to hold public office."[6]

Given the contradiction between Miranda's celebration of Hamilton as an immigrant and the reality of Hamilton's negative stance on immigration, the word "immigrant" was fraught. Miranda blatantly created a presentist hero in the guise of an immigrant, assuring his mostly liberal audiences that the story was their story, an immigrant story with an inspirational message to counter the toxic resurgence of nativism that would soon bring Donald Trump to the presidency. However, the real-life Hamilton responded to Thomas Jefferson's proposal to open doors for immigration and citizenship. "Hamilton protested, fretting about the corruption of national character, and (revealingly) claiming that if only 'native citizens' had voted in 1800, Jefferson wouldn't be president."[7]

Article I, Section 8 of the original 1789 US Constitution enumer-
ated the powers of Congress, including "to establish a uniform Rule
of Naturalization." Congress duly passed the Naturalization Act in
1798, requiring immigrants to wait fourteen years to become naturalized citizens. The law was passed under the guise of protecting national security, but most historians conclude that it was intended by
the ruling Federalists—Hamilton's party—to decrease the number
of voters. At the time, most immigrants supported Thomas Jefferson
and his Democratic-Republican party, the political rivals of the Federalists. The law had only limited effect, because many immigrants
rushed to become naturalized before it went into effect, and states
could at the time make their own more lenient naturalization laws.
In 1798, the Federalists pushed through the Naturalization Act, one
of the four Alien and Sedition Acts (the other three are the Alien
Friends Act, Alien Enemies Act, and Sedition Act). The Alien and
Sedition Acts were passed by the US Congress amid widespread fear
that war with France was imminent. The four laws—which remain
controversial to this day—restricted the activities of foreign residents in the country and limited freedom of speech and of the press.
Like the Naturalization Acts of 1790 and 1795, the 1798 act also
restricted citizenship to "free white persons"—*persons* being male.[8]

Hamilton was no scrappy immigrant as portrayed by Chernow
and Miranda. He arrived in New York when it was a British colony and
was a member of the elite ruling class, a prominent New York politician, a former state assemblyman, a longtime state resident, and
married into the prominent and influential New York Schuyler slaver family sixteen years before his resignation from the office of
secretary of the treasury. Although Chernow's and Miranda's dubious claims that Hamilton was an anti-racist abolitionist have been
effectively challenged, few appear to question the central theme of
Miranda's script: that Hamilton was an immigrant who thereby had
a larger view of the world and had sympathy for the underdog. But
Hamilton did not sympathize with immigrants or any kind of underdog. Hamilton took a hard line on the presence of foreigners and
naturalization of citizenship.

The view of Hamilton as immigrant and immigrant friendly was
not invented by Ron Chernow or Lin-Manuel Miranda. Even as

early as 1954, historian James Morton Smith criticized Hamilton biographers for insisting on Hamilton's liberalism, particularly regarding immigration, thereby absolving him from any involvement in invoking the draconian Alien and Sedition laws. In fact, most biographers explicitly deny that Hamilton was involved and portray him as a champion of civil liberties. Smith points out that one biographer even asserts that the Federalists "mutinied" against Hamilton's recommendation of moderation. In John C. Miller's heralded study of the Alien and Sedition Acts, he claims that Congress acted against Hamilton's advice. Even two of Jefferson's biographers credit Hamilton for opposing their passage, one characterizing Hamilton as having been an earlier and stronger opponent of the bills than Jefferson.[9]

Hamilton not only opposed liberal immigration, he also supported a forceful expulsion policy. "My opinion," he informed Pickering, who became the chief enforcement officer of the Alien and Sedition laws, "is that the mass [of aliens] ought to be obliged to leave the country." He suggested two exceptions, however, to his proposed policy of mass removal. "The provisions in a Treaty in favor of Merchants," he wrote, "ought to be observed and there ought to be *guarded* exceptions of characters whose situations would expose them too much if sent away and whose demeanor among us has been unexceptionable. There are a few such. Let us not be cruel or violent."[10] This letter, which is supposed to illustrate Hamilton's leniency, gives insight into Hamilton's ideas of cruelty and violence as applied to aliens. Hamilton did not object to the section in the bill that provided that any alien could be deported without trial by jury, or to the one that stipulated that any alien who returned to the United States in violation of a removal order by the president might be imprisoned for life at hard labor without trial by jury. His sole remedy for the cruelty of the bill was protection for foreign merchants and for the few aliens whose demeanor had been "unexceptionable." Hamilton apparently thought that it would be neither cruel nor violent to uproot the mass of peaceable aliens in the United States and deport them.[11]

Federalists in Congress had proposed bills to deny naturalized citizens the right to hold office or vote. The Alien Act of 1798 was a Federalist initiative pushed through Congress during the threat of war with France. The context in which the Federalists created laws to limit immigration was the ongoing French Revolution. As politicians, the Federalists were also responding to a base that wanted to restrict US citizenship to protect a homogeneous nation against influences represented by French universalism. The United States needed to resist foreign ideas that immigrants might bring with them. The Federalists had conjured an ideology of United States citizenship that celebrated its presumably revolutionary birth and that was unrestrained by traditional provincialism, but in an attempt to define and legislate a unique nationality, they envisioned the US as a bulwark against the threat of world revolution. Irish Republicans were particularly targeted, as they were enthusiastic supporters of international revolution.[12] Although most aspects of the Alien and Sedition Acts were repealed, the paranoia embedded in them remains a factor in US political culture, and a reality. President Franklin Roosevelt, following the Japanese attack on Pearl Harbor in 1941, invoked the Alien Enemies Act to give legal color to the internment of citizens of Japanese descent as well as those designated as enemy aliens from Japan and Axis countries, requiring them to register and be subject to arrest.

Nancy Isenberg, author of *Fallen Founder: The Life of Aaron Burr*, takes exception to Miranda's portrayal of Aaron Burr in the musical as an envious and power-hungry man without a moral compass and who is obsessed with diminishing Hamilton, leading to the duel and Hamilton's death. In reality, Burr was the opposite. Devoted to the values of the Enlightenment, he advocated criminal justice reform, press freedom, and the rights of women and immigrants. The Federalists accused Burr of "revolutionizing the state," because as a member of the New York State Legislature, he backed funding for internal improvements of roads and bridges and for debtor relief, and establishing a more democratic method of electing state senators. And significantly, given the musical's characterization of Hamilton as pro-immigrant, it was actually Burr who, among the politicians, was uniquely friendly to immigrants. Burr gave an eloquent speech in the New York State Assembly saying that "America stood with open arms and presented an asylum to the oppressed of every nation."[13]

NOT AN ABOLITIONIST

Chernow and Miranda have been mostly lauded by audiences and theater critics, but they have also received sharp criticism regarding race and slavery and the portrayal of Hamilton as an abolitionist. Ishmael Reed, an African American writer, poet, novelist, playwright, and founder of the American Book Award, wrote, directed, and produced a two-act play, *The Haunting of Lin-Manuel Miranda*, which premiered in 2019.[14] As a writer, he clarifies, "I agree with my critics the 'Hamilfans' that Miranda has the right to take liberties with their [the founders] histories, but in doing so, he covered up their crimes. Some of those who should know better have endorsed this billion-dollar entertainment. President Obama aided the production by recording George Washington's Farewell Address with a Black choir humming softly in the background. George Washington raffled off slave children to pay his debts." Reed effectively challenges the characterization of Hamilton as an abolitionist, noting that when the successful 1791 slave revolt in Haiti occurred, Hamilton sided with the French slaveholders, not the self-emancipated slaves.[15] Reed also condemns Miranda for casting Black and Latino actors for the roles of Hamilton and the other "founding fathers," most of them slavers, yet having no actual enslaved Africans appear in the musical.[16]

Annette Gordon-Reed, Harvard professor of history and law, who won the Pulitzer Prize for her book *The Hemingses of Monticello*, writing nearly a year after the musical debuted, observed how little serious criticism the musical had received. She recognized that it was amazing theater but worried that audiences were absorbing it as accurate history. She wonders what the musical's effect would be if played, accurately, by all white actors.[17] Historian Lyra Monteiro is troubled by all the Black and Brown bodies on stage without a single enslaved character or even a free Black person. Although a few mentions of slavery are scattered in the lyrics, mainly concerning Jefferson, it's very likely that one viewing the musical could assume that slavery did not exist or, if it did, played little role in the lives and wealth of the men who created the United States. Yet, although slavery is hardly mentioned in the musical, antislavery is central to the portrayal of Hamilton. Following Hamilton's death in the musical, his wife, Eliza, sings, "I speak out against slavery. / You could have done so much more if you only had / Time."[18]

Although the family Hamilton married into was the ultrawealthy, slaveholding, and slave-trading New York Schuylers, the source of their wealth is not mentioned in the musical, nor is Hamilton's role in the family slave trade revealed. As Sarah Churchwell writes, "Anyone who didn't know better would finish *Hamilton* innocent of the fact that George Washington owned slaves, much less that Alexander Hamilton himself bought and sold them on behalf of his wife's family. Such stories try to have it both ways: for their heroes to be representative Americans, while erasing the vicious ways in which they truly were representative. The fact that everyone was doing it is not a defense, it merely measures the scale of the crime."[19]

In the fall of 2020, a researcher at the Schuyler Mansion found evidence that had long been overlooked in letters and Hamilton's own account books indicating that he not only bought and sold slaves but also personally owned slaves. The researcher, Jessie Serfilippi, was unequivocal: "Not only did Alexander Hamilton enslave people, but his involvement in the institution of slavery was essential to his identity, both personally and professionally. . . . It is vital that the myth of Hamilton as 'the Abolitionist Founding Father' end."[20] The headline of the story published in the *San Francisco Chronicle* read "New Research Paper Claims Abolitionist Owned Slaves," continuing to insist that Hamilton was an abolitionist, which he never was. Abolitionists by definition did not own or trade slaves.[21]

Four years before *Hamilton* opened, in her critique of two biographies of Hamilton, Michelle DuRoss, a historian of Early America, challenged the characterization of Alexander Hamilton as having been an antislavery activist or abolitionist or having had a sympathy for or even identification with enslaved Africans. She clarifies that although Hamilton was not a vocal advocate for slavery, when the issue of slavery conflicted with his personal ambitions and his nearly fanatic belief in property rights, Hamilton chose those goals.

Regarding his ambitions, Hamilton was tenacious in his desire to rise to the highest position possible, first in New York society, then in the United States once it was established. Most of the wealthy and influential men in positions of power who could assist him in that ambition were slave owners or slave traders. As for Hamilton sympathizing or identifying with enslaved Africans, such claims are consistently from secondary sources, and there are no existing documents that would support the claim. In his extensive correspondence, there is no mention of the horrors of plantation slavery in the West Indies. Historians describe the horrors and then attribute to Hamilton an opinion that he never expressed or alluded to.[22] That Hamilton did not describe the horrors of slavery and the slave trade in the Caribbean surely could more accurately be interpreted to mean that he took the situation for granted, as normal.

Ron Chernow's biography of Hamilton on which Miranda based his script claimed that Hamilton "saw emancipation of slaves as an inseparable part of the struggle for freedom."[23] Chernow, as have other Hamilton biographers, base this view on the fact that Hamilton was a member of the New York Society for the Promotion of the Manumission of Slaves. A previous Hamilton biographer, conservative journalist Richard Brookhiser, wrote that "the society did successfully push to make slavery illegal in New York—a considerable achievement in a state where slavery was a real presence."[24] However, DuRoss faults both biographers for citing evidence of the society's impact on New York laws, as New York did not abolish slavery until 1827. She also points out that Hamilton's devotion to property rights was not compromised by voluntary manumission of slaves, as the members of the society could still own slaves. Hamilton's membership in the New York Antislavery Society gave him yet another opportunity to be a part of upper-class New York society.[25] Historian Phil Magness writes, "Keep in mind that Hamilton was a prolific newspaper editorialist, penning hundreds of typically pseudonymous tracts on all manner of political issues of his day. A striking feature of the Hamiltonian corpus is the general absence of any clear, unequivocal exposition of the 'abolitionist' viewpoint so many of his biographers have attributed to him."[26]

BOOTSTRAPS ASCENDENCY

Hamilton supported the infamous three-fifths clause in the Constitution, which gave slavers voting representation that increased their voting and legislative power based on three-fifths of every individual they held in slavery. Hamilton believed that the right to vote should be based on property ownership, and the more property one owned, the greater the power of representation. The musical and the book use a version of the historical character Hamilton to promote a classic US "bootstrap" narrative, as in the rap stanza that attributes success to working hard and being smart and a self-starter. As Monteiro points out, the musical is "insidiously invested in trumpeting the deeds of wealthy white men, . . . and though it makes fun of Jefferson, he is nonetheless a pivotal figure."[27] It is the perfect entertainment to popularize the rampant neoliberalism of the late twentieth and early twenty-first centuries and to lay the burden of failure on those who don't make it in a system designed to benefit inherited wealth.

In an interview with the *Wall Street Journal*, *Hamilton* cast member Leslie Odom Jr., who is Black, said, "I was a student of African-American history. I cared way more about the achievements and hard-won battles of black people in this country than I did about the founding fathers. But this show has been such a gift to me in that way because I feel that it's my history, too, for the first time ever. We all fought in the Revolutionary War. I think this show is going to hopefully make hundreds of thousands of people of color feel a part of something that we don't often feel a part of."[28] Monteiro asks essential questions: "But is it necessarily a good thing to feel ownership over a celebratory, white narrative of the American past? Is it a good thing for people of color to feel connected to the story of Hamilton, Washington, Jefferson, Madison, and Burr? Or is this the historical version of the Clarks' Doll Test that was so pivotal in the *Brown v. Board of Education* decision, encouraging people of color to see the important past as limited to the deeds of white men, while further silencing the historical role of people of color?"[29]

While the show was on Broadway and as the play appeared in

other venues around the country, Miranda provided free performances for young people, with whole classes attending. Due to the phenomenal embrace of *Hamilton*, foundation money poured in to develop curricula based on the play for school districts. Young people of color, and especially immigrant youth, were enraptured by the validation offered them in what Miranda presented as the true America, providing a hero to emulate by working hard, always being in the room where "it happened." The modern Horatio Alger myth had been created. It seems cruel to delude aspiring young people by offering a myth; it also appears cynical, as Miranda stated in the coffee table book he created to accompany the play: "Ron [Chernow] tells you a story and he's the star of the story. I tell you a story and I'm the star of the story. History is entirely created by the person who tells the story."[30] Yes, and in Chernow's and Miranda's telling, that's the problem, reinforcing as they have the liberal version of the US triumphant origin story.

THE FISCAL-MILITARY STATE

US economic conservatives have long admired Alexander Hamilton, while in the past, liberals have favored Jeffersonians. With Miranda's play, liberals en masse rallied, mainly due to the play's celebration of immigrants, portraying Hamilton as a founding immigrant. But neither conservatives nor liberals nor Hamilton biographers have dealt with Hamilton's role in creating a Constitution that has been characterized as establishing the first "fiscal-military state"—that is, a state created for making war.[31] This aspect of Hamilton's role is crucial to understanding the structure of the settler-colonial state entirely dependent on imported labor, both enslaved (African) and free (immigrant). The United States was thus founded as the first constitutional capitalist state and an empire on conquered land, with capital in the form of slaves and land (real estate). It is crucial to understand that this was exceptional in the world at that time and has remained exceptional. The capitalist firearms industry was among the first successful modern corporations, an initiative of Alexander

Hamilton. This was the Springfield armory in western Massachusetts established by the Continental Congress in 1777.[32] Arms production is one of the few industries that survived late twentieth-century deindustrialization. By 1840, the United States was the leading economic powerhouse in the world, having expanded its claimed territory beyond the Mississippi and establishing the Cotton Kingdom.

Stanford law professor and historian Gregory Ablavsky emphasizes the centrality of Indian affairs in creating the Constitution, particularly provisions concerning federalism and the fiscal-military state. He highlights how ratification created a Constitution committed to the violent expropriation of the Indigenous territories bordering the thirteen states. The Constitution created a people empowered to sustain a powerful military to carry out conquest of the continent, with the full participation of the settlers. This was what the war for independence was fought for, with great sacrifices; this is what the Anglo-American settlers desired.

For his analysis of the Constitution, Ablavsky borrowed historian Max Edling's term "fiscal-military state." Edling took the term from the historical literature on British state formation, in which it refers to "a state primarily designed for war." Edling writes that the United States did not adopt the British model wholesale, rather the Constitution created a national government that was "light, and inconspicuous," but which "held the full powers of the 'fiscal-military state' in reserve."[33] US historians make much of the fact that the founders did not create a large military, and thereby ignore military history. But the initial importance of the US military was mainly for the gradual taking of the continent, not for engagements with European militaries. The immediate objective of the Washington administration's policy was to secure the Ohio territory that the British had relinquished to the United States. However, lands of this territory were owned and densely inhabited by Indigenous nations, among them the Miami and the Shawnee, with extensive village networks, transportations routes in roads and rivers, and meticulously tended farmlands. Although committed to appropriating these already inhabited lands, the administration desired to buy off rather than fight the Native peoples. British colonists had already forged into Ohio country before the revolution, against British prohibition to do so, and the Washington administration realized that the interests of the settlers and the Natives were at odds. Washington believed that the government had to be the arbiter of the conflict. Edling writes, "In the end, however, the government never managed to reconcile these clashing interests but used the army to destroy the Indian tribes, thereby setting a pattern that would often be repeated as the republic pursued its westward course of empire."[34]

Hamilton argued the federal military was too weak to overawe the "savages." The expansionist states of Georgia, Pennsylvania, and New York sought and gained federal protection of settler land claims. Hamilton and other Federalists invoked "savages" to justify a stronger federal state and a standing army. This elevated the dispossession of Indigenous peoples into a constitutional principle.[35] Ablavsky writes, "The 'savages' Hamilton referenced at the Convention were thus both impetus and justification for the creation of a federal standing army supported through direct taxation. This militarist constitutional solution to Indian affairs sought a fiscal-military state that would possess the means to dominate the borderlands at Indians' expense. While Madison's argument for centralization languished, Hamiltonian invocation of the 'savage' threat, embraced partly out of expediency, became an important part of Federalist rhetoric."[36]

Hamilton was right, of course. Native nations did resist settler spread and were an existential threat to settlers' ambitions of "free land" and empire for the entire nineteenth century. The first attempted military moves against the Indigenous confederacy in 1790 and 1791 were catastrophic. The United States spent $5 million to triple the size of the army, making up five-sixths of all federal expenditures from 1790 to 1796. The Militia Act of 1792, the forerunner of the Insurrection Act of 1807, mandated a genocidal policy against the Indigenous nations of the Northwest Territory, allowing for federal troops to eliminate the resistant communities in order to allow settlers to occupy the land. The Militia Act was used two years later against Appalachian settlers in western Pennsylvania who were protesting an unfair tax on their distilleries. This was the sole work of Hamilton. Although secretary of the treasury, he was still a military commander who led twelve thousand federal troops to crush the minor "whiskey" rebellion.[37] Only with unlimited counterinsurgent war—destroying Indigenous towns, burning crops and food storage, driving inhabitants into peripheries as refugees—did the United States prevail, seizing most of present-day Ohio. Military historian John Grenier writes, "For the first 200 years of our military heritage, then, Americans depended on arts of war that contemporary professional soldiers supposedly abhorred: razing and destroying enemy villages and fields; killing enemy women and children; raiding settlements for captives; intimidating and brutalizing enemy noncombatants; and assassinating enemy leaders. . . . In the frontier wars between 1607 and 1814, Americans forged two elements—unlimited war and irregular war—into their first way of war."[38] Unlimited US wars against Native nations remained a near constant for the next century. This is the military aspect of the fiscal-military state created by the Constitution.

Simple military conquest was only one part of the process. The framing of the bloody wars to come cast the Indians as aggressive "savages" with the Anglo settlers as victims. Seventy years later, the US Army had jackbooted across the continent to the Pacific, incorporating seventeen new states and ethnically cleansing the continent east of the Mississippi by forcibly removing Native peoples. Although the legal term "genocide" did not exist until the mid-twentieth century, it was embedded in the conscious designs of the Constitution's drafters. Ablavsky notes that the Constitution was not a document of restraint, as many argue; rather it was the foundation of a powerful early national state, whose authority was strongest on its peripheries.[39]

> In short, the Constitution created a national state that was simultaneously weak and strong. . . . This was precisely what the expansionist states and Anglo-American settlers wanted. Their libertarian streak ran only as far as self-interest, for they welcomed a strengthened federal state as long as it was an imperialist one, focused on projecting power against the Indians

rather than against its citizens. The Hamiltonians would solve the problem of Indian affairs by committing the federal state to empowering, not restraining, the inexorable westward tide.[40]

HAMILTON, A MILITARY MAN

Conquest of the continent, including the military conquest of México, which ceded half its territory to the United States, was only the beginning of US imperialism. Native nations were the first subjects of US empire, but not the last. When the founders were writing the Constitution, Indian affairs were a central site of nation-state formation, establishing a template for later imperial projects. Ablavsky writes that "the Federalists' strategic deployment of the rhetoric of savagery anticipated future debates, as Indians became the stock template for America's subsequent cross-cultural encounters, their supposed primitiveness evolving into a free-floating discourse to justify rule over other purportedly inferior peoples." The constitutional structures that were created to take Indigenous lands and control the continent—the definition of the national fiscal-military state—became the basis of US overseas imperialism.[41] The "savage" as enemy has endured as the justification for US military intervention. President George W. Bush's Justice Department employed that precedent from nineteenth-century "Indian wars" to legitimize military actions and torture in its "War on Terror."[42] An arc can be drawn from that formative time to the 2011 SEAL Special Forces Operation Neptune Spear to kill Osama bin Laden, which was code-named "Geronimo." Once bin Laden was killed, one of the commanders reported "Geronimo E-KIA," E-KIA being code for "enemy killed in action."

Historian William Hogeland, writing before Lin-Manuel Miranda had conceived *Hamilton*, observed that "Neo-Hamiltonians of every kind are blotting out a defining feature of his thought, one that Hamilton himself insisted on throughout his turbulent career: the essential relationship between the concentration of national wealth and the obstruction of democracy through military force. . . .

Using the military to trounce the rule of law and violate civil rights was integral to his vision of federal power, national wealth, and a strong union." Hogeland sees Hamilton's success in the Whiskey Rebellion as inspiring an almost obsessive militarism as he grew older. The Whiskey Rebellion of 1794 was a mass settler protest to taxation in western Pennsylvania, which Washington and Hamilton violently put down at the head of twelve thousand troops. "Out of office, Hamilton continued to order around his hacks in the Adams cabinet (or as the PBS biography puts it, he 'advised' them), hoping to contrive an all-out war with France. Hamilton also envisioned leading the U.S. army into Spanish Florida, then continuing into Central and South America."[43] As Hogeland told an interviewer, "They just aren't getting what was important about him. It was the intertwining of military force and wealth concentration as almost the definition of nationhood."[44] That's the fiscal-military state, a capitalist state created for war.

A hundred years' war followed, and hardly a day passed without counterinsurgent war against one Native nation or another, or many at once. The road map (literally, the maps) for the conquest of the continent was the Northwest Ordinance promulgated by the Continental Congress in 1787, which drew up plans and military strategies for seizing this vast region of dozens of Native nations, whose citizens lived in villages surrounded by their self-subsistent food crops of maize, corn, squash, and pumpkins. During the previous two decades, George Washington, leading the Virginia colony militia, had encroached into this territory through the Appalachians, mapping the land and selling plots to land-poor white farmers, who then illegally settled on the unceded lands. Although Britain claimed the territory, in a 1763 proclamation, it barred settlement west of the thirteen colonies. The drive of colonial settlers to expand over the mountain range to appropriate this territory was a primary motivation for independence from Britain. With the establishment of the United States, the first structure of settler colonialism was erected.

The Society of the Cincinnati, a hereditary society that still exists, was founded in 1783 and composed of the military officers of the Continental Army. General George Washington was the founding president general and served as such until his death in 1799. General Alexander Hamilton succeeded him as president general in 1780. The badge of office was a diamond eagle. The society was named after Cincinnatus, a fifth-century Roman Empire war hero.[45] The city of Cincinnati, chartered by the United States in 1802 on the Ohio River and the border of Kentucky, was also named after Cincinnatus. The locale had been the heart of the Shawnee Nation. It was the crucible of the founding of the United States in genocide.

CHAPTER 2

SETTLER COLONIALISM

As the late Patrick Wolfe emphasized in his groundbreaking research, settler colonialism is a structure, not an event.[1] Wolfe was an Australian anthropologist and historian, one of the initial theorists and historians of settler colonialism. He researched, wrote, taught, and lectured internationally on race, colonialism, Indigenous peoples' and Palestinian histories, imperialism, genocide, and critical history of anthropology. He was also a human rights activist who used his scholarship and voice to support the rights of oppressed peoples.

But in the case of the United States, settler colonialism was more than a colonial structure that developed and replicated itself over time in the 170 years of British colonization in North America preceding the founding of the United States. The founders were not an oppressed, colonized people. They were British citizens being restrained by the monarch from expanding the thirteen colonies to enrich themselves. They were imperialists who visualized the conquest of the continent and gaining access to the Pacific and China. Achieving that goal required land, wealth, and settler participation. They devised a unique plan, manifest in the 1787 Northwest Ordinance, which was created during the War of Independence by the Continental Congress and reenacted at independence by the US Congress in 1789. Designed as what historian Howard Lamar called "an internal colonial system for the West," its provisions were borrowed in part from the British system of settler colonialism in Ulster, Ireland, and the thirteen North American colonies. However, this invention was something new, the constitutional construction of the fiscal-military settler state, with both ethnic cleansing of the Native presence and chattel slavery producing racial capitalism.

The Northwest Ordinance provided for eventual settler self-government once European American settlers outnumbered the Indigenous population. This land act guaranteed to the settlers property, civil rights, religious freedom, trial by jury, representational legislation, and public education. That ultimate conclusion, however, was preceded by successive stages of colonial development, from military ethnic cleansing and control to a federally appointed territorial government to a semi-representational government to, finally, admission into the United States as a state. This constituted a unit of the fiscal-military nation-state. Lamar observes that apologists for US expansionism do not see the ordinance as a reflection of colonialism but rather as a means of "reconciling the problem of liberty with the problem of empire."[2] The founders were unapologetic imperialists, chips off the old block of British imperialism, but with the added conceit of an "empire for liberty," as Thomas Jefferson conceived the future. Historian David Reynolds writes that Jefferson believed the US empire was destined to assume the responsibility to spread freedom around the world, starting with the North American continent and intervening abroad. US foreign policy was stamped with this concept and has provided the ideological motivation for all US wars and interventions.[3]

Through the Northwest Ordinance, the United States created a unique land system among colonial powers, including Britain. In the US system, land itself—not just what was produced from the land, such as agriculture, mining, logging, grazing, and so on—was the most important exchange commodity for the accumulation of capital and building the national treasury. In order to comprehend the apparently irrational genocidal policy of the US government toward the presence of Native nations on the land, the centrality of land sales in building the economic base of the US capitalist system must be the frame of reference. This policy was embedded in the design of the fiscal-military state. As Wolfe summed up the issue, "Tribal land was tribally owned—tribes and private property did not mix. Indians were the original communist menace. . . . Whatever settlers may say—and they generally have a lot to say—the primary motive for elimination is not race (or religion, ethnicity, grade of civilization, etc.) but access to territory. Territoriality is settler colonialism's specific, irreducible element."[4]

However, Wolfe didn't quite understand the difference for the US founders between territory and land and the centrality of land as real estate, but he makes a correct point about US American obsession with private property. Regarding the communal nature of Native societies, Senator Henry Dawes, arguing in the 1880s for allotment of collectively held Indigenous lands, said, "The defect of the [reservation] system was apparent. It is Henry George's system and under that there is no enterprise to make your home any better than that of your neighbors. There is no selfishness, which is at the bottom of civilization. Till this people will consent to give up their lands, and divide among their citizens so that each can own the land he cultivates they will not make much more progress."[5]

PRIVATE PROPERTY ON STEROIDS

Although private property in land had long been a fact of life in Europe, it was demarcated by the contour of streams, rivers, tree lines, rock formations, and mountains and was reserved for the economic and political elite. The United States, being founded as a settler-colonial, fiscal-military state, created something new under the sun, the plat system of privatizing land into marketable units. The Northwest Ordinance spawned the Public Land Survey System (PLSS), a unique surveying method to plat, that is, divide land, transforming it into property for sale and settling, plots of 160 acres with sections of four plots, or 640 acres. As the US took more land with the Louisiana Purchase, the Oregon Territory, and half of México, the government promised "free land" to Europeans and European Americans for the purpose of recruiting and motivating settlers to squat on Indigenous peoples' lands. With Indigenous resistance to the squatters, the army would be dispatched.[6] The pieces of paper, deeds representing units of land, made up the commodity market that built the United States capitalist system and remains its central factor. The other main commodity until 1860 was human, the enslaved African body with its deed of sale.

Historian Donald Harman Akenson aptly describes the implementation of the Land Ordinance:

> Its importance was equal to that of the trumpet-toned Constitution of 1787. It did not deal with ethereal concepts such as the pursuit of happiness but instead declared in practical terms how the land from the Appalachian Mountains up to the Mississippi River was to be conquered. This was to be done by surveyors' chains, each twenty-two yards in length. The measuring began at an arbitrary point in the Ohio Territory, and invisible lines were drawn on the land to form a grid of perfect rectangles marked by cairns, iron bars, and the occasional brass plate cemented onto a masonry base. Each of the rectangles had its own map reference, and as the U.S. imperium expanded, the grid eventually reached the Pacific coast and stretched between Mexico and British North America. The lines on the land not only conquered natural topography but also made possible the liberation of parcels of land from their previous occupants and their efficient allocation to newcomers.[7]

This was the implementation of the fiscal-military state, the state made for war in order to appropriate property.

From the beginning of surveys in the newly claimed Northwest Territory to the Pacific Ocean, the lands claimed by the surveys were already populated with Indigenous peoples, but the land was treated as *terra nullius*, unpopulated land, while the Indigenous nations and communities, reduced in numbers by genocidal warfare that caused displacement, starvation, crowded refugee situations, and resultant infectious diseases, were forced onto army-guarded reservations, dependent on government rations. The Indigenous peoples of the large Native agricultural nations of the South were forcibly relocated to west of the Mississippi. This is important for understanding not only how settler colonialism defines the United States and all its institutions, but also, as Mahmood Mamdani has documented,

that "all of the defining institutions of settler colonialism as practiced in the nineteenth, twentieth, and twenty-first centuries were
first developed in North America. The US tribal homeland was the
prototype not only for the South African reserve but also the Nazi
concentration camp."[8]

FREE-SOILER IMPERIALISM

During the Civil War, President Abraham Lincoln did not forget his
Free-Soiler base who brought him to that high office. "Free-soil"
meant free of chattel slavery for white commercial farmers, like Lincoln's family, who could not afford to purchase enslaved bodies.
Congress, at Lincoln's behest, passed the Homestead Act in 1862, as
well as the Morrill Act, the latter transferring large tracts of Indigenous land to the states to establish land grant universities. The Pacific
Railroad Act provided private companies with nearly two hundred
million acres of Indigenous land.[9] With these massive land grabs,
the US government broke multiple treaties with Indigenous nations
whose people were still living there. It would take genocidal military force to evict them. Most of the western territories, including
Colorado, North and South Dakota, Montana, Washington, Idaho,
Wyoming, Utah, New México, and Arizona, were delayed in achieving statehood, because Indigenous nations resisted appropriation of
their lands and outnumbered the settlers—until they didn't. So, the
colonization plan for the West established during the Civil War was
carried out over the following three decades of war and land grabs.

Under the Homestead Act, 1.5 million homesteads were granted
to settlers west of the Mississippi, comprising nearly three hundred
million acres (a half million square miles) taken from the Indigenous
collective estates and privatized for the market. The dispersal of
landless settler populations from east of the Mississippi served as an
"escape valve" for the ruling class, lessening the likelihood of class
conflict as the Industrial Revolution accelerated the use of cheap immigrant labor. Little of the land appropriated under the Homestead
Act was distributed to actual single-family homesteaders. It was
passed instead to large operators or land speculators. The land laws
appeared to have been created for that result. An individual could

acquire 1,120 or more acres of land, even though homestead and preemption (legalized squatting) claims were limited to 160 acres.[10] A claimant could obtain a homestead and secure title after five years or pay cash within six months. Then he could acquire another 160 acres under preemption by living on another piece of land for six months and paying $1.25 per acre. While acquiring these titles, he could also be fulfilling requirements for a timber culture claim of 160 acres and a desert land claim of 640 acres, neither of which required occupancy for title. Other men within a family or other partners in an enterprise could take out additional desert land claims to increase their holdings even more. As industrialization quickened, land as a commodity—"real estate"—remained the basis of the US economy and capital accumulation.[11]

The federal land grants to the railroad barons—carved out of Indigenous territories—were not limited to the width of the railroad tracks, but rather formed a checkerboard of square-mile sections stretching for hundreds of miles on both sides of the right of way. This was land the railroads were free to sell to settlers in parcels for their own profit. The 1863–1864 federal banking acts mandated a national currency, chartered banks, and permitted the government to guarantee bonds. As war profiteers, financiers, and industrialists such as John D. Rockefeller, Andrew Carnegie, and J.P. Morgan used these laws to amass wealth in the East, Leland Stanford, Collis P. Huntington, Mark Hopkins, and Charles Crocker in the West grew rich from building railroads with cheap Chinese and Irish labor and eastern capital on land granted by the US government.[12]

SETTLER COLONIALISM AS GENOCIDE

The history of the United States is a history of settler colonialism. The objective of settler colonialism is to terminate Indigenous peoples as nations and communities with land bases in order to make the land available to European settlers. Extermination and assimilation are the methods used. This is the very definition of *genocide*. The word and its definition were created by Raphael Lemkin in 1944, published in his book *Axis Rule in Occupied Europe*.[13]

Lemkin was Polish, of Jewish descent, and a respected lawyer and prosecutor in Poland until the 1939 German invasion. Although Lemkin escaped to Sweden, forty-nine of his relatives perished in the Holocaust. Lemkin became an advisor to the chief counsel of the Nuremberg trials, during which his concept of genocide as a crime in international law did not yet exist and was not one of the legal bases for the trials. Then, for two years, with the support of the Truman administration, Lemkin lobbied the member states of the new United Nations to adopt the Genocide Convention, which the General Assembly did in the same session as the passage of the Declaration on Human Rights. "Genocide" is a legal term with a precise definition, enshrined in the international treaty the United Nations Convention on the Prevention and Punishment of the Crime of Genocide, presented in 1948 and adopted in 1951. Although President Truman signed the convention, it went into effect in the United States only in 1988 when the US Congress finally ratified it, the only member state of the United Nations that had not done so.

The convention is not retroactive, so the United States is not liable under the Genocide Convention before 1988. The Truman administration had lobbied in favor of it at the United Nations, and President Truman signed the Convention and sent it to the Senate for ratification. There, the all-white Senate expressed concern that genocide charges might result from the history of racial segregation, lynching, and Ku Klux Klan activities. In addition, although the treaty was not retroactive, senators expressed fear that it would be used to define the nineteenth-century US treatment of Native Americans as genocide. As the senators feared, in 1951, the Civil Rights Congress, led by the cofounder of the National Association for the Advancement of Colored People (NAACP) W. E. B. Du Bois and the opera star Paul Robeson, filed a petition in the United Nations titled *We Charge Genocide: The Historic Petition to the United Nations for Relief from a Crime of the United States Government Against the Negro People*, in which they stated:

> Out of the inhuman black ghettos of American cities, out of the cotton plantations of the South, comes this record of mass slayings on the basis of race, of lives deliberately warped and

distorted by the willful creation of conditions making for premature death, poverty and disease. It is a record that calls aloud for condemnation, for an end to these terrible injustices that constitute a daily and ever-increasing violation of the United Nations Convention on the Prevention and Punishment of the Crime of Genocide.[14]

Thereafter, when ratification would be proposed in the Senate, similar, more nuanced, arguments would be aired. They included the possibility that the actions of the US military in Korea and Vietnam might be cause for a genocide charge. Native American intellectuals and scholars of the 1950s onward also discussed the possibilities of international human rights law, and after the US signed the Genocide Convention in 1988, work on developing cases began. Finally, pressure on the Reagan administration by the Jewish and Armenian lobbies broke the US holdout. But by that time, the radical civil rights and Black Power movements had waned and dispersed, and even when a movement for reparations for slavery developed in the 1990s, the Genocide Convention was not referenced.

Challenging Native American discussions and publications, especially since the 1992 Columbian quincentenary, US historians and other mainstream scholars and intellectuals, including some human rights activists, have exerted considerable energy in attempting to redefine the Genocide Convention in ways that conclude that it in no way applies to the United States either historically or currently. But the Genocide Convention is not a complex document for which the meaning can easily be misinterpreted, and its terms align with US policies and actions.[15]

In the convention, any one of five acts can be considered genocide if "committed with intent to destroy, in whole or in part, a national, ethnic, racial or religious group." These acts are

(a) Killing members of the group
(b) Causing serious bodily or mental harm to members of the group
(c) Deliberately inflicting on the group conditions of life calculated to bring about its physical destruction in whole or in part

(d) Imposing measures intended to prevent births
     within the group
(e) Forcibly transferring children of the group
     to another group

. . .

The followings acts are punishable

(a) Genocide
(b) Conspiracy to commit genocide
(c) Direct and public incitement to commit genocide
(d) Attempt to commit genocide
(e) Complicity in genocide

The 1951 Civil Rights Congress petition *We Charge Genocide*
pointed out:

> It is sometimes incorrectly thought that genocide means the
> complete and definitive destruction of a race or people. The
> Genocide Convention, however, . . . defines genocide as any
> killings on the basis of race, or, in its specific words, as "kill-
> ing members of the group." Any intent to destroy, in whole or
> in part, a national, racial, ethnic or religious group is geno-
> cide, according to the Convention. Also, the Convention states,
> "causing serious bodily or mental harm to members of the
> group," is genocide as well as "killing members of the group."[16]

The analytical tools provided by the Genocide Convention are essential for historical investigations into the effects of European and European American colonialism, particularly settler colonialism, which
led to the establishment of the United States and was inherently committed to elimination of the Indigenous nations, but also including the
transatlantic slave trade, slavery, the situation of descendants of enslaved Africans, and the annexation of half of México and the treatment of Mexicans. But most important, the Genocide Convention
is applicable to US policies and actions since 1988, when the United
States ratified the convention. There is no statute of limitations.

The term "genocide," both in popular use and often by historians and other scholars, even legal scholars, is often misused to indicate only extreme examples of mass murder, the death of vast numbers of people, as in the Holocaust, or in the midst of aggressive warfare, as, for instance, in Cambodia, thereby dismissing Native and African American claims of US genocide. What is important—and no doubt surprising to many—is that the United Nations' organized war crimes tribunal did not prosecute the Khmer Rouge's mass killings of hundreds of thousands of Cambodians, the ethnic Khmer who comprised the majority of the population and the largest number of victims,for genocide. The specific charges of genocide related solely to the Khmer Rouge's actions against one Indigenous group, the Cham, and to the ethnic Vietnamese population, who were also targeted for elimination because they were not Khmer. Lars Olsen, the tribunal's legal communications officer, explains that is because the definition of genocide in law "is different from what many people would regard as genocide." Simply put, the 1948 Genocide Convention defines genocide as having the intention to eliminate, in part or in full, a group of people based on their race, religion, ethnicity or nationality, and need not be accompanied by warfare, therefore not in the category of war crimes per se.[17]

The Khmer Rouge slaughter of the majority Khmer population in Cambodia violated several international war crime statutes and crimes against humanity. The Khmer Rouge former officials who were responsible were tried, convicted, and sentenced, but they were not tried solely for violations of the Genocide Convention. Not all war crimes constitute genocide, and not all genocides are war crimes, as is clear in the Genocide Convention. To qualify as genocide, a case does not require governmental acts of mass murder simply worse than anything else but rather it requires a specific kind of act. The Genocide Convention is not a war crimes convention, rather a human rights convention, approved by the United Nations in the same session as the Declaration of Human Rights, which refers to individual, not group, rights. The Genocide Convention is the only international law that applies to collective rights, which is why it is uniquely important to Indigenous peoples and other groups.

Although clearly the Shoah is the most extreme of all genocides, the bar set by the Nazis is not the standard required to be considered genocide. The 1948 Genocide Convention did not yet exist for the Nuremberg war crimes tribunal, although Raphael Lemkin, who had already created the concept, attended and lobbied for a genocide convention, influencing the tribunal members. Lemkin made clear that the convention, which he helped draft and lobbied for, should not replicate German Third Reich policies and actions, because, for one thing, he was as committed to the prevention of future genocide as to its punishment. Centuries of European monarchies, states, and people carrying out pogroms against Jewish individuals and communities led to the Holocaust. The title of the Genocide Convention is the Convention on the *Prevention* and Punishment of the Crime of Genocide (emphasis mine). The law is also about preventing genocide by identifying the elements of government policies or actions that could lead to genocide, rather than only punishment after the fact. Most important, genocide does not have to be complete to be considered genocide, nor does it have to include actual death. Forced assimilation is genocidal, forcibly removing children from their families is genocidal, creating conditions that make it impossible for the group to maintain its integrity is genocidal, all of which can be carried out without death. The Trump administration immigration policy of separating children from their parents or guardians is subject to the charge of genocide, although not likely to occur in the short term.

US history, as well as inherited Indigenous trauma and that of descendants of enslaved Africans, cannot be understood and accounted for without acknowledging the genocide that the United States committed against the Native nations and enslaved Africans, both of whose descendants survive in US-claimed boundaries under conditions that constitute genocide. From the colonial period through the founding of the United States and continuing into the twentieth century, this has entailed torture, terror, sexual abuse and rape, massacres, systematic military occupations, removals of Indigenous peoples from their ancestral territories, forced removal of Native American children to military-like boarding schools over a period of a century, children stripped of languages and cultures, as well as allotment of land (that is, privatization of Indigenous territories), and from 1953 to 1974, congressionally legislated policy, the Indian Termination Act.

Within the logic of settler colonialism, genocide was the inherent overall policy of the United States from its founding, but there are also specific, documented policies of genocide on the part of US administrations that can be identified in at least five distinct periods:

(1) the Revolutionary War period through 1832
    in the Ohio Country
(2) the 1830s Jacksonian era of forced removals
(3) the 1850s California gold rush era in Northern California
(4) the Civil War and post–Civil War era (up to 1890)
    of the so-called Indian wars west of the Mississippi
(5) the 1950s termination and relocation period

Additionally, there were genocidal policies and practices that overlapped those time periods, in particular, the compulsory federal boarding schools from the 1870s to 1960s. The Carlisle boarding school, founded by US Army officer Richard Henry Pratt in 1879, became a model for others established by the Bureau of Indian Affairs (BIA). Pratt said in a speech in 1892, "A great general has said that the only good Indian is a dead one. In a sense, I agree with the sentiment, but only in this: that all the Indian there is in the race should be dead. Kill the Indian in him and save the man."[18] That is the definition of genocide.

Cases of genocide carried out as policy may be found in historical documents as well as in the oral histories of Indigenous communities. An example from 1873 is typical, with General William T. Sherman, hero of the Civil War, writing, "We must act with vindictive earnestness against the Sioux, even to their extermination, men, women and children . . . during an assault, the soldiers cannot pause to distinguish between male and female, or even discriminate as to age."[19] Although Sherman demurred that the US did not desire to totally destroy the Natives, it would be necessary if they did not comply and give up. The nearly three-centuries-long "Indian wars" technically ended around 1880, although the Wounded Knee Massacre, of some three hundred starving Lakota Sioux refugees, occurred a decade later. Clearly an act with genocidal intent, the Wounded Knee Massacre is still officially listed as a victorious "battle" in the annals of the US military. Congressional Medals of Honor were bestowed on twenty of the soldiers involved. A monument was built at Fort Riley, Kansas, to honor the soldiers killed by friendly fire. A battle streamer was created to honor the event and added to other streamers that are displayed at the Pentagon, West Point, and army bases throughout the world.

Not all the acts iterated in the Genocide Convention are required to exist to constitute genocide; any one of them suffices. In cases of United States genocidal policies and actions, each of the five specific acts have taken place, some still present in current policies and actions.

The old Northwest Territory was the initial site of genocidal policy enacted by the founders of the United States. By the time of the War of Independence that created the United States, British settlers and armed white citizen militias had 170 years of experience in ethnically cleansing and dominating the thirteen original colonies. Employing this intergenerationally practiced and unlimited war against civilians and their resources, the government and settlers intensified and accelerated those practices from 1787 to 1832 in the invasion and conquest of the Ohio Country—the Northwest Territory—which comprised the future states of Ohio, Indiana, Illinois, Michigan, Wisconsin, and Minnesota. The genocidal campaigns carried out by the new US Army were resisted by a confederation of Indigenous nations, but by 1803, ethnically cleansed Ohio became a state, followed by Indiana thirteen years later, and the others following.[20]

In the next period of the US, the army under Andrew Jackson pursued genocidal wars in the South against the Muskogees and Cherokees and into Spanish Florida, where the US Marines and Army mounted three major wars against the Seminole Nation between 1816 and 1858, albeit without succeeding in removing the Seminole people. And when Jackson was president in the 1830s, he ordered, and the army carried out, the forced removal of all the Native people from east of the Mississippi. During the Civil War, the Union Army forced the removal and four-year incarceration of the Navajo, resulting in the death of half their population. During the same time the Dakota Nation was forced by the Union Army out of their homeland in Minnesota, while unarmed Northern Cheyenne were massacred in their reservation at Sand Creek in Colorado.

After the Civil War, six of the seven divisions of the US Army were stationed west of the Mississippi, where they carried out genocidal wars against the Plains and southwestern Indigenous nations, including the intentional extermination of tens of millions of bison. These troops were pulled out of the South, where they were supposed to be occupying the defeated former Confederate states to allow for land distribution to former slaves and for their political participation in democratic elections. Without sufficient US Army troops to stop them, the Ku Klux Klan made Reconstruction impossible, imposed a reign of terror, and restored the ex-Confederate elite.

But the "wild west" originated in the Northwest Territory, east of the Mississippi, not in the West. Defining the West as the site of genocidal conquest erases its origins at the very founding of the United States, when and where its leaders were intent on building world power based on land theft, genocide, and slavery, the pillars of the US fiscal-military state.

It is essential to understand that aggressive white nationalism and settler colonialism form the bedrock of US institutions and historical and continuing white nationalism—a culture of violence, a gun culture, a militaristic culture—and that genocidal policy toward Indigenous nations and descendants of enslaved Africans always looms inside the US and has been extended globally by genocidal US policies and wars in the Pacific and the Caribbean, including Central America, Southeast Asia, the Middle East, and increasingly in Africa.

WHY DOES THE GENOCIDE CONVENTION MATTER?

Although many do consider US actions and policies historically and today to fall within the Genocide Convention, most question why the Genocide Convention matters, or why international human rights law matters at all, regarding international law and institutions as without having any effect, given United States' domination and flouting of international treaties and norms, as it has historically and it continues today in its treaties and agreements with Native nations. The United Nations itself is generally known to most

US citizens as the Security Council, in which the five most powerful nation-states have veto power over any resolution. However, the UN General Assembly is the actual governing body that produces international agreements and treaties. But Native nations are still here and remain colonized and vulnerable to US genocidal policy, as are descendants of enslaved Africans and Mexicans, particularly undocumented migrant workers. International human rights law and institutions are the only instruments available to oppressed peoples. This isn't *just* history that predates 1988, when the US signed the 1948 Genocide Convention. But the history is important and needs to be widely aired and discussed, included in public school texts and particularly in US law schools, in order for citizens to comprehend the present and develop knowledge and skills to deconstruct the fiscal-military state.

The shadow of genocide lies in the Doctrine of Discovery, which remains a fundamental law of the land in the United States, the legal framework that informs the US colonial system of controlling Indigenous nations. And the US is a nation of laws, and that's the law. But the international human rights treaties that the US has ratified are also US law. From the mid-fifteenth century to the mid-twentieth century, most of the non-European world was colonized under the Doctrine of Discovery, one of the first principles of international law that Christian European monarchies promulgated to legitimize investigating, mapping, and claiming lands belonging to non-Christian peoples outside Europe. It originated in a papal bull issued in 1455 that permitted the Portuguese monarchy to seize West Africa and enslave the inhabitants, the beginning of the transatlantic slave trade.

Following Columbus's landing in the Caribbean—his enterprise funded and sponsored by the king and queen of the infant Spanish state—another papal bull extended similar permission to Spain to claim the land and enslave the people. Disputes between the Portuguese and Spanish monarchies led to the papal-initiated Treaty of Tordesillas (1494), which divided the planet equally between the two Iberian empires.[21] Protestant monarchies challenged Iberian-papal domination and staked out their own claims, but maintained the Doctrine of Discovery as their legalistic justification for doing so. Not only monarchies participated. Following the French

Revolution, French republics invoked the Doctrine of Discovery for their nineteenth- and twentieth-century settler-colonialist projects in Southeast Asia and Africa, as did the newly independent United States when it continued the colonization extending from the thirteen former colonies.

In 1792, not long after US independence, then secretary of state Thomas Jefferson claimed that the Doctrine of Discovery developed by European states was international law applicable to the new US government as well. Then, in the 1820s, the Doctrine of Discovery was engraved in constitutional law by the US Supreme Court under John Marshall in decisions regarding the Cherokee Nation. Writing for the majority, Chief Justice Marshall held that discovery had been an established principle of European law and of English law in effect in Britain's North American colonies, and was also the law of the United States. The court defined the exclusive property rights that a European country acquired by dint of discovery: "Discovery gave title to the government, by whose subjects, or by whose authority, it was made, against all other European governments, which title might be consummated by possession." Indigenous rights were, in the court's words, "in no instance, entirely disregarded; but were necessarily, to a considerable extent, impaired." The court further held that Indigenous "rights to complete sovereignty, as independent nations, were necessarily diminished." Indigenous peoples could continue to live on the land, but title resided with the discovering power, the United States. The decision concluded that Native nations were "domestic, dependent nations," which means captive colonies.[22] The Doctrine of Discovery was a one-sided assumption of dominion that gave the discovering European entity first rights over other European entities to land and resources of the Native nations. However, the Native people did not wish to part with their land. Preemption sanctioned European priority but not Indigenous freedom of choice to sell.[23] "The American right to buy always superseded the Indian right not to sell."[24]

It is a troubling reality that most citizens of the United States have never heard of the Doctrine of Discovery, although it is honored annually on Columbus Day, which became a federal holiday only in 1937, the same year the Buffalo or Indian Head nickel was introduced, apparently as implicit war trophies in those dark days of the Depression. Celebrating Columbus is a celebration of the Doctrine of Discovery. The Doctrine of Discovery is so taken for granted that it is rarely mentioned in historical or even legal texts published in the Americas. And yet, the United States has used the Discovery doctrine to rationalize its colonial dominion over Indigenous peoples throughout its history, citing the Marshall court precedent as recently as 2005 in the US Supreme Court case of *City of Sherrill v. Oneida Nation of Indians* in denying the Oneida Nation land claim. Although this was the Republican-dominated court of Antonin Scalia, Samuel Alito, and Clarence Thomas, the Oneida case was decided unanimously, with Justice Ruth Bader Ginsburg writing the decision.[25]

THE SETTLER MOVE TO INNOCENCE

A kind of innocence characterizes the erasure of continued settler colonialism. Romanticizing settler sovereignty is a way of erasing colonialism and Indigenous nations, and is a tendency as much on the left or liberal spectrum as the right or conservative.[26] Just as John F. Kennedy's book *A Nation of Immigrants* ushered in a new liberal era, so too did his romantic rhetoric about settlers as he reached the presidency. In accepting his nomination as the 1960 Democratic presidential candidate in Los Angeles, he said, "I stand tonight facing west on what was once the last frontier. From the lands that stretch three thousand miles behind me, the pioneers of old gave up their safety, their comfort and sometimes their lives to build a new world here in the West. . . . We stand today on the edge of a new frontier."

Echoing Kennedy in an attempt to revive frayed liberalism, Barack Obama in his 2009 presidential inaugural address also romanticized settlers, even including enslaved Africans as settlers: "In reaffirming the greatness of our nation, we understand that greatness is never a given. It must be earned. Our journey has never been one of shortcuts or settling for less. . . . It has been the risk-takers, the doers, the makers of things. . . . For us, they packed up their few worldly possessions and traveled across oceans in search of a new life. For us, they toiled in sweatshops and settled the West, endured the lash of the whip and plowed the hard earth. For us, they fought and died in places like Concord and Gettysburg; Normandy and Khe Sanh."[27]

Settler colonialism is in the present, as Alyosha Goldstein observes; it is not "a relic of the past but a historical condition remade at particular moments of conflict in the service of securing certain privileges and often to symbolically negotiate inequalities among white people."[28] A deep psychosis inherent in US settler colonialism is revealed in settler self-indigenization.[29] The phenomenon is not the same as the practice of "playing Indian," which historian Philip Deloria brilliantly dissected, from the Boston Tea Party Indians to hobbyists dressing up like Indians to New Age Indians.[30] Settler self-indigenization's genealogy can be traced to the period of the mid-1820s to 1840s, what historians call the Age of Jacksonian Democracy, marked by, among other phenomenon, the blossoming of US American literature.[31] The giants of the era are well known to every US high schooler who has had to suffer through American Lit classes—Thoreau, Emerson, Whitman, Longfellow, Hawthorne, and dozens of others.

Among them was James Fenimore Cooper (1789–1851), who conjured the United States' origin story in his *Leatherstocking Tales*, made up of five novels featuring the hero Natty Bumppo, also called variously, depending on his age, Leatherstocking, Pathfinder, Deerslayer, Hawkeye. Together the novels narrate the mythical forging of the new country from the 1754–1763 French and Indian War to independence to the settlement of the plains by migrants traveling by wagon train from Tennessee. At the end of the saga, Bumppo dies a very old man on the edge of the Rocky Mountains as he gazes east. But it is *The Last of the Mohicans*, subtitled *A Narrative of 1757*, that relates the self-indigenization myth that has endured. *The Last of the Mohicans* was a best-selling book throughout the nineteenth century and has been in print continuously since, along with a half dozen Hollywood movies, the first in 1911, plus several television series made in the US, Canada, and Britain. The most recent Hollywood production was a blockbuster that appeared in 1992, the Columbus Quincentenary.

Cooper conjured the birth of something new and wondrous, literally, the US American race, a new people born of the merger of the best of both worlds, the Native and the European, not a biological merger but something more ephemeral involving the disappearance of the Indian. Cooper has Chingachgook, the last of the "noble" and "pure" Natives, die off as nature would have it, handing the continent over to Hawkeye, the indigenized settler and Chingachgook's adopted son. The publication arc of the *Leatherstocking Tales* parallels the Jackson presidency. For those who consumed the books in that period and throughout the nineteenth century—generations of young white men mainly—the novels became perceived fact, not fiction, and the basis for the coalescence of US American settler nationalism, the settler ideology that justified the fiscal-military state.

DANIEL BOONE, FIRST PIONEER

Behind the legend was Daniel Boone, a looming real-life figure, the archetype that inspired Cooper in the creation of his hero. Boone is the icon of settler colonialism. His life spanned from 1734 to 1820, precisely the period covered in the Leatherstocking series. Boone was born in the shadow of the Appalachians in Berks County, Pennsylvania, on the edge of British colonial settlement. He was an avatar of the moving settler-Indigenous frontier. To the west lay "Indian Country," claimed through the Doctrine of Discovery by Spain, Britain, and France but free of European settlers, save for a few traders, trappers, and soldiers manning colonial outposts. Daniel Boone himself was of Welsh heritage, born in Pennsylvania, but most of those who followed his migrations west were Scots Irish, Ulster Scots. The Scots Irish had been the settler colonialists of Northern Ireland. Beginning in the early 1600s, the British decided to force Protestantism on the Catholic Irish. They chose to use Lowland Scotland Presbyterians. When British colonization of North America began, many of these Ulster Scots chose to join. They were seasoned usurpers of Indigenous property.

The westward migration of Scots Irish settlers represented a mass movement between 1720 and the War of Independence. During the last two decades of the eighteenth century, first- and second-generation Scots Irish settlers continued to migrate to the Ohio Valley, West Virginia, Kentucky, and Tennessee. They cleared forests, built log cabins, and killed Indians, taking their cultivated land. Historian Carl Degler writes, "These hardy, God-fearing Calvinists made themselves into a veritable human shield of colonial civilization."[32]

Richard Slotkin finds the origin of US nationalism in the late eighteenth-century treks of these settlers over the Appalachian-Allegheny spine. Daniel Boone, he writes, "became the most significant, most emotionally compelling myth-hero of the early republic," the US American hero as "the lover of the spirit of the wilderness, and his acts of love and sacred affirmation are acts of violence against that spirit and her avatars." In the twentieth-century reformation of this archetype, promoted notably in the writings of Theodore Roosevelt and, of course, in Western novels and films, Slotkin identifies the archetypes of the "hunter" and the "farmer," or "breeder," and especially "the man who knows Indians."[33] Indeed, it is rare even today to meet a descendant of the old-settler trekking culture who does not identify Daniel Boone as a direct ancestor.

Just as Boone had been hired by land speculators in 1775 to lead settlers—illegally under British law—over the Appalachians to what later became Kentucky in 1799, he led settlers from Kentucky to Spanish-claimed "Upper Louisiana," which was seized by Napoleon in 1803 and sold to the United States as the Louisiana Purchase. Boone died in 1820 in Missouri, a year before it became a state of the United States. His body was ritually taken for burial in Frankfort, Kentucky, the covenant heart of the Ohio Country, Indian Country, the Shawnee homeland for which the revolution had been fought and in which he had been the trekker superhero, almost a deity.

Daniel Boone became a celebrity in 1784 at age fifty, a year after the end of the War of Independence. Real estate entrepreneur John Filson, seeking settlers to buy property that was inhabited by Indigenous farmers and their villages in the Ohio Country, wrote and self-published *The Discovery, Settlement and Present State of Kentucke,* along with a map to guide squatters. The book contained an appendix about Daniel Boone, purportedly written by Boone himself. That part of the book on Boone's "adventures" subsequently was published as "The Adventures of Col. Daniel Boone" in the *American Magazine* in 1787, then as a book. Thereby a superstar was born—the mythical hero, the hunter. "The Hunters of Kentucky," a popular song that swept the nation in 1822–1828, helped elect Andrew Jackson as president by associating him with Boone, the hero of the West.[34] Yet Cooper's positive twist on genocidal colonialism was based on the reality of invasion, squatting, attacking, and colonizing of the Indigenous nations. Neither Filson nor Cooper created that reality. Rather, they created the narratives that captured the experience and imagination of the Anglo-American settler, stories that were surely instrumental in nullifying guilt related to genocide and set the pattern of narrative for future US writers, poets, and historians.

The site of the mythology that Cooper channeled was the Appalachian Mountains with their passages to the rich lands of the Ohio Valley, where British settlers were barred from making claims after the French and Indian War. The 1763 royal proclamation ordered all those who had moved into that region to return to the colonies. Defying the proclamation, George Washington, who was head of the Virginia colonial militia, took survey teams into the area to map the territory for future settlement, which by definition meant the extension and expansion of slavery. By the time he was in his mid-twenties, George Washington was already a notoriously successful slaver and land speculator in unceded Indian lands.[35] The wealthy slavers of the Southern colonies, particularly those in Virginia, were most incensed by the order, since their wealth relied on accessing more and more land as they depleted the soils with intensive monocrop, non-food production for the market. The slavers also had an interest in decreasing the growing numbers of disgruntled landless white settlers, many of whom had already trekked into and illegally squatted in the Appalachian part of the Cherokee Nation. These mostly Scots Irish settlers in the Appalachians became the mythologized settler archetype identified with Daniel Boone, claiming to be the original settlers, a self-indigenizing process. This is what has been called the "settler move to innocence."[36]

SETTLER CLAIMS TO INDIGENEITY IN APPALACHIA

In the newest iteration of the mythologizing of white Appalachian settlers and their descendants, historian Steven Stoll first acknowledges the brutality of the forced removal of Indigenous nations from east of the Mississippi, and concedes that as aboriginal nations, Indigenous peoples differed from the plight of the Scots Irish settlers. He recognizes that Native nations were uprooted and removed by the federal government as peoples, whereas the Scots Irish were individual settlers who took what Stoll implies was ethnically cleansed vacant land and created their own agrarian civilization. Stoll then leaves the tragic past of Indigenous presence and settler-colonial violence and posits a new people—echoes of Cooper's tales—the people of the mountains who he claims resemble the peasants of feudal England who experienced foreclosure of the commons that had been provided by their lords. Yet, Stoll continually argues that there are parallels in US policy toward the "peasants" of Appalachia and the experience of Native nations. He writes,

> Both groups were cast as degenerate races with no capacity for historical progress. Neither Scots Irish cattle herders nor Chickasaw maize gardeners could be brought into the circulation of capital without shedding their rootedness in locality and their household sufficiency. Indian territorial sovereignty conflicted with the expansion of cotton and slavery. Mountaineer kinship made some of the same kinds of claims on the landscape as homeplace. Neither group made much sense to an emerging conception of land as a commodity. Most of all, perhaps, both underwent an intellectual dispossession that preceded the one that actually took away the land.[37]

Stoll portrays the white, mostly Scots Irish settlers in the middle and southern Appalachians as subsistence agrarians and hunters. He concedes that they engaged in market exchange, selling livestock and lumber, but claims that they did not become dependent on the cash and credit economy that dominated the rest of the United States. He characterizes them as "swiddeners," an anthropological term indicating slash and burn agriculture, another Indigenous marker. After drawing a picture of this near-idyllic society, Stoll launches into a global history of enclosures of "the commons." Throughout the book, he applies the already somewhat romanticized histories of the feudal period of the English commons and the enclosure movement that fenced the commons and privatized the land, throwing the peasants into a surplus labor force, launching the British capitalist economy.[38] Stoll characterizes the colonial settlers of Appalachia and their descendants as "peasants" who experienced enclosure with the arrival of the coal and timber industries in the late nineteenth century. The final chapter is subtitled "The Fate of the Commons and the Commoners." He compares this process to the forced removal of all the Indigenous peoples east of the Mississippi to Indian Territory and to the Dawes Act that divided all common Native land into marketable allotments. In doing so, Stoll disappears the Native and bestows indigeneity upon these settlers.

Stoll didn't create the idea of self-indigenizing settlers. It is a phenomenon that harkens back to the mythologizing of Daniel Boone and the US origin story. Then it took new form in the aftermath of the Civil War when Reconstruction waned, as did the possibilities of Black equality. The mountain people as a pocket of whiteness took on a demographic category in the minds of northern elites when the railroads brought industry into the mountains. The whiteness of the population appeared as unspoiled Americana as opposed to the foreignness of the flood of Eastern and Southern European immigrants arriving. The coal mining industry took over and transformed the white settler population into heroic white miners, while labor organizing and union militancy marked the culture of whiteness.[39] With economic depressions and competition in the coal industry, the West Virginia coal industry waned as did the labor movement, leaving the mountain people impoverished, many migrating to Cincinnati, Chicago, and other industrial centers. In the late 1960s, the War on Poverty turned attention to white poverty in Appalachia.

The Black civil rights movement in the South branched out to the North and the entire country, radicalizing many young white people; at the same time, the US decade-long covert military intervention in Southeast Asia became outright war mobilization in 1964. Already, many on the left in the United States and Europe were committed anti-imperialists and supported the national liberation movements and antiapartheid in South Africa. At the intellectual level, development theory—that Europe had undeveloped the "Third World"—gained traction, so much so that the United Nations established the United Nations Conference on Trade and Development. Out of the thinking on development and underdevelopment, the concept of internal colonization was theorized by Mexican sociologist Pablo Gonzalez Casanova in 1964 and became popularized.[40] In general, the designation of "internal colony" was racialized, indicating the impoverishment and powerlessness of African Americans living in "ghettos," as well as Mexican Americans, particularly New México. But antipoverty scholars and activists also applied it to white Appalachians, coinciding with the revival of self-indigenization.[41]

What set off the current Appalachian settler appropriation of indigeneity was the 1962 publication of *Night Comes to the Cumberlands: A Biography of a Depressed Region* by Kentucky lawyer Harry Caudill.[42] In *Ramp Hollow*, Steven Stoll praises the book, writing, "After the book's publication, Caudill kept Appalachia before the public." In a 1967 article, Caudill wrote, "The colonialist sway in the rest of the world has ended. Only in our Appalachia does it proceed unchecked"[43] This was a period when most of Southern and West Africa remained under the boot of colonialism and thirteen years before Zimbabwe won independence. Caudill called white people of the Appalachians "indigenous mountaineers" who "have lived in the plateau since the beginning." He went on:

> Much of the pioneer society in this mountainous region had resided in the wilderness for three or four generations. . . . They had acquired much of the stoicism of the Indians and inurement of primitive outdoor living had made them almost as wild as the red man. . . . His "old woman" could endure harsh privations as well as the Indian squaw, and was far more fruitful. . . . He ate the Indian's corn and "jerked" meat. He wore the Indian's deerskin clothes. He even adopted his tomahawk, and here only, on the rampaging frontier, the white border man collected scalps with all the zest of the Choctaw brave.[44]

Appalachian scholar Stephen Pearson is one of the few intellectuals from the region to refute the concept of white Appalachians
being indigenous and colonized. Exploited by capitalism they have
been, but colonized they have never been. The colonial model, he
writes, "maintains that White Appalachians—positioned as the
region's 'Indigenous population'—are the victims of a form of colonialism analogous to that dominating American Indian nations.
As such, the colonialism model of Appalachian exploitation calls
for the 'decolonization of Appalachia.' "[45] He notes that the Appalachian case "offers an excellent illustration of how settlers can
employ indigenization in late settler-colonial contexts in order to negotiate land claims and other inequalities among White settlers. . . .
The Appalachian case shows that even in late settler colonies, Native
presence remains an unsettling factor challenging the legitimacy of
ongoing settler occupancy."[46]

Appalachian scholars developed and refined Caudill's work, using the internal colonialism theoretical context, going further than
Caudill in portraying white settlers as an Indigenous people. In
1978, scholarly articles were published in the book *Colonialism in
Modern America: The Appalachian Case*, which remains a fundamental text in Appalachian studies.[47] Pearson writes that in the
flagship essay of the collection, written by Helen Lewis and Edward
Knipe, the authors refer to the white residents as "the indigenous
population," while those of the residents who align themselves with
the coal companies are designated as "natives who become colonizers of their own people." They write of the "colonizers" manifesting
racism against an Indigenous population, referring to the white settler population, which the authors refer to as "the colonized." The
authors analogize regional development organizations to the Bureau
of Indian Affairs, claiming that the white population lives "on the
Appalachian Reservation." Pearson notes that this is a comparison
also made by other white Appalachian scholars. Most disturbing is
that Lewis and Knipe treat the original invasion of the Scots Irish
squatters as peaceful settlement rather than genocidal violence.
They portray an empty landscape that the settlers occupied, the Indigenous peoples somehow having disappeared with white settlers
inheriting indigeneity and the land.[48]

In another anthology, Edward Guinan writes of the Appalachian region, "whose indigenous Cherokee integrated, educated, and nursed the exiled Celtic arrivals into maturity, wisdom, and community."[49] Julie "Judy" Bonds, a well-known activist opposing mountaintop removal, has stated that "we're a distinct mountain culture, and our culture means something. This is a culture that has been handed down to us all the way from the Native Americans."[50]

David Whisnant, whom historian Steven Stoll acknowledges as one of the "historians of Appalachia whose work I read and admire," characterizes his scholarly mission as being one of Franz Fanon's "native intellectuals in a colony going through decolonization."[51] Another Appalachian scholar, Rodger Cunningham, asserts that "all native Appalachian scholarship, including mine, is like that of other colonized peoples in being engaged with history and praxis."[52] Pearson observes that "the colonialism model has allowed White liberals within the region to valorize themselves as Indigenous leaders in a struggle for decolonization—a supersessionist settler-colonial fantasy come to fruition."[53]

Razib Khan, an immigrant to the US from Bangladesh, is a writer in population genetics and consumer genetics. Although arriving as a child with his family, Khan finds aspects of the descendants of British settlers in the United States downright exotic, specifically the thirty million Scots Irish who make up around 10 percent of the US population. In an article titled "The Scots-Irish as Indigenous People," he writes, "What these people lack in cosmopolitan openness, they make up for in adherence to authentic values which can't but help earn some admiration. Substitute 'Scots-Irish' for 'Pashtun,' 'Hmong' or 'Berber' and you will see what I mean." Of course, the Scots Irish were the foot soldiers of the British and US empires, not a colonized people, although Khan appears to be referring to their unique characteristics rather than claiming they are actually indigenous. But it does mirror the self-indigenizing settler in Appalachia. Khan clarifies that

> though the Scots-Irish are not "Pilgrim stock" in their length resident on the American continent, the majority were not immigrants to the United States, they were settlers of the Amer-

ican colonies. Theirs was part of the founding culture of the
United States. . . . One aspect of Scots-Irish identity is that
to a great extent it has decoupled itself from any "Old Country" consciousness. A broad swath of the Eastern American
Uplands is dominated by people who give their ethnicity as
American. After 250 years, they have only the vaguest recollections of the nature of their British antecedents.

Although Khan implicitly erases the original and continued existence
of the actual Indigenous peoples, unlike self-indigenizing Appalachians and other descendants of original settlers, he acknowledges
that

the early American republic also saw the emergence of a white
man's republic, where implicit white identity gave way to the
expansion of suffrage to non-property holding white males as
a natural right, and the revocation of what suffrage existed
for non-whites based on their racial character. The Scots-Irish
were a major part of this cultural evolution, being as they were
generally part of the broad non-slave holding class. They may
not have had the wealth of lowland planters, but the Scots-
Irish were part of the aristocracy of skin. . . . It is true that
Scots-Irish Americans are arguably among the more racist
white ethnic groups.[54]

The memoir of Appalachia-born J.D. Vance, *Hillbilly Elegy: A
Memoir of a Family and Culture in Crisis*, quotes from Khan's commentary positively to define his own national origin as Scots Irish,
but does not quote the part about white supremacy and racism.[55]
Vance is a wealthy, self-defined political conservative, a graduate
of Yale Law School, and a Silicon Valley investor. *Hillbilly Elegy*
was a sensation from its release in 2016, with Oprah Winfrey's en-
dorsement. It remained on all best-selling book lists for two years,
selling a million copies. Although there were some negative reviews,
it received critical attention from the conservative *National Review*
to the liberal National Public Radio, as well as all major newspapers
and media. In the fall of 2020, *Hillbilly Elegy* premiered as a major
motion picture.

Vance's memoir is the second twenty-first-century Scots Irish memoir, after that of former US Navy secretary and US senator James Webb's *Born Fighting: How the Scots-Irish Shaped America*, published in 2005.[56] Vance is critical of his Appalachian family and community, invoking the self-blaming "culture of poverty" rhetoric, but as with Webb, he is extremely proud of his Scots Irish ancestry. Like many Scots Irish men in the United States, both are proud of their service in the US Marine Corps. Webb's story is more interesting as he traces the Scots Irish trek from the Appalachians to the Arkansas Ozark region, where he grew up. The majority of the white settlers in Missouri, Oklahoma, and Texas were also Scots Irish.

Vance writes that there is an "ethnic component" in his story, noting that ethnic differences extend beyond skin color. "I may be white, but I do not identify with the WASPs of the Northeast. Instead, I identify with the millions of working-class white Americans of Scots-Irish descent who have no college degree." He describes the entrenched poverty among his ancestors who were day laborers in the slave economy, not slavers, then they were sharecroppers, then machinists and millworkers. "Americans call them hillbillies, rednecks, or white trash. I call them neighbors, friends, and family."[57] Vance characterizes the Scots Irish as "one of the most distinctive subgroups in America," with good and bad traits, the good ones being a sense of loyalty and devotion to family and country, the bad ones being dislike of outsiders or "people who are different from us." He edges toward Appalachian indigeneity, remarking apparently magically, "When the first wave of Scots-Irish immigrants landed in the New World in the eighteenth century, they were deeply attracted to the Appalachian Mountains." The term "deeply attracted" is a deeply inappropriate conceptualization of the genocidal settler invasion of the agricultural homelands of several Indigenous nations, particularly the Cherokee.[58] However, actual Indigenous peoples do not exist in Vance's story, nor in Webb's.

Indigenous peoples, African Americans, and actual history do appear in a 2019 book of essays that critique Vance's *Hillbilly Elegy*.[59] Appalachian historian T. R. C. Hutton writes that *Hillbilly Elegy* is "inadvertently a book about race, more so than region or class, . . . about whiteness, and the failure of American capitalism to give whiteness the natural purchase it once promised." Hutton notes that Vance implies that whiteness is the absence of race, and Vance uses the term "hillbilly," which embodies whiteness, a term rarely applied to a person of color. And, he uses "hillbilly" interchangeably with Scots Irish.[60] Legal scholar Lisa R. Pruitt writes, "Reflecting the common practice of white default or transparency, and in the fashion of Appalachian studies, Vance elects merely to imply race. Even though that race is 'white,' the use of the 'hillbilly' label permits Vance to suggest a downtrodden minority."[61]

In a review of the 2020 Ron Howard movie based on *Hillbilly Elegy*, writer Ellen Wayland-Smith, who is white and hails from Appalachia, asks the pertinent question: "Why does Vance's memoir strike such a sensitive national nerve?" Donald Trump had been campaigning for the presidency in the year before Vance's book appeared, using racist language and catering to Appalachians, promising to bring back the coal industry. "During Trump's vertiginous rise in Obama's ostensibly post-racial America, Vance's memoir arguably served a similar role: tacitly excusing Trump's most egregious racist dog whistles, Vance reassured readers that his hillbillies' animus had nothing to do with race."[62]

RANCHER INDIGENEITY

Settler self-indigenizing is not limited to Appalachia.[63] Under the guise of "regional studies," descendants of Appalachian and other early settlers who migrated west and settled in Missouri, Oklahoma, and Texas, many of whom trekked on to the valleys of California and the Pacific Northwest, also carry with them the sense of being of the original people and often express an affinity for their version of Indianness, being men who claim "to know Indians." Another site is the intermountain west where white cattle barons dominate, many of them Mormon, who have their own indigenous origin story blessed by their God.

On the day after the 2016 new year, an armed gang of assorted, self-styled white nationalist militias, led by the son of an affluent rancher—some Hollywood-style on horseback, most in oversized and expensive pickups or SUVs—crashed into the Malheur National Wildlife Refuge in eastern Oregon, claiming it as their land, holding the refuge center and offices for forty days. They were an exponent of an organized effort to convert all federal lands to private property, called the Sagebrush Rebellion, that began like many of the white supremacist groups during the Reagan administration. The Malheur invaders were in fairly friendly territory with white ranchers dominating the region of eastern Oregon and Washington, abutting rancher-dominated Idaho and Nevada. They run their stock on federal lands, paying little in fees or refusing to pay any fees. The leader of this armed takeover, Ammon Bundy, owner of a truck fleet business in Arizona, is the son of Cliven Bundy, who in 2014 led a gang of armed men to stop Bureau of Land Management (BLM) officers from impounding Bundy's cattle. Bundy had been grazing his herds on federal land for two decades without paying the ridiculously low BLM fees. The unarmed BLM officers backed off, and neither Bundy nor his armed supporters were detained, and Bundy's cattle continue to graze on federal land without payment.[64]

The Malheur National Wildlife Refuge is operated by the US Fish and Wildlife Service and consists of nearly 190 thousand acres. Ammon Bundy claimed that all the land in the refuge once belonged to private ranchers and that the federal government acquired it illegally. Actually, in the nineteenth century, violent and armed white settlers and the federal government seized the land from the Indigenous Northern Paiute Nation, for whom the land was sacred. The federal government forcibly relocated the Paiutes when they resisted settler encroachment. Their residency dates back fourteen thousand years as part of the larger Paiute Nation of the intermountain area. In 1972, the 430 surviving Paiutes who had been relocated were able to obtain a federally protected small reservation on part of their original land base. The Bureau of Indian Affairs designated 771 acres as the Burns Paiute Reservation, Burns being the largest settler town in the area. The reservation did not include the already established Malheur Wildlife Refuge, which had been designated as such in 1908 by President Theodore Roosevelt in response to his ornithologist friend's request to protect the migratory birds that habituated the lakes there.[65]

During the four decades since the Northern Paiute community

returned to their homeland, they have developed a relationship with the US Fish and Wildlife Service to collaborate in the excavation and protection of their sacred objects that had been left in the ruins of the genocidal settler warfare that forced them out.

As the Bundy gang holding the refuge in 2016 grew in numbers, the FBI and other law enforcement presence increased as well. When one of the intruders left the site, he was detained, and when he reached for his sidearm he was shot by an FBI agent. Another intruder was wounded. In the end, after forty days of wrecking the center and grounds, opening drawers and handling the carefully excavated Paiute sacred items that were kept in the center as a secure place, they surrendered. A number of them were arrested and charged with felonies. At trial, twelve pleaded guilty and were given light sentences with probation or house arrest. Only seven received prison time. Bundy was tried by a jury and acquitted of all charges, once again victorious.[66]

Referring to the 2016 Dakota pipeline protests taking place during the same period as the trials, geographers Joshua F. J. Inwood and Anne Bonds wrote at the time,

> Nothing illustrates the fundamental contradictions of the United States settler state quite like the juxtaposition of a jury in Oregon acquitting Bundy and his supporters of the armed takeover . . . while peaceful and non-violent Native Americans in the Dakotas have been subject to state-supported violence while peacefully protesting the construction of a tar-sands oil pipeline through land ceded to the Lakota through a federally recognized treaty, . . . subject to tear gassings, attack dogs, have had rubber bullets fired into their protests as well as having been sprayed with fire hoses in freezing and dangerous conditions.[67]

During the takeover, Ammon Bundy was asked by a reporter about the Paiute people; his response expressed contempt for prior Paiute rights, stating a typical self-indigenizing settler refrain: "We also recognize that the Native Americans had the claim to the land, but they lost that claim. There are things to learn from cultures of the past, but the current culture is the most important."[68] In an interview a month after the occupation ended, retired Wyoming senator Alan Simpson, in response to a reporter's question about guns, said, "Without guns, there would be no West," adding that his grandfather was an original settler in the Wyoming Territory before it was a state, in 1874, two years before Custer's defeat by the Sioux and the Cheyenne nations at the Little Big Horn.[69] "The West" is a site of massive white self-indigenizing, as also reflected in the wildly popular Laura Ingalls Wilder's *Little House on the Prairie*. The self-indigenizing as first settlers is inherently genocidal with guns a central metaphor. As Simpson said in an earlier interview, "How steady you hold your rifle, that's gun control in Wyoming."[70]

ERASURE

Anishinabek historian Michael Witgen writes:

> The United States imagines itself as a nation of immigrants. . . . The United States aspired to be a settler colonial power, but the presence and persistence of Native peoples forced the republic to become a colonizer. The violence of settler colonial ideology is represented not only in the widespread dispossession of indigenous peoples but also in its attempt to affect their political, social, and cultural erasure. . . . To imagine the United States as a nation of immigrants, devoid of an indigenous population, is not only a form of erasure; it is also historically inaccurate. The United States was founded as, and continues to be, a nation of settler immigrants locked into a struggle over the meaning of place and belonging with the Native nations of North America.[71]

Criticizing US scholars for their erasure of the Indian, Mahmood Mamdani writes:

> Engaging with the native question would require questioning the ethics and the politics of the very constitution of the United States of America. It would require rethinking and reconsider-

ing the very political project called the U.S.A. Indeed, it would call into question the self-proclaimed anticolonial identity of the U.S. Highlighting the colonial nature of the American political project would require a paradigmatic shift in the understanding of America, one necessary to think through both America's place in the world and the task of political reform for future generations.[72]

Furthermore, Mamdani argues, regarding the conflation of immigration and settlement: immigrants join existing polities whereas settlers create new ones. "If Europeans in the United States were immigrants, they would have joined the existing societies in the New World. Instead they destroyed those societies and built a new one that was reinforced by later waves of settlement." The nation of immigrants rhetoric that avoids the dynamics of settler colonialism plays a role that "is essential to settler-colonial nation-state projects such as the United States and Israel. The political project of the settler—to create and fortify the colonial nation-state—becomes obscured by the nonpolitical project of the immigrant, who merely seeks to take advantage of what the state allows every citizen."[73]

Historian Lorenzo Veracini also distinguishes between settlers and immigrants, asserting that settlers are unique migrants made by conquest not by immigration. Settlers are founders of political orders and carry their sovereignty with them, whereas immigrants face a political order that is already constituted. Immigrants can certainly be individually co-opted within settler-colonial societies, and often are, but they do not enjoy inherent rights and are characterized by a defining lack of sovereign entitlement.[74]

Immigrants and refugees to the United States do have the option to resist becoming settlers, although in most cases they do not know the history of the United States or the political reality. The US Immigration and Naturalization Service policies based on exclusion make the new immigrant's life precarious, particularly for immigrants of color entering a racial order that renders them suspect already, so they may not want to know the reality or that they have a choice and that by default they become settlers.

CHAPTER 3

ARRIVANTS

Enslaved Africans did not come to the Americas as immigrants, nor as indentured servants, nor as settlers. They were indigenous agrarian villagers who were kidnapped or taken as captives in wars, force-marched in groups to the Atlantic coast, and transported across the ocean against their will and with violence so unbearable that many committed suicide. Parallel to the European invasions, enslavement, and colonization of the Indigenous peoples of the Western Hemisphere, the same European invaders were ethnically cleansing whole swaths of West and Central Africa by enslaving and transporting captives to sell in the colonies of the Americas. In both cases, vast regimes of genocide persisted for three centuries. European colonialism in Africa forms the context for the presence of two hundred million descendants of Africans in the Western Hemisphere in the twenty-first century. The second largest population is in the United States with forty-one million descendants, while Brazil ranks first with sixty-five million African descendants. The island states in the Caribbean that had been the European sugar colonies have majority African-descendant populations.

Although they were transported in the earliest years of European colonization of the Americas, enslaved Africans and their descendants cannot be categorized as "settlers." African Caribbean poet Edward Kamau Brathwaite introduced the term "arrivant" to describe the status of African people forced into slavery in the Americas.[1]

THE TRANSATLANTIC SLAVE TRADE

During the early 1500s, Genoese, Catalans, and Valencians raided the Canary Islands to enslave Africans or purchased them from Moroccan traffickers. Those living in the territories of the Holy Roman Empire were still primarily capturing Slavic people for forced labor, to the extent that the term "slave" was derived from "Slav" for the enslaved in the Byzantine Empire. Although the terms "slave" and "slavery" were used for those captured in war or penal offenses, these medieval European captives were not subject to permanent racial or caste codes nor were their offspring born into slavery. But in the mid-fifteenth century, Catholic Iberians had begun to view the "natural" slave as African. In 1444, the Portuguese were the first Europeans to sail south to West Africa to enslave 240 Africans to sell at the Lisbon slave market, initiating the transatlantic slave trade.[2] The Portuguese monarch Alfonso V made the first slave auction into a spectacle and show of power to other Christian monarchies. A few years later, papal bulls of 1452 and 1455 validated the Portuguese monarchy's dominion over West Africa and the subjugation of the residents.[3]

Ten million enslaved Africans arrived alive in the Americas during a span of three hundred years, while as many as half the number who began the voyage across the Atlantic perished. Millions more died in "seasoning" prisons in the Caribbean colonies after arrival. Millions of Africans died in Africa during mercenary slave raids, wars, and transport to the African coast where the survivors were sold to European traders. Millions surely died of infectious diseases in captivity and transport.[4]

During the early 1500s, millions of Indigenous North and Central Americans were enslaved and forcibly transported by Spanish and Portuguese colonizers to the mines of Perú and Brazil. The majority of the dense Nahua Indigenous agrarian population of the western half of El Salvador and of Nicaragua were either killed in colonial wars of conquest or enslaved and transported to the mines of Perú, as were the peoples of the Natchez Nation in the Mississippi Valley. The enslaved Natchez people were transported from the Gulf of México, down the length of South America over the Atlantic, and around Tierra del Fuego, then north to Perú, a longer passage than from Africa to America. Although the Spanish outlawed the enslavement of Indians in 1543, to be replaced with only enslaved Africans, the illegal practice continued throughout the following two-and-a-half centuries. In the British North American colonies, captured Natives were often sold to planters in the Caribbean.[5]

Britain began its transatlantic slave trade in the Caribbean in 1562, and in 1619 a merchant brought twenty enslaved Africans to the fledgling British Virginia colony of Jamestown.[6] In 1607, the English settlers had invaded what they called Jamestown, bringing with them Irish, Welsh, and Scots individuals who were indentured under contracts for various lengths of time. Their conditions of labor were exploitative and often cruel, but ultimately they were free to be social equals with the other English settlers. European indentured servants did not arrive as settlers, but they became settlers. During the twelve years before the introduction of enslaved Africans, the English colonists had violently appropriated the Powhatan villages and their carefully manicured gardens, food storage granaries, and oyster beds, pushing the people to the periphery. The colonizers relied on tobacco as a profit-making commodity, which the Indigenous peoples had invented and used only sparingly for ceremonial and medicinal purposes. Within a few years of exporting tobacco to Europe, a burgeoning addicted market flourished, making tobacco a lucrative industrial monocrop for Virginia planters. They had come in search of gold but grew wealthy off a toxic and addictive drug, the beginning of European and later US drug trafficking mixed with wars in Asia. The British settlers in Jamestown were no strangers to slavery, being familiar with the entrenched half century of the slave trade and slave colonies in the Caribbean. After a decade of unsuccessful attempts to force the resident Native people to do the work of tending their tobacco plantations, Virginia tobacco planters eagerly purchased the enslaved Africans and soon many more.

CODIFICATION AND ENTRENCHMENT OF
SLAVERY IN THE BRITISH COLONIES

The codification of African enslavement—the "Black" codes—developed over several decades. The Barbados Slave Code was passed by the colonial English legislature to provide a legal basis for establishing African slavery in the Caribbean island of Barbados, marking the beginning of England's legal codification of slavery in its American colonies.[7] It formed the template for all the colonies Britain established afterward.

By the 1670s, settler slave patrols to control enslaved Africans were established in the newly constituted Carolina colony and were quickly adopted in Virginia, indicating a deep entrenchment of slavery in the social order.[8] In the slave code, the term "white," Matthew Horton writes, "emerged as a definitive way to signify a settler superordination squarely opposed to 'Negroes' and 'Indians.' What distinguished 'White,' therefore, was not that it aligned 'European planters' with 'European laborers,' but that it created basic legal parity for 'Europeans' of all classes on global frontiers across imperial jurisdictions, languages, political ideologies, and religious sects, for the purposes of exploiting, dispossessing, and killing people of color."[9] The English slave codes were adopted from the long-established "cleanliness of blood" Spanish racial codes that designated Europeans (Criollos) at the top and "Indios" at the bottom, with "Negro" second to last, and a dozen mixtures in between, from "Mestizo" (white father, Indian mother) to "Zambo" (Black father, Indian mother).[10]

African American studies historian Robin D. G. Kelley points out that the massive forced transfer of people in the European transatlantic slave trade was a process of elimination: "eliminate the culture, identity, and consciousness while preserving the body for labor."[11] It was the loss of villages and fields, the land, a loss of extended family ties, and community. Yet, even with the horrors of attempted elimination, the late historian Cedric Robinson writes, "the cargoes of laborers also contained African cultures, critical mixes and admixtures of language and thought, of cosmology and metaphysics, of habits, beliefs, and morality. These were the actual terms of their humanity. These cargoes, then, did not consist of intellectual isolates or deculturated Blacks—men, women, and children separated from their previous universe. African labor brought the past with it, a past that had produced it and settled on it the first elements of consciousness and comprehension."[12] Africans also brought seeds; many were Muslims and brought copies of the Koran; they brought the banjo, the African drums, songs, poetry, and the oral tradition of storytelling, providing descendants of the enslaved with historical memory. These traces of African origins were instruments of both survival and resistance that created a new people in the cauldron of enslavement, rapacious capitalism, and colonialism under the fiscal-military state that continues today.

The Haitian Revolution that began in 1791 as a massive slave insurrection achieved Haitian independence from France in 1804, the first successful national liberation movement against European colonialism. The gestating liberation movements in the Spanish colonies received not only inspiration but also material assistance from independent Haiti. The Mexican, Central American (formed at first as the Republic of Central America), and Bolivarian independence movements in South America abolished slavery once they achieved independence. However, except for Haiti, the enslaved people of the other Caribbean sugar colonies—French, Spanish, and British—did not succeed in their powerful rebellions.

The late Haitian historian Michel-Rolph Trouillot points out that many more enslaved Africans were placed in the Caribbean sugar plantation islands and Brazil than in the thirteen English colonies. "Enslaved Africans worked and died in the Caribbean a century before the settlement at Jamestown," and the Caribbean as a whole imported the greatest number of enslaved Africans, the second being Brazil.[13] This is true, but it was also intentional on the part of British, then European American slavers who trembled in the wake of the Haitian Revolution, even banning the transatlantic slave trade, believing rightly that newly arrived enslaved Africans, such as the Angolans in Haiti, were more likely to rebel while their cultures and languages and memories of freedom were intact. Even before US independence and the Haitian Revolution, British slavers in North America kept a wary eye on slave insurgency in the Caribbean, where enslaved people comprised the overwhelming majority of the population. The North American slavers took care to maintain a majority European population and mandated intense policing that involved all European colonists, whether or not they owned enslaved Africans. Only the South Carolina colony came close to an enslaved African majority at US independence.

The sugar industry in the Caribbean made up the largest agricultural industry in the world. It was perfectly legal under the British in the Caribbean to violently abuse the enslaved by torture, electrocution, maiming, decapitating, drawing and quartering, roasting alive, even publicly starving to death while suspended in iron cages ("gibbeting"). In addition, slavers were free to inflict torture, kill, rape, or mutilate the enslaved. Thereby, the enslaved were worked to death or killed in great numbers, requiring a replenishing of the supply through the transatlantic slave trade of two million in the eighteenth century alone. Historian Fara Dabhoiwala points out that even at the time, John Locke concluded that, in fact, "slavery itself was always a state of war" and no slave defeat was ever final.[14] There were multiple maroon communities outside slavers' control that carried out effective, organized warfare against the colony, some gaining legality through treaties. "Enslaved men, women, and children fought not only to win freedom, or territory, or simply a space to live their own lives, but to uphold their human dignity: to fight was to raise hope, to create possibilities, to refuse to be subjected. And it always inspired others. Well into the next century, when newly captured Africans arrived in Jamaica, their fellow plantation slaves would instruct them in the history of Tacky's Revolt."[15] Tacky's Revolt, 1760–1761, called the Coromantee War by the British, was a war of the enslaved in Jamaica that was led by experienced African combatants.

The Haitian Revolution and other insurrections in the Caribbean convinced North American slavers to breed slaves rather than relying on importation of Africans. Consequently, both the British and the new United States outlawed the transatlantic slave trade in 1807.[16] Thereby, in the North American colonies and after independence, enslaved people were outnumbered by European settlers. Although not all European settlers were slavers, all were obligated to defend the settler communities from threats and all had a vested economic interest or they would not have been in the colonies. Although there were large plantations in the British colonies in North America with one hundred or more enslaved people, the average number was four to six, so the enslaved Africans were physically separated. By the late 1700s, most were born in North America and had not experienced a previous life of freedom. Revolts and acts of sabotage occurred constantly, but actual war was limited to joining forces with Indigenous peoples' resistance movements, as with the Seminole Nation in Florida from 1815 to 1859.

The slave colonies created and codified a thoroughly racial capitalist slavery that was hardened following the US War of Independence with the new nation's fiscal-military constitution and the rise of the Cotton Kingdom, building the wealth of the nation on enslaved African labor and the land violently wrenched from the Native peoples. By 1810, the number of enslaved Black people in the United States had nearly doubled to one million since the beginning of the war, and it doubled again by the beginning of the Civil War.[17] With the beginning boom of cotton in the Mississippi Valley, the old slave colonies of Virginia and South Carolina—their soil depleted from monocrop commercial agriculture—operated a thriving and profitable slave reproduction industry that created a lucrative domestic market. It was a form of industrial production that predated twentieth-century cattle and hog factory farms; however, it was the forced breeding of human beings.

RACIAL CAPITALISM

Like *Hamilton*, another blockbuster Broadway hit, *The Lehman Trilogy*, was promoted as a history lesson and an immigrant story but omitted slavery in narratives that are, in fact, all about slavery.[18] Sarah Churchwell writes, "Ever since the 2008 collapse of Lehman Brothers precipitated a global financial crisis, the bank's dramatic reversal of fortune has been treated as an allegory of the history of American capitalism." The play begins with a rags-to-riches immigrant-bootstrapping narrative elevating an antebellum nineteenth-century German-Jewish family to great wealth, thanks to their hard work and the welcoming warmth of US Americans. Then the narrative turns dark as the Lehmans lose touch with their humble mercantile roots and are tempted by the possibilities of financial speculation. Rather than selling useful objects, they are in the world of abstract mathematics. Created during the Trump administration, the play moves on to make the point that immigrants like Lehman were being barred from energizing the US economy. Churchwell observes that the story is "a cautionary tale for our times: the rise and fall of the American Dream," one in which soaring inequality and stagnation destroy dreams of thriving prosperity.[19] Although Black slavery was the economic bedrock of the United States, as with the *Hamilton* musical, slavery is not a theme of the *Lehman* narrative.

When the Lehman brothers arrived in Mobile, Alabama, in the mid-1840s, the Cotton Kingdom in the Mississippi Valley was at its height, the center of capitalism both in the United States and the world. After New Orleans, Mobile was the second largest port for the export of cotton to the textile mills in England and the northeast United States. To operate the cotton industry required vast supplies, and the Lehman brothers built a fortune fulfilling that need. The play makes much of the dry goods provided by the Lehmans' mercantile business but no mention of the most valued commodity, which was the Black human body. Debt instruments had been created in the Cotton Kingdom that used enslaved bodies as collateral, which could be transferred into mortgages and bonds; they were simply a common financial asset that could be sold nationally and internationally, even in places where slavery was outlawed. Between 1840 and 1860, the cotton and slave economy made up half of the total goods exported from the United States and formed the basis of institutions that are fundamental in the present: policing and the prison system and the real estate, insurance, and finance systems.[20] A year before Lehman Brothers' 2008 collapse, the House Judiciary Committee conducted a hearing on the legacy of the slave trade and slave labor, naming prestigious financial firms involved in the slave trade, including Lehman Brothers as well as Aetna, New York Life Insurance, Brooks Brothers, and J. P. Morgan Chase.[21]

That said, in the US South when the Lehmans arrived, when the numbers of enslaved people were at their apex, there were only one hundred twenty Jews among the forty-five thousand slaveholders owning twenty or more slaves, and only twenty Jews among the twelve thousand slaveholders owning fifty or more slaves.[22] The conspiracy pseudo-theory of Jewish domination of the African slave trade and Jews as a major slaver element in the Americas, such as the 1991 Nation of Islam two-volume publication "The Secret Relationship of Jews and Blacks," is part of the larger anti-Jewish mythology of economic control. In Western Europe and Britain, Catholics and Protestants were the drivers of the transatlantic slave trade and made up the overwhelming majority of slavers. Some Jews were slavers and some were involved in the slave trade, but most who were involved in the slave economy, which was the basis of the US economy, were, like the Lehmans, merchant suppliers of goods.

At the eve of the Civil War, almost a third of Southern families were slavers, and in Mississippi and South Carolina 50 percent were. In the 1950s, only 2 percent of US families owned corporation stocks equal in value to the 1860 value of a single slave. On a typical plantation (more than twenty slaves) the capital value of the slaves was greater than the capital value of the land and implements. Slavery was profitable, although a large part of the profit was in the increased value of the slaves' bodies. And although the population of the South was only 30 percent of the US population, the South had 60 percent of the wealthiest individuals. The 1860 per capita income in the South was $3,978; in the North it was $2,040.[23]

Enslaved-labor production of wealth and the wealth accrued from the commodification of enslaved bodies added to the wealth amassed in the sale of land taken from deported Native nations. Enslaved bodies and real estate in land seized by the military combined to create the giant fiscal-military state that the founders envisioned. Eric Williams, the noted African Caribbean historian who also served as the first prime minister of the independent state and former British colony Trinidad and Tobago, published the first text documenting the origins of capitalism as emerging out of the institutionalization of African slavery and the transatlantic slave trade in his 1944 book, *Capitalism and Slavery*.[24] Subsequent US and European historians built upon the concept of the institution of slavery as embedded in the development of capitalism, but the late African

American historian Cedric Robinson in the late twentieth century dug deeper and theorized "racial capitalism" that went beyond simply the period of slavery to the essence of capitalism today.[25] Slavery and the slave trade constituted the basis of US capitalist development and articulates racial capitalism today.

In 1807, the US Congress prohibited the international slave trade. Illicit smuggling thrived, however, accounting for likely tens of thousands of imports from Africa. The US government was complicit in the illegal trade, refusing to allow British ships—in implementing the ban on the international slave trade—to search US flagged ships at sea. Thereby, US flagged ships continued shipping enslaved Africans so that by 1845, as W.E.B. Du Bois pointed out, "a large part of the trade was under the stars and stripes; by 1850 fully one-half the trade, and in the decade, 1850–1860 nearly all the traffic, found this flag its best protection."[26] Historian Walter Johnson is one of the few historians of slavery in the United States to identify the Cotton Kingdom as the site for the rise of the fully articulated US capitalist state. It began with appropriation of the land that made the Cotton Kingdom possible. Following the 1815 Battle of New Orleans, Johnson writes, "Andrew Jackson spent the next fifteen years—first as a general in the U.S. Army, then as the military governor of Florida, and finally as the president of the United States—supervising the ethnic cleansing and racial pacification of the southeastern United States. . . . The homelands of the Indigenous nations had, through military force, been converted into a vast reserve for the cultivation of whiteness." With forced removal, ethnic cleansing was complete, and slaveholders—with their reserve of capital, enslaved African bodies—transformed the Mississippi Valley into the Cotton Kingdom which formed the basis for US capitalism and world trade. "The extension of slavery into the Mississippi Valley gave an institution that was in decline at the end of the eighteenth century new life in the nineteenth." The population of enslaved Africans in the Deep South states increased from 100,000 in 1800 to 250,000 in 1840, and to more than 750,000 in 1860.[27]

Johnson writes, "The fortunes of cotton planters in Louisiana and cotton brokers in Liverpool, of the plantations of the Mississippi Valley and the textile mills of Manchester, were tied together through the cotton trade—the largest single sector of the global economy in the first half of the nineteenth century"[28] Although there were already some enslaved Africans in the area before the boom, a domestic slave trade developed, transforming the original Atlantic plantation states into slave exporters. Approximately a million slaves were brought to the Mississippi Valley between 1820 and 1840, some with their migrating slavers, but the majority bred for the purpose of enslavement. Slave traders walked the slaves southward, bound wrist to wrist in a coffle (chained together in a line).

An industry emerged with firms competing with individual slave traders, maintaining offices with jails that could keep up to one hundred slaves at a time. Around the jails were large spaces where the enslaved people were forced to exercise, as well as attached exhibition rooms where interested buyers could assess the property and decide on purchases. Slave traders developed a formal system of grading slaves: "Extra Men, No. 1 Men, Second Rate or Ordinary Men, Extra Girls, No. 1 Girls, Second Rate or Ordinary Girls," and so on, allowing the traders to quantify physical distinctions between the bodies into a comparative scale, then base the price on those factors. But, Johnson writes, the so-called domestic slave trade was never just that: "The price of Southern cotton that the price of slaves so surely tracked was, as every planter was repeatedly told by every factor, set by the prices that cotton buyers in markets as distant as New York and Liverpool were willing to pay. The value of the ground beneath the feet of the new white inhabitants of the Mississippi Valley, as well as that of the slaves whom they drove westward and then out into the fields every morning, pitched and rolled in response to the rhythm of distant exchanges."[29] That is racial capitalism as provided for by the founding fiscal-military state; the Cotton Kingdom was also a war zone of surveillance and slaver counterinsurgency.

SLAVE PATROLS

Slave patrols did not originate in the Cotton Kingdom, but they were more efficiently brutal in the capitalist order than in the original slave colonies. They appeared in the South Carolina colony in the late 1600s. As historian Sally Hadden writes of slave patrols, "People other than masters or overseers had legitimate rights, indeed, legal duties, to regulate slave behavior."[30] They originated with the 1661 and 1688 slave codes in the British Caribbean colony of Barbados, which extended policing of enslaved Africans from slavers and overseers to the public. Any enslaved person outside the direct control of the slaver or overseer was required to carry a pass and subjected to questioning by a slave patroller, as well as by any member of the European population. Slave patrols were separate from the traditional English constables who policed European residents. Many of these Barbados slavers, with their enslaved subjects, moved to the British South Carolina colony, which had been established in 1651.[31] Slave patrols were then established in Virginia and in other colonies. Most white males were required to serve in slave patrols, but the commanders were property owners. Impoverished white men were not allowed to be patrollers as they would be unable to compensate a slaver for lost property if a death or injury occurred during an attempted capture. Slave patrols were not the same as the later entrepreneurial individual "slave catchers," who were bounty hunters that proliferated in the Cotton Kingdom and beyond.[32]

After US independence, rapid expansion of slavery into newly conquered Indigenous territories brought a surge in slave patrols, but the basic structure remained. An 1860 judicial hornbook, *The Practice at Law in North Carolina*, is an example:

The patrol shall visit the negro houses in their respective districts as often as may be necessary, and may inflict a punishment, not exceeding fifteen lashes, on all slaves they may find off their owner's plantations, without a proper permit or pass, designating the place or places, to which the slaves have leave to go. The patrol shall also visit all suspected places, and suppress all unlawful collections of slaves; shall be diligent in apprehending all runaway negroes in their respective districts; shall be vigilant and endeavor to detect all thefts, and bring the perpetrators to justice, and also all persons guilty of trading with slaves; and if, upon taking up a slave and chastising him, as herein directed, he shall behave insolently, they may inflict further punishment for his misconduct, not exceeding thirty-nine lashes.[33]

In late nineteenth-century criminal digests, arrests made by slave patrollers before the Civil War continued to be used as legal precedents. In the segregated Jim Crow South, sheriffs continued the work of slave patrols, and those practices formed the culture of twentieth-century policing nationwide.

Horses played a central role in pursuing runaways. Horses were a symbol of power for slavers, not only for show and racing but also as a physical symbol of racial power. Johnson writes, "The words 'slave patrol' summon to mind a vision of white men on horseback, an association so definitive that it elides the remarkable fact that the geographic pattern of county governance in the South emerged out of circuits ridden by eighteenth-century slave patrols."[34] It was not only the advantage of height and speed that a horse provided in pursuing a person on the run, but also the nature of the animal itself, its own power, the fear the huge, galloping animal could evoke, and the severe bodily harm it inflicted when it trampled a person or when the patroller tethered a bound captive to the horse. And, of course, slavers used dogs. Resistant Africans marooned in the swamps or, if fleeing, rested there. Horses could not navigate swamps, and most settler personnel were afraid to enter them. Bloodhounds were trained from pups to identify and hunt Black people. Johnson writes, " 'Loyal' to their masters (or those to whom their masters hired) and able to travel more rapidly than any human being across even the most difficult ground, these weaponized dogs were implacable enemies, driven by a purpose beyond that of even their owners." Another tool was the widely distributed "Wanted" flier that alerted the public to be on the lookout, which attracted white men from hundreds of miles away to hunt freedom seekers for bounty.[35]

By the 1820s, there were 230,000 free Black people in the United States. Thomas Jefferson originated the idea of how to get rid of them and came up with the destination: Africa. Jefferson, with other like-thinking slavers, created the American Colonization Society as a private company in 1817, which established the colony of Liberia on the west coast of Africa in 1822, becoming an independent state in 1847. The indigenous people who lived there were not consulted. The Black Americans spoke only English, and they were essentially settlers.

Henry Clay became the leader of the colonization movement in the 1820s. He envisioned drawing funds from Native land sales west of the Mississippi in order to colonize indigenous land in West Africa. Johnson makes the important point that the issues addressed by the elite US proponents of Black colonization were not related to slavery per se, but rather to their problem with the presence of free Black people. "Colonization was less a program for racial purification than one designed to maintain the internal frontier between black and white, master and slave, even while making it possible to imagine that boundary someday meeting its natural limit—the territorial boundary of an all-white United States."[36]

FROM SLAVERY TO JIM CROW

By 1860, there were a half million free Black people in the United States. In the midst of the Civil War, Abraham Lincoln also entertained a scheme to get rid of emancipated Black people.[37] Johnson writes, "The history of the nineteenth-century United States was marked by repeated efforts to expatriate free blacks, to identify the space of US national sovereignty with the process of white racial purification, and to harness the property (in the form of the value of enslaved people) to the purpose of white supremacy."[38]

The Thirteenth Amendment, ratified in 1868, made millions of enslaved people legally free, while the Fourteenth Amendment mandated their citizenship and the citizenship of every person born in the United States.[39] However, the Thirteenth Amendment included an exception to freedom from servitude: "Neither slavery nor involuntary servitude, except as a punishment for crime whereof the party shall have been duly convicted, shall exist within the United States, or any place subject to their jurisdiction." Although the amendment abolished slavery, it allowed the exception that involuntary servitude

remained punishment for a crime. The Virginia Supreme Court decision in *Ruffin v. Commonwealth* affirmed that convicts had the status of slaves: "He [the defendant] has, as a consequence of his crime,
not only forfeited his liberty, but all his personal rights. . . . He is for
the time being the slave of the State. He is civiliter mortuus; and his
estate, if he has any, is administered like that of a dead man."[40]

Michelle Alexander, in her book *The New Jim Crow*, theorizes
about the effect of this exception on the mass incarceration of African Americans. In 2016, African American filmmaker Ava DuVernay directed the documentary *13th,* in which Alexander, Angela
Davis, law professor Bryan Stevenson, and others, describe in detail
how the Southern elite, within a few years after the US military
occupation that was to protect the process of Reconstruction and
empower the emancipated people, abandoned that effort. Alexander's text and DuVernay's documentary link the conviction loophole
of the Thirteenth Amendment to the incarceration of vast numbers of
mainly young men in the twentieth century, starting with convict
leasing in the former Confederate states under the Jim Crow segregation regime. In that way, the former slavers rebuilt cotton production and wealth using the unfree labor of Black convicts, a practice
that spanned the entire era of Jim Crow segregation legislation
until 1951 when Congress explicitly outlawed the practice.[41] The
presumed connection between convict leasing and contemporary
disproportionate incarceration of Black people is dubious, although
the Thirteenth Amendment inclusion of incarceration as slavery is
undoubtedly a factor of the mass incarceration, as are modern urban
police forces grounded in slave patrols.

Surveillance and control of most Black people continued during
Reconstruction. The occupying US Army took no concerted action against the patrols in most places, forcing formerly enslaved
Africans to remain and work on plantations. Even with military
vigilance, "patrolling" Black people continued as a form of organized terrorism, perpetrated especially by the Ku Klux Klan, which
was founded for that very purpose nineteen months after the Civil
War ended. The intensive military training and experience over four
years of fighting in the Confederate Army produced a militaristic
character to local police forces and patrol techniques under the

post-Reconstruction Jim Crow regime. Freed African Americans no longer even had the protection of being valued as property and collateral by former slavers, allowing for extreme forms of revenge, violence, and terror against them.

During Reconstruction, when the US Army was an occupying force, Black Republicans were elected to state and local offices and attempted to reform the all-white local and state militias, requiring all males to serve regardless of race. Few Anglo-Americans were willing to serve with Black people. But African Americans did serve in the state militias as well as founding their own local volunteer militia groups. Former slavers spread rumors that Black people were forming insurrectionary armies to kill white people. Former slavers created their own armed gangs to intimidate other white farmers and merchants who traded with Black farmers and artisans, the threats and acts of violence putting white merchants out of business. Most ominously, elite white Southerners formed volunteer militias under the guise of private rifle clubs. By 1876, South Carolina had more than 240 such clubs. This allowed thousands of Confederate combat veterans, along with former Confederate guerrillas, to mobilize quickly. The KKK was the most violent syndicate, its purpose being to subdue the Black population and to exploit their labor.

Either by their absence in many places or by their actions in others, some of the US Army officers in charge made these failures of Reconstruction possible. One character that stands out, but is also representative, is US general Edward R. S. Canby, a Kentuckian who was the army occupation commander of the Carolinas. Canby refused use of the soldiers under his command to enforce the new laws and instead relied on white Southern law enforcement to maintain order. He had to have known what would happen. Like many US Civil War commanders assigned to the occupation army of the former Confederacy, he was reassigned in 1872 to the Army of the West, where he commanded troops to round up several dozen Modoc families in Northern California who refused to be forced into an Oregon reservation. The Modocs waged a yearlong resistance to the US Army's counterinsurgency, finally killing General Canby.[42] One factor that led to the US pulling troops out of the South prematurely was the dozens of wars the United States was initiating against Indigenous nations in the Northern Plains, Southwest, and West, led by former Union Army officers—in addition to Canby, William Tecumseh Sherman, Phillip H. Sheridan, George Crook, Nelson Miles, George Armstrong Custer, and others. Undoubtedly, engrained white supremacy among the white army officers contributed to their poor performance as enforcers of desegregation.

Southern slavers were grounded in generations of enforcing slavery, which had continued where possible during the Civil War. What was different after the war ended, compared to the slave regime, was accessibility to the tons of technologically advanced guns and ammunition and the tens of thousands of militarily seasoned and violent men who made ideal candidates for the Klan. When the Confederate war hero and former slaver Nathan Bedford Forrest joined the Klan, it gained a chivalric image that attracted other war heroes. Although Congress enacted laws forbidding secret groups, they were rarely effectively enforced. In fact, the United States never broke with the slaveocracy, as exemplified in the career of Forrest. He lost his parents and economic security at seventeen, but became a slave trader, land speculator, and finally a wealthy slaver with his own large plantation. He was the epitome of the "self-made" man that was the vaunted ideal of white settler mythology. In the Civil War, Forrest was a Confederate cavalry officer and was infamous for having led the massacre of hundreds of disarmed Black Union soldiers in 1864, a war crime even at that time. Yet President Andrew Johnson granted Forrest a presidential pardon in 1868 while he was a hero of the Klan.[43]

Illegal as it was, the Klan operated like a reconstituted, albeit much more heavily armed, slave patrol, requiring African Americans to carry written permission to travel to and from the plantations where many continued to work. The Klan established curfews for gatherings of African Americans, as well as limits on the number who could gather. The Klan burned the homes of Black families, confiscated their guns, and inflicted punishment similar to slave patrols' beatings, but they also had far more freedom to torture and murder their victims, since the Black body no longer carried monetary value that the murderer would have to compensate the slaver for. Black people organized and resisted, as they had resisted slavery and slave patrols. However, the Klan was a private terrorist organization, not a public entity, and had no legal status or accountability. Now and then, a Klansman would be put on trial by the occupying US Army, but no one would ever be convicted for Klan violence, even murder. Occasionally, the US Army would declare martial law, but as one army commander said in 1871, "The entire United States Army would be insufficient to give protection throughout the South to everyone in possible danger from the Klan."[44] The Klan was effectively the reconstituted Confederate Army.

JIM CROW GOES NATIONAL

In the late nineteenth-century South, arrests made by slave patrollers before the Civil War continued to be used as legal precedents. From the perspective of African Americans who survived the organized violence, there was no distinction between past slave patrols, the Klan, and white policemen, whether rural, in towns, or in the cities. In the first four decades of the twentieth century, some six million African Americans fled the hideous terror of the Jim Crow South, but Jim Crow followed them.

Between 1940 and 1950, one and a half million Southern Black people migrated north and west, more than three hundred thousand to work in the war industry in the greater Los Angeles and San Francisco Bay areas.[45] During the same period, a wave of Southern and Southwestern Anglo-Americans migrated to those locales for jobs in war production. They joined the nearly half million mostly white migrants from Oklahoma, Texas, Arkansas, and Missouri who had fled the Depression and droughts of the 1930s to work in the agribusiness fields of the California Central Valley. Many of them also joined the wartime workforce. Following the war boom in jobs, many of the white people who had come from the South and border states were able to buy homes and moved into the white working-class communities in South Central Los Angeles. When Black families began buying homes in those neighborhoods, the white people moved on to Orange County and the San Bernardino and San Fernando Valleys.

In 1950, William Parker became chief of the Los Angeles Police Department (LAPD) for the following decade and a half, ending his reign after the 1965 Watts uprising. The LAPD, like most US urban police forces, was already virtually all white and mostly Irish American when Parker took control. But now there was a sizable population of African American workers living in blue-collar South Central Los Angeles. With the goal of controlling the Black population, Parker began building the ranks of the force with white people who had moved to the area from the South and Southwest. The new, powerful technology of television brought the LAPD-produced drama series *Dragnet* to homes in every part of the country, extolling the LAPD and attracting recruits, as well as influencing other urban police forces nationwide. During this time, the LAPD became the most notorious racist police operation ("police culture") in the country, with nearly every aspect of the Southern tradition of slave patrols woven into the system.[46] A similar police force was formed in Oakland, where many Black veterans and war-industry workers had made their homes.

FROM THE CIVIL RIGHTS REVOLUTION
TO THE CARCERAL LANDSCAPE

Several decades of the Black civil rights movement efforts made widespread gains in the 1950s and '60s, with school integration mandated by law in 1953 and civil rights legislation in 1964. There was growing Black resistance to police violence in the South, in Northern cities, and in Los Angeles and Oakland. During the summer of 1965, police killed thirty-one people in the Watts Los Angeles uprising, while over four thousand were arrested. President Lyndon Johnson declared a "war on crime," and with the Law Enforcement Assistance Act, the federal government would provide to local police forces military weapons that were being used in the US war in Vietnam, and many Vietnam veterans upon their return would join those forces. Police mainly patrolled Black neighborhoods and arrested Black people.[47]

The Black Panther Party (BPP) formed in Oakland, California, in 1967 and quickly spread to Los Angeles and other cities, challenging police violence primarily but also building mutual aid in Black communities and providing inspiration for predominately white radical movements, including the anti–Vietnam War movement. Criminalization of members of the BPP by the nearly all-white urban police forced the organization's national and local leaders into multiple criminal court cases, while the FBI instrumentalized its counterintelligence program (COINTELPRO), that is, a domestic counterinsurgency operation that led to BPP internal divisions and even deaths. The decimation of the BPP took place during President Richard Nixon's administration. Police violence and accelerated incarceration of African Americans soared and was continued by subsequent administrations. Multiplied by the discriminatory sentences for drug possession in the "war on drugs," mainly marijuana, the era of prison construction and mass incarceration of Black people was launched and ballooned.[48]

By the turn of the twenty-first century, a carceral landscape spread across the continent, with federal, state, and local prisons in deindustrialized sites as well as chronically impoverished rural areas functioning as a jobs program. One out of every one hundred people in the US was behind bars, the total number over 2.3 million—172,000 in 102 federal prisons, 1,200,000 in 1,700 state prisons, and 680,000 in 3,200 local jails, plus 942 juvenile facilities and 79 Native American jails, plus immigration detention centers and military prisons. Some 150,000 more inmates were in privately owned and operated prisons. African American male inmates made up 37 percent of the male prison population, while Black males make up 6 percent of the US population. White males made up 32 percent of the prison population, exactly their percentage of the US white male population. Only Native Americans are incarcerated at a higher rate than African Americans, 38 percent higher than the national average.[49]

In a study of California, Ruth Wilson Gilmore documents incarceration in what is generally considered a liberal state. Between 1982—the Reagan era—and the turn of the century, the prison population grew nearly 500 percent. African Americans and Latinos, mostly Mexican, made up two-thirds of the 160,000 inmates in the state's prisons. Most were from urban centers, especially the larger Los Angeles basin, and more than half were employed before the arrest but were soon indigent, with 80 percent being assigned state-appointed lawyers. During that time, the state built twenty-three major new prisons, whereas between 1852 and 1964, there were only twelve state prisons. In addition to the prisons, the state ran five less restrictive prison camps and thirteen community corrections facilities, each with five hundred beds. The cost to the state's general fund went from 2 percent in 1982 to 8 percent in the early 2000s. The California Department of Corrections became the largest state agency, with 54,000 employed.[50]

Gilmore, along with Angela Davis and dozens of other scholars and activists, has developed the research and analysis that calls for abolition of prisons. Gilmore writes, "The purpose of abolition is to expose and defeat all the relationships and policies that make the United States the world's top cop, warmonger, and jailer. Practicalities rather than metaphors determine the focus and drive the analysis, because the scope of prison touches every aspect of ordinary life. . . . Abolition is a movement to end systemic violence, including the interpersonal vulnerabilities and displacements that keep the system going . . . by putting people before profits, welfare before warfare, and life over death."[51]

Every Black inmate, whether they were jaywalking or breaking into a convenience store or driving a car, began the journey to incarceration by the actions of one or two or more men with guns. These gunmen had badges and totalitarian authority at the moment of encounter, and the Black person often ended up dead at the scene. Law enforcement boomed in the 1980s and '90s, consuming up to half of cities' budgets. Police unions functioned as parallel agencies without any public scrutiny, successfully defending any of their members from punishment for murder or other abuse. Programs of reform, retraining, antibias training, and ethnic and racial diversification failed to change a police culture of anti-Black bias in the United States. As Alex Vitale writes, "Any effort to make policing more just must address the problems of excessive force, overpolicing, and disrespect for the public. Much of the public debate has focused on new and enhanced training, diversifying the police, and embracing community policing as strategies for reform, along with enhanced accountability measures."[52]

POLICE KILLING BLACK PEOPLE

Police in the United States kill civilians at a far higher rate than any other wealthy country: per ten million people, US police kill 35.5 individuals while Canadian police, which have a negative reputation for violence and targeting among Native people, kill 9.8 individuals per ten million. Australian police kill 8.5 per ten million; the Netherlands, 2.3; New Zealand, 2.0; Germany, 2.3; the United Kingdom, 0.5; Japan, 0.2; Iceland and Norway, zero.[53]

Although not new, police abuse and killings of Black individuals became visible with the advent of the home video recorder, first appearing on evening television news programs in March 1991, thanks to the video that recorded the brutal beating and arrest of Rodney King by Los Angeles police. The video, made by a neighbor from his balcony, was widely viewed and denounced. Within three days of outcry and demonstrations, the LAPD released King without charges, and soon after the four officers who administered the brutal beating were indicted by a grand jury. However, the seventeen officers who stood by and watched the beating were not indicted. As preparations were being made for trial in Los Angeles, a superior court judge ordered the trial moved to the northern suburb of Simi Valley, which happened to be a white, middle-class community where many LA police officers lived or retired to. It was also the site of the Ronald Reagan library. It was unlikely that a Simi Valley jury would convict police officers, and they did not. The jury was composed of eight men and four women. Nine of the jurors were white, two were Black, and one, Latino. On April 29, 1992, the officers were acquitted, and a massive uprising began in South Central Los Angeles, lasting six days. It spread beyond predominately Black South Central to other parts of Los Angeles, including the predominately Korean district, where a Korean woman shopkeeper shot and killed a fifteen-year-old girl who was Black, exacerbating the already tense relations between the more affluent Korean immigrant community and the Black community.[54]

Intense policing in Black communities and unpublicized police killings of Black people continued in the 1990s, monitored closely and protested by Copwatch, which was founded in 1990, and Critical Resistance, founded in 1997 by Angela Y. Davis, Ruth Wilson Gilmore, and Rose Braz, and other anti-racist activist groups. The protests grew beyond activists when twenty-two-year-old Oscar Grant was shot and killed by a San Francisco Bay Area Transit cop, who was found guilty of involuntary manslaughter and spent only eleven months in a county jail. In early 2012, seventeen-year-old Trayvon Martin was murdered in Sanford, Florida, by George Zimmerman, a self-appointed neighborhood watchman of a mostly white gated community. Martin was visiting his Black father, who was a resident there. Zimmerman was acquitted by a jury.

In mid-July 2014, forty-four-year-old Eric Garner, who was an asthmatic, was killed in a chokehold by a Staten Island, New York, police officer. The officer accused Garner of illegally selling cigarettes, which he denied. He asked the officer to leave him alone; instead, the officer pushed Garner to the sidewalk. The video of the incident showed officers holding Garner face down on the ground while he repeated "I can't breathe" eleven times before he lost consciousness. He lay unconscious for seven minutes without medical aid from the officers awaiting an ambulance and was pronounced dead on arrival at the hospital. A grand jury determined not to indict the police officer, and he continued as an officer until he was fired five years later.

Less than a month after the Garner murder, eighteen-year-old Michael Brown Jr. was shot by a police officer in Ferguson, Missouri, a predominately Black suburb of St. Louis. A week of round-the-clock demonstrations in Ferguson ensued. The local police, backed by police from nearby St. Louis, and the National Guard behaved like military in a war zone, although they were never under threat. In the months after the killing, there were more than fifty demonstrations against police brutality nationwide. In the widely televised protests in Ferguson, the militarization of civilian police was on view for all to see.[55]

The militarization of the police was directly related to the endless US wars in Afghanistan and the Middle East that began after the 9/11 disaster, creating a surplus of military weaponry, which was offered to police forces across the country. In his indispensable book *The Rise of the Warrior Cop*, Radley Balko tells an illustrative story of the 91 percent white town of Keene, New Hampshire, population twenty-three thousand, and their surprise when, in 2011, the town government was offered a $285,933 grant from the Department of Homeland Security to purchase a Bearcat, an eight-ton armored personnel vehicle, for its small police department. A sizable group at the city council meeting considering the offer opposed taking the equipment, but the defense contractor representative presented terrorism scare scenarios that dismissed the opposition. Keene was hardly the only recipient of war machinery from the government. Balko writes, "Since the September 11 attacks, Homeland Security has been handing out antiterrorism grants like parade candy, giving cities and towns across the country funds to buy military-grade armored vehicles, guns, armor, aircraft, and other equipment." The military-industrial complex has thrived, "creating yet another class of government hardware contractors, and a new interest group to lobby Washington to ensure the process of police militarization continues." By 2011, Homeland Security had spent $34 billion in domestic military grants to police forces, going to all-sized cities.[56] Balko traces the militarization and increased violence of the police back to the postwar civil rights and anti-war organizing and demonstrations, particularly the Nixon administration's war on drugs, which led to a gradual increase in the size, scope, and culture of the police.

The militarized police were on full display, along with armed white nationalist thugs, after the May 25, 2020, police killing of forty-five-year-old George Floyd in Minneapolis. It was a particularly gruesome incident captured on video, all nine minutes and twenty-nine seconds showing the police officer pressing his knee with full body weight on Floyd's neck, with the victim repeating "I can't breathe" and calling for his mother until he was lifeless, and still the cop's knee remained on his neck. The two other police officers did nothing to intervene while bystanders yelled at the cop, who appeared to savor the attention. Protests broke out across the country. A little-publicized police killing of a Black woman, Breonna Taylor, two months earlier in Louisville, Kentucky, came to national and international attention with massive months-long demonstrations in Louisville and nationwide. Taylor was killed in her bed when narcotics police rammed the door of her apartment in the middle of the night, having used the wrong address. Between 2015 and 2020, forty-eight Black women were killed by police and only two police officers were charged.[57]

Led by Black Lives Matter, demonstrations exploded across the country during the spring and summer of 2020, at first in large urban centers but, over several weeks, erupting in small- and medium-sized towns and cities, many of them with large white majority populations. The demonstrations were met with militarized police and National Guard troops. The Movement for Black Lives emerged in 2012, following the police killing of Oscar Grant in Oakland, California. The hashtag #BlackLivesMatter began on Twitter and was created by young Black activists, led by Alicia Garza, Opal Tometi, and Patrisse Cullors, three Black women in Oakland.[58] These women were acting in the tradition of the historical leadership of Black women, from Sojourner Truth and Harriet Tubman to Fannie Lou Hamer and Ella Baker to Angela Davis and the women of the Black Panthers and the Combahee River Collective that was founded in 1974.[59]

AFRICAN AND AFRICAN CARIBBEAN IMMIGRATION

In 1965, President Lyndon Johnson signed into law a new immigration act that replaced the exclusionist 1925 law. For the first time, a supposedly nondiscriminatory policy went into effect that allowed immigration from Africa, the Caribbean, Asia, and other non-European regions. Albeit laden with national origins quota systems, more immigrants of color did immigrate to the United States, many of them fleeing US wars and interventions in their countries. In 1980, Black immigrants from the Caribbean and Africa made up only 3 percent of the US Black population, but by the twenty-first century, Black immigrants and their offspring comprised nearly 20 percent of the US Black population, or one in five African Americans. Being Black in the United States is a marker of slavery, and a Black individual is the principal target of racial discrimination and violence, mimicking the violence imposed on Black bodies under slavery. Black immigrants and refugees from Africa and the Caribbean, like all other immigrants to the United States, arrive knowing little about the United States but often are drawn to Hollywood movies and the American Dream rhetoric. For those coming from majority Black societies, the reality of anti-Black racism is often unexpected.

Somalian refugee Mohamed Abdulkadir Ali writes, "In Somalia, we knew African Americans only through popular Hollywood movies, like *Rambo* and *Rocky,* in which they were the comic sidekicks or inept villains. They were peculiar, alien caricatures to us."[60] Ali's family had had contact with US diplomats in Somalia who had given him and his brothers gifts, figurines of the Statue of Liberty, the Empire State building, the Golden Gate Bridge. He writes, "Then, in 1989, civil war broke out. As violence began to spread throughout the country, my family and many others were forced to flee abroad. And so we were pitched across the Atlantic, to the America I'd long imagined, of Coca-Cola, cowboys, and grinning white men who spoke of wealth, ambition, and towering buildings that touched the sky."[61] Temporarily placed in a small white town in Vermont, Ali became aware that he was Black: "In Somalia, my blackness was like the blueness of the sky; it was always there, an immutable fixture in the world, and so there was no reason to dwell upon it. . . . In America, though, I became acutely conscious of it. How it shaped and twisted my path through the world. How it came to determine the texture and flavor of every moment in life, from the very small to very big. How it shaded every human connection I sought to make."[62]

Ali's family, like many Somalian refugees to the US, was placed in a poor Black neighborhood in Columbus, Ohio, with forty thousand other Somalis already there. That neighborhood, like other poor, Black ones, had a legacy of crime, imprisonment, and overpolicing.

He writes, "We looked at how our neighbors suffered, and we thought we are not them, we will not become them. To assimilate was to become black, and to become black, well, that was unimaginable. And so we encased ourselves in our Somali identity, as a shield against becoming black in America."[63] Later, trained as a lawyer and in New York to interview for a prestigious position, he was profiled and slammed against the wall by police, finally understanding the "rage that fills you up, winds you up, and holds you so tightly you sometimes feel you cannot think or breathe. . . . But you hold onto it so tightly, for it is better than the alternative: a crippling fear. . . . I am Somali, I am African, I am a refugee of war. This is my history. But every time I go out my door in America, a 400-year history of generational pain, anger, and trauma is foisted upon me. It has weighed down every step I've taken there. It made me stumble when I sought to stride."[64] Ali returned to Africa to live, where, he writes, "I have come to have a lightness in my step, long forgotten, that has made me wonder: Is this the way white people feel in America?"[65]

Anti-Black racism permeates US society—not only from white people but also from Asian, Latino, and Native American communities. Profiled by law enforcement and by employers, every Black person in the country lives a precarious life from a very young age and throughout life. Black African and Caribbean immigrants are not immune from anti-Black racism in the United States.[66] African and Caribbean immigrants and refugees to the US are themselves descendants of people who were enslaved and colonized by Europeans and the United States, but the countries they come from have majority Black populations and are independent states—at least since the 1970s—with seats in the United Nations, unlike Black people in the United States, who make up a little over 12 percent of the population and have no autonomous status.

Writer Edwidge Danticat, a Haitian immigrant to the United States, writes, "Describing the reaction of some of Minnesota's Somali refugees to the sadistic killing of Floyd, Fartun Weli, the executive director of Isuroon—a nonprofit organization that supports Somali families—told the Minneapolis *Star Tribune,* 'They were like, "We can't believe it. This is America."'" Danticat explains that brutal police killings of Black people in the US comes to resonate for Black immigrants, as it did for Ali. She tells of her own tragic loss when in 1997 a family friend, Abner Louima, also a Haitian immigrant, was detained in Brooklyn and dragged to the precinct where he was assaulted, several police officers beating him with their fists and with flashlights and nightsticks, then sexually assaulted him with a wooden broom handle, requiring three major surgeries. His arrest was due to mistaken identity; he was not the Black suspect the police were pursuing. Danticat writes:

Some black immigrant parents harbor the illusion that if their émigré and U.S.-born children are the most polite, the best dressed, and the hardest working in school, they might somehow escape the brunt of systemic racism. But the myth of the good immigrant as exempt from police assault and murder kept getting shattered around us. By the February 4, 1999, killing of Amadou Diallo, a twenty-three-year-old Guinean, slaughtered on his doorstep by nineteen of the forty-one police bullets aimed at him as he reached for his wallet; by the March 16, 2000, shooting of Patrick Dorismond, the twenty-six-year-old son of Haitian immigrants, by undercover officers.[67]

The US government does not welcome Haitian immigrants, who have one of the highest deportations rates. The United States Marines invaded Haiti in 1915 and militarily occupied the country to 1934, nearly two decades. Two generations of Haitians grew up under US military occupation, which was oppressive and often violent. The majority of Haitians are desperately poor, and a large percentage are homeless in their own country following the devastating 2010 earthquake that killed nearly a quarter of a million people. For eight years, from 1916 to 1924, during the same period of the occupation of Haiti, the border country of the Dominican Republic was also occupied by the US military. In both countries, chaos, instability, and impoverishment resulted in emigration, much of it undocumented, to the United States. Historian Ryan Fontanilla, who also served in the US Coast Guard, had the unsavory task of participating in the rough and often violent pursuits of Haitian asylum seekers crowded in rickety boats attempting to reach US territory. He writes that the legal structure of Coast Guard techniques is rooted in the transatlantic slave trade. "A disquieting intuition repeated in my head: the USCG cutter, the Haitians' sailing vessel, and European slave ships represented a triad of homologous instances in which people of African descent have suffered involuntary concentration in small spaces upon the Atlantic. I dreaded that I was in closer proximity to the enslavers of the past, and to the cops and jailors of the present, than I ever would be to those Haitians."[68]

Indian American Suketu Mehta notes, "The world grows ever more horrific for human beings caught in conflicts, internal or international. In 2012, there were 930,000 newly registered asylum seekers driven out from their countries. Three years later, there were 2.3 million." The United States ranks nineteenth in the number of immigrants per capita it takes in annually.[69] The wealthiest country in the world and the one most responsible for wars in Africa, Asia, and Latin America is unwilling to allow the refugees they generate to move to the United States.

AFRICAN AMERICANS
POST-SLAVERY AND REPARATIONS

The US republic was from its birth the engine of capitalist accumulation in expropriating Native land to sell to land speculators, slavers, and later the railroads and white settlers, under the Homestead Act, thereby financing the government and its military, which carried out the expulsions and crushed enslaved people's resistance. The plantation economy that developed in the Mississippi Valley was fully realized capitalism. The planters' capital was human, bodies were fungible private property, the value of which was more than all other private property, machinery, infrastructure, manufacturing, and free labor combined in the United States at that time. Indeed, the question of whether imported enslaved Africans could be counted as immigrants in "a nation of immigrants" ideology gives discomfort; so, the answer for Lin-Manuel Miranda in the *Hamilton* fantasy was to make everyone Black and everyone an immigrant.

Native scholars have written on, and largely rejected, the notion that enslaved Africans or their emancipated descendants were settlers in the framework of settler colonialism, although some freedmen and families did receive land grants in Indian Territory, and others later purchased allotments after the forced federal allotment of Native lands there. One designation for the status of enslaved Africans that rarely appears is that of being the first proletariat in the United States. US labor history is Eurocentric, but what were slave revolts if not labor strikes? Of course, they were about more than that, as they were about freedom from bondage, but they were also about labor exploitation and powerlessness and self-organizing.

Due to the centuries-long resistance of North American Indigenous nations and the work of Native scholars, it is clear to most progressive US educators and intellectuals that the US is a settler-colonial state, attempting genocide in seizing nearly all the land bases of the original inhabitants who now remain under a colonial regime. But what of descendants of enslaved Africans in the United States? Civil rights legislation and affirmative action have been capable of creating a professional elite, but cultural and economic oppression persist. The Black Power movement of the 1960s and '70s broke away from the civil rights movement's limitations in light of national liberation movements and formal United Nations decolonization in Africa, Asia and the Pacific, and the Caribbean. Black nationalists theorized the Black colony in the South, but the theory was incomplete and did not present a strategy for a liberated future while it ideologically eliminated the Native.

Descendants of enslaved Africans in the Western Hemisphere have a common history that binds them and crosses borders, as do the Indigenous peoples of the hemisphere. In 2001, the Declaration of the United Nations World Conference Against Racism, Racial Discrimination, Xenophobia, and Related Intolerance, held in Durban, South Africa, acknowledged that common history:

We acknowledge that slavery and the slave trade, including the transatlantic slave trade, were appalling tragedies in the history of humanity not only because of their abhorrent barbarism but also in terms of their magnitude, organized nature and especially their negation of the essence of the victims, and further acknowledge that slavery and the slave trade are a crime against humanity and should always have been so, especially the transatlantic slave trade and are among the major sources and manifestations of racism, racial discrimination, xenophobia and related intolerance, and that Africans and people of African descent, Asians and people of Asian descent and indigenous peoples were victims of these acts and continue to be victims of their consequences.[70]

Although legalized racial enslavement has ended for Black people in the United States, oppression continues in institutionalized racism, discrimination, police profiling and killing, and myriad other ways. Trouillot observes that slavery is a ghost in the United States, "both the past and a living presence; and the problem of historical representation is how to represent that ghost, something that is and yet is not."[71] These past horrors require societal remembrance, and reparations are necessary, but Trouillot cautions that "focus on The Past often diverts us from the present injustices for which previous generations only set the foundations." Trouillot is concerned that for white liberals, feeling guilt about the past can be comfortable "inasmuch as it protects *them* from a racist present."[72] Western historical narratives about colonialism and slavery are filled with silences. As a Haitian historian, Trouillot was well aware of the absence of the Haitian Revolution in those narratives, but as he points out, "History does not belong only to its narrators, professional or amateur. While some of us debate what history is or was, others take it in their own hands."[73]

However, in the United States the process of Americanization of immigrants is one of erasing history with the presentation of a canned narrative of greatness and goodness and expectation of immigrant gratitude for being a part of it, threatening the immigrant's legitimacy in the absence of birthright citizenship. There is a similar expectation that, somehow, Black Americans should be grateful for Lincoln and the Civil War that brought emancipation from slavery, ignoring the tradition of enslaved African resistance and free Black abolitionism. Police killings of Black people, particularly young

Black men, simply cannot be understood without knowledge of the workings of enslavement and slave patrols. The existence and resilience of white supremacy makes no sense without understanding invented racial codes to justify genocide of Indigenous inhabitants, enslavement of Africans, and establishment of settler colonialism and continental imperialism. Racial capitalism and violence are embedded in the US fiscal-military state, the Constitution, and institutions. US historians know this history, but for professional credibility and advancement, they must obfuscate under the demand for "balance." For oppressed people to take history into their own hands, they have to know that history. The protests led by Black Lives Matter supporters during the summer of 2020 revealed a deep knowledge on the part of those who rallied and produced a process of intense education.

How immigration and the machinery of Americanization has presented barriers to structural change in the United States is pertinent but incomplete without the acknowledgment that the United States is a settler-colonialist state.

CHAPTER 4

CONTINENTAL IMPERIALISM

Although he was likely unaware of the reasons why, John F. Kennedy was right not to include Mexicans as immigrants in his "a nation of immigrants" scheme. People conquered by war and dominated by an imperialist power are not immigrants. The United States is the only rich country that has a long border with a poor and formerly European-colonized country, which provides a permanent reserve of surplus labor. And that border was imposed by an imperialist war.

US IMPERIALISM FROM THE BEGINNING

The story begins not with the 1846 US military invasion of México but in 1806 with a US military spy mission illegally entering México, which remained at that time, after nearly three centuries since the Europeans' arrival, a colony of Spain.[1] This spy mission, in preparation to annex México in order for the US to reach the Pacific and dominate the continent, took place just before the Mexican people initiated their successful war of independence. With early and incessant US intervention, as historian Greg Grandin writes, "It's a wonder México survived the nineteenth century at all."[2]

For most US historians, the United States' invasion and colonization of the Spanish territories of Cuba, Puerto Rico, and the Philippines in the late 1890s—also US interventions in those peoples' independence movements to throw off Spanish colonialism—mark the era of United States imperialism, which they portray as a period, not a persistent reality from the nation's founding and continuing into the twenty-first century. US historians traditionally have used euphemisms such as "expansion" or the "moving frontier" or "manifest destiny" rather than US imperialism to describe the three-decade process that culminated in the annexation of half of México. Yet, at the same time that President Thomas Jefferson was sending marines and warships to North Africa, he was sending military spy missions to the Spanish colony of México when the Mexican people were beginning their decade-long war of national liberation. A century later, the Marine Corps captured the period as imperialism in their hymn, "From the halls of Montezuma to the shores of Tripoli."

US historians employ passive terms such as "manifest destiny" or "westward movement" or "expansion" in conceptualizing the invasion, conquest, and colonization of Indigenous nations across the continent, as well as the invasion and occupation of the Republic of México, as natural; not colonialism, not imperialism. But they know better. Historian Frederick Jackson Turner, the author of the "frontier thesis" of US democracy, observed in 1897: "Our colonial system did not begin with the Spanish war; the United States had had a colonial history and policy from the beginning of the Republic: but they have been hidden under the phraseology of 'interstate migration' and 'territorial organization.'"[3] Turner was not criticizing that reality, only stating it. However, the subsequent academic history field "The West" ignored its founder's truth through most of the twentieth century.

Exploring the origin of United States colonialism, exceptional historian Howard Lamar traced its roots to the Northwest Ordinance enacted by the Continental Congress in 1787 and reenacted by the United States Congress in 1789, which specified successive stages of colonial development, from an imposed territorial government to a semi-representational government to, finally, admission to the Union as a state.[4] After his 1803 purchase of the Louisiana Territory from Napoleon, President Thomas Jefferson claimed that its boundaries extended to the Rio Grande, which was then a part of Spanish-occupied México. Soon after the founding of the Republic of México in 1821, US officials and newspapers began to hint that the Río Grande marked the border between the United States and

México, and there was great public conviction behind the attempt to "reunite" and "reacquire" the territory, the term "manifest destiny" being coined in 1845.[5]

In 1803, the Jefferson administration, without consulting any affected Indigenous nation, purchased the Louisiana Territory from Napoleon Bonaparte. The 828,000 square miles doubled the size of the United States. The territory encompassed all or part of multiple Indigenous nations, including the Lakota, Cheyenne, Arapaho, Crow, Pawnee, Ponca, Osage, Arikara, and Comanche, among other peoples of the bison. It also included the area that would soon be designated Indian Territory (Oklahoma), the site of forced relocation of Indigenous peoples from east of the Mississippi in the 1840s. Fifteen states would be carved out of the Louisiana Territory during the following decades—all of present-day Arkansas, Missouri, Iowa, Oklahoma, Kansas, and Nebraska; Minnesota west of the Mississippi; most of North and South Dakota; northeastern New México and north Texas; the portions of Montana, Wyoming, and Colorado east of the Continental Divide; and Louisiana west of the Mississippi River, including the city of New Orleans. The territory bordered lands occupied by Spain, including Texas and all the territory west of the Continental Divide to the Pacific Ocean. These would soon be next on the US annexation list, but it would require a two-year war, followed by more than three decades of Indigenous peoples' resistance.[6]

In preparation for US domination of the western half of North America, President Thomas Jefferson commissioned military spy missions into the newly acquired territory of the Louisiana Purchase. Setting off from St. Louis, Meriwether Lewis and William Clark traveled from August 31, 1804, to September 25, 1806, through the northern Plains and west near the Canadian border to the Pacific, gathering information about the numerous Indigenous nations and mapping the topography.[7] Jefferson then ordered two spy missions led by Lieutenant Zebulon Montgomery Pike Jr., in 1806 and 1807, into the southwest part of the Louisiana Territory, to map and assess Spanish assets and military strength. Pike's expedition provided the first documentation of United States interest in the northern provinces of México. And although the expedition led to Pike's arrest by Spanish officials when he supposedly accidentally crossed into Spanish-held New México, he took copious notes while traveling more than six hundred miles to Chihuahua as a prisoner. Pike's notes on the terrain, the flora and fauna, the behavior of his guards and the villagers along the route provided valuable information. The 1810 publication of Pike's report, which became a best-selling book, also afforded motivation for entrepreneurs to enter the area for trade.[8]

Pike's report coincided with the beginning of the Mexican war of independence, an armed national liberation movement that began in 1810, with massive peasant uprisings leading to victory and independence in 1821. Two years later, in December 1823, President James Monroe, in the annual message to Congress, included what came to be known as the Monroe Doctrine, stating "that the American continents . . . are henceforth not to be considered as subjects for future colonization by any European powers."[9] In speaking at a meeting of his cabinet, in 1825, President John Quincy Adams said,

> The world should be familiarized with the idea of considering our proper domain is to be the continent of North America. From the time we became an independent people, it was as much a law of nature that this should become our pretension that the Mississippi should flow to the sea. Spain had possession of our southern border and Great Britain was upon our north. It was impossible that centuries should elapse without finding their territories annexed to the United States.[10]

It became and remains the cornerstone of US foreign policy, distilling Thomas Jefferson's 1801 declaration that "however our present interests may restrain us within our own limits, it is impossible not to look forward to distant times, when our rapid multiplication will expand itself beyond those limits and cover the whole northern, if not the southern continent, with a people speaking the same language, governed in similar form by similar laws."[11]

US SLAVERS COLONIZE TEXAS

Nearly a year before Monroe's claim of the hemisphere as being United States–dominated territory, in January 1823, Stephen F. Austin was indemnified by the nascent and poverty-stricken Republic of México with a land grant that his father had received from Spanish authorities. Austin, a slaver in Missouri, brought three hundred other slaver families to the Texas province of México and began colonization of the region of the Brazos River in southeast Texas. Austin's father had received an impresario grant from Spain to settle in Texas, and Stephen Austin obtained recognition of the grant from México. Some thirty thousand Anglo-Americans arrived during the 1820s and '30s, many of them small farmers owning one or a few slaves but with prospects for greater wealth in property in Texas. México outlawed slavery in 1830 and banned further immigration to Texas. The Anglo slavers ignored both laws.

In 1823, Austin employed ten men initially to kill the Indigenous residents who did not comply with being pushed out of their homelands. This marked the birth of the Texas Rangers. They grew as a force, and when Texas claimed independence in 1835, they were constituted as the state militia with military titles. Historian Gary Clayton Anderson writes,

> Politicians supported Texas Ranger units that became the agents of ethnic cleansing. Rangers did act occasionally on their own, and politicians found them difficult if not, at times, impossible to control. Nevertheless, many politicians in the state had been rangers, and the paramilitary groups that forced removal or committed the occasional genocidal act were an extension of the Texas political system. . . . Anglo political elites likewise encouraged a great distrust of "the other" (which could be Indians or Tejanos), even at times in speeches individually calling for extermination of Indians.[12]

The Texas Rangers warred against the communities and nations of the Karankawa, Waco, Tehuacani, Tonkawa, and Cherokee, and their war against the Comanches and Kiowa continued to the 1880s.

With skirmishes and battles starting in 1832 that became a war of Anglo slavers' secession from México, the slavers and US mercenaries like Davy Crockett suffered a humiliating defeat that ended with their retreat into a former Franciscan mission in San Antonio, called the Alamo, in February 1836. But the slavers declared independence the following month. México did not recognize the self-styled Republic of Texas and tried to regain the territory without success. Following Texas's illegal independence, the number of enslaved Africans soared, and by the time of the Civil War they made up one-third of the Texas population and the main source of wealth.[13]

President James Polk, revealing his intentions to invade México, sent the Third Infantry Regiment to Anglo-controlled Corpus Christi in June 1845. Then, in December, with the agreement of the Anglo-Texas illegal government, the US Congress annexed Texas as the twenty-eighth state. Polk then moved the Third Army Infantry to the Rio Grande in February 1846, poised for the invasion in June.[14]

ANGLO INFILTRATION INTO NEW MÉXICO

In 1835, US Army captain Lemuel Ford of the First Dragoons wrote in his diary, "These Spaniards (Mexicans) are the meanest looking race of people I ever saw, don't appear more civilized than our Indians generally. Dirty, filthy looking creatures."[15] He was referring to comancheros that he encountered, Mexican citizens in northern México who traded and intermarried primarily with Comanches on the plains. Waddy Thompson Jr., who served as a US diplomat to México from 1842 to 1844, wrote of the people of México, "That the Indian race of México must recede before us, is quite as certain as that that is the destiny of our own Indians."[16] Army officers like Ford and diplomats like Thompson were not exceptional in their racist views of Mexicans. Indian hating and white supremacy were part and parcel of "democracy" and "freedom," and central to US foreign policy then, as it is today.

The instability of the new Republic of México as it emerged from over three centuries of Spanish colonialism and a decade of war for independence placed it in a weak position to defend its territory from US aggression. But emphasizing internal contradictions in México, as historians of the US West tend to do, distracts from the pertinent issue of merchants tied to the US economy determining and dominating the economy of northern México as the US government planned a war to annex the country in order to complete its continental imperialist ambition. Racial capitalism was at work using the playbook of the fiscal-military state. With Spain out of the way, the United States could pursue its own militaristic imperialism in the Western Hemisphere and Pacific without risking hopeless wars with European powers.

Hundreds of US traders like Waddy Thompson were involved in diverting northern New México trade from the old Camino Real, a route from Taos to Chihuahua and on to the port of Veracruz, continuing world trade with Europe. The merchant center established in Taos by Anglo residents turned trade northeastward from Taos to St. Louis. Merchants tied to the US economy soon dominated all trade. After this "conquest of merchants," it was a short step to military and political control.[17] St. Louis was established for that purpose. The city was connected to the merchant houses of the east by the Cumberland Road and to the rest of the world down the Mississippi, so that Missouri traders had the advantage of superior variety and quality of domestic and imported goods, at lower cost, than did Chihuahua traders who depended on the declining port of Veracruz.[18] Walter Johnson sees St. Louis as the crucible of US history—that much of that history unfolded from the juncture of empire and anti-Blackness that is centrally framed by the history of genocide, removal, and the expropriation and control of land, all justified in the name of white supremacy. It "rose as the morning star of US imperialism." From St. Louis, Lewis and Clark, then Pike, set out to survey territory that contained dozens of Indigenous nations as if they were not there. And it was from St. Louis that the US waged genocidal wars to destroy their presence. Early on, the US Army's Department of the West was headquartered at St. Louis's Jefferson Barracks, and for a period after the Civil War, the entire US Department of War was relocated from Washington, DC, to St. Louis.[19] New México was the gateway to the Pacific, so the two decades of trade through St. Louis built a bond between the American Party in Taos and the United States.

This development of "mobile capitalism" bred a nouveau New México Hispano elite as an increasingly commercial, self-interested class.[20] Traders and mercenaries were to have an enormous influence in paving the way for US control of New México, constituting the core of what Father José Martínez of Taos called the American Party of Taos, of which the padre was an active member. Carlos Beaubien, for instance, a French Canadian from a noble French family, had migrated to Missouri and, like many other French Canadian traders, had become involved in the lucrative Southwest fur trade. By 1823, Beaubien had visited Taos and decided to settle there. Within a few years he was an established Mexican citizen and married into the elite Hispano Lovato family. Through his children's marriages he also became linked with the Maxwell, Trujillo, Abreu, Clouthier, and Muller families, surnames indicating the presence of several nationalities connected with the US economy. Another French Canadian, Ceran St. Vrain, traveled to Taos in 1825. In the early period, few traders and commercial trappers remained in New México during the winter, but St. Vrain did, making great profits by staking Anglo-American trappers with supplies in return for a percentage of their catch.

With the aid of family connections in Missouri, St. Vrain and the Anglo-American Charles Bent, with their brothers, established a trading center, Bent's Fort, in 1832 on the Colorado River at a strategic intersection of Indian, trapper, and trader routes. Their goal was to establish a monopoly of frontier trade in the Southwest by attracting all Indian and fur trade to their establishment. Contacts were made with Indian traders and trappers who were attracted by their low prices. A branch store was established in Taos, and agents traveled to the interior of México. Bent's Fort became the economic center for the fur trade in the Southwest and was second in North America only to Astor's American Fur Company. Bent himself moved to Taos, and by the mid-1830s had married into the New Mexican Jaramillo family. Another influential foreigner living in Taos was the US mercenary Kit Carson, who was hired by Bent and became related to him by also marrying into the Jaramillo family, thereby establishing himself socially.[21]

Not only traders and trappers but also Anglo-American crafts-men were moving into the area. A Mexican lawyer, Antonio Bar-reiro, commented in 1831 that the towns of New México were becoming the homes of Anglo tailors, carpenters, blacksmiths, pot-ters, shoemakers, gunsmiths, and others.[22] In an 1826 report to the nascent México national government, New México governor An-tonio Narbona expressed concern about the growing foreign pop-ulation: "In the aforementioned port of Taos, which is the frontier, there commonly reside a greater number of foreigners. By it being the edge of our populated area, it affords a refuge which many take advantage of without giving knowledge of their presence."[23]

The trade was becoming increasingly capitalized and now in-volved the manipulation of capital, credit, and labor.[24] Militarism followed trade and missionaries under any European imperialist project, including that of the US. As early as 1824, Missouri senator Thomas Hart Benton petitioned the US Senate on behalf of the citi-zens of Missouri to provide facilities for the Santa Fé Trail "to draw from the bosom of the wilderness an immense wealth which now must be left to grow and perish where it grows, or be gathered by the citizens of some other government."[25] In 1825, US consuls were appointed to Santa Fé and Chihuahua, and in 1832, President An-drew Jackson began using US troops to protect caravans of citizens traveling on the Santa Fé Trail. Generally, merchants provided their own protection, sometimes even carrying cannons. The US mounted infantry accompanied caravans in times of particularly intense Na-tive resistance to trespass, especially in 1834 and 1843.[26]

Members of the provincial Hispano elite were not only silent partners to foreign land ventures; they too prospered with the open-ing of the Santa Fé trade and acquired increased landholdings. Al-ready controlling vast amounts of land that Spain had appropriated from the Indigenous Pueblos and disbursed through land grants, the leading families of New México continued to prosper from cattle and sheep operations, with the added element of money exchange, which allowed them to accumulate capital for trading ventures. In the years before the Santa Fé trade opened, New Mexican ranchers were driving hundreds of thousands of sheep each year to the Chi-huahua market to exchange for manufactured items.[27] The numbers diminished for a few years after Mexican independence, but then grew rapidly with the opening of the Santa Fé trade. The large stockmen bought sheep at low cost from small operators and sold them for two or three times the amount offered at Chihuahua. Most of the wealthy ranchers resided in the Río Abajo area around Albuquerque with their extended families, servants, and workers, although a few wealthy families lived in the Río Arriba area around Taos.[28]

As early as 1824 some two dozen New Mexican Hispano merchants had established trade relations with merchants in St. Louis, and by 1840 they were sending their sons to parochial schools in Missouri to learn English and to receive training in business establishments there.[29] Beginning in 1826, New Mexican merchants organized their own caravans, combining their trading ventures with ranching.[30] The Perea, Otero, Armijo, Chaves, and Sandoval families each sent from $17,000 to $60,000 worth of merchandise to Chihuahua in 1844, most of which had been purchased with cash.[31]

Mexican villagers and the Indigenous Pueblos, who lived by subsistence agriculture and barter, were increasingly impoverished by the introduction of a cash and credit economy. Although more capital circulated in the province, the poor had no means of accumulating it or for that matter purchasing manufactured items with cash.[32] The standard of living of the elite was enhanced by trade, but the Paris styles, cosmetics, books, medical supplies, and household implements never reached the poor Mexican farmers, shepherds, and Indigenous Pueblos. Furthermore, their trade with neighboring Indigenous peoples was seriously impaired by monopolistic establishments like Bent's Fort and the stores of Santa Fé. The poor had to rely on trade with Plains Indians and on sheep contracts (partido), similar to sharecropping, with the large operators.[33] They became increasingly dependent on credit and employment at Bent's Fort. Bent was able to capture most of the Indigenous trade. Many became indebted and remained at Bent's to join the hundreds of other laborers who were practically indentured.[34]

ONWARD TO THE PACIFIC AND WAR

In addition to their efforts in New México, some of the same prominent US citizens laid groundwork for the annexation of California as well. Missouri senator Thomas Hart Benton; his son-in-law, US Army captain John C. Frémont; and Kit Carson were key to paving the way for the invasion of Northern California, the seat of the Mexican government there. In the early 1840s, Benton and his daughter, Jessie—Frémont's wife—built a booster press to entice settlers to the Oregon Territory as well as to the Mexican state of California. Historian Walter Johnson writes, "Benton was not so much the architect of the US Pacific empire as he was its prophet." A year after Mexican independence, Benton advocated for US military forts in the Rocky Mountains, which was at the time in Mexican territory. As a senator, beginning in 1821, Benton sponsored four expeditions out of St. Louis to designate and survey a route through Mexican territory to San Francisco. Benton's son-in-law, Captain Frémont, was in charge of the expeditions of 1842 and 1843–1845, the ultimate goal of which was access to the Pacific and Asia.[35] Frémont's third expedition illegally entered the Sacramento Valley region from the north in early 1846, just before the United States declared war against México. Frémont encouraged Anglo settlers in the California Central Valley to side with the United States, promising military protection if war broke out. Once a US warship was positioned for war, Frémont was appointed lieutenant colonel of the California Battalion, as if it had all been planned in advance.[36]

In the mid-nineteenth century, the population of México was six million, that of the United States was twenty-three million, not counting the more than three million enslaved people or the Native nations' population. México's population was made up of three million Indigenous people of sixty-two distinct communities, two million Mestizos, and a million Criollos, that is, European American–identified and propertied citizens who had seized political power once the peasantry, made up of Indigenous and Mestizos, succeeded in ousting the Spanish. Most of the resistance to the US invasion was guerrilla warfare carried out by the peasantry, including the Indigenous, while the Mexican Army was defeated in most regular battles with US forces.

The US Army in México had the highest desertion rate of any army in US history—8 percent. Foreign-born immigrant soldiers made up almost half of the army, and half of those were Irish.[37] Three US Army forces, operating independently, invaded México. Colonel—later Brigadier General—Stephen W. Kearny led a hardened force of dragoons to invade México from the east, covering over a thousand miles from Fort Leavenworth, Kansas, to the New México province of México, and on to California and the Pacific. In occupying New México and California, the US American residents in those provinces played a vital role.

Concurrently, Brigadier General Zachary Taylor invaded México from the Rio Grande in Texas. With those forces, accompanied by Texas Rangers, they assaulted the fortified town of Monterrey, defeating México's Army of the North at Buena Vista. Major General Winfield Scott directed the third and decisive campaign, mainly against civilian Mexican guerrillas, not armies. Scott's army, accompanied by marines, landed at Veracruz on the Gulf of México, which was México's major export port. With no regular Mexican armed forces to defend Veracruz, Scott's forces and marines laid siege for twenty days fighting civilian resisters. Scott then proceeded along the main highway in México from Veracruz to the Valley of México facing peasant guerrilla resisters every step of the way, with US victories at Cerro Gordo, Contreras, Churubusco, Molino del Rey, and ending with the seizure and occupation of México City.[38]

The official US Army annals of the war, written immediately after it ended, admit to the depredations of the Mexican-hating Texas Rangers:

Throughout the war, both Taylor and Scott also relied heavily on special companies of mounted volunteers: the Texas Rangers, who acted as the eyes and ears of the Army by conducting crucial reconnaissance, collecting intelligence, and carrying messages through Mexican lines. They also launched raids against specific targets, especially guerrilla encampments.

Technically state militia and not mustered into federal service, the Texans voluntarily agreed to serve in México. Their depredations on the Mexican citizenry were often excessive, however, and their behavior, along with that of other volunteers, did much to spark local Mexican resistance.[39]

Between 1840 and the 1920s, the Texas Rangers and other law enforcement in the United States, along with vigilantes and white citizen mobs, lynched some five hundred Mexicans and Mexican Americans and killed thousands more in Texas and in the former Mexican lands that became the states of New México, Arizona, California, Nevada, Utah, and Colorado. And the Texas Rangers were not finished with brutalizing and oppressing Mexicans back home; that continued along with their paramilitary wars against the Comanches.[40]

The lyrics "the halls of Montezuma" from the US Marine Corps' trademark hymn immortalized their invasion of México. While the US Army invaded and occupied what is now California, Arizona, and New México, the Marines were a part of the forces that invaded by sea and occupied Veracruz, using counterinsurgency tactics in their march to México City, burning fields and villages and murdering and torturing civilian resisters. They were a part of the occupation force in México City supporting the US Army divisions and the marauding Texas Rangers that had converged there, until the Mexican government, under brutal occupation for six months, signed a dubious treaty in February 1848 that transferred the northern half of México to the United States. The September 1847 Battle of Chapultepec is legend. Chapultepec Castle was used as a military training school, and in the "battle" a handful of teenaged Mexican cadets—with few weapons and little ammunition—held off the marines, killing most of them over two days of endless fighting in the castle, until the cadets themselves were all dead. The remaining marines raised the US flag and later their official hymn traced their genealogy back to the 1806 invasion and occupation of Tripoli in North Africa to the occupation of Mexico City.[41]

The war against México was a training ground and a rehearsal for the Civil War twelve years later. Five officers who led the war in

México went with the Confederacy as generals: Robert E. Lee, Braxton Bragg, Thomas "Stonewall" Jackson, James Longstreet, and P. G. T. Beauregard, while six stayed with the United States Army: Ulysses S. Grant, William Tecumseh Sherman, George McClellan, Ambrose Burnside, John C. Frémont, and George Meade. Jefferson Davis, a colonel in the war against México, returned to serve as Secretary of War, from 1853 to 1857, in the Franklin Pierce administration before he became president of the Confederate States of America in 1860.

THE AFTERMATH IN MÉXICO

In México, following a decade of internal conflict and recovery from the war, a liberal reform government organized a strong central government, curbing the power of the Roman Catholic Church and guaranteeing universal male suffrage and freedom of speech. The new constitution was met with violent conservative opposition that led to a devastating three-year civil war, which defeated the conservatives and brought Benito Júarez to the presidency in 1861. Among other reform acts, Júarez suspended payment of all foreign debts, which led to France, under Napoleon III, occupying México for six years. Invoking the Monroe Doctrine, the US pressured the French to leave. In 1877, Porfirio Díaz seized control of México, ruling as a dictator for most of the following thirty-four years until he was overthrown by a massive revolution that began in 1910. Díaz had opened the country to rampant foreign investment, and by 1910, practically all large businesses were owned by mostly US and British nationals and corporations.[42]

Historian Juan Mora-Torres writes, "The imposition of the Río Bravo (Grande) as the boundary between México and the United States was so extraordinary in its transformative powers that it marked at once an end and a beginning. . . . The 1848 boundary created by war and violence would remain unpoliced by both the Mexican and U.S. governments until decades later because of their lack of capacity to control the area."[43] This was not due to an absence of immigration laws; rather, as George Sanchez writes, "The presence of a strong border culture in which passage had been largely unregu-lated mitigated against stringent enforcement of these regulations."[44] Most of the population flow at the border was local. Mexicans and Indigenous communities that straddled the border, now sep-arated, found it easy to visit family or friends on the other side, especially as railroads were built in the early 1880s. By 1890, Mex-icans were working in the developing Anglo agribusiness industry in the Southwest, as well as in the mines, without being required to hold documentation. As the population began to grow, surveillance increased.[45] This border openness tightened with the Mexican Revo-lution of 1910–17, which was largely due to US fear of a radical rev-olution spilling over the border during a period of intense socialist labor organizing the United States.

US COLONIAL OCCUPATION

The US invasion and occupation of México ended with the Treaty of Guadalupe Hidalgo in 1848; Article VIII promised that "property of every kind, now belonging to Mexicans now established there shall be inviolably respected. The present owners, the heirs of these, and all Mexicans who may hereafter acquire said properties by contract, shall enjoy with respect to its guarantees equally ample as if the same belonged to citizens of the United States."[46] Much of the story of this article in the following half century is one of dispossession of the former Mexican citizens and Indigenous nations and communi-ties in the cession area.

Article XI of the treaty embodied a declaration of war and a requirement for México to participate in genocidal wars against the resistant Comanche, Apache, and Diné (Navajo) nations that ended with the 1886 surrender and incarceration of Geronimo and his peo-ple. The four decades of war against the Apaches was a part of the US Army's genocidal war making that continued unabated during the Civil War, during which Kit Carson, the handyman of US em-pire, was credentialed by the US Army to head an army contingent to round up and force-walk ten thousand Diné men, women, and children 450 miles from their homeland to a desert concentration camp near the New México-Texas border. In the three years of incarceration, half their number died of exposure, starvation, disease, and abuse.[47]

In Northern California, where the Indigenous peoples had been affected but never colonized by the European intruders, immediately after the war and under the protection of the US Army, crazed gold seekers from all over the world brought death, torture, rape, starvation, and disease to the Indigenous peoples whose ancestral territories included the sought-after goldfields northeast of San Francisco. As poet Alejandro Murguía describes it, unlike the Native peoples for whom gold was irrelevant, the forty-niners "hungered for gold with a sickness": "They would do anything for it. They left families, homes, everything behind; they sailed for eight months aboard leaky, smelly ships to reach California; others, captains and sailors, jumped ship at San Francisco, leaving a fleet of abandoned brigs, barks, and schooners to rot by the piers. They slaughtered all the game they could find and so muddied the rivers and creeks with silt that the once plentiful salmon couldn't survive. The herds of elk and deer, the food source for Native Americans, were practically wiped out in one summer. The miners cheated and killed each other in the goldfields."[48]

In a true reign of terror, US occupation and settlement saw the extermination of more than one hundred thousand California Native people in twenty-five years, reducing the population to thirty thousand by 1870. Described by scholars as the most extreme demographic disaster of all time, it has also been defined as genocide in terms of the Genocide Convention.[49] From the onset of the California gold rush, crazed "gold bugs" invaded Indigenous territories, terrorizing and brutally killing those who were in their path. The settlers ran roughshod over unarmed Indigenous residents of fishing communities in a bountiful paradise of woods, rivers, and mountains, as well as former Mexican citizens who were farmers or ranchers. The role left for the US Army was to round up the starving Indigenous refugees to transport them to already established reservations in Oregon and Oklahoma.

INDIGENOUS RESISTANCE

Yet, against impossible odds, the Indigenous peoples resisted and survived to tell the story. Had they not resisted, there would be no Indigenous peoples remaining in Northern California, because the objective was to eradicate them. In 1872, the Modoc people were rounded up and incarcerated on a reservation across the Oregon border with the refugees of several other Indigenous communities. A Modoc leader, Kintpuash, nicknamed Captain Jack, led his people back to their homeland that included the lava beds area now called Lassen National Park. More than a thousand troops commanded by General Edward R. S. Canby, a former Civil War general, attempted to capture the resisters, but had no success as the Modocs engaged in effective guerrilla warfare and knew the territory well. Before the Civil War, Canby had built his military career fighting in the Second Seminole War and later in the invasion of México. Posted to Utah on the eve of the Civil War, he had led attacks against the Navajos and then began his Civil War service in New México. Therefore, Canby was a seasoned Indian killer. In a negotiating meeting between the general and Kintpuash, the Modoc leader killed the general and the other commissioners when they would allow only for surrender.

In response, the United States sent another former Civil War general in with more than a thousand additional soldiers as reinforcements, and in April 1873 these troops attacked the Modoc stronghold, this time forcing the Indigenous fighters to flee. After four months of fighting that cost the United States almost $500,000—equal to nearly $10 million currently—and the lives of more than four hundred of its soldiers and a general, the nationwide backlash against the Modocs was vengeful. Kintpuash and several other captured Modocs were imprisoned and then hanged, and the Modoc families were scattered and incarcerated on reservations as far away as Indian Territory, Oklahoma. Kintpuash's corpse was embalmed and exhibited at circuses around the country. But the descendants of these Modoc resisters reconstituted themselves as the Pit River Nation and have survived.[50]

There was also Indigenous resistance in New México. Kearny's army was able to enter Santa Fé in September 1846 without a shot being fired. He set up a provisional government, drawn from the American Party and their Hispano associates. After promulgating a legal code, Kearny set out for the California conquest, taking most of his troops and leaving Colonel Sterling Price in command of three hundred army troops. However, Taos Pueblo, the northernmost of the Pueblo city-states, organized resistance against the hated American Party that had dominated their lives and livelihood for more than a decade. They ambushed and killed Kearny's appointed governor, the exploitative proprietor of Bent's Fort, George Bent, in January 1847, and the revolt quickly spread, with actions in nearly every Pueblo and Mexican village in the north. They organized an army and government, appointed leaders, and sent circulars all over the territory calling for people to fight against United States occupation. All the towns of the north, except Las Vegas and Tecolote, joined the resistance. They destroyed distilleries and other enterprises of the American Party, and apprehended and executed other prominent members of the collaborators. They also destroyed Spanish land grant documents. They numbered over a thousand Mexican and Pueblo villagers, along with uncolonized Apache allies. Fearing being ruled by the Pueblo Indians and their allies, the New México Hispano elite joined with US army troops and resident commercial hunters and fur traders in putting down the revolt. Armed with the most modern rifles and four twelve-pound mountain howitzers, they engaged the rebels, forcing them to retreat under direct attack. They escaped to Taos Pueblo but were defeated after two days of hard battle. The leader of the resistance, Tomasito of Taos Pueblo, was taken prisoner but allegedly was killed by a guard before being tried. Other captured rebels were tried, and one was found guilty of treason against the United States.[51] Hipolito Salazar, who was of a mixed Indigenous people called Genízaros, was executed for treason, the only person ever charged and executed for treason by the US government. Law professor Carlton F. W. Larson writes, "In 1847, New México did not belong to the United States, but to México. It would not be formally transferred to American jurisdiction until the 1848 Treaty of Guadalupe Hidalgo. Hipolito Salazar was a Mexican citizen who had never set foot in the United States."[52]

After the defeat of the Taos Pueblo–led armed resistance, New

México was ruled for four years by a military dictatorship directly under the United States Army. Taos Pueblo itself was occupied by a standing army. Military rule was crucial to the consolidation of United States authority in the area. Historian Lawrence Murphy wrote, "As an army of occupation, troops prevented dissidents among the populace from mounting a successful revolt against the foreign invaders."[53]

The first territorial governor was inaugurated in March 1851 and the policies of colonialism were put into effect—the US Congress defined the boundaries, divided the territory into nine counties, and established a territorial assembly according to the land ordinances already established for US colonization east of the Mississippi. Wealthy Hispano ranchers in the central part of the territory made up the majority of the delegates, along with land speculators and American Party associates, lawyers, and the Roman Catholic Church. Although limited in power, the assembly members controlled their constituencies and gained experience in Anglo-American politics, and they were usually successful in blocking policies that were opposed to their interests. For more than sixty years, New México remained a territory in which the highest positions of political authority were by appointment, not elective. Territorial delegates to US Congress were appointed so that representation of the territory in Washington, DC, was not answerable to a local electorate; territorial judges were also appointed. These officials were all Anglo-Americans until 1897, when one Hispano was appointed.[54]

THE FORMER MEXICAN CITIZENS

US and European gold seekers and other entrepreneurs flooding sparsely populated California quickly overwhelmed the Indigenous and Mexican communities. The Mexican settlers in California were a combination of new settlers after Mexican independence and descendants of Spanish settlers who began arriving in 1769, mostly as ranchers, shopkeepers, and craftsmen. This was a double-layered settler colonialism in which Anglo-Americans became quickly dominant and violently oppressed and discriminated against the

Californios, as the former Mexican citizens and their descendants self-identify in California. In the twentieth century, with the development of commercial agriculture, Mexican migrant farmworkers would far outnumber the descendants of the Californios, in the twenty-first century making up nearly half the population in California, and few if any identifying with the original Spanish settlers.

The rise in pride in Spanish colonial roots in California did not come so much from the resident Californios but from the Roman Catholic Church, which grew with Irish immigration to the state beginning with the gold rush. It is estimated that the gold camps were 10 to 20 percent Irish, and much more in some. Out of their numbers in Northern California, especially the largest California city at the time, San Francisco, some powerful Irish entrepreneurs and politicians emerged, as well as Irish organizations in the 1860s, such as the Hibernian Society, the Sons of the Emerald Isle, and in 1903 the Irish-founded fraternal Catholic organization the Knights of Columbus. San Francisco saw its first St. Patrick's Day parade in the early 1850s, and within two decades six thousand people joined the procession with over fifty thousand spectators.[55] In the late nineteenth century, Catholic organizations raised funds to restore the Franciscan missions—still owned by the Roman Catholic Church—as tourist sites, which were strung along El Camino Real—the Royal Road—from San Diego to Sonoma, as well as creating a founding cult around the Franciscan friar Junípero Serra, who established the first nine of the twenty-one missions. Lobbying by the California Catholic church led to the Vatican's beatification of Serra in 1988 and his advancement to sainthood in 2015. A statue of Serra was erected at the California state capitol in 1965, when Governor Edmund "Pat" Brown, who was Catholic, was serving his second term as governor.[56] Perhaps more bizarre, a paired statue of Columbus and Castilian queen Isabella had been installed at the California capitol in 1883. In July 2020, all three of the Spanish colonizer statues were toppled by protestors in support of Indigenous peoples.[57]

New México's Spanish heritage was unique in the former Mexican territories taken by the United States. There had been migration from México in the twentieth century, especially in mining in the southern part of the state, but the migrant population did not outnumber that of the descendants of the Spanish colonizers, as was the case in California. The Hispano elite in the New México Spanish colony never identified with the Republic of México during the twenty-five years of its existence in New México before the US invasion and annexation. New México was the first Spanish settler-colony in the northern territory of México that was seized by the United States. And there, the double-layered settler colonialism was and continues to be problematic. Hispano land grantees certainly have a grievance: the Spanish and Mexican land grants made to Hispano settlers in New México were largely denied by the Court of Private Land Claims that the federal government set up to hear the claims. Only settled villages and surrounding farmlands were recognized, while the vast pastures and alpine grazing lands and the woods and streams included in the grants for common use were denied. For instance, the San Miguel del Vado grant of 315,000 acres in the north, dotted with small settlements, was reduced to 5,024 acres; the Cañon de Chama grant was reduced from nearly a half million acres to 1,422 acres.[58]

The citizens of the nineteen Indigenous Pueblos who officially became US citizens because they had held citizenship status in the Republic of México also failed to obtain title to all their territories that had been recognized by both the Spanish colonial regime and the Mexican government.[59] The only possibility for protecting their land base, already reduced to small islands by past Hispano settlement, was to seek federal trust status as American Indians. They fought in the courts for decades, and finally, in 1913, the US Supreme Court reversed an earlier decision and declared the Pueblos wards of the federal government, stating, "They are essentially a simple, uninformed, inferior people."[60] US settlers who had purchased Pueblo lands took action to evade the decision. The Pueblos were able to lobby Congress successfully to investigate the situation, which ascertained that there were around three thousand non-Pueblo claimants representing twelve thousand individuals who were squatting on Pueblo lands. In 1924, Congress enacted the Pueblo Lands Act, and by the 1930s, all the land titles had been settled with many of the non-Pueblos evicted, but the final settlement was much less than what had been originally patented.[61] As attorney Felix

Cohen wrote, "The Pueblos had faced the choice of being treated like other Indian tribes and subjected to federal control of their internal affairs or being treated like non-Indians and finding themselves cut loose from federal services and their lands cut loose from federal protection."[62]

The rapid industrialization of mining and cattle ranching beginning in the late nineteenth century destroyed much of the irrigated subsistence farming that had dominated the land and forced both Pueblos and non-elite Hispanos into the labor market. The landscape of the Rio Grande Valley changed dramatically; prior to 1880 the grass cover was four to eight feet high, but by the turn of the century, only random patches of grass remained. Rain runoff, which once provided the valley with moisture for planting, now cut trenches hundreds of feet wide and thirty feet deep, causing catastrophic flooding.[63] Many of the rural Hispanos and Pueblos who did not abandon subsistence agriculture during the drought and Depression years did so during World War II. Many of those located in central New México, especially the people of Acoma and Laguna Pueblos, worked for the Santa Fé railroad, others in the uranium mines. Over half the young men of the Hispano villages and Pueblos joined the military or moved their families to California, where defense facilities offered wage labor. Villages were deserted, though few landowners who left sold their land, and, of course, extended families and clans remained in the Pueblos. Most residents who moved away returned, usually only to leave again in search of jobs.

The impoverishment and dislocation experienced by the former Mexican citizens was due to Anglo economic dominance. By World War II, the average acreage of irrigable lands for the Anglo-American in the northern Río Grande Valley was fifty to two hundred acres, compared with an average of five to fifteen acres for the subsistent Hispano farmer. The large operators also could afford to lease federal lands, which subsistent farmers could not afford. Except for uranium mining, not many jobs were created with the federal government's establishment of Los Alamos and the nuclear war industry in the heart of Pueblo lands. Instead, there was more displacement and far more dangerous pollution.[64]

New México is often compared to land areas that were colonized by Europeans in Asia, Latin America, and Africa.[65] The colonial mode presented itself in the United States' conquest of northern México and in the conditions in New México during the territorial period with the entrance of speculative capital and settlers from the United States. The Anglo intruders became dominant but never the majority of the population in the north. Economically, northern New México had been brought into the mainstream of the US economic system and resembled other depressed rural areas of the United States—parts of the Deep South and Appalachia—more than colonies of the "Third World." Only the Indigenous Pueblos and the Apache and Navajo reservations in New México retained a colonialist relationship with the US government. The Hispano-Anglo dichotomy has an ethnic and a class element, but that does not adequately explain the land question of New México today, which configures as both Hispano settler colonialism and Anglo settler colonialism.

HISPANO LAND GRANTS

In the early 1960s, Hispano land grantees began a campaign that continues in the twenty-first century to repossess the land lost under United States occupation. Lorena Oropeza writes, "In August 1962, Reies López Tijerina announced his intention to resurrect the *Treaty of Guadalupe Hidalgo*, which, he rightly claimed, the United States had violated the treaty in terms of property rights, the land grants that both Spain and independent México had bestowed upon the Hispano settlers. He accused the United States of colonialism, comparing its actions to those of European states colonization of Africa and Asia."[66]

Tijerina was a Texas-born Mexican American evangelical preacher whose wife was a New México Hispano land grantee. In 1963, he formed the Alianza Federal de Mercedes, later called the Alianza Federal de Pueblos Libres, to pressure the US government to reconsider the land grant settlements and loss of the common lands. The Alianza grew and was composed of many poor as well as affluent land grant heirs. In June 1967, the National Guard was dispatched with tanks, helicopters, and infantry to Río Arriba County in northern New México in search of the agrarian Hispano rebels who had participated in the Courthouse Raid. Earlier that month, Tijerina had led an armed raid on the Rio Arriba county courthouse to free the imprisoned members of his group. The incident occurred in the tiny and remote Hispano town of Tierra Amarilla on the edge of national forest land that had been a land grant before it was denied by the US government. The incident and government response briefly focused international and national attention on northern New México, and the land grant issue, which had been resolved in the courts of law for more than sixty years, was once again a live issue. It remains so in the twenty-first century.

The Alianza was behind the several years of actions that culminated in the 1967 US military assault on the mountain settlements of the old Tierra Amarilla community land grant. Land was the fundamental if not the single issue of the Alianza.[67] Along with such actions, the organization and others undertook community projects to decrease the economic suffering and dependency of the villagers in the original grant area. Proposals were formulated that would establish a new land claims court to reopen the land grant settlements. Another proposal would establish, based on the requirements of the Treaty of Guadalupe Hidalgo, a federal agency to protect the property of the former Mexican citizens. Lawsuits were drawn for the reopening of land grant settlements.

In a parallel development, the Pueblos continued their vigorous battles for land and water rights, which often conflicted with Hispano land claims. Land tenure, along with water rights, without exception remain the major political and social issues of northern New México. Federal land comprises 30 percent of the state, or 25.7 million acres, most of it the result of the settlement of Hispano land grants. These forested areas, lava beds, and mountains are all areas that Pueblos traditionally considered sacred and contain particular sites of ritual; they are analogous to what Christians call churches and cathedrals and pilgrimages. The various federal agencies—Forest Service, Bureau of Land Management, National Park Service, and others police the lands and create barriers to Pueblo traditional usage.

Meanwhile, without much attention paid by the Alianza, Pueblos in New México were continuing their ceaseless claims to land and water, with Taos Pueblo winning a major victory in 1970, thanks to decades of pressure bolstered by the Native rights movement and the more militant Red Power movement. After more than a half century of litigation, mass struggle, and congressional debate, forty-eight thousand acres of land, including Blue Lake, were returned to Taos Pueblo, land and water sacred to the Taos people that had been appropriated by the United States Forest Service as the Carson National Forest in 1906. The victory of Taos was one of the few instances of land being returned to its Indigenous owners rather than monetary compensation being made.[68] An opponent of the return of Blue Lake testifying before the Senate subcommittee invoked the 1967 Courthouse Raid and the Hispano land grant movement:

> The history of the land squabbles in New México among various groups of people, including Indian Americans and Spanish Americans is well-known. Substantially every acre of our public domain, be it national forest, state parks, or wilderness areas is threatened by claims from various groups who say they have some ancestral right to the land to the exclusion of all other persons. Recently one of the more notorious claimants Reis [sic] Tijerina, was convicted in the Federal District Court for appropriating one of our national park areas and assaulting a park ranger who sought admission to the area. The group not only claims the park area as its own, but it has sought to set up that area as a completely separate country outside the United States and to establish its own government therein. This is only one example of the dangerous condition existing in this state which can only be fostered and encouraged by the present legislation if passed.[69]

Senators sitting on the subcommittee expressed fear that a precedent might be set by returning land to claimants based on ancient use, treaties, and aboriginal ownership. Though the senators finally agreed that the Taos claim was sufficiently unusual to avoid establishing a precedent, the case has, in fact, set a precedent.[70] In a study of Indian land claims, a legal authority pointed out, "It would seem that rather than being a unique case, the return of Blue Lake has, as opponents predicted, established a precedent."[71]

Hispanos gained considerable political power in New México, dominating local and county governments and law enforcement, as well as the state legislature. And in 2001, after decades of pressure from the Hispano land grantees, the US government's General Accounting Office (GAO) began a study of New México land grants, completing a preliminary report that year and issuing its final 220-page report in 2004. It concluded:

> Based on all of these factors, we have identified a range of five possible options that Congress may wish to consider, ranging from taking no additional action at this time to making payment to claimants' heirs or other entities or transferring federal land to communities. We do not express an opinion as to which, if any, of these options might be preferable, and Congress may wish to consider additional options beyond those offered here. The last four options are not necessarily mutually exclusive and could be used in some combination.[72]

The proposed GAO options are these:

(1) Consider taking no additional action at this time because the majority of community land grants were confirmed, the majority of acreage claimed was awarded, and the confirmation processes were conducted in accordance with US law.

(2) Consider acknowledging that the land grant confirmation process could have been more efficient and less burdensome and imposed fewer hardships on claimants.

(3) Consider establishing a commission or other body to reexamine specific community land grant claims that were rejected or not confirmed for the full acreage claimed.

(4) Consider transferring federal land to communities that did not receive all of the acreage originally claimed for their community land grants.

(5) Consider making financial payments to claimants' heirs or other entities for the non-use of land originally claimed but not awarded.

The report adds, "As agreed, in the course of our discussions with land grant descendants in New México, we solicited their views on how they would prefer to have their concerns addressed. Most indicated that they would prefer to have a combination of the final two options—transfer of land and financial payment."[73] Pueblo Indian governments in New México did not participate in the GAO study, and Pueblo leaders are cautious about acknowledging the treaty made between the United States and México, neither of which recognized their full sovereignty.

In 2018, the US House of Representatives introduced a bill, H.R. 6365, titled Treaty of Guadalupe-Hidalgo Land Claims Act of 2018. Its stated purpose was "to establish the Treaty of Guadalupe Hidalgo Land Grant-Merced Claims Commission and other Federal policies for the restoration of land for hardships resulting from the incomplete and inequitable implementation of the Treaty of Guadalupe Hidalgo, to affirm Land Grant-Merced property rights protected by the Treaty of Guadalupe Hidalgo, and for other purposes." The bill was introduced in September 2018 but was not enacted.[74]

Oropeza, Tijerina's biographer, captures the contradiction of descendants of one colonizer claiming to be colonized by a succeeding one: "Thus in leading an anticolonial movement, Tijerina was forced to navigate a complex history in which Alianza members objected to the consequences of a colonization begun in 1848, while seeking to secure the benefits of another begun in 1598."[75] Although the Hispano case has elements similar to Appalachia and other Anglo sites of settler colonialism and self-indigenization, it is also distinctive in the details. Laura Gómez uses the term "double colonization," explaining that with the US annexation of half of México, in New México the various groups were obligated to deal with various "racial regimes" at the same time—the Hispano, Pueblos, and other Indigenous groups within the Anglo-American racial order and the influx of Anglo settlers. Double colonization refers to Hispanos being descendants of the Spanish colonizers who appropriated most of the Pueblos' territory, then themselves were colonized by the United States, thereby losing much of their landholdings, while Pueblos experienced a new colonizer on top of the old Hispano one. Gómez claims that this double colonization resulted in everyone having to compete for "status."[76] However, it was not an even playing field, what with both the Anglo and the Hispano colonizers' Indian hating and the very real possibility of genocide for the numerically fewer and still colonized Indigenous peoples, including the Apache and Navajo nations that span both Arizona and New México.

Historian John M. Nieto-Phillips, himself New México Hispano, argues that the Spanish American identity of New México Hispanos evolved out of a medieval rhetoric about blood purity, or *limpieza de sangre*, along with a desire to be accepted into the United States' white body politic.[77] In an interview, Nieto-Phillips explained,

> In aligning themselves with whiteness, some Hispanics advocated for "pure" Spanish blood to be perpetuated by pushing a eugenics movement, treating those with mixed backgrounds as "mongrels who couldn't govern themselves." . . . Whiteness figured very prominently into the creation of Hispanics, at least in the context of New México. If it were to truly be in allyship to Indigenous communities, I think we need to acknowledge our complicity in the roles that we've played historically, that our forebears have played, and understand that Latinx people are both the protagonists in historical justice and the progeny of colonization.[78]

HISPANO SETTLER COLONIALISM IN NEW MÉXICO

Chicano and Indigenous activism declined during the Reagan era, following nearly two decades of converging alliances between Indigenous and Chicano activists. The traditional Hispano elite of New México became more vocal in expressing pride in their Spanish colonial (not Mexican) heritage, and a younger generation of New Mexican Hispanos grew up in the new order of the 1990s. While the anniversaries that celebrate the 1598 founding and 1692 refounding of the Spanish colony in New México had long been marked by parades, they reached a new level of aggression leading up to the tricentenary of the 1692 reconquest of the Pueblos of New México led by Diego de Vargas. Official New México state celebrations of that event coincided with the 1992 quincentenary of Columbus.[79] It only became more fraught with the four-hundred-year anniversary in 1998 of the first bloody conquest of the Pueblo Nation of the northern Rio Grande, led by Juan de Oñate, which reduced the ninety-eight Pueblo city-states to only twenty-one within a few decades.

The 1992 Pueblo-made film *Surviving Columbus* featured a segment on the de Vargas parade in Santa Fé, criticizing the Hispano community's lack of sensitivity to the Pueblos, who were victims of renewed Spanish colonization following the successful 1680 Pueblo revolt that had driven the Spaniards out.[80] The 1692 reconquest of the Pueblos in New México was violent, but in the subsequent 130-year occupation, the Spanish colonial officials no longer interfered with the internal affairs of the Pueblos, that is, discontinuing suppression of the rituals and self-governance that had marked the first era of colonization and led to the revolt. However, Pueblos were required to have official passes to leave Pueblo demarcated grounds, and they were not allowed to ride horses. The Pueblos were required to provide men to serve as foot soldiers in the Spanish colonizers' unending attempts to colonize the Apaches and Navajos, which they never succeeded in doing. Nor did México defeat the Apache and Navajo resistance in its twenty-five-year governance. After US annexation, it took the post–Civil War US Army forty years of genocidal warfare to confine the surviving Apaches and Navajos in reservations.[81] The Mescalero Apache reservation is in southeast New México, the Jicarilla Apache in the north, and the Chiricahua Apache Mimbreno Nde in the Southwest, as well as a segment of the Navajo Nation in the northwest. The Apache and Navajo three-hundred-year resistance to European and European American colonialism may have been the longest continuous resistance to European colonialism in the world, with Geronimo, the final leader, a global icon of resistance.

In 1998, the New México Hispano community successfully pressed the state government to acknowledge and celebrate the four-hundred-year anniversary of the founding of the first Spanish colony. Nearly a half million in state tax dollars were set aside for the Cuarto Centenario of the Spanish conquest of New México, led by Juan de Oñate in 1598. One project was the establishment of the

Oñate Monument and Visitors Center outside Espanola, New México, which featured a statue of Oñate twelve feet in height. Just as the festivities were to begin in January 1998, unidentified persons sawed off one of the statue's large bronze feet: "We took the liberty of removing Oñate's right foot on behalf of our brothers and sisters of Acoma Pueblo. . . . We see no glory in celebrating Oñate's fourth centennial, and we do not want our faces rubbed in it."[82]

The foot as a symbol of the violent Spanish invasion of the city-states of the northern Rio Grande refers to the Spanish army's genocidal attack on the Pueblo of Acoma in November 1598, three months after the Spanish had occupied the largest and most central of the small city-states, Ohkay Owingeh, renaming it San Juan. When several abusive Spanish soldiers were killed at Acoma, Oñate sent seventy heavily armed soldiers to punish the people. The Acomas surrendered after several days of assault that left over five hundred men and three hundred women and children dead. The survivors were charged with treason against the Spanish monarchy, and Oñate personally imposed the sentences: all males over twenty-five were sentenced to have one foot cut off and to serve twenty years enslaved; males between the ages of twelve and twenty-five years and women over twelve were sentenced to twenty years of slavery; and young girls and boys were given to missionaries, who were to supervise their distribution "in this kingdom or elsewhere."[83] Although Acoma was effectively depopulated, many of those who were enslaved managed to escape, and by 1601 they had reestablished Acoma, however, with greatly reduced numbers. This kind of extreme exemplary violence, a common practice of all European colonizers, was meant to give warning to others of the high cost of resistance.[84]

Hispano writer Juan Estevan Arellano, then director of the Oñate Monument and Visitors Center, responded with extraordinary tone deafness to the statue foot cutting by blaming the Anglos, arguing that no Pueblo could have done the deed. Arellano wrote to the *Santa Fé New Mexican*:

A lot of people have said just leave off the foot so that they can make a statement. But what statement? The ones who were yelling the most were the Anglos. It was not so much the Native

Americans, it was the Anglos. They don't say anything about Kit Carson. Kit Carson probably killed more Indians than Oñate or a lot of the Spanish *conquistadores* did. I think you have to find a middle ground between the extremes. It has become a cliché about the feet cut off the Acoma by Oñate. The ones who are fueling that debate are the Anglos. What we are seeing now is that the Anglos are trying to revive the Black Legend. They are trying to create the schism between Native Americans and the Indo-Hispanos, so they can exploit it. I know even though I can't prove it, I know it wasn't done by Native Americans or Hispanos, it was done by some extreme environmental group. I think the environmentalists are the ones responsible because they don't want some of the things we are doing here at the Center in relation to the land grants and water rights, are things they are trying to appropriate for their agenda.[85]

Arellano appeared to be unaware that Kit Carson settled in Taos and married into an elite Hispano family when it was still a part of México, and the entire Hispano ruling class collaborated with the Anglo invasion while Pueblos resisted it. Anglo-American historian Marc Simmons's biography of Oñate is gushing in its praise for the man, calling him "the George Washington of New México."[86]

According to Hispano historian Michael Trujillo, Arellano was influenced by early Chicano ideas and Mexican literature and framed the Oñate Center as blending both, referring to the center as an "Indo-Hispano cultural center in the heart of Hispano culture."[87] The Chicano influence, which included great respect and solidarity with Native peoples, had opened up the "pure" Spanish identification of the Hispano to a claim of indigeneity. Racializing indigeneity to be about blood quantum is another way of eliminating Indigenous nations whose indigeneity is not based in genetics but in their citizenship in a Native nation based on ancestry, not race. Scholar Kim TallBear shows how DNA testing, although useful in identifying close biological relatives, is problematic. Tribal citizenship is a legal category. TallBear notes that the "markers" that are identified and applied to Native nations reflect the misinterpretations of the researcher.[88]

Arellano found it difficult to fathom why the Pueblos make so much of Spanish invasion and colonization. Hispanos resent and compete with the Anglo-Americans who took their place as colonizers. They think the Pueblos should make common cause against the dominance of Anglo-Americans and forget about the centuries of Spanish settler colonialism that reduced their population by 90 percent and their land base to 5 percent of its original size. And, of course, the Indigenous peoples of New México are in constant conflict and negotiations with the US government and are hardly Anglophiles.

Maurus Chino, an artist and activist from Acoma Pueblo, was the founder of the Southwest Indian Alliance and cofounder of the Tricentennial Truth Alliance, the latter formed to counter the three-hundred-year anniversary of the founding of the city of Albuquerque in 1706. He responded to Arellano's statement:

> Many Spanish are afraid to admit that the courageous and powerful act of cutting a butcher's foot could not have been done by Indians. They have always feared any Indian uprising, and so they blame the Anglos. Even now to keep the people in ignorance of our violent history, they make claims to our "friendship" before the Anglos came and ruined everything. And where are all these Anglos Mr. Arellano is talking about? I wish I knew. I might ask them to help me "fuel the debate." . . . "We were friends," they claim, and now they can't seem to understand where this anger is coming from and how the People still have this resentment, this generational grief and anger. And always they go back to the "peace" before the Americans came. There was never "peace." There was only quiet, and now the voices are starting to rise again. They cannot see how offensive bringing up the savage past is to the People. They can't see the anger of the theft of lands, in many cases the best lands from the People, and so stupidly they have the knuckle-headedness to ask Indians to support the Spanish land grant system.[89]

CHICANISMO AND AZTLÁN

In 1998, on the anniversary of the 1598 violent Spanish conquest of the Pueblos, a New México Chicano-identified group stated, "Why should we celebrate the 400th Anniversary of the first Spanish settlement of New México? 1598 marks the first permanent settlement in the present day United States by Europeans. In New México, this was the beginning of the mixture of Spanish and Indian blood. This marks the birth of the Chicano/a people."[90]

Dating the "birth of the Chicano/a people" to 1598 was an extreme departure from the original concept of Chicano that emerged in the mid-1960s and launched the radical embrace of "Chicano" as a rallying cry of young Mexican Americans. It meant simply those Mexicans born or raised in the United States who, of course, despised the border, as do the people of México, but in no way identified with the Spanish colonizers. In 1965, historian Jack Forbes, cofounder of the Native American studies program at University of California, Davis, and author of the 1960 classic book *Apache, Navajo, and Spaniard*, wrote and distributed a paper, "Aztecas del Norte," a concept he had first proposed in 1961 and which was published as a book in 1973. Aztlán, the original homeland of the Nahuatl-speaking Aztecs, was located in the region of New México, Arizona, and Colorado. The Aztecs migrated south during the early thirteenth century and dominated Central México when the Spanish invaded and overthrew them in 1519–1521. During the three centuries before the Spanish invasion, the Aztecs, who called themselves Mejica, had maintained ties with the north with road building and trade. When the Spanish arrived in New México, they were surprised that the language of Central México was widely spoken as a second language, the language of trade.[91]

Records of Oñate's 1598 violent invasion of the Pueblo homeland along the northern Rio Grande contained lists of some two hundred Spanish settlers, including families, soldiers, and priests who were meticulously recorded and identified (mostly blue-eyed and fair, being primarily Basques who had settled in Chihuahua), along with seven thousand head of cattle. But the records did not list the number or names of captive Indigenous servants who most likely outnumbered the Spanish soldiers and settlers. The servants were surely scattered to work on the many Spanish ranches and settlements, but by 1610, the majority of them resided in the Spanish capital, Santa Fé, in a section the Spanish named the Barrio de Analco, serving the officials and ruling class in households as day laborers and as army auxiliaries.

From this history, Forbes posed an origin story, theorizing that the birth of the "Chicano" took place in the Barrio de Analco in Santa Fé during the 1680 Pueblo revolution that drove out the Spanish colonizers for twelve years. By 1680, eight decades after the Spanish invasion, the descendants of the servants brought from México had multiplied. They were joined over those decades by Apaches and Navajos who had been captured and enslaved by the Spanish, while some captives were sold in slave markets that thrived deeper in México. The Analco servants and laborers comprised a mixed Indigenous people the Spanish referred to as Genízaros, deculturated Indigenous individuals who practiced Catholicism and whose language was Spanish. When the Pueblo revolutionaries, led by Popé from San Juan Pueblo, having been joined by resistant Apaches and Navajos, had driven the Spanish settlers from the outlying areas, they surrounded Santa Fé and upon attacking the capital, the Genízaros in the Barrio of Analco rose up and joined the Pueblos in driving out the remaining Spanish elite, officials, and military.[92] When the Spanish colony was reestablished in 1692, the authorities dispersed the Genízaro population from Santa Fé to the northern frontier, providing them community land grants and requiring them to defend the colony from Apache and Navajo attacks.[93]

Therefore, during the 1980s and '90s, the origin story of self-identified Chicanos in New México was transformed from being embedded in the 1680 Pueblo revolution against the Spanish to celebrating the 1598 Spanish invasion and colonization of the Pueblos as the birth marker of the Chicano.[94]

The American Indian Movement (AIM) was founded in 1968, and its offshoot, International Indian Treaty Council (IITC), was established in 1974. Both embraced Pan-Indianism, which modeled past Native confederations such as that led by Tecumseh in the early 1800s and Crazy Horse in the 1870s.[95] From the beginning, Chicanos were active in AIM and the IITC. In New México, the

1960s generation of young Hispanos, especially college students, also identified as Chicanos, most notably the prize-winning author of the 1972 novel *Bless Me, Ultima*, Rudolfo Anaya.[96] Many still do identify as Chicano, but in the context of that shift at the turn of the century that connected Hispanos to the Spanish invasion, self-indigenizing their Spanish-settler heritage as Indo-Hispano. As noted above, this was not the case in other parts of the Southwest and California or nationally. Most self-identified Chicanos in other locales were first- or second-generation children of Mexican citizens who migrated to the United States for work, not descendants of the original Spanish settlers, although some Californios and Tejanos—descendants of Spanish settlers—were involved in the Chicano movement. There are also Mexican immigrants and their descendants in New México, but mostly as migrant workers, particularly in the zinc mines in southern New México and in agribusiness. They are outnumbered by the Hispano population.[97]

DESCENDANTS OF ORIGINAL SETTLERS' CLAIMS OF INDIGENEITY

Early on in this neo-Hispano era, in 1993, the El Paso, Texas, city government commissioned a giant statue of Oñate on a rearing horse. Thanks to Pueblo protests, it was not completed until 2006 and was placed in front of the tiny El Paso airport. El Paso had been the site where Oñate's 1598 colonizing project was organized and the site to which the surviving Spanish settlers and officials retired when they were driven out by the Pueblo revolution. In the wake of strong protests by both Mexican Americans and Pueblos against honoring Oñate, the El Paso city council voted to drop Oñate's name from the statue and renamed it *The Equestrian*, an unnamed Spanish conquistador.[98]

In 2005, leading up to the planned celebration of the tricentenary of the Spanish founding of Albuquerque in 1706, another statue of Oñate was commissioned and placed in front of the Albuquerque Museum. A group of Pueblo and other Native Americans established the Tricentennial Truth Alliance to counter the celebration. Members of the Spanish royalty from the city's namesake traveled to New México for the celebration in April 2006.[99] Following a protest by the Tricentennial Truth Alliance, a Hispano citizen wrote a letter to the *Albuquerque Journal* objecting to a quote from the group: "We equate the conquistador Juan de Oñate and his soldiers with Hitler and the Nazis. Both practiced genocide." Orae Dominguez claimed that the Tricentennial Truth Alliance was "spreading racist lies about Spanish and American colonization" and that "genocide" did not apply.[100]

A few days after the May 25, 2020, police killing of George Floyd in Minneapolis, in the midst of a pandemic, Black Lives Matter called for nationwide protests that met with an unprecedented response, including in New México. Soon statues of racist figures, including Columbus, were removed by protestors. The decades-long demand by Native Americans for removal of statues and place names of Columbus was realized by protestors across the country, and statues of the Spanish missionary and colonizer of California, Junípero Serra, who was made a saint by the Roman Catholic Church in 2014, was also removed. In New México, the Native organization the Red Nation had joined with Black Lives Matter beginning in late May in protesting police violence.[101] When the statues began falling nationwide, Native protestors in New México toppled the Oñate statue in the town of Alcalde. A call to protest the Oñate statue at the Albuquerque Museum brought a large crowd of determined but peaceful protestors. They rallied while several of their number using a pickaxe and a chain tried to topple the statue. An armed group of white nationalists, calling themselves the New México Civil Guard and which included Hispanos, arrived to protect the statue and threatened the protestors. The Albuquerque police sided with the armed gang. Steven Ray Baca, a Hispano man and the son of a deputy sheriff, who would later claim he was not with the self-styled militias, knocked down a woman protestor and was chased by other protestors. He pulled a firearm and shot one of the protestors, who was hospitalized but survived. Baca was charged with aggravated battery, but the charges were soon dropped.[102] The museum removed the statue for safe keeping.

Coincidentally, also in June 2020, a collection of essays appeared in book form, *Querencia: Reflections on the New México Home-*

land, published by University of New México Press. Notwithstanding a few Indigenous commentaries, the book is a Hispano version of a similar collection of Appalachian writers published in 1978, *Colonialism in Modern America: The Appalachian Case*,[103] discussed in chapter 2. In both cases, the logic of settler colonialism is on display, invoking the "feeling" of belonging. *Querencia* is a Spanish word that Levi Romero, Hispano poet laureate of New México and coeditor of the collection, describes as "the traditional northern New México concept to define the relationship between place and identity," and, in the words of Juan Estevan Arellano, to whom the book is dedicated, *querencia* "is that which gives us a sense of place, that which anchors us to the land, that which makes us a unique people."[104] As Jake Kosek puts it, "Nature is central to these senses of belonging: as attachment, as possession, and as appendage."[105]

As with the Appalachians who claim indigeneity, the Hispano writers take great pains to express their gratitude to the Natives for having bequeathed them their *querencia*. Rudolfo Anaya, referring to a Hispano elder, writes, "Cleofes Vigil understood how much the Pueblos had shared with the españoles. They helped them survive those years after 1598. The Pueblo love of querencia was shared with the españoles through hard work, stories, songs, ceremonies, fiestas. I think it is fair to say that the Pueblo World's subliminal knowledge of querencia became part of our birthright."[106] Echoing *The Last of the Mohicans*, the great gift-giving Indian is a refrain of settler colonialism in the United States.

But much more is at stake in New México than in Appalachia, where the Cherokee presence is ghostly but not present, the area having been ethnically cleansed by the Scots Irish ancestors of the contemporary residents. In New México, the descendants of the Pueblos who were brutally colonized by the Spanish are very much present, as are the descendants of the Spanish colonizers. The remaining nineteen Pueblo city-states in New México are located on miniscule remnants of their original land base and are surrounded by Hispano and Anglo settlers. The Hispano movement for regaining land their ancestors lost to US occupation constitutes a project of settler colonialism and recolonization as that land should be restored to the relevant Pueblos.

In the aftermath of the demonstrations in Albuquerque, University of New México professor Dulcinea Lara cites the United States' annexation of New México as an example of how Hispanos were able to benefit from their European ancestry. Lara finds that many younger-generation Hispanos among her students are acknowledging the settler-colonial stance of Hispano nationalism: "There's a lot of crying in my classes, with students saying, 'Here I am in this body, talking about the discrimination my family and I have experienced, but at the same time, historically my ancestry has been involved in the oppression of Indigenous people,'" Lara says. "We have to have these conversations in a compassionate way, because it's not so much about the statues. It's about challenging systems of oppression and its symbols."[107]

A few weeks later, Ralph Arellanes, the executive director of the New México branch of the rather conservative League of United Latin American Citizens (LULAC), sent a letter to the president of the University of New México requesting a meeting to discuss the university's Chicano studies and Native American studies departments, claiming that both programs teach Latino students "self-hate" about their Spanish heritage: "We will be calling for the removal of these courses and programs that are teaching our New México students this kind of hate and complete propaganda." The university quickly rejected Arellanes's call, and the New México state director and national LULAC made clear that this was not the position of the national organization.[108]

Although New México history presents as unique in the United States, it is well within the contours of US settler colonialism and the fiscal-military state, with Hispanos having reasserted their dominance after more than a century of having lost their colonizer status due to US invasion and Anglo domination. A younger generation of radicalized young Hispanos may eschew the stance of settler colonialism, joining in solidarity with Indigenous peoples.

CHAPTER 5

IRISH SETTLING

During the fall of 1974, court-ordered school desegregation in Boston began with white rioting, and the predominately Irish American working-class neighborhood of South Boston vied with Selma, Alabama, of 1964, assuming the mantle of virulent anti-Black racism. "Wild, raging mobs of white men and women confronted armies of police, while youths in their teens and younger hurled rocks, bottles, and racial epithets at buses carrying terrified black youngsters to school."[1] The situation continued for three years. The length of time and violence incurred by Boston antibusing was far greater than had occurred in any other US city. Although seemingly uncontrolled, there were organized groups, primarily Restore Our Alienated Rights (ROAR), which was dominated by Louise Day Hicks of South Boston.

Hicks had opposed desegregation through busing since 1963, when she was chair of the Boston school committee. South Boston's population of 38,500 was 98 percent white, majority Irish Americans. It had a higher percentage of families on welfare than the rest of Boston and also a higher school-dropout rate, higher unemployment, and income well below the city's average. At the time, there were four housing projects in South Boston, which had a high percentage of single-mother families. As in most impoverished communities, alcohol abuse was common.[2] The ideology of the Boston antibusing movement was that it was ordinary working people against the "elites," and this ushered in a new era of right-wing populism.

How could it be that descendants of long-suffering and impoverished Irish Catholics fleeing Protestant England–colonized Ireland, being starved out, did not see a reflection of their own historical existential misery as analogous to the descendants of enslaved Africans?

ENGLISH COLONIZATION OF IRELAND

The twelfth-century Christian Crusades against Muslims and their expulsion from Spain in the early fifteenth century and the Anglo Norman twelfth-century invasion and occupation of Ireland mark the beginnings of European colonialism. Spain became a world imperialist power by invading and occupying most of the Western Hemisphere. England invaded and began the colonization of Ireland in 1155, which was not completed until 1801.[3]

England emerged as a world imperialist power a century after Spain, absorbing aspects of the Spanish racial caste system into its colonialist rationalizations, particularly regarding African slavery; it did so within the context of Protestantism, which imagined a chosen people founding and raising a New Jerusalem in North America, establishing providence or manifest destiny. The English did not just adapt the habits and experiences of Spanish colonization; they also had their own prior experience, which in their colonization of Ireland constituted overseas imperialism.

During the 1600s, while establishing colonies in North America, the British declared a half million acres of land in the north of Ireland open to settlement, forming the plantation of Ulster, the two combined creating the template of settler colonialism. The settlers who served this early settler colonialism came mostly from western Scotland, but also from Wales and England. Many of these Protestant Scots settlers in Catholic Ireland, the Scots Irish, became a settler class in North America in the 1700s.

The settler-colonial occupation of Northern Ireland was brutal—the ancient Irish social system was systematically attacked, traditional songs and music forbidden, whole clans exterminated, and families crushed with debt and hunger. The British colonization of Ireland, like its colonizations in Africa, Asia, and the Americas, wreaked misery on the majority of the populations. English economist-statistician William Petty estimated that by 1641 there were a quarter million Scots Protestant settlers in the Ulster plantation, whom the Irish called "undertakers," among the million and a half Irish Catholics. That year, a rebellion in Ireland that lasted eight years was violently crushed under Oliver Cromwell, who continued the ethnic cleansing. During the following half century, English colonization formed the characteristics that persisted into the twentieth century: loss of small landholdings, absentee land ownership, Catholic persecution and Protestant privilege, corrupt administrations, and official terror. English legislation was enacted that prohibited Irish marketing products and goods such as cattle, woolens, linens, and glass, creating dependency and impoverishment.[4]

In the 1830s, Frenchman Gustave de Beaumont visited Ireland and published an ominous account of what he witnessed:

> Misery, naked and famishing, that misery which is vagrant, idle, and mendicant, covers the entire country; it shows itself everywhere, and at every hour of the day; it is the first thing you see when you land on the Irish coast, and from that moment it ceases not to be present to your view; sometimes under the aspect of the diseased displaying his sores, sometimes under form of the pauper scarcely covered by his rags; it follows you everywhere, and besieges you incessantly; you hear its groans and cries in the distance, and if the voice does not excite profound pity, it importunes and terrifies you.[5]

De Beaumont attributed the situation to English colonialism, writing, "The dominion of the English in Ireland, from their invasion of the country in 1169, to the close of the last century has been nothing but a tyranny. During the three first centuries, they covered Ireland with deeds of violence, the object of which was the completion of the conquest. . . . When the wars which the Irish maintained for the defence of their religion and country terminated, English oppression did not cease."[6] From this account, it is clear that the Irish already lived with hunger long before the potato crop was struck by blight in 1845, and would continue to live with and flee hunger through the rest of the century.

FAMINE

By the time of the famine, nearly half the population depended almost solely on the potato for food and as a cash crop. With Spanish colonization of the Andes in South America, the potato had been dispersed all over the world, arriving as a staple for poor Irish families in the late 1700s. The potato did alleviate hunger. However, only one genetic strain of the hundreds cultivated by the Quechua people in the Andes was planted, what came to be known as the "Irish potato," and the lack of diversity made it vulnerable to the spread of blight.[7]

The homes of most of the rural Irish population were windowless mud huts without furniture. Large, productive farms on vast estates of land were owned by an absentee Anglo-Protestant gentry who rented small parcels to the Irish tenants, who could barely eke out a living and were indentured by debt.[8] English rulers' response to the potato famine and the plight of the Irish was inaction. Food was available, but the English colonial masters claimed that food assistance would create Irish dependency, whereas in reality they considered the Irish a surplus population. The potato famine was a form of colonial genocide.[9] This can be seen in the words of Charles Edward Trevelyan, who was the British assistant secretary to the Treasury and oversaw relief for the victims of the potato famine. In 1848, three years into the famine, he published *The Irish Crisis*, defending the continued export of food from starving Ireland. As a follower of Thomas Malthus, the British theorist of population control, Trevelyan saw the famine as the work of God, culling the Irish population through natural disaster. He wrote, "The judgement of God sent the calamity to teach the Irish a lesson, that calamity must not be too much mitigated. . . . We must not complain of what we really want to obtain. If small farmers go, and their landlords are reduced to sell portions of their estates to persons who will invest capital we shall at last arrive at something like a satisfactory settlement of the country."[10]

Mid-nineteenth-century Ulster Scot scientist Robert Knox, apparently welcoming the famine, spelled out a case for genocide very similar to that being attempted in the United States at the time: "The race [Celtic] must be forced from the soil; by fair means, if possible; still they must leave. England's safety requires it. . . . The Orange club of Ireland is a Saxon confederation for the clearing the land of all papists and jacobites; this means Celts."[11]

The German transplant to England Friedrich Engels traveled to Ireland for the first time in 1856 and wrote to Karl Marx:

"Strong measures" are visible in every corner of the country, the [British] government meddles in everything, of so-called self-government there is not a trace. . . . I have never seen so many gendarmes in any country . . . armed with carbines, bayonets and handcuffs. . . . I never thought that famine could have such tangible reality. Whole villages are devastated, and there among them lie the splendid parks of the lesser land-lords, who are almost the only people still living there, mostly lawyers. Famine, emigration and clearances together have accomplished this. . . . The country has been completely ruined by the English wars of conquest from 1100 to 1850.[12]

The Irish rebelled in every way possible, one by leaving Ireland, but also with violence and boycott, the term itself referencing the English land agent in the west of Ireland, Charles Boycott. Rebelling Irish sharecroppers and tenants targeted the County Mayo estate that Boycott managed. They pressured migrant farmworkers to strike at harvest, as well as harassed businesses he patronized. The Irish parliamentarian Charles Stewart Parnell had recommended the tactic in a speech, saying,

When a man takes a farm from which another has been evicted, you must shun him on the roadside when you meet him—you must shun him in the streets of the town—you must shun him in the shop—you must shun him on the fair green and in the market place, and even in the place of worship, by leaving him alone, by putting him in moral Coventry, by isolating him from the rest of the country, as if he were the leper of old—you must show him your detestation of the crime he committed.

If a rebel were arrested, at trial it was difficult to find witnesses to testify as they feared being targeted as well.[13] Historian Samuel Clark, author of *Social Origins of the Irish Land War,* clarifies that "the practice was obviously not invented by Irish farmers in 1880. For centuries, in all parts of the world, it had been employed by active combinations for a variety of purposes"; rather, what was new was "the spread and development of this type of collective action on a scale so enormous that the coining of a new term was necessary. Boycotting was becoming the most awesome feature of the agitation."[14]

THE STIGMA OF BEING IRISH AND CATHOLIC

By the time of the famine that began in 1845, impoverished and colonized Ireland had already been bleeding its population through emigration, mostly to the United States. By the 1830s, Irish Catholics outnumbered Scots Irish Protestants in the United States. By 1840, Irish Catholic immigrants constituted a third of the immigrant population, which increased to half the immigrant population with the arrival of the famine refugees after 1845. Many well-off Irish Catholics as well as Scots Irish Protestants immigrated to the United States both before and after US independence, but poverty was the rule for the famine refugees, and anti-Catholicism in the United States was virulent.

Irish American historian Patrick Higgins points out that early on in their North American and Caribbean colonies, the British exported colonized Irish as a surplus population, creating a kind of "pressure valve."[15] As Cecil B. Rhodes famously said in the late nineteenth century,

I was in the East End of London (a working-class quarter) yesterday and attended a meeting of the unemployed. I listened to the wild speeches, which were just a cry for 'bread! bread!' and on my way home I pondered over the scene and I became more than ever convinced of the importance of imperialism. . . . My cherished idea is a solution for the social problem, i.e., in order to save the forty million inhabitants of the United Kingdom from a bloody civil war, we colonial statesmen must acquire new lands to settle the surplus population, to provide new markets for the goods produced in the factories and mines. The Empire, as I have always said, is a bread and butter question. If you want to avoid civil war, you must become imperialists.[16]

Ireland's population in 1841 was 8.2 million. Ten years later, it had sunk to 6.6 million and to 4.7 million in 1891. Irish Americans came to outnumber Ireland's population sevenfold, and a greater number of Irish lived in New York City than in Dublin. Most of the immigrants settled initially in the large eastern urban centers of New York, Boston, and Philadelphia. In 1850, the US census reported nearly a million Irish in residence. By 1860, Irish Catholics made up 16 percent of the population of St. Louis, and by then were associated with the Democratic proslavery party.[17]

British neglect had contributed to the deaths of over a million Irish, who perished from starvation or from famine-related diseases. Another nearly two million fled Ireland.[18] Most refugees from Ireland's famine arrived in the United States nearly destitute and with few skills. Settling in northeastern cities, they took whatever unskilled jobs they could find, working on the docks, pushing carts, digging canals, and building the railroad, as well as petty theft and prostitution. Their mortality rates were high, especially the children, more than half of whom born to famine refugees in Boston died before the age of six. Adult immigrants lived an average of only six years after their arrival in the United States.[19] They did not starve as they would have at home, but there is much evidence that they did not regard themselves as willing immigrants or the US as the American Dream but saw themselves as exiles, having been forced out of their homeland. They blamed the English government and the landlord system; as one woman from Limerick put it, "Due to the suppression of the English, the Irish were practically driven from their homes." Another said, "We didn't want to leave Ireland, but we had to."[20]

Irish Catholics had been racialized under English colonial rule that regarded them as biologically inferior. During the 1870s, influenced by social Darwinism, some English scientists even promoted the theory that the Irish (and all people of color) had descended from apes, while the English were descendants of "man," who had been created by God "in his own image." Thus, the English were "angels" and the Irish (and other colonized peoples) were apes, a lower species. Today in the United States, Christian Identity white supremacists call Black people and other people of color "mud people," inferior products of the process of evolution, while white people were created by the Christian deity.[21] Even prosperous Irish Catholics were subjected to the Penal Laws, which criminalized being Catholic Irish. These derogatory attitudes and behaviors toward the Irish famine refugees prevailed in the United States as well. American-born Anglo-Saxons called the Irish immigrants "low browed," "savage," "bestial," "lazy," "wild," "simian," "sensual," "Celtic Beast" with "prehensile paws" rather than hands, and other such insults, similar to their descriptions of Black people. Political cartoonists made their "Paddy" character resemble an ape. Historian David Roediger writes, "In short, it was by no means clear the Irish were white."[22]

Many Irish families in the shantytowns and tenements of the Northeast lost their children or the children lost their parents to early deaths, producing many Irish orphans. Between 1854 and 1929, a quarter million children were transported from New York to the Southwest. Some 25 percent were Irish. In the 1870s, the Roman Catholic Church was so concerned that the children were being placed in Protestant homes that it set up its own program, Placing Out.[23] Historian Linda Gordon writes that in 1904, Catholic nuns in New York transported forty Irish orphans to an isolated Arizona mining camp to place them with Catholic families, who were Mexican and part of the majority of the border area population. However, the local Protestant Anglo-Americans expressed horror about "interracial" mixing. They formed a vigilante raid that was successful in kidnapping the children, and in the fray nearly lynched the nuns and the local priest. The Roman Catholic Church sued for return of the children, but the courts all the way to the US Supreme Court ruled in favor of the Anglo-Americans.[24]

HOW THE IRISH BECAME SETTLERS

The late historian Noel Ignatiev, in his 1995 book, *How the Irish Became White*, theorizing whiteness as a social construct, did not take into account the very bedrock of the United States as a settler-colonial, fiscal-capitalist state.[25] Ignatiev expressed frustration that Irish immigrants did not identify with enslaved Africans and express solidarity, becoming abolitionists, and especially why they did not unify with the free Black population in the eastern cities where the refugees lived in squalid poverty. In Ireland itself, antislavery was widespread. Given the desperate condition of the Irish famine refugees and given that they were fleeing not only famine but also brutal English colonization, his assessment was naïve.[26] Ignatiev's query as to how the Irish became white assumes that the United States was a republic marred only by the smudge of racial slavery. As Irish scholar Mary Mullen has observed, the question is not how the Irish became "white," rather how the Irish became settlers.[27]

In the lead-up to the formation of the United States, Protestantism in the form of Puritanism refined already-existing European white supremacy as part of a political-religious ideology in defense of settler-colonial genocide of Indigenous inhabitants and the codification of Blackness as slave status. Irish famine immigrants, then, arrived in the United States as inferiorized and stigmatized people. This was the time of the violent ethnic cleansing of the Southeast Indigenous commons in the 1840s and appropriation of land and human property by slavers. The result was the Cotton Kingdom, a vast commercial-agricultural construct made up of factory-like plantations surrounded by concentration camp conditions to control enslaved Black workers, elevating the US economy to the wealthiest among European states. This was the birth of fully developed racial capitalism, the fiscal-military state. Despite their lowly state, the Irish refugees, because the majority were light-skinned in a US culture obsessed with whiteness, became US Americans inheriting the privileges of white settler. The stigma of Catholicism was resolved through settler-colonial extreme patriotism, which they came to embrace.[28] A major factor in Irish acceptance of US patriotism was Irish republicanism, as they saw the United States as a prior colony of Britain that revolted and became a republic, not recognizing the settler colonialism in the US that was patterned after the English settler colonialism in Ireland.[29]

Anti-Black racism was also required for acceptance. By the 1850s, Irish Catholic famine refugees, having fled brutal and racialized English colonization, would flock to minstrel shows, which often showcased Irish immigrants in blackface.[30] The integration of millions of Irish immigrants into the white republic formed a template for the absorption of the twenty million, mostly destitute or persecuted Eastern and Southern European immigrants, predominately Catholic and Jewish, who arrived between 1880 and 1920. Although neither the Irish nor the later European immigrants left their homes and countries and arrived in the United States in pursuit of the American Dream, a concept invented in 1931, they surely were not aware of, or were in denial about, the racial capitalist order they were entering.[31] It was a superior social order based on whiteness that they could join, even if they remained working class or poor, as part of the dominant settler class by virtue of being of European origin. As the inventor of the American Dream meme explained, "That dream of a land in which life should be better and richer and fuller for everyone, with opportunity for each according to ability or achievement." In other words, a sense of superiority, not prosperity, was the guaranteed reward.[32]

Unlike earlier Irish Catholic settlers who had arrived as individuals or families in the eighteenth-century British colonies or in the four decades after US independence, the Irish famine refugees were not simply a mass of impoverished, starving individuals or families; they were also a conscious, colonized people escaping British colonization. Although not pursuing any kind of dream in their exodus, they regarded the United States positively as having expelled the hated British Empire. They had either no knowledge or incorrect knowledge of the Indigenous nations that were resisting US genocidal colonization, nor knowledge of the central role of racial slavery that was at its apex in the Cotton Kingdom on their arrival. Yet, in escaping Ireland, being free of colonization, they soon gained the privilege of whiteness, of Europeans and European Americans in the United States, especially after the Civil War.

W. E. B. Du Bois wrote in his 1935 book *Black Reconstruction in*

America, 1860–1880 that normal labor unity did not work, due to "a carefully planned and slowly evolved method, which drove such a wedge between the white and black workers that there probably are not today in the world two groups of workers with practically identical interests who hate and fear each other so deeply and persistently and who are kept so far apart that neither sees anything of common interest." Du Bois added his oft-quoted concept of the white worker's "psychological wage," writing, "They were given public deference and titles of courtesy because they were white. They were admitted freely with all classes of white people to public functions, public parks, and the best schools. The police were drawn from their ranks, and the courts, dependent upon their votes, treated them with such leniency as to encourage lawlessness."[33]

Noel Ignatiev and other whiteness studies scholars and activists make much of the psychological wage without acknowledging adequately the much greater importance of the material rewards of maintaining the wedge, which is a major factor in the ascendency and continued success of US capitalism that is based on surplus labor supply and exploitation of labor. Formerly enslaved abolitionist Frederick Douglass traveled as an abolitionist leader extensively throughout Ireland, publishing his analysis of the colonization of the Irish.[34] However, he acknowledged the stark contrast between the political views of the Irish in Ireland and Irish Americans, lamenting that "the Irish, who, at home, readily sympathize with the oppressed everywhere, are instantly taught when they step upon our soil to hate and despise the Negro."[35]

Irish Americans' climb to political access depended on their numbers. Roediger points out that how immigrants voted in the US had little impact through 1830, as the foreign born accounted for only one in thirty ballots. But Irish Americans, by sheer numbers, gained political attention between 1830 and 1855, during which they made up nearly half the total immigrants. By the early 1830s, Irish Catholics were aligned with Andrew Jackson and the Democratic Party.[36] Andrew Jackson was the archetype Protestant Scots Irish settler, the family from County Antrim. Nevertheless, in the 1832 election, the Pennsylvania Scots Irish who had championed Jackson turned against him, while the Irish Catholics supported him.[37]

The Scots Irish went on, together with Anglo-Saxon fundamentalists, to form the nativist Know-Nothing Party, a rabidly anti-Catholic, anti-immigrant political party. At its height in the 1850s and operating nationwide, it included more than a hundred elected congressmen, eight governors, a dominant share of state legislatures from Massachusetts to California, and thousands of local politicians. Starting as a cult-like society, the Order of the Star-Spangled Banner, the Know-Nothing Party had an initiation rite they were not allowed to discuss outside the society, so if asked about it, members would reply, "I know nothing." The party supported a naturalization period of twenty-one years for immigrants, mandatory Bible reading in schools, and the expulsion of Catholics from public office, and they were in favor of temperance, Protestantism, self-reliance, and US nationalism.[38] Although the Know-Nothing Party faded as a party, the ideological tendency continued in US politics, becoming dominant in the mid-twentieth century in opposition to the civil rights movement and immigration, including among white Catholics when they were no longer the target.

THE SAN PATRICIO BATTALION
AND IRISH AMERICANS IN US WARS

The military is another avenue for immigrants to become Americanized. Irish famine refugees had an added misfortune of arriving as the United States prepared to invade México. The US Army heavy-handedly and with false promises recruited Irishmen and others into military service upon their arrival in the United States. The Whig Party, along with the Jacksonian Democrats and the ideology of manifest destiny, whipped up Protestant pride against Catholic Mexicans and instilled fear of a papal takeover, fueling Mexican hating. Irish immigrants' loyalty was questioned.[39] Most Irish soldiers in the Mexican war remained loyal to the United States, and in the battle to take México City, their performance was praised by US officers as "the extremest of bravery." But around seven hundred mostly Catholic famine refugee soldiers deserted the US Army at the Rio Grande under the leadership of Irish American John Riley, forming a battalion within the Mexican Army. Two-fifths of the battalion were Irish born, and the rest were Polish, German, and other Catholic immigrants. They were motivated by revulsion of the Texas slavers, the anti-Catholicism of the US soldiers and officers, and for the Irish immigrants, anticolonial solidarity with a poor country like their own, plus the Mexican government distributed flyers urging desertion with promises of land and citizenship.[40]

Dubbed by Mexicans as the San Patricio Brigade, they fought in a number of battles before the Mexican Army's key defeat on August 20, 1847, at the Battle of Churubusco on the outskirts of México City, which allowed the US Army to occupy the capital. Some Irish and other immigrant soldiers were killed and others escaped, but eighty-five were captured and tried for desertion. The commander, John Riley, was wounded and captured. At trial, Riley spoke in defense of the Irish American troops that joined the Mexican Army and of the vicious treatment of Irish and other Catholic immigrants in the US Army, attributing their desertion to US anti-Catholicism. Because Riley was a US citizen and already a regular in the US Army and had defected before the declaration of war, he was not eligible to be sentenced to death; rather, a *D* for deserter was branded on his cheek and he was then released. Riley became a Mexican citizen and continued to serve in the Mexican Army. The Irish soldiers who, like Riley, had joined the Mexican Army before the official declaration of war on México were sentenced to receive fifty lashes on their bare backs, to be branded with the letter *D*, and to wear iron yokes around their necks for the duration of the war. Those Irish who deserted after the war was declared were hanged.[41]

Although more than nine thousand US soldiers deserted the army during the war, only the Patricios were punished by hanging, a firing squad being the official, more dignified means of punishment for desertion. William S. Harney was the US Army commander delegated to carry out the sentences of the deserters, staging a mass lynching of thirty of the San Patricios. Harney was also of Irish Catholic descent and was the son of an early Irish immigrant. Historian Walter Johnson writes that Harney carried out his duty "by placing the men on the backs of wagons and forcing them to watch the climactic battle of the war unfolding in the distance with nooses hanging around their necks. At the culmination of the battle, the wagons were driven forward. Harney left the bodies hanging from the gallows. 'I was ordered to hang them, and have no orders to unhang them,' he said."[42] This was excessive behavior even by the US military standards of the 1840s.[43]

Harney was typical of many of the US military men in the US war against México, such as Robert E. Lee, Braxton Bragg, Jefferson Davis, and Ulysses S. Grant, having fought in the counterinsurgent wars against the Seminole Nation in Florida, the Sauk and Fox in the Great Lakes area, the Arikara in the Central Plains, and other Indigenous nations in the 1830s before the war in México. Then, in the Civil War, Lee, Davis, Bragg, and others fought for the Confederacy, while Grant and others fought for the Union. Harney was born in Tennessee in 1800, the son of an early Irish Catholic settler who had been a military man in the colonies, killing Indians and fighting in the War of Independence. William Harney got his start in the army under Andrew Jackson. Johnson describes him as "white supremacy and empire embodied." Harney was in the First Battalion of the US Mounted Rangers (First Dragoons), founded at Jefferson Barracks at St. Louis in 1832. Officers included captains Jefferson Davis and Nathan Boone, son of Daniel Boone. While posted in St. Louis, Harney married one of seven daughters of a local, wealthy Irish Catholic merchant and rejoined the Roman Catholic Church. In 1834, he murdered an enslaved woman in St. Louis by publicly beating her to death. He was acquitted and soon promoted and given command of the Second US Dragoons. During the Second Seminole war, in 1839, Harney wrote of the indigenous Seminoles, "Ere must be no more talking—they must be hunted down as so many wild beasts. Let everyone taken be hung up in the hoods to inspire terror in the rest."[44] Harney's cruelty to the Patricios was nothing new and continued in the "Indian wars" up to his retirement before the Civil War.[45]

Nearly a quarter million Irish Americans fought in the Civil War, 20 percent of them for the Confederacy. The Union's Conscription Act of 1863 made all white men between the ages of twenty and forty-five years eligible for the draft. Free Black men were not subject to the draft but were permitted to "volunteer through the provisions of the Emancipation Proclamation." White men with money could illegally bribe doctors for medical exemptions, legally hire a substitute, or pay for a commutation of a draft. Lower-class white men, many of them Irish American Catholics, engaged in riots against the draft, targeting enrollment officials and free Black men, as well as well-dressed white men. The largest riot took place on June 11, 1863, when an angry mob murdered more than a hundred people. They set fire to a draft office and attacked police officers. But most of their anger went into attacking and killing Black people.[46]

On the other hand, the goal of the Irish-nationalist Fenian movement was to train a fighting force of Irish people in the US who could assist in the liberation of Ireland. They encouraged Irish gun ownership and organization of citizen militias in the US. When the Civil War started, they flocked into the Union Army and formed dozens of autonomous Irish brigades. It was an extension of older strategies the Fenian movement had promoted for Irish men to join military forces of friendly foreign powers, as they had done in Spain and France and even as Vatican guards, and to enlist in the British army to obtain military training and battle experience, after which they would defect, mutiny, or work as double agents. After the Civil War, many of Custer's soldiers were Irish, and he would have the band play his favorite song, which was Irish. And Irish Catholics are notably represented both as troops and as officers in US imperialist wars.[47]

THE IRISH BECOME THE POLICE

When Black people today are asked how the Irish became white, they often knowingly respond, "when they became the police." By sheer numbers in the major northeastern cities, the Irish American Catholic population pioneered ethnic politics that spread to other cities across the country, followed by similar ethnic patronage of Italians, Greeks, Slavs, Germans, and Jews, although none as numerous or successful in the Northeast cities as Irish Americans. Irish American political power began with the vote and their support for the Democratic Party, but it was first institutionalized by coming to dominate fledgling urban police forces in the Northeast.

Although Irish Americans are no longer the majority of rank-and-file police officers, they continue in the twenty-first century to run police departments and wield powerful influence in police unions. All police commissioners in the New York Police Department have been Irish except for two.[48] Across the United States, city police departments honor Irish American police with Emerald Societies. Founded in the 1950s, Emerald Societies were made up of autonomous chapters and extended to Irish members of fire departments and other public agencies. In the first surge of Irish American police in the second half of the nineteenth century, Irish immigrants went from being viewed as the major source of crime to becoming the police who fought it.

Historian Livia Gershon observes that "to a large extent, northern US cities invented their police departments as a way to control the 'Irish problem.'" Irish immigrants populated shantytowns and slums of cities, and many, for lack of employment or income, turned to petty theft and sex work. Drunkenness, domestic abuse, and gangs were the fruit of impoverishment. There were many poor Irish Americans in the cities even before the influx of millions of famine refugees. In 1837 in Boston, there was a Protestant-led, anti-Irish Catholic riot of fifteen thousand people, which was about a fifth of Boston's population, that destroyed the Irish neighborhood. Only the Irish Americans were prosecuted while the assailants went free. The next year the Boston Police Department, the first in the country, was established to control the "dangerous classes." Unsurprisingly, nativist panic flourished with the arrival of masses of Irish refugees in the 1840s and '50s. One Boston Irishman was hired by the police force in 1851, but was ousted after three years when the nativist and anti-Catholic Know-Nothing Party took control of the Massachusetts legislature. Hiring predominately Irish Americans for the police force was a result of Irish political power through the Democratic Party in cities over the next decades.[49]

Organized police departments were established in New York City in 1845; Albany, New York, and Chicago in 1851; New Orleans and Cincinnati in 1853; Philadelphia in 1855; and Newark, New Jersey, and Baltimore in 1857; and by the 1880s all major US cities had municipal police forces in place.[50] Hiring a few Irish Americans led to more, as Irish American policemen helped friends and family members obtain work on police forces. James R. Barrett explains that the structure of Irish American social relations, based on where Irish members' families came from in Ireland, lent itself well to networking with close-knit Catholic parishes and county organizations. Barrett's father was a police officer and told him that it was common within police departments for people to ask what county in Ireland you were from well into the twentieth century. In 1855, of the 1,100 police in the New York Police Department, three hundred were born in Ireland, seven hundred were second-generation Irish Americans, and thirty-six had served prison terms.[51]

In 1872, Irish American John Kelly took over New York City's powerful political organization Tammany Hall, which had been exclusively Protestant. Irish American street gangs and organized crime syndicates flourished, and often Irish police joined Irish gangs attacking Italian and Jewish immigrants and Black people.[52] Patrick Higgins points out that gangs and police have a symbiotic relationship and neither represents working-class power.[53]

IRISH AMERICAN WORKERS, UNIONS, AND POLITICAL POWER

On May 8, 1970, four days after the National Guard fired on unarmed and peaceful anti-war protestors at Kent State University in Ohio, killing four and wounding nine, two hundred union construction workers were mobilized by the New York State AFL-CIO to attack a thousand college and high school students. The students were protesting in Lower Manhattan against the United States' expansion of the war in Vietnam to bombing Cambodia. Most of the construction workers were of Irish Catholic descent. Peter J. Brennan, an Irish American Catholic from New York City and a painter by trade, was the president of the Building and Construction Trades Council of greater New York and vice president of the New York State AFL-CIO. George Meany was AFL-CIO national president. Meany was born into an Irish Catholic family in Harlem in 1894, the second of ten children. His parents were both US-born. The families of both parents had been famine refugees who immigrated to the United States in the 1850s. George Meany was raised in a union family, his father a plumber and active in the union local and in the local Democrat Party.[54]

After beating up the demonstrators and chasing them through the financial district, injuring around seventy, the workers stormed city hall and forced officials to raise the US flag to full-staff from half-staff, where it had been placed days before in mourning for the Kent State dead. The intruders sang "The Star-Spangled Banner" and yelled at the police standing by to take off their helmets, with which they dutifully complied. The workers went on to attack the nearby Pace College, smashing windows with clubs and crowbars and beating students. They ripped a Red Cross banner from the gates of Trinity Church and attempted to tear down the flag of the Episcopal church, where volunteer nurses were caring for the injured. The police, mostly of Irish descent, did not intervene.[55]

Patrick Buchanan, Irish American, then president Richard Nixon's aide, wrote in a memo to Nixon that "these, quite candidly, are our people now."[56] Peter Brennan denied that the union had any role in the mayhem, telling a reporter that "the unions had nothing to do with it, the men acted on their own. They did it because they were fed up with violence by anti-war demonstrators, by those who spat at the American flag and desecrated it." He added that his office had received calls and letters from all over the country praising the workers for their patriotism. It is now known that the Nixon administration initiated planning for the counterprotest with New York labor leaders and helped coordinate it and several others that month. Local shop stewards encouraged workers to join the protest, and in some cases offered cash bonuses. Brennan became secretary of labor in Nixon's second term. The hard hat Brennan gave to Nixon is on display at the Nixon presidential library. When he had ceremoniously presented it to Nixon soon after the riot, Brennan said, "The hard hat will stand as a symbol, along with our great flag, for freedom and patriotism to our beloved country."[57]

Irish Americans, who comprise 10 percent of the total US population, have long made up a larger percentage of the blue-collar workforce and, as indicated above, have been active trade unionists and officials. Union workers in most countries are considered a progressive if not left-wing force. But the US working class is different. Mike Davis offers three main reasons. First, by the mid-nineteenth century, workers' geographic mobility in the United States substituted for collective action; that is, if working conditions or poor pay created intolerable conditions, the worker could move on. British settler colonialism was based on attracting settlers to gain free land, property; so, as Friedrich Engels observed, US culture was the "purest bourgeois culture."[58] Second, Davis cites the cultural division of the US working class, writing that the most disastrous obstacle to labor unity in the 1850s was the reaction of native workers to the arrival of several million impoverished Irish migrants. They provided cheap labor for the growth of New England factories as well as armies of raw muscle for western railroads and the Pennsylvania coalfields. They were met by universal nativist hostility and riots against them, evicted from workplaces, refused admission into trade unions, and excluded from voting. Protestantism in the United States was not simply a majority religion but a constituent militant element of US nationalism.[59]

The millions of Irish Catholic famine refugees arrived in the aftermath of the half century of Protestant fervor after the second "Great Awakening," the first having swept through the British colonies in the 1730s and linked the separate settler colonies by fanatic religiosity up to the founding of the United States. In the 1795–1835 Second Great Awakening, large meetings were held in small towns and big cities but also in camp revival gatherings of the mainly Scots Irish frontier trekkers in Kentucky and Tennessee, the US foot soldiers of Empire who fed their genocidal guilt with feverish evangelism. The core of this religious fervor was a personal experience with Christ, and that could take many forms—speaking in tongues, handling snakes. In 1801 in Cane Ridge, Kentucky, following bloody massacres of Indigenous farmers and the burning of their crops and towns, the settlers from the newly established white settler communities, built on the bones of dead Indians, came from a wide area to hold a weeklong revival. The event drew more than ten thousand regular attendees and many more attended for a day or two. Seven itinerant Presbyterian, Baptist, and Methodist preachers worked the crowd.

The masses screamed and writhed and sang themselves to unconsciousness and oblivion, clearing their relationship with the devil. But surely the guilt remained, unnamed, even unknown. Patriotism was its perfect expression and justification. The Protestant religious awakenings formed a type of purging, in what Richard Slotkin characterizes as "regeneration through violence."[60] Davis writes that the Irish famine refugees arriving in the most militant Protestant nation in the world, rivaling even Britain, were bringing a particular form of Catholicism unlike the European continental and monarchical church. The lower tier of the Irish Catholic church was antimonarchical and for Irish independence, thereby allied with the aspirations of the poor Irish people and therefore a fusion of religion and Irish nationalism, although the Irish church as an institution collaborated with the Crown and against republican movements.

The colonized Irish were an agricultural proletariat—sharecroppers, tenants, day laborers—not peasants as in England and the European continent.[61] Roediger misunderstands the difference, noting that Irish Catholic immigrants came from rural areas, "in which place mattered tremendously, contributing to a relationship with the past, to a sense of kinship and even to religious faith. Torn from their homes, they resettled in places remarkably different from Ireland," not only in cities but also in crowded quarters, so that "Irish-Americans maintained only the most tenuous of ties to nature," noting that they kept pigs.[62] The Irish certainly cared about place and their land and country and counties and clans; however, this characterization implies bucolic lives tied to "nature" in Ireland. But rural Irish Catholics were colonized and desperately poor, living in miserable huts in countrysides scarred by deforestation, commercial agriculture, and water pollution and working as day laborers and sharecroppers on commercial Anglo-Irish plantations. Although some Irish immigrants took up farming in the Midwest, it should be no surprise that most of them eschewed the countryside when they immigrated to the United States. Many did work in the coal mines of Pennsylvania and the railroads and canals located in rural areas, but these occupations were not likely to be described as work that allowed them to experience nature.

The third divisive force Davis identifies in the US working class was and is white supremacy, which Irish immigrants to the United States inherited. Davis writes, "American democracy was, after all, the most spectacularly successful case of settler-colonialism and the correlative condition for 'free soil, free labor' was the genocidal removal of the indigenous population."[63] White supremacy had been fully foundational for two-and-a-half centuries in North America when the Irish famine refugees arrived. Most nativist workers eschewed any move for social equality and suffrage for Black freedmen before and after emancipation. The Republican Party Free-Soilers did not attempt to alter white supremacy. Allying with the Irish republican activist Daniel O'Connell, radical abolitionists William Lloyd Garrison and Frederick Douglass developed a strategy in the 1840s for an abolitionist alliance between Irish Americans and the movement in Ireland. But O'Connell received angry negative replies from Irish American supporters. In a letter from an assembly of Irish coal miners in Pennsylvania, they denounced the call to accept Black people as "brethren," writing, "WE do not form a distinct class of community, but consider ourselves in every respect as CITIZENS of this great and glorious REPUBLIC—that we look upon every attempt to address us, otherwise than as CITIZENS, upon the subject of the abolition of slavery . . . as base and iniquitous, no matter from what quarter it may proceed." Davis writes, "The refusal of Irish miners in an anthracite hell-hole of eastern Pennsylvania not only to sympathize with the slaves, but to accept the implication—even from their own national hero—that they were in America anything less than 'CITIZENS,' speaks volumes about the ideological impact of American exceptionalism and the difficulties of building a class-conscious movement."[64]

By 1880, the social structure of Irish Americans had been transformed, especially the structure of the working class. Labor activist and scholar Bill Fletcher Jr. stresses that labor organizing in the United States took place within the settler state's ideology of property ownership and was based on white-exclusive trade unions that took for granted the existence of the settler state. White supremacism was inherent in the labor movement, not only against Black people but also Chinese immigrants; whereas with Irish Americans, organized labor was "willing and able to configure itself in such a way ultimately to legitimize these immigrant workers and their descendants."[65] There were over a million Irish American male wage-workers in industry and transportation, around 65 percent of all Irish American males, while they made up only 15 percent of unskilled manual laborers, most of them recent immigrants. Irish Americans were 7.5 percent of the total US workforce but had more representation as iron- and steelworkers, teamsters, masons, skilled textile workers, and other trades in which unionization was dominant.[66]

By the turn of the twentieth century, Irish Americans had attained considerable political power, with thirty-six Irish American Congress members, four senators, the first Irish Catholics in the cabinet and on the Supreme Court, as well as appointments in the diplomatic service and political machines in the large cities. The hierarchy of the US Catholic Church was three-fourths Irish American. There were more than twenty thousand Irish American manufacturers and a number of millionaires funding twenty Catholic universities.

IRISH SELF-INDIGENIZING

The transformation of Irish Catholic immigrants to settlers sometimes is overtheorized as a phenomenon that originated once they were in the United States. That is because most narratives are concerned with the Irish embrace of the prevailing anti-Black racism, omitting the strain of anti-Native American racism that existed in Ireland, which Irish Catholic immigrants brought with them. Irish studies scholar Mary Mullen writes that scholars of Ireland have long noted that Irish nationalists have tended to identify more with white settlers than with Indigenous peoples. Young Ireland's emphasis on "native feeling" and the Fenian Brotherhood's articulation of "the right of distinct peoples to self-government" did not extend to Indigenous groups.

> But Irish settler identity is not merely a matter of identification. It is a structural position: even when Irish nationalists identify with Indigenous peoples or their experience, they reinforce and reproduce the structures of settler colonialism. . . .

Irish nationalists use analogies between Irish and Indigenous peoples to assert the reality of Irish colonial history through depictions of unreal American Indians. In the process, they question settlement in Ireland while legitimating and participating in the settlement of America.

Mullen calls this stance a "doubleness of Irish transnational identity" in which the Irish nationalists want it both ways, enjoying US settler status while claiming an affinity with Indigenous peoples, thereby making Indigenous peoples a metaphor, a form of erasure.[67]

Irish scholar Luke Gibbons writes that Irish historians turn to origin stories, seeking an "original Irish civilization" to counter the English view of both the Irish and Indigenous peoples as savages lacking in history. In doing so, they instrumentalize indigeneity whereas Indigenous peoples in the Americas are made up of hundreds of distinct nationalities with varied cultures, religions, and languages, and are not an inchoate race. And, although these analogies of wildness and savagery originate with English settlers, they also shape Irish anticolonial thinking that then relies on racializing and celebrating mythic origins.[68] The Irish nationalists regarded property in Ireland as rightfully theirs with their culture embedded in it, but "when this vision of property crosses the Atlantic, it suggests that merely identifying with America could justify Irish ownership of Indigenous land." An 1852 article by an Irish nationalist categorized the Celt as "aboriginal," yet goes on to characterize the Celt as natural colonizers: "Within a century, the Celtic element will inevitably be sovereign in America. . . . We see in America the natural inheritance of such a race." The article goes on to claim that Irish people's "love of land and love of arms" makes them a good fit for the United States where "land is as free as air." Mullen writes, "The fact that the Irish flourish in places of 'free' land allows them to claim ownership of the land. Such an argument erases Indigenous peoples from the land while nevertheless finding the origin of American culture in this land."[69]

As is the case of the Protestant Scots Irish settlers in Appalachia and Hispanos in New Mexico, Irish American Catholics as immigrants also carried with them from Ireland a myth that claimed Irish discovery of America as well as a myth of Indigenous peoples in North America as descendants of the Irish. John F. Kennedy hinted at the myth in his book *A Nation of Immigrants*, claiming that the American Indians who were present when British colonialists arrived were not the original people.[70] Mary Mullen writes, "The most explicit version of Irish nationalists' 'native feeling' that contributes to the dispossession of Indigenous peoples' lands is the myth of Irish origins for Indigenous tribes."[71] The myth was proposed in the series "Letters from America" in the Irish nationalist *Nation* in 1843.[72] The series sought to form political connections between Ireland and Irish Americans, offering advice also to prospective emigrants. The author celebrated that the United States was free from the British Empire that oppressed the Irish but also expressed sympathy for the Native peoples who were being deprived of their lands and pushed west. He warned that the white population, even the Irish, were the "natural enemies" of the Indigenous. He then narrates a "tradition extant that some tribes of those Indians are of Irish descent," asserting that, in 1169, the son of a Welsh prince and an Irish princess gathered a number of ships and crew and set out west to "discover lands then unknown," therefore "discovering America" before Columbus. Patrick Higgins observes that the United States came to form a "blind spot" for Irish nationalists, even among those with a stated record of opposing British colonialism around the world. An example of this is Roger Casement, who wrote at length against Belgium's actions in the Congo and the British Empire's crimes in Africa and Asia, yet regarded the United States positively.[73]

Mullen notes that the myth of Celtic Indians triggers a form of "native feeling" that extends to the United States and can be found across Irish history. Thomas D'Arcy McGee, a contributor to the Irish *Nation* and founder of the New York *Nation*, offered another version of the myth. It draws on thirteenth-century accounts that argue that a long time before Columbus, the land between Virginia and Florida was "peopled by the Irish" and constituted a "Great Ireland beyond the western sea." McGee conceded that it might not be grounded in fact but is a way of perceiving Irish immigration, writing, "The dates and details we must leave to the antiquarians, while we endeavor to show what modern emigration has done to accomplish the legend."[74] Mullen points out that the myth serves multiple purposes, that it separates the Irish from the white population that oppress the Indigenous, and it bestows the right of discovery prior to Columbus, allowing the Irish to define themselves both through the colonial oppression they live under and their right by discovery to be Indigenous in the new land.[75]

Throughout the Irish periodical *Nation*, analogies between Irish and Indigenous peoples take various forms, one being an expression of fear, particularly during the famine that the Irish will suffer the same fate as the "Red Indians," which stresses the inevitable disappearance of the Indigenous nations, situating them in the past without a future. But there is also a narrative of celebration of Irish survival in the face of British oppression, that the Irish had overcome British plans for Irish extinction, partly due to their success in the United States.[76] Similarly, the Irish republican newspaper *Irish People* carried statements of Irish survival that contrast Irish and Indigenous peoples. One article states, "We must be allowed mildly to observe, that it may not be quite so easy to get rid of us as of the Bushmen and Maoris. There is something in belonging to the Caucasian races, even in its Celtic branch."[77] Mullen concludes, "Claiming racial superiority for the Irish people, the article reinforces the sense that Indigenous peoples are a mere metaphor for their own disappearance." Therefore, the English in denying food to the famine-stricken Irish intend genocide, but unlike the Indigenous peoples, the Irish block the plan successfully by emigrating. Actually, they thereby become a factor of Indigenous dispossession. The authors do not take note that the Native peoples did not disappear despite attempted genocide.[78] The *Nation* portrays Irish and Native similarities and differences, both in ways that grant innocence to Irish settlers.

Many Irish studies scholars and activists have acknowledged race and settler colonialism as social structures rather than simply events of the past. However, Mullen notes that many continue to reference "Native American" as a racial category rather than "Native peoples" as a post-colonization term encompassing distinct nationalities.[79] Indigenous studies scholar Mark Rifkin traces United States law as constructing "racial Indianness" in the nineteenth century, transforming Native nations into a "population" as a part of the colonization process.[80]

Irish Americans are not unique as settler-immigrants in self-indigenizing; it is a trait of settler colonialism that looms large in the United States, with an extremely reduced Indigenous presence and an enduring white republic that stigmatizes immigrants of color. Patrick Higgins argues that the positive aspects of the tradition of Irish republicanism has been "surgically removed" from Irish Americans. Priests played a large role, the church being a "bastion of anti-communism." Higgins cites the pioneering role of the Irish American priest Charles Coughlin, who, as Father Coughlin, used the radio to spout pro-Nazi fascist propaganda, forming a blueprint for right-wing jocks like Rush Limbaugh.[81] But, as Mullen shows, Irish nationalism itself diminished Indigenous peoples' aboriginalism and resilience.

THE IRISH SLAVERY MYTH

However exploited, oppressed, colonized, demonized, and starved the Irish were—and they were—they were never subjected to chattel slavery as experienced by enslaved Africans who were deported to the European colonies in the Western Hemisphere and their descendants. Even after the emancipation of enslaved Africans in the United States, Jim Crow laws of segregation continued, as did intergenerational trauma and police profiling. The myth of Irish enslavement has been documented and debunked by Irish librarian and researcher Liam Hogan, who asserts, "The conflation of indentured servitude with chattel slavery in the 'Irish slaves' narrative whitewashes history in the service of Irish nationalist and white supremacist causes. Its resurgence in the wake of Ferguson reflects many Americans' denial of the entrenched racism still prevalent in their society."[82]

Historian Brian Kelly astutely notes that, while imperialism oppressed and tortured the Irish and others who were colonized for centuries, raising that point at this time is a classic case of diversion. Irish immigrants in the nineteenth century were transported to America in "coffin ships." Some arrived in such a state that port officials had to check whether they were alive or dead as they sorted out the bodies. But, once ashore, they were accorded a status denied to African Americans. The Irish were never slaves. To posit a parallel between the experiences of Irish Americans and African Americans is to reveal either awesome ignorance or outright racism. The incorporation of the Irish into the American State helps explain the over-representation of the Irish in the repressive institutions of the US today.[83]

Hogan even sees a distortion of Irish history that damages the actual history of oppression. "There is no need to exaggerate what our ancestors endured. . . . This refusal to differentiate between indentured servitude and racialized perpetual hereditary chattel slavery via the transatlantic slave trade, only feeds white supremacist myths."[84] This myth is a pernicious one that is used to create a false equivalency to support anti-Black racist claims that white people experienced slavery too and emerged from it successfully and without complaint, while descendants of enslaved Africans claim damage and liability and demand reparations.[85]

Matthew Horton explains that Irish nationalists in Ireland originated the "Irish slavery" discourse in the eighteenth century, rather loosely equating the documented horrors of contractual, time-limited indentured servitude or penal servitude with racialized perpetual, hereditary chattel slavery with Africa as the source. It was raised again in the twentieth century as a strategy to build Irish solidarity around a common historical experience of "slavery" with militants in South Africa and from the African diaspora. In the 1980s and '90s, a number of leftist scholar-activists in the United States conflated time-limited indentured servitude, however brutal and onerous, and perpetual, inherited, commodified, and legalized chattel slavery, perpetuating the myth of Irish slavery. Their goal was to appeal to poor and working-class white people in the United States to envision Black-white solidarity, and as Horton observes, they drew from Marx's descriptions of European working conditions as a form of "slavery."[86] This conflation had the unintentional effect that allowed some Irish Americans to claim that they overcame the trauma of past enslavement, criticizing the Black civil rights struggles. Tom Hayden, cofounder of the Students for a Democratic Society, civil rights activist, and anti-war leader during the US war in Vietnam who was of Irish Catholic heritage, also endorsed the "Irish slavery" myth in his 2001 memoir, *Irish on the Inside: In Search of the Soul of Irish America.* Hayden envisioned splitting the white working class by organizing Irish Americans to identify as radical anticolonial republicans, using the Irish slavery discourse apparently as a means of creating solidarity between the Black community and Irish Americans, writing, "If Irish America goes green, there goes white America. . . . When the Irish leave whiteness, there goes the neighborhood."[87]

Between 1840 and 1900 the number of Catholics in the United States had increased from fewer than seven hundred thousand to over three million, most of that increase being Irish immigrants.[88] Many were drawn to the Knights of Columbus, a fraternal society founded by Irish Catholics in 1881 for Catholic men. As the organization spread in the Northeast with the support of elite Irish Americans, it focused on developing "citizen culture" and had much to do with Americanizing the immigrants. By centering Columbus as the paragon of virtue and Catholic devotion, the organization could counter the accusation that the Roman Catholic Church had allegiance only to Rome by attaching Columbus to the founding of the United States. In 1892, in New Haven, Connecticut, the four-hundred-year anniversary of Columbus's landing brought together forty thousand people, six thousand of them Knights of Columbus, plus a thousand-piece band conducted by the West Point musical director "in a joint celebration of holiness and patriotism."[89] The idea of Columbus as founding father only grew with Italian Catholic immigration in the late nineteenth and early twentieth centuries.

CHAPTER 6

AMERICANIZING COLUMBUS

Mahmood Mamdani, in *Neither Settler nor Native,* locates the founding moment of the modern nation-state at 1492, noting it emerged out of two developments in Iberia. "One was ethnic cleansing, whereby the Castilian monarchy sought to create a homogeneous national homeland for Christian Spaniards by ejecting and converting those among them who were strangers to the nation—Moors and Jews. The other development was the taking of overseas colonies in the Americas by the same Castilian monarchy that spearheaded ethnic cleansing." Mamdani emphasizes that modern colonialism didn't suddenly start occurring in the eighteenth century but that European colonialism and the modern state were co-constituted.[1]

"DISCOVERY" AND THE CULT OF COLUMBUS

A few months after Catholic entry into ethnically cleansed Granada, the Spanish monarchs contracted with a Genoese seaman who promised he could reach India by a shorter route by sailing west. Columbus landed not at already European "discovered" India but, rather, on an island of what is now called the Bahamas. The thriving Indigenous residents informed him that to the north and south and east and west stretched a huge landmass, two massive continents teeming with cities and tens of millions of acres of farmlands that would come to constitute the major portion of humanity's food production. The rapacious crusade-hardened mercenaries representing Christendom were skeptical, until some voyages later they reached the continent at Central America, which they named Cabo Gracias a Díos (Thanks to God Cape). Two decades later a Spanish army would possess the heart of that landmass, destroying the most populated city in the world at the time, Tenochtitlán, in the valley of México.

October 12, 1492, is etched in the brains of many as the day of "discovery," but the Indigenous peoples of the Western Hemisphere and of Africa and descendants of enslaved Africans regard the date as the symbol of infamy, domination, slavery, and genocide. Haitian historian Michel-Rolph Trouillot writes, "To call 'discovery' the first invasions of inhabited lands by Europeans is an exercise in Eurocentric power that already frames future narratives of the event so described. . . . Once discovered by Europeans, the Other finally enters the human world."[2]

The first formal celebration of Columbus in the United States came five years after the Constitution was ratified—the tricentenary of discovery on October 12, 1792. It was organized by the Tammany Society, also called the Columbian Order, that was founded in 1789 by a group of wealthy men in New York City. An obelisk dedicated to Columbus was erected in Baltimore in 1792, the first known public monument to Columbus in North America. Although Bolivarian revolutionaries named Gran Colombia after Columbus, the independent states founded from the former Spanish colonies did not take up celebrating Columbus until the 1920s, even then and now not as a formal holiday. In 1937, at the behest of the Knights of Columbus, President Franklin D. Roosevelt proclaimed Columbus Day an official federal holiday.[3]

So, why did the United States, which at its founding had no direct geographical, calendar, or colonizing link to Columbus, embed the event and date as the very founding of the United States? Historian Claudia Bushman thinks the cult of Columbus rose in part because it eschewed the British source of US existence and located it origins to first founder of the Americas.[4] At first, "Columbia," meaning the land of Columbus, rather than "Columbus" was used for honoring Columbus. Columbia College, now University, was founded in 1754 as King's College and was renamed Columbia College when it reopened in 1784 after independence. And the federal capital was named the District of Columbia. The 1798 hymn "Hail, Columbia" was the early national anthem and is now used whenever the vice president of the United States makes a public appearance. By 1777, a year after the settlers of the thirteen British North American colonies declared independence, the poet Philip Freneau named what would become the United States of America "Columbia, America as sometimes so called from Columbus, the first discoverer." There were others who advocated that the thirteen states should adopt the name Columbia. South Carolina named its capital Columbia.[5]

Brian Hardwerk observes, "Columbus also provided a convenient way to forget about America's original inhabitants."[6] Bushman notes that "in early American textbooks from the 1700s Columbus is the first chapter. Columbus starts American history. There's nothing about the Indians. . . . Some of these books even show pictures of Columbus in colonial era clothing."[7] And, of course, Columbus was not even his name. David Vine asks, "Why do we call the man who some celebrate today as 'Christopher Columbus' when that wasn't his name?" pointing out that his only known name historically is Spanish—Cristóbal Colón—not difficult to pronounce, but definitely not an English name. Because Colón was being repurposed to be the founder of the United States, his name was anglicized to Christopher Columbus.[8]

Most significant, though, is that Columbus represented colonialism and imperialism that the original founders and future ruling classes fully embraced. In 1846, US senator from Missouri Thomas Hart Benton, who was basking in the glory of the US Senate's declaration of war against México, explained to Congress that the war was a continuation of Columbus's vision, "the grand idea of Columbus" who in "going west to Asia" provided the United States with its true course of empire, a predestined "American Road to India." Benton also explained the racial impact of the arrival of the "White race" on the west coast, "opposite the eastern coast of Asia" would be a benefit claiming that the "White race" was unique in having received "divine command, to subdue and replenish the earth," being the only "race" that searched for new and distant lands.[9]

In 1861, a twenty-by-thirty-foot mural was installed in the US Capitol building, titled *Westward the Course of Empire Takes Its Way*, symbolizing continental imperialism, which had come to be called manifest destiny. The US was mired in war with the secessionist Confederacy, but regarding imperialism, the two warring sides were in total agreement. The mural's painter, Emanuel Gottlieb Leutze, was born in Germany in 1816, his family immigrating to the United States in 1825. His first work was titled *Columbus Before the Council of Salamanca*, followed by a companion piece titled *Columbus in Chains*. In a tribute to the European radical revolutions of 1848, which he supported, Leutze painted *Washington Crossing the Delaware* in hopes the revolutionists would be inspired by the US War of Independence establishing the white republic.[10]

Mamdani's argument that the nation-state was born in 1492 is validated by the conscious mythical founding of the United States as a white republic that like the establishment of the Spanish nation-state was founded on white supremacy and ethnic cleansing. Required courses in history were incorporated into US school curricula in the early nineteenth century introducing children and young people to Columbus practically as an ancestor. But clearly Columbus took on a renewed significance and purpose with the increasing presence of the Roman Catholic Church in the United States with the arrival of millions of Irish immigrants and the millions of Eastern and Southern European immigrants, many of them Catholic, particularly the four million Italians who arrived between 1890 and 1920. Trouillot writes that "ethnicity gave Columbus a lobby, a prerequisite to public success in U.S. culture." In 1866, there were fewer than four thousand Italian Americans and only a few Spaniards in the United States, yet they already celebrated October 12 as Columbus Day in New York, and commemorations subsequently spread to Philadelphia, St. Louis, Boston, Cincinnati, New Orleans, and San Francisco. But the real boost for Columbus came from another source: Irish Americans and the Roman Catholic Church, with the 1882 establishment of the Knights of Columbus.[11]

THE KNIGHTS OF COLUMBUS AND AMERICANIZATION

In the February 11, 1882, edition of *Connecticut Catholic*, an Irish American newspaper owned and edited by a Catholic layman, came the news, "Pursuant to a call issued by Rev. Fr. McGivney—over sixty young men assembled in the basement of St. Mary's Church last Tuesday evening, February 7, 1882 and formed a cooperative benefit order to be known as the Knights of Columbus." Father McGivney proposed Columbus as patron to the organization while James T. Mullen, who became the first "Supreme Knight" suggested the full name Knights of Columbus to better evoke the ritualist character of the order. Matthew C. O'Connor, the first "Supreme Physician," asserted that Columbus was to signify that as Catholic descendants of Columbus, they "were entitled to all rights and privileges due to such a discovery by one of our fathers."[12] Although the Knights attracted Italian immigrants later in the century, the founding was largely an Irish American Catholic project.

Notre Dame historian Thomas Schlereth notes that the Irish American founders "apparently never entertained the idea of naming themselves after St. Brendan." He explains that for the Catholics of New Haven it had to be Columbus, mainly because Columbus was already embraced as a symbol of the authentic US American and helped remove from them the stigma of nativism. It was a symbol providing, as they put it, "social legitimacy and patriotic loyalty." As Catholic descendants of Columbus, they were entitled to "all the rights and privileges due such a discovery by one of our faith."[13] Father Michael McGivney was only thirty years old when he founded the Knights of Columbus and died eight years later. In October 2020, Pope Francis beatified McGivney, paving the way to sainthood, the highest tribute possible that the Roman Catholic Church could bestow upon the Knights of Columbus, illustrating the Vatican's continued support for its fifteenth-century doctrine of discovery.[14]

By the time of the four-hundred-year anniversary of their namesake in 1892, the Knights of Columbus were located in every state and soon would spread all over Canada, México, and the Philippines and become the largest body of Catholic laymen in the world with over two million members at the turn of the twenty-first century. Catholic historian Christopher J. Kauffman writes, "By adopting Columbus as their patron, this small group of New Haven Irish American Catholics displayed their pride in America's Catholic heritage, evoking the aura of Catholicity and affirming the 'discovery' of America as a Catholic event." But it was also a patriotic event; Kauffman notes, "The society's ceremonials led the initiates on a journey into council chambers where, with symbol, metaphor, and Catholic fellowship, they were taught the lessons of Columbianism: a strong attachment to the faith, a pride in American Catholic heritage, . . . and a duty to understand and defend the faith against its enemies, in short to display loyalty to Catholicism and to the flag." In 1882, Thomas Cummings said to fellow members of the newly formed Knights of Columbus, "Under the inspiration of Him whose name we bear, and with the story of Columbus' life as exemplified in our beautiful ritual, we have the broadest kind of basis for patriotism and true love of country."[15]

The organization spread rapidly in the Northeast with the backing of well-to-do Irish Americans and emphasized the shaping of "citizen culture." Trouillot notes that "Columbus played a leading role in making citizens out of these immigrants. He provided them with a public example of Catholic devotion and civic virtue, and thus a powerful rejoinder to the cliché that allegiance to Rome preempted the Catholics' attachment to the United States."[16] This was the beginning of the Americanization project at work, capped by the quadricentennial celebrations of Columbus in 1892–1893.

COLUMBUS IN THE WHITE CITY

By 1892, twenty-eight monuments to Columbus had been erected in cities around the United States, more than in any other country. Some were statues on pedestals, others were fountains and arches, and some freestanding columns. Many depicted Columbus holding or viewing a globe or sometimes an American eagle. In the 1860s, various cities began holding Columbus Day festivities, so by the time of the quadricentenary, the Columbus cult was firmly in place.[17] Throughout 1892 there were local celebrations all over the country, leading up to the quadricentennial national celebration of Columbus extravaganza in Chicago. It was a love fest for Western European and US American triumphal colonialism and imperialism, which was at its genocidal apex with the US government's total colonization of its now full continental shape, the triumph of manifest destiny. The World's Fair Columbian Exposition in Chicago launched in 1890 around the time of the US Seventh Calvary's massacre of hundreds of Lakota refugees at Wounded Knee, marking the occasion not only as a celebration of Columbus but of colonial genocidal victory.

The official guide to the event, which was funded by the US Congress, downplayed the preceding 280 years of European American history in North America, stating that it was only a "preparatory period" to the rise of the United States: "Most fitting it is, therefore, that the people of the greatest nation on the continent discovered by Christopher Columbus, should lead in the celebration of the Four Hundredth Anniversary of that event."[18] The site of the fair in South Chicago was nicknamed the "White City" for the massive and glistening white fake-marble buildings constructed specifically for the fair, not meant to be permanent, but rather templates for how a future city should appear, grandiose and imposing, as well as symbolizing the triumph of capitalism.

On the carnivalesque midway of the White City was the Ferris wheel, which was invented for the occasion. Not far away, the historian Frederick Jackson Turner delivered his thesis, "The Significance of the Frontier in American History," to the American Historical Association, which had convened its annual meeting at the exposition. Nearby, Buffalo Bill's Wild West performed.[19] Without mentioning the 1890 Wounded Knee Massacre, Turner chose the year 1890 as the demarcation of the end of the frontier, warning that the seemingly endless moving frontier of white settlement that had formed US wealth, character, and culture had closed, and the future was not clear without the frontier escape valve for the teeming landless masses. Buffalo Bill had the answer: fantasy, reenactment, premiering the soon-to-be-born western movies.

Self-identified Christian socialist and ordained Baptist minister Francis Bellamy wrote a pledge of allegiance to the US flag in 1892, which was a presidential election year in addition to being the quadricentenary of Columbus. Both presidential candidates, Benjamin

Harrison and Grover Cleveland, urged the use of the new pledge as a way of honoring Columbus. Bellamy's stated goal for the pledge was to advance patriotism by flying the flag in every school in the country along with mandatory reciting of the pledge. Bellamy led the way in organizing teachers to use a packaged Columbus Day educational kit he assembled. In an amazing feat, on October 21, 1892, Bellamy and his volunteers were able to involve twelve million schoolchildren around the country, including a hundred thousand Chicago schoolchildren, to simultaneously salute the flag and recite the pledge of allegiance.[20] In 1954, thanks to the Knights of Columbus' intense lobbying of the Eisenhower administration, the words "one nation under God" were added to Bellamy's secular pledge of allegiance.[21]

The United States' eugenics-influenced racial ideology was on display in the form of live enactments of levels of humanity. Nearest to the White City were the Teutonic and Celtic races, represented by two German and two Irish displays, illustrating the Celtic climb to whiteness. Below Christian Europeans were the Muslim and Asian people, descending to Africans on view in the Dahomean Village, and then at the remotest location in the display, North American Indians. Frederick Douglass was present at the fair representing the government of Haiti and was incensed by the Dahomean Village. He castigated the organizers, complaining that his race was being misrepresented by the "barbaric rites" of "African savages brought here to act the monkey."[22]

A measure of the success of the Chicago extravaganza was the naturalization of Columbus as first founder, which rationalized and justified the US occupation of the continent. In 1892, historians were already projecting a century ahead to celebrate the Columbus quincentenary, suggesting that Columbus, Ohio, be the center for the occasion, which actually happened with the AmeriFlora exposition in Columbus, Ohio, in 1992. As Trouillot observes, to make Columbus the discoverer of the United States, it was necessary to whiten him. Anglo-American was the definition of whiteness, and clearly Columbus was not Anglo, was not American, and did not speak English. While Columbus was becoming whiter, racism against Italian Americans was at its height in the United States.[23]

INDIGENIZING ITALIANS

Like the mass of Irish famine refugees who preceded them four decades earlier, the majority of the four million Italian immigrants to the US were fleeing grinding rural poverty in Southern Italy and Sicily. They were peasants stuck in medieval socioeconomic relations, while others were proletarian sharecroppers and migrant farmworkers, all without skills beyond agriculture. Most were motivated by jobs in the booming US Industrial Revolution, with plans to earn money to return to Italy and buy land or start businesses. In the United States, Italian migrants were met with endless insults in newspapers and magazines, which described them as "swarthy," "kinky haired," and criminally inclined, and regarded as racially impure in an era of the pseudo race theory of eugenics. Their children were often refused access to schools, and adults were turned away from public places and labor unions, and even in church, forced to sit in segregated church pews set aside for Black people. They were catcalled on the streets with epithets like "dago" and "guinea"—the latter a term of derision applied to enslaved Africans and their descendants—and more racist insults like "white nigger" and "nigger wop." In 1912, the US House Committee on Immigration debated whether Italians could be considered "full-blooded Caucasians," and immigrants coming from Southern and Eastern Europe were considered "biologically and culturally less intelligent."[24]

Employers often preferred light-skinned Slovaks and Poles to Italians. Railroad bosses wouldn't hire them because of their small stature. In the mining industry, English-speaking workers held the skilled and supervisory positions while Italians were hired as laborers. Even those who were educated and skilled were unable to secure any jobs besides manual labor. Only in the 1920s did Italians become more integrated into the workforce. More Italian immigrants were employed in semiskilled jobs in factories as well as skilled positions, but a third remained in unskilled positions. Even Italian American union members faced prejudice with meetings held in English, and Italians were not elected to official positions.[25]

Three years after the Chicago fair, a group of Italians in New

York formed the Sons of Columbus Legion to celebrate future Columbus anniversaries, mingling with the Irish and the Knights of Columbus who had succeeded in getting the seventy-six-foot Columbus Monument installed in the center of Columbus Circle in New York in 1892. By then the Irish had spread throughout the country, as Trouillot notes, "with the full benefits of white status . . . Columbus himself . . . became more Irish than ever— until Italian Americans made new gains in the continuing contest for racial and historical legitimacy."[26] The Knights lobbied state legislatures to establish October 12 as a legal holiday, and by 1912, they had succeeded in fourteen states and two decades later convinced the Franklin Roosevelt administration to make it a federal holiday.

The oppressed masses of Italian immigrants would find the attachment to Columbus an avenue to acceptance. They realized that the accepted representation of Columbus as "first founder" of the United States served to connect being Catholic and being Italian with the very birth of the United States; therefore, Italian immigrants could present themselves as Italian descendants of the original Italian founder, not so much as immigrants but returnees, as part of the origin story of the United States. Historian Danielle Battisti shows how casting Columbus as "the first immigrant" rewrote history, even though he never set foot on the continental landmass that became the United States and was never an immigrant himself, and even though the English colonies that became the United States did not exist in 1492. Later, in 1965, when Italian Americans campaigned to overturn immigration exclusion restrictions, they employed the origin story based on Columbus to great effect.[27]

Matthew Frye Jacobson observes that "race is absolutely central to the history of European immigration and settlement." That centrality was based in the founding 1790 naturalization law—An Act to Establish a Uniform Rule of Naturalization—that "white persons" were allowed to immigrate and become citizens. "The Europeanness—that is to say, whiteness—was among the most important possessions one could lay claim to. It was their *whiteness,* not any kind of New World magnanimity, that opened the Golden

Door."[28] In 1971, James Baldwin wrote, "I had my fill of seeing people come down the gangplank on Wednesday, let us say, speaking not a word of English, and by Friday discovering that I was working for them and they were calling me nigger like everybody else."[29] Baldwin critiqued the tragedy of how the immigrants' pursuing the lie of white supremacy "helped to steal the vitality from immigrant communities. . . . And in the debasement and defamation of Black people, they debased and defamed themselves."[30] He writes, "White people are not white; part of the price of the ticket is to delude themselves into believing that they are."[31] Baldwin characterized the United States as a destination where Europeans of all sorts could be melded in contrast to "Negroes" and "Indians." He writes, "No one was white before he/she came to America"; rather, they were Irish, German, Italian, Jewish, English, French, Swiss, Norwegian.[32] In the white Republic, one is either white, or not.[33]

Italian American journalist Christine Grimaldi laments what she calls the "paesanos of shame," Italian ancestors and contemporary Italian Americans, such as Rudy Giuliani and Mike Pompeo, who celebrate Columbus as an ancestor and embrace right-wing ideology and white supremacy: "Those of us who challenge whiteness through activism and essays still benefit from it, too. We will never experience the racist COVID-19 backlash against Asian American people and their businesses, though the virus overtook Italy and traveled from Europe to New York."[34]

CENTRAL AND EASTERN EUROPEAN IMMIGRANTS

Late-nineteenth- and early-twentieth-century European immigrants to the United States were in search of jobs. Many German immigrants were socialists fleeing political persecution, and Jewish immigrants were fleeing violent pogroms in Eastern Europe, but they all had to find work. At the turn of the twentieth century, nearly 60 percent of the US industrial workforce was foreign born, most being the nine million immigrants from Southern, Central, and Eastern Europe, as well as those continuing to emigrate from Ireland.

Unlike the British, Irish, and German early settlers in the colonies or early United States, immigrants to the Industrial Revolution—mostly rural Italian, Polish, Hungarian, Jewish, Czech, Slovak, Serb, Greek—lacked skills suited for industry. For instance, in 1907, of the fourteen thousand common laborers at the US steel mills in Pittsburgh, nearly twelve thousand were Eastern Europeans. They worked twelve-hour days, seven days a week, at low pay and made up the lower and poorly paid ranks of the urban sweatshops and the mills, factories, and mines.

Except for the Jewish immigrants who had fled Jew-hating, violent pogroms in Russia and Poland, many of the immigrants had hopes of returning home. None had the mythical American Dream in mind. In 1908, more Austro-Hungarians and Italians left the US than arrived. Those immigrants working in the large cities were packed into crowded slums, making up nearly 60 percent of the population of cities with more than a hundred thousand, and even larger percentages in the major industrial centers like Chicago, Philadelphia, and New York. Outside the cities, there were company towns where single corporations dominated every aspect of workers' lives, such as Gary, Indiana, and Butte, Montana, as well as dozens of steel and coal towns. In many locales, workers had to buy food and other goods at company stores at high prices. The United States as the industrial powerhouse of the world made it a magnet. Eastern European immigrants to the United States were either Catholic or Jewish; although most German immigrants were also Catholic or Jewish, many were Protestant.[35]

By the turn of the twenty-first century, German Americans made up 14 percent of the US population. Like the Irish, Germans had immigrated to the colonies and to the US after independence in significant numbers, important enough that during the writing of the Constitution, there was a movement to make German an official second language. Between 1820 and 1870, and especially after the failed 1848 European revolutions, more than seven and a half million Germans had immigrated, and many of them were socialists. In St. Louis alone by 1860, a third of the city's population had been born in the Catholic German-speaking territories of Europe.

Walter Johnson, in a history of St. Louis, relates that the German-speaking immigrants experienced nativism and violence and that the politics of the city in the 1850s revolved around nativist and immigrant divisions. The German immigrants were targeted by the anti-immigrant Know-Nothing Party that took control of the St. Louis government in 1855.[36] Throughout the nineteenth century and well into the twentieth, German immigrants arrived in the US with the goal of owning land and farming, but many were already skilled workers and craftsmen. German speakers lived in many parts of Central and Eastern Europe, many of them family farmers. Depending on their location, they were Protestant or Catholic or Jewish. Of those who did work in industry and cities in the late nineteenth century, some were communists and some were anarchists. In the 1887 trials of Chicago anarchists in the Haymarket bombing the year before, five of the eight defendants and three of the four hanged were German immigrants.

Czech immigrants in the late nineteenth century were known as Bohemians from Bohemia, Moravia, and Czech Silesia and self-identified as Americans of German Bohemian descent. Their descendants numbered nearly two million. Members of the Moravian Brethren were Protestant religious dissidents who migrated in the early 1700s to the North American British colonies and missionized among the Indigenous communities before and after US independence. Nineteenth-century Czech Catholics immigrated after the failed 1848 revolutions, and a larger number in the late 1800s. Like German immigrants, many were farmers and sought land, although many others worked in industry.

Like the Germans and the Irish, smaller numbers of Polish people were early settlers in the North American British colonies, but the largest number of Polish immigrants came in the decades leading up to World War I. Millions of landless and impoverished Polish peasants fled Germany, Austria, and Russia, many migrating to the United States in search of land to own, although the majority ended up working in industry. Catholicism was central to their identity, so the Columbian effect resonated. Like Italian immigrants, many Poles—up to a third—returned to Poland, although immigration continued.

JEWISH IMMIGRATION

In 1880, the number of Jews in the United States was around a quarter million, many having migrated to the British colonies before US independence. Most were tradesmen and artisans of moderate means. During the pre–Civil War years, Jewish and Lebanese Christians (Syrians at the time) were overland merchants who supplied settlers in the US colonized Southwest with goods, as well as establishing supply houses that eventually became department stores, including in St. Louis, El Paso, and other regional urban centers. They acquired scarce currency to purchase foreign goods, and they carried goods over vast areas to their destinations. The merchants became not only a source of commodities in remote regions but also the dominant source of credit.[37] During the three decades after 1880, more than two million mostly Ashkenazi Yiddish-speaking Jewish people fled Tsarist Russia and Eastern Europe, escaping vicious pogroms.[38] Most settled in industrial areas of the Northeast. By 1915, Yiddish newspapers had a half million subscribers in New York. Many Jewish immigrants joined theater and other entertainment groups, and of course, made up a large presence in the motion picture industry.[39]

In the 1880s, a quarter million Jews fled Eastern Europe to the United States, and in the 1890s, three hundred thousand more followed. In the twentieth century, one and a half million more arrived in the United States. The flow was halted by the restrictive immigration laws of the 1920s. While the German-speaking Jews who arrived earlier in the century were mostly merchants, the Eastern European Jews fleeing pogroms were from rural areas, many of them farmers with few industrial skills.[40]

Jewish immigrants to the US may have escaped pogroms and death, but they lived with a barrage of anti-Semitism. The leader of the pack was the odious plutocrat Henry Ford, who published his own newspaper in the 1920s specifically for disseminating anti-Jewish propaganda. The newspaper, the *Dearborn Independent*, warned of "a Jewish plan to control the world, not by territorial acquisition, not by military aggression, not by governmental subjugation, but by control of the machinery of commerce and exchange."[41] Ford was not the only widely admired US American to spout Jewish conspiracies of world domination, with famed aviator Charles Lindbergh and Father Coughlin chiming in. In response to the 2018 white supremacist massacre of Jews in Pittsburgh's Tree of Life synagogue, where the killer yelled "All Jews must die," Princeton historian Julian Zelizer wrote about late-nineteenth-century populist leaders who railed against Jewish bankers as a threat to the security of workers and political cartoons of that time that conjured images of Jews with big noses and crooked faces. Early in the twentieth century, the Ku Klux Klan targeted Jews, as did Irish Catholic gangs doing "Jew Hunts." Jews were excluded from law firms, the medical professions, universities, fraternities, country clubs, and hotels, with one hotel boasting "No Hebrews or tubercular guests received." And as with Black people, Jews were subject to restrictive real-estate covenants in certain neighborhoods.[42]

The main reason that capitalist giants like Henry Ford maligned Jews had less to do with banking than with the fact of their labor militancy. This was the time of the rise of the US Socialist Party and militant trade unionism, as well as the Bolshevik Revolution. By 1915, there were one and a half million Jewish residents in New York City, around 30 percent of the population. The clothing industry employed around a quarter million Jews and some Italians. The pay was by piece produced rather than by the hour, and with sixty- to seventy-hour workweeks in poorly ventilated, dirty, badly lighted work spaces, the work regimen was grueling. Most of the unskilled labor was done by young, single women. Twenty thousand of the young women went on strike in 1909, only to be brutalized and arrested on the picket line and replaced by others. The International Ladies' Garment Workers Union had formed in 1900 and gained some contracts after the strike.[43]

Writer and poet Emma Lazarus, best known for her poem with the lines "Give me your tired, your poor, / Your huddled masses yearning to breathe free," inscribed posthumously in 1903 at the base of the Statue of Liberty, was born in 1849 to a wealthy industrialist father of Sephardic Jewish heritage and a mother of Ashkenazi roots. She took up the cause of the masses of Jews fleeing persecution in the 1870s. During her short life—she died in 1887 at thirty-eight—

Lazarus studied Hebrew and Jewish history, established the Hebrew Technical Institute for vocational training, and, a decade before Theodore Herzl's Zionist movement, championed a homeland for Jews in Palestine, even traveling to England to lobby the British authorities. The Nazi genocide of Jews and the Rosenberg executions were in the future, but Jews had been suffering persecution as the enemy since Christianity took hold in Europe. This was the generational experience that the flood of Jewish immigrants, really refugees, was bringing.

Emma Lazarus wrote the poem "The New Colossus" in 1883, while the Statue of Liberty was nearing construction and three years before it was finished and dedicated, clearly referencing the monolith. Indeed, Lazarus wrote the poem as a means of raising money for the installation of the statue.

> Not like the brazen giant of Greek fame,
> With conquering limbs astride from land to land;
> Here at our sea-washed, sunset gates shall stand
> A mighty woman with a torch, whose flame
> Is the imprisoned lightning, and her name
> Mother of Exiles. From her beacon-hand
> Glows world-wide welcome; her mild eyes command
> The air-bridged harbor that twin cities frame.
> "Keep, ancient lands, your storied pomp!" cries she
> With silent lips. "Give me your tired, your poor,
> Your huddled masses yearning to breathe free,
> The wretched refuse of your teeming shore.
> Send these, the homeless, tempest-tost to me,
> I lift my lamp beside the golden door!

In 1903, the poem, engraved on a bronze plaque, was placed on the pedestal of the Statue of Liberty.[44]

During the 1886 dedication, attended by President Grover Cleveland and US and French dignitaries, neither the poem nor immigrants nor Jews were mentioned in the speeches or literature.[45] The French intention in the gift of the statue and the US official reception were solidly Eurocentric and focused on one concept, liberty.

The statue is of Libertas, the Roman goddess of liberty. She holds a plaque in her left hand inscribed with July 4, 1776, in Roman numerals, the date of the Declaration of Independence. Her feet are circled with a broken shackle and chain celebrating US abolition of slavery. France's original idea for the gift occurred at the end of the Civil War. But the idea of liberation of the formerly enslaved rang hollow to those under the boot of a restored Southern order of racist repression. As the editor of the Black-owned newspaper the *Cleveland Gazette*, put it:

> "Liberty enlightening the world," indeed! The expression makes us sick. This government is a howling farce. It cannot or rather *does not* protect its citizens within its *own* borders. Shove the Bartholdi statue, torch and all, into the ocean until the "liberty" of this country is such as to make it possible for an inoffensive and industrious colored man to earn a respectable living for himself and family, without being ku-kluxed, perhaps murdered, his daughter and wife outraged, and his property destroyed. The idea of the "liberty" of this country "enlightening the world," or even Patagonia, is ridiculous in the extreme.[46]

And it is certain that "liberty" was laughable to the captive Geronimo and his people, who at the time were being shipped in chains to a dungeon prison at Fort Marion, Florida, or to those Indigenous nations that had been incarcerated in reservations carved out of their former homelands, learning that Congress was set to divide the reservation lands into marketable allotments, which would end up privatizing three-fourths of the already shrunken Native land base. Or for that matter, those teeming masses of Lazarus's poem, huddled in the overcrowded slums of the Lower East Side in New York City, who were doubtfully even aware of the festivities celebrating liberty.

Paul Auster writes that the statue was to celebrate republicanism, but the poem "reinvented the statue's purpose, turning Liberty into a welcoming mother, a symbol of hope to the outcasts and downtrodden of the world."[47] The Statue of Liberty was a marker on the path to the twentieth-century myth of the American Dream.

THEODORE ROOSEVELT,
EUGENICS, AND AMERICANISM

More than twenty million immigrants arrived in the United States
between 1880 and 1915, making up 15 percent of the then total
US population. Most Southern European immigrants were motivated by desperate poverty, while Central and Eastern Europeans
fled both poverty and religious and political persecution. Between
1850 and 1930, five million German-speaking people immigrated,
and in a four-year period, from 1881 to 1885, a million German
speakers settled primarily in the Southern Plains, Missouri, and the
Midwest. A million and a half Swedes and Norwegians, which was
some 20 percent of the Scandinavian population, immigrated during
the late nineteenth century. The Roman Catholic Church became
the largest religious denomination. Americanization as assimilation
was on the agenda.[48]

Columbus could go a long way in Americanizing Catholics, but
more was needed to ground US patriotism. Theodore Roosevelt led
the charge using the ideology of Americanism and militarism, which
he laid out in some detail in a 1915 speech to the Knights of Columbus. Given on Columbus Day 1915 as war raged in Europe, the
speech rings of preparation to join the war as a means of better fus-
ing a collective Americanism, the lack of which appeared to be much
on his mind. Roosevelt first paid tribute to the patron of the Knights
of Columbus and his descendants, the Italians:

Four centuries and a quarter have gone by since Columbus
by discovering America opened the greatest era in world history. . . . Three centuries have passed since, with the settlements on the coasts of Virginia and Massachusetts, the real
history of what is now the United States began. All this we
ultimately owe to the action of an Italian seaman in the service
of a Spanish King and a Spanish Queen. It is eminently fitting
that one of the largest and most influential social organizations of this great Republic—a Republic in which the tongue
is English, and the blood derived from many sources—should,
in its name, commemorate the great Italian. It is eminently

fitting to make an address on Americanism before this society. We of the United States need above all things to remember that, while we are by blood and culture kin to each of the nations of Europe, we are also separate from each of them. We are a new and distinct nationality.

Roosevelt made clear that "there is no room in this country for hyphenated Americanism. . . . For an American citizen to vote as a German-American, an Irish-American or an English-American is to be a traitor to American institutions; and those hyphenated Americans who terrorize American politicians by threats of the foreign vote are engaged in treason to the American Republic." Allegiance must go purely to the United States. German or Irish or English or French is to be condemned, but "if he is heartily and singly loyal to this Republic, then no matter where he was born, he is just as good an American as anyone else.[49]

This speech reflects an adjustment in Roosevelt's conception of humanity and what characteristics made up a member of the "American race." Roosevelt was born in 1858 in New York City, son of a wealthy businessman and a wealthy socialite mother from Georgia, his father descended from the original Dutch settlers in New York and Scottish settlers in Pennsylvania. They were related to the Upstate New York slave-trading family the Schuylers, the family Alexander Hamilton married into and managed the family's slave trade. Roosevelt's mother was a Southern belle and socialite from a wealthy former-slaver plantation family of Scottish heritage. Roosevelt was a sickly asthmatic child who early on turned to strenuous physical activity to overcome his weakness. He seemed headed for a life in academia or law, tutored at home, then graduating from Harvard, then Columbia Law School, marrying into the wealthy Cabot Lodge family (whose wealth came from the Atlantic slave trade), researching and writing books, as well as traveling extensively. But early on he was attracted to politics and later claimed that it was while in law school that he decided he wanted "to be one of the governing class."[50]

Roosevelt's first interest was naval power, which he researched and published on, gaining recognition as a naval historian. However, he became obsessed with the Anglo-Saxon conquest of what became the United States, and during the decade 1885 to 1894, he published the seven-volume *The Winning of the West*. During that time, he purchased and operated a cattle ranch in North Dakota, where he spent a good deal of time learning to be a rancher and trophy hunter. He wrote and published three books on hunting, proud that he had helped in the slaughter of the bison, which was the life sustenance of the Plains peoples. He even became a deputy sheriff and chased outlaws. He began to consider himself an heir to hunter icons such as Daniel Boone and Davy Crockett, another mythologized figure, who died at the Alamo. In 1887, Roosevelt and his closest family friend and political ally, Henry Cabot Lodge, founded the Boone and Crockett Club for trophy hunters like themselves. The membership included politicians, professionals, and businessmen, as well as the famous painters of the romanticized West, Albert Bierstadt and Frederic Remington, and the popular western novelist Owen Wister.[51]

Roosevelt was an early convert to "social Darwinism," which led to the racist pseudoscience of eugenics. In his view, all the darker peoples were inferior, particularly Native Americans, who were destined to disappear completely. But he also regarded poor whites as inferior and distinguished himself from those "game butchers" who hunt and kill animals for profit or food. He identified with James Fenimore Cooper's character Hawkeye and embraced the Boone myth, as men killed animals or other humans only to test and prove their manhood. Roosevelt's hunting was for aristocrats, to revitalize the superior class of the species. Furthermore, he theorized that a new race was born with testing of settlers' survival skills in nature, creating a new kind of aristocracy destined to rule the world. The settler "stock" that morphed into that superior species, Roosevelt asserted, was composed of Anglo-Saxons, Scots Irish, French Huguenots, and German and Dutch Protestants.[52]

However lowly and savage on Roosevelt's scale, Native peoples played a key role in his theory of the genesis of US-settler white supremacy. He theorized that the superior European American was strengthened by not intermarrying with their defeated enemies, the Indians, which would have caused loss of vigor. Slotkin summarizes the genocidal violence inherent in the perspective: "American settlers must regain that vigor by repelling and exterminating their barbarians. Instead of biological exchange with savages of another race or folk, the Americans participate in a *spiritual* exchange, taking from the enemy certain abstract ideas or principles but accepting no admixture of blood." The settlers must become "men who know Indians," embracing the "savage" rules of warfare that Roosevelt thought necessary in order to destroy the enemy. Slotkin views overseas US imperialism, of which Theodore Roosevelt was a major booster and actor, as a "regeneration through violence," or recovering the frontier spirit, becoming the hunter, embracing the martial tradition.[53] Historian Nancy Isenberg sums up Roosevelt's motto in three words: "work-fight-breed."[54] And it was urgent for Roosevelt, who worried about the future: "If white civilization goes down, the white race is irretrievably ruined, . . . carrying with it to the grave those potencies upon which realization of man's highest hopes depends."[55]

Theodore Roosevelt was president of the United States from 1901 to 1909 and received the 1906 Nobel Peace Prize. He was undoubtedly the most famous of many well-known advocates of the ideology of eugenics, which its proponents regarded as scientific. Eugenics dominated ruling-class and intellectual thinking in the United States from the late 1880s to 1915, paralleling the massive influx of Eastern and Southern European immigrants. Although the pseudoscience and its practices were largely debunked by World War I, they left an indelible mark with the continuation of IQ and other testing, as well as the rise of a more sophisticated eugenics in the academic field of sociobiology in the 1970s, which continued to enjoy respectability in the twenty-first century.[56]

Proponents of eugenics argued that the genetic makeup of a person and that person's station in society were interrelated; that is, if a person was poor, it meant they were genetically defective. Their Puritan Calvinist forefathers had embraced the notion of the "elect," who were predestined to join the Christian God in heaven, those whose worldly wealth and success reflected their destined status. In US culture, with its deep racial coding from its founding, race and eugenic theory were inseparable, although, as Theodore Roosevelt argued, poor whites were included as genetically inferior.[57] Roosevelt advocated sexual sterilization of criminalized individuals and those with cognitive differences from the norm, alleging that otherwise the United States would be committing "race suicide." Roosevelt-appointed Supreme Court justice Oliver Wendell Holmes upheld compulsory sexual sterilization laws, which gave the state of Virginia, thereby all states, the power to regulate the breeding of its citizens.[58] A few years after the Supreme Court decision, the Nazi regime that took power in Germany in 1933 adopted US race law and eugenics as a fundamental platform for their governance, as well as embracing US continental imperialism and ethnic cleansing as the basis for their program of *Lebensraum*, which led to death camps for Jews, Roma, communists, and the disabled.[59]

OVERSEAS IMPERIALISM

Theodore Roosevelt was William McKinley's vice president when they took office in 1897, and Roosevelt became president when McKinley was assassinated in September 1901. In 1898, with prodding from Roosevelt, the United States military intervened in ongoing wars of liberation against Spanish-occupied territories in the Caribbean and Pacific, crushing those anticolonial movements while expelling Spain from the hemisphere and the Pacific. Spain ceded Puerto Rico, Guam, and the Philippines to the United States and allowed Cuba independence, which then fell under US indirect colonialism. The US intervention in Cuba and the Philippines undercut the national liberation wars that would have driven out the Spanish colonizers.

The United States had purchased the Russian Empire's colony, Alaska, in 1867, and had imposed military control of Hawai'i in 1874. During the military invasions in the Pacific, the US forcibly annexed Hawai'i after overthrowing Queen Liliuokalani.[60] In 1901, Roosevelt took over as president and commander in chief of the armed forces. Spain had ceded the Philippines to the US in 1898, so from the beginning the US was fighting an "Indian war"; that is, a

US military counterinsurgency against the massive liberation resistance that had been fighting the Spanish. Admiral George Dewey led the US Navy in the war. He referred to Filipinos as "the Indians" and vowed to "enter the city [Manila] and keep the Indians out."[61] It took the United States three more years to crush the Filipino "Indian" resistance to US occupation, the army using counterinsurgency techniques practiced against Indigenous nations of the North American continent, including new forms of torture such as water boarding, and under many of the same army commanders. The death toll of civilian Filipinos was 250,000, with multiple sites of genocidal actions.[62] Twenty-six of the thirty US generals in the Philippines had been officers in the "Indian wars." Major General Nelson A. Miles, who had commanded the army in campaigns against Indigenous peoples, was put in general command of the army in the Philippines war.[63]

The US occupied the Philippines until 1946, while Puerto Rico today remains a colony. The US imposed statehood on Hawai'i and Alaska in 1959. Since that time, the Kanaka Maoli indigenous Hawaiians have challenged the legitimacy of statehood and organized for independence. As an island colony, Hawai'i was on the 1946 United Nations' list for decolonization with the right of self-determination and independence, as was Puerto Rico. The US government sat on the committee at the UN in 1953 that removed Hawai'i from the list. At that time, prior to the 1960s and '70s independence movements in Africa, Asia, and the Caribbean, the UN was primarily European and funded mainly by the United States, where its headquarters are located.[64]

During his last year as president, Roosevelt addressed the Methodist Episcopal Church in Washington, DC, in a speech he titled "The Expansion of the White Races," saying, "There is one feature in the expansion of the peoples of white, or European, blood during the past four centuries which should never be lost sight of, especially by those who denounce such expansion on moral grounds. On the whole, the movement has been fraught with lasting benefit to most of the peoples already dwelling in the lands over which the expansion took place."[65]

THE SECOND KU KLUX KLAN

On February 8, 1915, D.W. Griffith's film *The Birth of a Nation* had its gala premiere at Clune's Auditorium in Los Angeles and subsequently opened in theaters in major cities across the country.[66] Griffith, who is lionized as the father of modern film making, grew up in rural Kentucky, the son of a Confederate officer. The nearly three-hour silent film was adapted from Thomas Dixon Jr.'s 1905 novel *The Clansman*, a romanticized portrayal of the Ku Klux Klan that demonized Reconstruction in the former Confederate states. Dixon was from the rural North Carolina Piedmont region and was an avowed racist. He had been a classmate of President Woodrow Wilson's at Johns Hopkins University and arranged for Griffith to do a special screening of the movie in the Wilson White House ten days after it opened nationally. Wilson had been in office for two years and had exhibited his own deeply racist views by resegregating the federal civil service. Although Washington, DC, was a totally segregated city, federal civil service had been desegregated since Reconstruction.[67]

The Birth of a Nation had some Black actors, although they received no credit, but most of the Black characters were portrayed by white actors in blackface and were depicted uniformly as lazy, ignorant, and violent. The central message of the movie was that Black people were not fit for citizenship and were a threat to the security and purity of the white race. Most importantly, the KKK was extolled as the savior of righteous white dominance. The KKK portrayed in the film had been founded by former Confederate general Nathan Bedford Forrest. It operated as a loose network of terrorists, most of them former Confederate soldiers and officers. The film was blatant propaganda that glorified the Klan and inspired the rebirth of the twentieth-century KKK. Jim Crow laws and mass incarceration of Black men had been institutionalized when Reconstruction ended. The Klan, having done its job, was replaced by white sheriffs, who continued to control Black people. The Klan and the subsequent sheriffs behaved much like the slave patrols under legalized slavery, with all white citizens obligated to assist in suppression of Black individuals and communities with public lynchings and other civilian terrorism.[68]

Dixon and Griffith achieved their objective. At Stone Mountain, Georgia, twenty-five miles from Atlanta, on Thanksgiving night, November 25, 1915, nine months after *The Birth of a Nation* appeared in packed movie houses across the country, fifteen men in white robes and hoods met to establish the second Ku Klux Klan, this time with the innovation of the burning cross and hoods, which had not been a part of the first Klan. On December 4, 1915, Georgia granted a charter for the fraternal organization, the Invisible Empire: Knights of the Ku Klux Klan, Inc. The second Klan spread across the country, unlike the original KKK. They paid full-time recruiters and operated in every state from its national headquarters in Georgia. At the peak of its popularity in the early 1920s, the organization claimed four to five million men as members, or about 15 percent of the white male population, along with Klan women auxiliaries. It espoused Americanism, attacking any group it deemed "un-American," such as Catholics, Jews, labor activists, socialists, and communists and worked to enforce Jim Crow segregation with threats and violence, including lynchings. But the KKK focus was on the "foreign born," especially Catholics.[69]

Historian Linda Gordon writes that the second Klan was not secret and was highly visible everywhere. Nor was it regional and Southern based; rather, it spread over the continent, having added the foreign born, who were mostly workers in northern and western industries. The organization published recruiting ads in newspapers, and members were proud of their affiliation, while hundreds were elected to public office, including the governorship of Texas. The Klan owned or controlled 150 magazines and newspapers, two colleges, and even a movie production company. Most important was their popularity, with millions of dedicated members and many millions more who participated in Klan activities and embraced their cause. Gordon suggests that possibly even a majority of white citizens supported the Klan, that it did not appear as extreme to most people; rather, it appeared ordinary and respectable. Its members included rich and poor, professionals, businessmen, farmers, and wage workers, but its core constituency was lower-middle-class and skilled-working-class white men and their families. Building on the politics of resentment, they blamed immigrants and Jews for taking jobs from "true" Americans. They did not hate the rich; rather, they respected men of wealth and status, instead blaming the "elite" city people, professionals, and intellectuals, the latter often used as a euphemism for Jews.[70] Fundamentally, the second KKK was an anti-immigration movement. For descendants of early Protestant English and Scots Irish settlers, nativism was not new. It descended from earlier movements, such as the Know-Nothing Party reacting to Irish Catholic immigrants, and jumping to the twenty-first century, white nationalists who brought a president to power in 2016. The KKK adopted the language of the anti-immigrant Daughters of the American Revolution, creating the category of "pure Americans."[71] They channeled the racialist writings of Theodore Roosevelt discussed above.

The Klan's Americanism was little different in ideology and general acceptance in Anglo-America from the Americanism in the 1893 White City or that of Theodore Roosevelt, but it was viciously violent. The second KKK received the green light from the Wilson White House and the ruling class, as well as masses of ordinary citizens. Americanization had fallen short of its goals, and although some leaders of the late-nineteenth- and early-twentieth-century workers' movements were descendants of early settlers, many immigrant workers had become internationalists, trade unionists, socialists, and communists. The KKK was an acceleration of Americanism that contributed mightily to the crushing of workers' movements and political socialism. Red-scare anticommunism did not begin with the mid-twentieth-century Cold War; rather, it began at the beginning of the century, even before the 1917 Russian Bolshevik Revolution.

ANARCHY, SOCIALISM, WAR, AND REPRESSION OF WORKERS' MOVEMENTS

US wars that were never ending—from the War of Independence to the wars to take the continent, followed by the wars to colonize and dominate the peoples of the Pacific and Caribbean—served to bolster Americanism, but the European war that began in August 1914 had no such potential. However, with workers' movements raging

across the country and the founding in 1901 and subsequent success
of the grassroots Socialist Party, and the founding four years later
of the Industrial Workers of the World (IWW), United States workers, many of them immigrants, were the vanguard of world socialism, contemporaneous with the Mexican Revolution of 1910–1920
and the Bolshevik Revolution in 1917. The IWW and the Mexican
anarcho-syndicalist Partido Liberal Mexicano, led by Ricardo
Flores Magón and his brothers, collaborated with Mexican and Indigenous workers on both sides of the US-México border, as well as
with Emma Goldman and other US-based anarcho-syndicalists.[72]

On April 2, 1917, President Wilson asked Congress for a declaration of war against Germany, and on April 6, Congress granted it
and Wilson signed the declaration, nearly three years after the war
had begun. On June 15, 1917, Congress passed the Espionage Act,
which was "an act to punish acts of interference with the foreign relations, the neutrality and the foreign commerce of the United States,
to punish espionage, and better to enforce the criminal laws of the
United States, and for other purposes." Even failure to purchase or
speaking against war bonds was criminalized. Mexican revolutionary Magón was the first arrested under the Espionage Act in 1918.
He was convicted and sentenced to twenty years. Imprisoned in Fort
Leavenworth Penitentiary, he died under mysterious circumstances
four years later.[73]

On August 2, 1917, Black, white, and Indigenous Seminole sharecroppers and tenant farmers in eastern Oklahoma cotton fields took
up arms against military conscription. Living hand to mouth, as they
did, without their young sons working the cotton fields, they would
starve. The Socialist Party in Oklahoma had the largest percentage
of members of any state and had elected many of its members to local
offices and school boards throughout the state. The IWW had successfully organized migrant oil workers, wheat thrashers, and miners in the state. And although the Socialist Party organized tenant
farmers, the more radical Working Class Union had influenced the
Green Corn rebels, who declared themselves in favor of a revolution
to overthrow the US government and to establish a commonwealth.
They were able to blow up bridges and create a liberated zone, but
the rebellion was crushed by local deputies and landowners.[74]

On September 5, 1917, using the Espionage Act, the Department of Justice raided forty-eight IWW meeting halls, arresting 165 IWW members, including founding leader William "Big Bill" Haywood, for "conspiring to hinder the draft, encourage desertion, and intimidate others in connection with labor disputes."[75] In April 1918, Haywood and a hundred other Wobblies who had been arrested went to trial. It was the longest criminal trial in US history at the time, spanning five months, Haywood himself testifying for three days. All were found guilty, with varying sentences; Haywood and fourteen others received twenty years.[76] Then the administration went for the socialists, arresting Eugene Debs, the Socialist Party cofounder and four-times presidential candidate, on June 30, 1918. A few days before, Debs had given a speech in Canton, Ohio, urging resistance to the draft and the war. He was charged with ten counts of sedition under the Espionage Act. He was convicted and sentenced to serve ten years in prison. While in prison, he ran for president on the Socialist Party ticket in 1920. He died in 1926.[77]

The infamous Palmer Raids in November 1919 and January 1920 constituted a massive attack on Southern and Eastern European immigrant workers. A. Mitchell Palmer was the US attorney general in the Wilson administration and instructed authorities to arrest all leftists, especially anarchists and communists. One of his most dedicated assistants was J. Edgar Hoover, who would go on to create and head the Federal Bureau of Investigation (FBI) for the next half century. On December 21, 1919, Emma Goldman was among the 248 radicals deported to the Soviet Union under the Immigration Act of 1918, called the "Alien Act," which specifically mandated expulsion of any noncitizen associated with anarchism.[78] The IWW leader Bill Haywood was free on bail while fighting in courts to overturn his conviction, but he failed, and in April 1921, when he was to report to prison, he skipped bail and fled to the Soviet Union, where he lived until his death in 1927.[79] Immediately after the end of World War I, on November 11, 1918, Allied intervention, including the United States, in the Russian Civil War attempted to overthrow the new Bolshevik regime, established in November 1917, to stop the perceived threat of communism worldwide.[80]

EXCLUSION, INCLUSION, AND ERASURE

World War I slowed European immigration to the United States. Then in 1921, with the immigrant-, Catholic-, and Jew-hating Ku Klux Klan at its apex, the United States imposed restrictions that led to the National Origins Immigration Act of 1924, giving priority to Western and Northern European immigrants.[81] Among other hardships, it made family reunion nearly impossible. The quota for all of Germany and Austria combined was 27,000. One insidious and deadly result of this was the quota applied to German and Austrian Jews in the 1930s. A number of President Franklin Roosevelt's appointees to the State Department expressed support for the Nazi exclusion of Jews from public life and did not favor admitting Jewish refugees to the United States. Roosevelt's War Department was not concerned with the development of concentration camps. Historian Richard Rothstein writes that the assistant secretary of state in charge of immigrant affairs, William J. Carr, referred to Jews as "kikes" and, after a visit to Detroit, complained that the city was full of "dust, smoke, dirt, Jews." To obstruct the entry of Jews fleeing Germany, the State Department rigidly enforced a law that required immigrants to present a supportive police affidavit from their home countries, which, of course, was impossible for Jews fleeing the country. The diary of Breckinridge Long, head of the State Department's visa department, was filled with invective against Jews, Catholics, New Yorkers, liberals, and in fact everybody who was not of his own particular background. William F. Dodd, the US ambassador to Germany, said that while he did not "approve of the ruthlessness that is being applied to the Jews here, . . . I have said very frankly that they had a very serious problem. . . . The Jews had held a great many more of the key positions in Germany than their numbers or their talents entitled them to."[82]

The self-indigenizing narrative of being first settlers or discoverers, like the Hispanos of New Mexico, the Scots Irish in Appalachia, the Irish Catholics, the western US white ranchers, and the US states adopting Columbus as first founder, appears as a requirement for citizenship acceptance, erasing the still living, still colonized Indigenous nations, the majority of whom had been removed from the eastern United States where the European immigrants made their homes. While violence pressured Eastern and Southern European immigrants to assimilate, erasure of Indigenous presence allowed immigrants to become settlers, Americanized. In the process of rooting the US founding with 1492, the Roman Catholic Church in the United States itself became Americanized, eventually shedding the Protestant bigotry of the past. In 2014, the Spanish colonizer of California, Junípero Serra, the Franciscan architect of the concentration camps to incarcerate California Indigenous peoples called "missions," was canonized as a saint. The ceremony took place in the US at Washington National Cathedral (Protestant) with Pope Francis officiating and was attended by President Obama and family, his entire cabinet, and congressional members while Indigenous peoples protested outside. By 2019, six of nine Supreme Court justices were Catholic while two were Jewish, along with one lone Episcopalian who had been raised as a Catholic.

Reliance on founding myths and pursuing whiteness were not options for Chinese immigrants who began arriving on the West Coast and in New York at the same time as the Southern and Eastern European Catholic and Jewish immigrants were populating the industrial centers of the east.

CHAPTER 7

"YELLOW PERIL"

The discovery in Wuhan, China, of COVID-19 in the fall of 2019, and its detection in the United States two months later, brought on a barrage of Sinophobia and attacks against Asian Americans. During the year 2020, there were 2,800 reports of harassment against Asian Americans in the United States, with some 240 physical assaults.[1] Princeton professor Anne Anlin Cheng observes, "This recent onslaught of anti-Asian violence can partly be attributed to our former president [Donald Trump], who spoke nonstop of the 'Chinese virus' and even the 'kung flu,' but he could not have rallied the kind of hatred that he did without this country's long history of systemic and cultural racism against people of Asian descent." Scholar Iyko Day points out that the attacks reveal "the fraudulence of the model minority myth and the assimilationist paradigm that legitimizes state violence against Black and Brown bodies." Day argues that anti-Asian racism in the US indicates something deeper that is engrained in the US capitalist system: "The idea of Asians—particularly the Chinese—as viral transmitters of disease [is] part of a longer history of romantic anticapitalism that remains a key ideology of white settler colonialism in North America."

The United States was the first state birthed as a capitalist state, the fiscal-military state, and since the 1840s has constituted the largest economy in the world, dependent on immigration to meet the needs of the labor market. Yet, immigration has always been fraught with suspicion of newcomers, none more extreme than Sinophobia. Although democracy is equated with the ideology of capitalism and free markets, a deep strain of white nationalism demonizes globalization and especially focuses on China. "For them, only the restoration of white racial purity can save the planet." Day points out that although these racial rantings appear extreme, they "form the bedrock of white settler ideology" and fear of white disappearance.[2]

As Day stresses, targeting Asia and mainly China as the source of disease in the world did not begin with COVID-19. "Asian" flu is a given to most in the West, although the deadly 1918–1919 flu pandemic originated in the central United States, and since then from several locales. The 1996 "mad cow" virus originated in England. During the 1876 smallpox outbreak in San Francisco, the thirty thousand Chinese residents were branded as a "laboratory of infection" and quarantined. Renewed calls to exclude Chinese immigration contributed to the 1882 Chinese Exclusion Act. Marie Myung-Ok Lee writes, "This yellow peril, pest-adjacent imagery of Asians remains deeply embedded in our national psyche." When COVID-19 appeared in the liberal San Francisco Bay Area, the University of California, Berkeley's student health center stated that "fear of interacting with those who might be from Asia is a common and normal reaction to fears" of the virus.[3] In 2015, President Barack Obama announced a "pivot to China" for the US military and national security apparatus. His successor, President Donald Trump, doubled down on the move, imposing tariffs and positioning warships.[4] The 2021 Democratic Party ascendance to the presidency showed no signs of ratcheting down the suspicions of China's actions and motives. Abuse of Asian elders on the West Coast actually increased.[5]

"Yellow peril" took a more dangerous turn in the twenty-first century with the growth of China's economy coming to rival that of the United States, the US economy being 40.75 percent of the world's economy while China held 34.27 percent in 2019.[6] The trope of "Wuhan virus" added to the economic panic of a weakened US empire reliant more on military might than economic.

THE LONG HISTORY OF "YELLOW PERIL"

The fear and demonization of Asia and Asian peoples are acute in the United States in the twenty-first century, as has been the case for nearly two centuries of US existence and much longer for Europeans.

Marco Polo warned of the peril he believed the Chinese represented: "From these qualities, so essential to the formation of soldiers, it is, that they are fitted to subdue the world, as in fact they have done in regard to a considerable portion of it."[7] Historian Gary Okihiro argues that Western belief that the Chinese threatened European civilization and Christianity is based on fear of nonwhite people, as well as being a justification for European expansion, domination, and colonization.[8]

The moniker yellow peril can be traced to the 1880s, when German Kaiser Wilhelm II referred to yellow peril following a dream in which he saw the Buddha riding a dragon threatening to invade Europe. Sometimes it's called "yellow terror" or "yellow specter." Leung Wing-Fai writes that the concept "blends western anxieties about sex, racist fears of the alien other, and the Spenglerian belief that the West will become outnumbered and enslaved by the East."[9] Spenglerian refers to the German historian Oswald Spengler's wildly popular and much translated 1918 book, *The Decline of the West*, and a second volume in 1922.[10] The 1948 Chinese Communist revolution's success recharged "yellow peril," with a book to explain the horrors of "oriental despotism." In 1956, Karl August Wittfogel published *Oriental Despotism: A Comparative Study of Total Power*. Under the scholarly guise of a dubious comparative study of irrigation societies, including ancient Egypt, Greece, Rome, and the Inca, along with the Muslim caliphates and Mughal period in South Asia, the focus is clearly "despotic" China, which in fact was never an irrigation society. The Chinese, according to Wittfogel, are about "total power" and "total terror."[11]

Yellow peril centered on China but also included the entire Asian continent and North Africa. In the late 1970s, Palestinian scholar Edward Said conceptualized "Orientalism" to critique Western views of the Middle East, principally the Arab Muslim world as one of harems, opulence, polygamy, and domineering patriarchs.[12] But his thesis also gives insight into Western conceptions of that entire vast continent that is peopled by the majority of humanity of which Western Europe forms a tiny western peninsula. European colonialism ideologically reduced that majority of humanity to the past as ancients who began civilizations but stopped developing with European ascendance and were viewed as sick and decayed. Said writes that Orientalism expresses "the relationship between Occident and Orient" as a relationship "of power, of domination, of varying degrees of a complex hegemony, . . . the hegemony of European ideas about the Orient, themselves reiterating European superiority over Oriental backwardness."[13] Orientalism is an ideological tool of imperialism. "Neither imperialism nor colonialism is a simple act of accumulation and acquisition. Both are supported and perhaps even impelled by impressive ideological formations that include notions that certain territories and people *require* and beseech domination, as well as forms of knowledge affiliated with domination, . . . with words and concepts like 'inferior' or 'subject races,' 'subordinate peoples,' 'dependency,' 'expansion,' and 'authority.' "[14]

In 1905, President Theodore Roosevelt wrote his son regarding the difference between the US sport of wrestling and Japanese judo, arguing that wrestling was a sport with rules while judo was designed simply to kill or disable the opponent. Sociologist Wendy Rouse observes that Roosevelt's comparison reflected the US American attitude toward Japanese culture, a certain admiration of the Japanese for their martial skills—Japan had just won in the Russian-Japanese war—yet, confirming that Western wrestling and boxing was high art, and US men were physically and morally superior. "Still, the Japanese and their martial art worried men like Roosevelt as they pondered the future of the United States and the potential threat of the new 'Yellow Peril.' "[15]

CHINA, FROM WEALTH TO DEBT, CHAOS, AND FAMINE

Beginning before Christianity existed, the Chinese had developed far-flung trade routes. Although known as the "Silk Road," it had many routes, not just one, linking China and Southeast Asia with India, Persia, and the Nile in North Africa. Although the route is named after silk, a major Chinese export, the trade relationships included many commodities cultivated or crafted in China—tea, spices, rice, porcelain, paper, gunpowder, medicines—as well as technologies, ideas, and the spread of Buddhism. When the Ottomans (Turkey) cut off the land routes in the mid-fifteenth century, new routes involving Western European seafaring traders were developed.

By that time, Western Europe was firmly under the rule of the Holy Roman Empire. Christianity was fervently evangelical and inherently imperialistic with its centuries of military crusades against Muslims in west Asia and North Africa. Christian missionaries and Western merchants formed the advance of European colonization of East Asia. Augustinian missionaries, then Benedictines, and others expanded beyond Europe. In 1289, the pope sent a hundred Christian scholars to China, then others arrived, but in the mid-fourteenth century, the Ming regime in China excluded foreigners. By 1500, Christianity had spread extensively with the Franciscans, Dominicans, and Augustinians establishing missions. Despite the Vatican's efforts, in 1500 there were no practicing Christians in China. Enter the new Jesuit Order, the Society of Jesus, founded in 1540. Franciscans and other orders arrived in China, and with the rise of Protestantism, other denominations joined in the evangelical racket beginning in 1807.[16] With Europe and the United States, when Christian missionaries arrive, gunboats are not far behind. During the next two decades, China became the main target for US and European Protestant missionaries of every denomination, accompanying parallel US and European economic domination.[17]

By the 1830s, China had the largest population of any country in the world with four hundred million people. The Qing regime ("Manchu") had ruled for two centuries and would prevail until the 1911–1912 revolution led by Sun Yat Sen. The regime, as well as the previous Ming regime, which ruled from 1368 to 1644, had managed robust trade with large surpluses. But then came the opium trade. The British East India Company established a monopoly on opium production in India. Chinese tea, porcelain, silk, and cotton were in high demand in Western Europe, although the West had little to offer in trade to China. Soon after US independence, merchants in Philadelphia, New York, and Boston became active in trade with China, sending ships across the Atlantic to buy and sell in Europe, then around Africa and across the Indian Ocean to China. Philadelphia merchants found a source of opium in Turkey and began to include it with other goods to sell in China. By the 1830s, this trade was integral to the US economy, and opium made up around a quarter of the total sales that US traders made in China. Although the US share of opium sold to China was only 10 percent, it was still lucrative.

Opium had been introduced to China by Muslim traders in the 1600s, being used medicinally and sparingly. But in the next century, North American Indigenous tobacco had been highjacked by British colonizers from its Indigenous ceremonial and medicinal use to being cultivated and marketed worldwide. Smoking the highly addictive tobacco also spread to China, and opium smoking became popular. Opium addiction increased during the first century of Qing rule, and in 1729, the regime prohibited, without effect, the sale and smoking of opium. Later in the century, importation and cultivation were outlawed, but opium continued to be imported illegally. By 1773, the British East India Company had established an opium cultivation monopoly in colonized Bengal with China as the targeted market. Soon, the opium trade reversed the trade imbalance with China in favor of Europe.

European and United States imperialism became increasingly aggressive, and China experienced severe trade deficits, having to make concessions to the imperialist powers. British and US military interventions in 1839–1842, called the First Opium War, ended in humiliating defeat for China and Britain's occupation of the strategic peninsula of Hong Kong, where Britain established a military base, exiting only in 1997. The devastation led to widespread famine and related diseases caused by malnutrition, with some fourteen million people perishing in 1849 and another twenty million between 1854 and 1860. This is the same period when Britain shored up its colonization of India and, in 1858, established direct rule of the subcontinent (including what is now India, Pakistan, Bangladesh, and Afghanistan).

The British Empire, along with the French, launched the "Lorcha War," often called the Second Opium War, from 1856 to 1858, triggered by the British complaint over what they deemed mistreatment of a British flag on a Chinese lorcha ("junk"). This questionable warmongering over a dubious symbol, along with the previous military intervention, garnered vast trade concessions from China. To top off the devastation, the European powers attacked and destroyed Beijing in 1860.[18] A social revolution in China (Taiping Rebellion), lasting from 1850 to 1871, offered a program for radical reform with a call to abolish private property, to advance gender equality, and to prohibit opium. Although it had a mass base and dominated southeast China, the movement was crushed by the Qing regime, which pleased the British.

From the 1860s to the 1930s, the Shanghai waterfront was the rich and powerful base of the Western imperialists in China, operating as a legally protected port. Britain and the United States occupied a section of the main trade port, the Shanghai International Settlement or Bund, extracted through forced treaties that allowed their unfettered presence. In 1896, the British- and US-controlled commercial enclaves merged and were joined by other European states. In addition to the United States and Britain (which included Australia, New Zealand, Canada, Newfoundland, and South Africa), Denmark, the Netherlands, Belgium, France, Italy, Germany, and Japan were represented, each with their own massive buildings that housed banks and other commercial operations, each distinguished with its national flag. They set up municipal councils, including a police force, and ruled the territory, dominating Chinese trade. The only Chinese allowed to enter the zone were servants of wealthy foreign masters. In 1941, the Japanese occupied Shanghai, joining the Axis powers in World War II, putting an end to the European Bund.[19]

CHINESE NEEDED BUT NOT WANTED

Given the famines and chaos of imperialist intervention, as well as the disintegrating Qing regime, mass exodus of emigrants from China from the mid-nineteenth century into the twentieth century should come as no surprise. Few of those fleeing sought promised lands, rather, survival as China sank into a colonized backwater. Many Chinese migrants to the United States, mostly men, sent a portion of their earnings from gold seeking or labor back to families at home and living under dire circumstances.[20]

The first Chinese individuals who arrived in the US in large numbers were men joining thousands of others from around the world and from every part of the United States in the 1850s to seek wealth in gold. The first Chinese gold seekers numbered around three hundred, arriving in Northern California in 1849, then more than four hundred joined them. The numbers increased every year, so that in 1852, there were some twenty thousand Chinese in the gold fields. With the construction of the first continental railroad, beginning in 1865, Chinese workers were recruited, and in 1870, there were sixty-three thousand Chinese in the US—three-fourths in California and others in parts of the country along the railroad routes as well as in northeastern cities. By 1870, Chinese immigrants made up nearly a third of the total population of Idaho, 10 percent in Montana, and 9 percent in California, where they comprised a quarter of the entire workforce. Initially, during the gold rush and railroad building, the Chinese had to reside in rural areas, but in the later nineteenth century they became increasingly urban.[21]

By 1900, nearly half of all Chinese in California lived in the urban San Francisco Bay Area. Although Chinese workers made up a large part of the labor force in California, some 40 percent of Chinese residents in San Francisco and Sacramento were shopkeepers and merchants, along with a significant number of professionals and artisans. By 1900, half the Chinese population in the United States lived in California, while fifteen thousand were developing Chinatowns in the cities of the Northeast. Historian Ronald Takaki observed that as the first Asian group to immigrate to the US in substantial numbers, close attention needs to be paid to what happened to the Chinese in the second half of the nineteenth century, as their treatment set the template for how immigrants from other Asian countries would be viewed and treated.[22]

Leland Stanford was the eighth governor of the state of California, serving one two-year term. He took office in 1862 in the midst of the US Civil War as a member of the party of Lincoln, a Republican. He would become one of the "big four" railroad barons, along with Charles Crocker, Mark Hopkins, and Collis P. Huntington. In his inaugural address as governor, he said,

> To my mind it is clear, that the settlement among us of an inferior race is to be discouraged, by every legitimate means. Asia, with her numberless millions, sends to our shores the dregs of her population. Large numbers of this class are already here, and, unless we do something early to check their immigration, the question, which of the two tides of immigration, meeting upon the shores of the Pacific, shall be turned back, will be forced upon our consideration, when far more difficult than now of disposal. There can be no doubt but that the presence of numbers among us of a degraded and distinct people must exercise a deleterious influence upon the superior race, and, to a certain extent, repel desirable immigration. It will afford me great pleasure to concur with the Legislature in any constitutional action, having for its object the repression of the immigration of the Asiatic races.[23]

At the time Stanford spoke those racist words, there were only thirty-five thousand Chinese immigrants among the United States' thirty-one million population, most of whom, along with tens of thousands of other non–US citizens, had joined the gold rush in Northern California in the 1850s.[24] Five weeks after Stanford's inauguration, the US Congress and Lincoln administration approved "An Act to Prohibit the 'Coolie Trade' by American Citizens in American Vessels," specifying that "coolies" were defined as individuals "disposed of, or sold, or transferred, for any term of years or for any time whatever, as servants or apprentices, or to be held to service or labor." A year later, Stanford and his business partners were recruiting Chinese workers from China to build the transcontinental railroad, ignoring the prohibition Stanford had initiated.[25]

RAILROAD BUILDING, CHINESE LABOR,
AND US IMPERIALISM

Indeed, profits appeared to soften Stanford's "yellow peril" paranoia. With the 1862 Congressional Pacific Railway Act, the Central Pacific Railroad Company was chartered to build the western portion, starting at Sacramento. Work began in the fall of 1863, cutting through the Sierra Nevada mountain chain, blasting out fifteen separate tunnels and trestles across deep canyons. In the beginning, the workers were white, but they began abandoning the dangerous and hard work and living conditions. The railroad barons decided to recruit Chinese workers, and by late 1865, Chinese men made up the majority of the workforce. Stanford wrote President Andrew Johnson, "Without them it would be impossible to complete the western portion of this great national enterprise, within the time required by the Acts of Congress."[26]

In 1865, Stanford praised the Chinese workers as "quiet, peaceable, industrious, economical—ready and apt to learn all the different kinds of work." Stanford's partner Charles Crocker even went so far as to proclaim, "They prove nearly equal to white men in the amount of labor they perform and are much more reliable," and surely most important of all, "no danger of strike among them."[27] Within two years, Crocker hired twelve thousand Chinese workers, 90 percent of the entire workforce. Takaki notes that the savings in hiring Chinese rather than white workers was huge. Chinese workers made thirty-one dollars a month and were on their own in obtaining food and lodging, while white workers would have required higher pay and their room and board covered, which would have increased labor costs by a third.[28] Historian Manu Karuka, in his extraordinary book *Empire's Tracks*, writes, "To be a Chinese worker on the Central Pacific was definitely not to be a slave, the property of another. It was, however, a reduction to the status of a tool for grading earth and drilling a mountain. It was to be expendable, interchangeable, replaceable. Chinese workers were instruments of labor, constant capital for the Central Pacific Railroad Company. The quality of their lives interfered with their essential function, as a quantity of labor."[29]

Historian Gordon Chang makes the important observation that China was embedded in the vision of a transcontinental railroad from the moment it manifested as a possibility in the 1840s. One of its foremost boosters was the wealthy US merchant Asa Whitney, who made a fortune in China in the 1840s through the lucrative and unbalanced export trade. He and other railroad boosters like Thomas Hart Benton saw the intercontinental railroad as the extension of continental imperialism to overseas imperialism, in which the US would dominate the Pacific.[30]

The railroad was also a colonial process of ethnic cleansing, the federal government taking Indigenous lands guaranteed by treaties to hand over to the railroad tycoons. As Karuka observes, the railroad transformed California from an overseas possession of Spain to a continental possession of the United States, completing the century-long process of continental imperialism. Soon after Chinese railroad labor was no longer needed, Chinese exclusion was implemented: "The railroad, and exclusion, were core infrastructures of continental imperialism."[31]

ALL-INCLUSIVE YELLOW PERIL

US imperialism had long extended to Latin America and the Caribbean, starting with their independence movements soon after US independence. By the 1870s, the elites in those countries were hosts to US and British mining interests and yellow peril paranoia and exclusion that accompanied Chinese, Japanese, and South Asian immigration. In the late nineteenth century, the demand for workers on Hawai'i plantations and in agribusiness in California drew Japanese labor migrations. Around thirty thousand Japanese had entered California by 1900, and within a decade, more than a hundred thousand more migrants had arrived. With labor shortages in the California fields, labor recruiters lured Japanese workers in Hawai'i to California. The 1910 census tallied 41,356 Japanese in California, less than 1 percent of the population but enough to cause yellow peril alarm with exclusionists calling for restrictions. The anti-Japanese movement was much like the anti-Chinese, focused on perceived threat to health and morality of the white population, but the real fear was economic and the effect on white workers.[32]

Historian Erika Lee notes that Asian immigration was fraught with what she calls "hemispheric Orientalism." Lee documents the interconnected debates about Asian immigration in the US, Canada, Hawai'i, Mexico, the Caribbean, and parts of Latin America, beginning in the mid-nineteenth century.[33] Between 1868 and 1941, 42 percent of Japanese migrants in the Americas settled in Latin American countries. By 1941, 33 percent of the Chinese population in the Americas lived in Latin America and the Caribbean, while 46 percent were in the US and 21 percent were in Canada. The first Chinese immigrants in Mexico arrived in 1864 from the United States to work in railroad construction and the Sonoran mines, mostly owned by US corporations.[34] Because the United States had established the racialized template for yellow peril, it played an important role "in the circulation of Orientalism abroad."[35]

In 1908, a year after anti-Asian riots took place up and down the Pacific coast from San Francisco to British Columbia, President Theodore Roosevelt called for "unity of action" among the Anglo states of the US, Canada, Australia, and Britain to promote a "White Pacific," in which white supremacy would dominate against ascendant Japanese power. Roosevelt dispatched the US Navy's sixteen-battleship Pacific tour to demonstrate Anglo unity against the yellow peril that Japanese immigration represented. Roosevelt told a reporter for the *New York Times* that the fleet would confirm that New Zealand and Australia were "white man's countries."[36]

MEASURING WHITENESS

As noted in the introduction, until 1875 the only legal guide to US immigration was the race-based Naturalization Act of 1790, which allowed citizenship only to "free white persons," a measure that remained on the books until the 1952 Walter-McCarren Act.[37] People simply arrived, many of them aggressively recruited for the newly ethnically cleansed territories seeking statehood, which desperately needed settlers to outnumber the Indigenous peoples who were being driven out or forced into reservations. In 1875, the US Supreme Court declared that regulation of immigration was a federal matter but did not specify the terms of immigration. The immigration service was established only in 1891. Tellingly, the first federal immigration laws, which created the foundation for US immigration, were based on exclusion. It is crucial to recognize that when and how "immigration" as such began, it was based on overt, blatant racism. That law was the Chinese Exclusion Act of May 6, 1882, which suspended Chinese immigration for a ten-year period and barred resident Chinese from US citizenship, and in 1902, was renewed indefinitely. The laws were widely evaded. Exclusion was repealed by the Magnuson Act on December 17, 1943, which allowed 105 Chinese individuals to enter per year.[38]

However, except for Chinese exclusion, prior to World War 1, as historian Mae Ngai points out, the United States had virtually open borders; immigration was encouraged and unfettered.[39] In the wake of the US entering the European war, xenophobia surged, and the US Congress in 1917 enacted an extremely restrictive immigration law that became the basis of the comprehensive Immigration Act of 1924 (the Johnson-Reed Act, Asian Exclusion Act, and National Origins Act), the primary determinant of eligibility for citizenship being whiteness, under the guise of "the nationality of the immigrant."[40] The 1917 law for the first time imposed a literacy test and increased the fee paid by arriving immigrants; it also gave more leeway to immigration officials to make decisions over whom to exclude. And, most restrictive of all, it excluded anyone from what was defined as the Asiatic Barred Zone, except Filipinos, who could travel freely to and within the US because of colonial status. There were no quotas or restrictions on Western Hemisphere populations. In 1921, Calvin Coolidge, who would become president in 1923 and sign the 1924 legislation, wrote in the popular magazine *Good Housekeeping* that "biological laws tell us that certain divergent people will not mix or blend. The Nordics propagate themselves successfully. With the other races, the outcome shows deterioration on both sides."[41]

In the 1924 immigration law, practically all immigration from Asia was prohibited, including from Japan, with the quota set at 165,000 for all of Asia. It limited the number of immigrants allowed entry into the United States through a national-origins quota. The quota provided immigration visas to 2 percent of the total number of people of each nationality in the United States as of the 1890 national census, which restricted Southern and Eastern Europeans while it had little effect on Western European immigration. This was to "preserve the ideal of U.S. homogeneity," in the words of the US State Department Office of the Historian.[42]

The process of measuring whiteness is illustrated by the treatment of Asian Indian immigrants. The first notable arrivals from South Asia were Sikh farmers and businessmen from the Punjab of then British-occupied India during the first decade of the twentieth century. They traveled the Pacific route from Hong Kong, arriving at San Francisco, established farms, initiating the rice industry to Northern California, and built lumber mills in the Pacific Northwest. In 1912, a Sikh temple opened in Stockton, California, the first in the United States. Most Punjabi men married into Mexican families.[43]

Other individuals from various parts of India arrived during the early 1900s. The first known India-born immigrant to become a US citizen was Bhicaji Franyi Balsara, a Parsi merchant from India. In 1909, circuit judge Emile Henry Lacombe of the Southern District of New York described Balsara as appearing "to be a gentleman of high character and exceptional intelligence." However, the judge had expressed reluctance in his decision regarding citizenship for Balsara, because the Congress that framed the original naturalization act "intended it to include only white persons belonging to those races whose emigrants had contributed to the building up on this continent of the community of people which declared itself a new nation." He realized he was broadening the concept of "free white persons" to include "all branches of the great race or family known to ethnologists as the Aryan, Indo-European, or Caucasian," which would bring in "Afghans, Hindoos, Arabs, and Berbers." The judge assured the public that the US attorney would appeal the decision, which he did, and that a higher court would decide, and the circuit court of appeals agreed that Parsis should be categorized as white. Several other South Asian individuals were naturalized, but in 1917, Congress passed the Barred Zone Act, overriding President Wilson's veto, that barred all Asians, and specifically Asian Indians, from entering the US. Then in 1923, the Supreme Court, in *United States v. Bhagat Singh Thind*, ruled that Asian Indian people were ineligible for US citizenship. The restriction was rescinded after World War II when Congress passed the 1946 Luce-Celler Act, allowing both Asian Indian immigration and citizenship.[44]

The Nazis' adoption of the US pseudoscience of eugenics has been well documented. They borrowed US race laws and also the US strategy of continental imperialism, ethnically cleansing the land in order to populate it with white settlers, what the Nazis called *Lebensraum*. Less well known is Nazi officials' interest in US racially determined immigration laws and citizenship requirements. Writing four years after the 1924 immigration act, Adolf Hitler, in the unpublished 1928 sequel to *Mein Kampf*, admiringly characterized the United States as "a race-state," referring to the US racist immigration measures that began with Chinese exclusion in 1882 and expanded to other nationalities in 1924. Hitler wrote, "American immigration policies provide confirmation that the previous 'melting pot' approach presupposes humans of a certain similar racial basis," and that approach "immediately fails as soon as fundamentally different types of humans are involved." When the Nazi lawyers began studying US race laws in depth in 1936, they were surprised that racial exclusion dated to the founding, one remarking that such was not common at the time.[45]

Yale law professor James Q. Whitman writes in his important book *Hitler's American Model: The United States and the Making of Nazi Race Law*, "The two new Nazi anti-Jewish measures that we remember today as the Nuremberg Laws . . . were the product of many months of Nazi discussion and debate that included regular, studious, and often admiring engagement with the race law of the United States." In a global history for German readers published in 1934, Nazi historian Albrecht Wirth hailed the founding of the United States: "The most important event in the history of the states of the Second Millennium . . . was the founding of the United States of America. The struggle of the Aryans for world domination received thereby its strongest prop." Another Nazi-era book in 1936, the translated title of which was *The Supremacy of the White Race*, characterized the US founding as "the first fateful turning point" in the worldwide rise of white supremacy, informing readers that the United States had assumed "the leadership of the white peoples" after World War I, without which "a conscious unity of the white race would never have emerged."[46]

THE TAINT OF WHITE SUPREMACY
IN WORKERS' MOVEMENTS

John Kuo Wei Tchen, historian of the New York Chinese experience in the nineteenth century, identifies an omen in 1870 of anti-Chinese furor that would lead to the next decade's Chinese exclusion. It was also a harbinger of the developing white supremacy in the nascent trade union movement. This was a lengthy front-page article in the main liberal Republican newspaper in the country, the *New York Tribune*, written by the chief editor and future prominent labor organizer, John Swinton. Eschewing debates over "coolies" in the workforce, Swinton addressed what he deemed unresolvable racial differences that led to a recent anti-Chinese protest:

The deepest dividing line between men is that of *race*. Deeper than politics or religion—deeper than the contemporary differences of laws or manners, are the depths and differences of *race*. . . . The people of the United States are of the white European race, the Japhetic stock, from which have sprung the Germanic, Celtic, and Latin varieties—all immediately related to each other by historical terms—all growing side by side for thousands of years, and all developing a progressive civilization through the changes of time.[47]

Swinton argued that labor must unite with capital to fight the scourge of the Chinese, against the threat of "the infusion and transfusion of the Chinese, Mongolian or Yellow race with the White American race." He claimed that experts were in agreement that the "Mongolian blood is a depraved and debased blood. The Mongolian type of humanity is an inferior type—inferior in organic structure, in vital force or physical energy and in the constitutional conditions of development." Swinton raised Darwin's theory of natural selection and warned that "a nation like ours would run a fearful risk from the degradation of its race—existence." As evidence, he wrote, "In the Spanish colonies on this continent, the European (Latin) race mingled with the Indian and the African, and we need nothing more than the direful and dismal history of Mexico and Central America as commentary on the fact."[48] Swinton did not factor in the United States' military and economic domination and interventions, including annexation of half of Mexico.

John Swinton was born in Scotland and as a child immigrated with his parents to the newly ethnically cleansed (of Indigenous communities) Illinois in the 1830s. Soon orphaned and an adolescent, he started working full time, apprenticing as a printer. He took a printing job in Canada, then returned to the US for various jobs in different cities. Early on, Swinton embraced radical abolitionism and even moved to the Kansas epicenter of abolition action in 1856 to work on the antislavery newspaper *Lawrence Republican.* Moving to New York at the start of the Civil War, he obtained a job at the *New York Times* where he remained for a decade, becoming chief editorial writer, then moved on to the *Tribune.* By the mid-1870s, he had immersed himself in the trade union movement in New York and was a popular orator. In 1883, he started his own trade union weekly, *John Swinton's Paper,* in which he upheld the workers' movement and attacked "Millionaires, Monopolists, and Plutocrats," as the masthead of each issue proclaimed.[49] Swinton represented the early articulation of white supremacy in the formation of US trade unions, which played a large role in the federal enactment of Chinese exclusion in 1882, as well as seeding a fatal flaw in the future of US trade unionism.

Historian Matthew Frye Jacobson writes, "An Irish immigrant in 1877 could be a despised Celt in Boston—a threat to the republic—and yet a solid member of The Order of Caucasians for the Extermination of the Chinaman in San Francisco, gallantly defending U.S. shores from an invasion of 'Mongolians.' "[50] Denis Kearney enacted that capsule description of the vile anti-Chinese obsession of white workers in the late nineteenth and early twentieth century. Kearney was born in County Cork, Ireland, during the potato famine. He took to sea at eleven and eventually ended up in the US, marrying an Irish American woman and settling in San Francisco, where he became a citizen. The majority of opposition to Chinese and Japanese immigration originated in labor unions and especially from Denis Kearney's Workingmen's Party on the West Coast. Their ravings warned of dire perceived threats to the health and morality of the white population. White workers' white supremacy barred any thought of organizing the Asian workers.[51]

Across the country in the mid-1870s, there was high unemployment and economic depression. Workers' rallies in San Francisco led to the formation of the Workingmen's Party of California in 1877, which was led by Kearney. Anti-Chinese immigration was at the top of the organization's agenda, with the party's slogan being "The Chinese must go!" The following year the party won eleven seats in the California Senate and seventeen in the State Assembly, playing a deciding role in rewriting the state constitution and denying Chinese citizens voting rights, which was later overturned as being unconstitutional. But it had the desired effect five years later with the federal Chinese Exclusion Act.[52] Kearney's speeches were filled with violent threats against capitalists. Many if not the majority of the unemployed workers associated with the party were Irish Americans, and Kearney was accused of being a foreign agitator by business leaders and other pillars of San Francisco. Anglo-American politician Frank Pixley, a former California attorney general and no defender of the Chinese, wrote of Kearney and the union in the newspaper he published, *The Argonaut:* "When an organization, composed almost entirely of aliens, who are themselves here by the sufferance of a generous hospitality, band themselves together in defiance of the law to drive out a class, . . . it is an act of insolent audacity that ought to move the indignation of every honest man."[53]

The party and Kearney's power didn't last for long, but Kearney was confident that their goals were met and justified. In an 1889 letter, he wrote,

> After the adoption of the new constitution and the passage of the Anti-Chinese Restriction Bills of 1879 and 1882 California began to move, and she is still a booming. Chinese immigration

is excluded. There are a few smuggled in over the borders. . . . My next fight will be to get Canada to pass an Anti-Chinese Exclusion law. At present, she is being made the dumping ground for Asiatic pests who are afterwards smuggled into our country. . . . I am a young man just turning 43. . . . I am in hopes of living long enough to see the Asiatic hordes excluded from this continent from Cape Horn to Icy Cape.[54]

In her study of myths about immigration taking away US Americans' jobs, Aviva Chomsky writes that it is "one of the most common arguments brandished to justify the need for a restrictive immigration policy."[55] Chomsky challenges the claim that immigration and immigrants reduce the jobs available, arguing that immigration is a minor factor in job loss and cites the US government and the US economic system itself as the main factors that maintain and exploit global inequalities. She points out that, due to the extremely restrictive quotas of the 1925 immigration law, immigration was very low when the Depression hit and unemployment soared to 20 percent, but the forced deportation of tens of thousands of Mexican workers during that time did not lower unemployment numbers. The post–World War II industrial boom shrank unemployment figures, again unrelated to immigration.[56]

White supremacy was embedded in the first labor confederation, the American Federation of Labor (AFL). In 1905, the president of the AFL, Samuel Gompers, made that crystal clear, writing, "Caucasians are not going to let their standard of living be destroyed by Negroes, Chinamen, Japs, or any others."[57] Gompers opposed US annexation of the Philippines not for anti-imperialist reasons; rather, arguing, "If the Philippines are annexed, what is to prevent the Chinese, the Negritos and the Malays coming to our country? How can we prevent the Chinese coolies from going to the Philippines and from there swarm into the United States and engulf our people and our civilization? . . . Can we hope to close the flood-gates of immigration from the hordes of Chinese and the semi-savage races coming from what will then be part of our own country?"[58] The United Mine Workers of America advocated upholding "Caucasian ideals of civilization," warning against the "yellow peril."[59]

Historian Alexander Saxton observed that Euroamerican workers in the US were organized in the nineteenth century through their competition and confrontations with three racialized groups: Native Americans, African Americans, and Chinese Americans.

> Central to each transaction has been a totally one-sided preponderance of power, exerted for the exploitation of nonwhites by the dominant white society. In each case . . . white workingmen have played a crucial, yet ambivalent, role. They have been both exploited and exploiters. On the one hand, thrown into competition with nonwhites as enslaved or "cheap" labor, they suffered economically; on the other hand, being white, they benefited by that very exploitation which was compelling the nonwhites to work for low wages or for nothing. Ideologically they were drawn in opposite directions. Racial identification cut at right angles to class consciousness.[60]

Bill Fletcher Jr. observes that beyond racial prejudice, there was also the silence of the labor movement on the objectives of the settler state itself.[61] Fletcher writes that "the 'official' labor movement, that is, the white-majority or white-exclusive formations, in effect pledged its loyalty to the racial settler state. In time this was treated as *patriotism*."[62] And that movement either supported or simply ignored the US wars against Indigenous peoples to take their land for settlers to replace them. "Free land" presented possibilities for white workers to own property. Fletcher writes, "Whether in openly white supremacist terms or by omission, the 'official' [labor] movement situated itself as a movement of white working people in struggle against the white employer class, but joined together by the framework of the white republic against all others."[63]

JACK LONDON'S OBSESSION WITH YELLOW PERIL

Jack London was a leading anti-Chinese bigot in the San Francisco Bay Area, where he was born in 1876. He died of alcohol-related disease at age forty in 1916, but he contributed a lot during his short life to yellow peril panic, mainly because he was a literary celebrity. London was not only a (white) workingman's advocate, but also an active and radical Marxist and socialist. Thanks to his best-selling books, he became wealthy. London's mother, descended from Puritan settlers in the Massachusetts Bay Colony, worked as a music teacher and spiritualist, but his birth father was Irish, which London was not proud of. In denial of his paternal Irish roots, he identified as pure Anglo-Saxon. London started working at fourteen when he borrowed money to buy a boat to use illegally to harvest oysters in the bay to sell on the streets. At seventeen, he spent eight months on a sailing schooner to Japan, and at twenty-one, he joined the Klondike gold rush—all material for his adventure novels and stories. He married and had children soon after, divorced and remarried, all the time writing and publishing stories and building wealth. In 1905, he was affluent enough to buy a ranch in Sonoma County, fifty miles north of San Francisco, and purchased adjacent land until it was a vast estate, where he lived the rest of his short life. He spent the equivalent of over two million dollars in twenty-first century currency to build a stone mansion, which was destroyed by fire before he moved in. He was recruited to join the elite men's Bohemian Club, in which he was active, and was a member of high society in the San Francisco Bay Area as a celebrity and despite his radical political views.[64]

London joined the Socialist Labor Party in 1896, when he was twenty, giving nightly radical speeches in a local park and once being arrested. Even before he joined the party, he had written an article promoting socialism for the *San Francisco Examiner*, "What Socialism Is." He also wrote a letter published in the *Oakland Times* recommending that people study Karl Marx's *Capital*.[65] In 1901, he left the Socialist Labor Party for the more radical, newly formed Socialist Party headed by Eugene Debs. The Socialist Party ran candidates for office, and in 1901, London lost a run for mayor of Oakland on the Socialist Party ticket, and again in 1905. He expressed admiration of the anarcho-syndicalist Industrial Workers of the World (IWW), but didn't join.[66] London was a celebrity socialist and writer, admired by Lenin and Trotsky. Famous anarchist Emma Goldman called him the "only revolutionary author in America." Even after his withdrawal from socialism and after his death, later socialist-minded writers

Tillie Olsen and Doris Lessing saw him as a working-class hero.[67] Once London became more successful and wealthy, he lost interest in socialism. California historian Kevin Starr calls this stage of London's life "post-socialist," writing that by 1911, "London was more bored by the class struggle than he cared to admit."[68]

In all his speeches and political writing, even his fiction, London railed against Chinese immigration. Like most of the elite and intellectuals of the Progressive Era, including those in highest political office, such as Theodore Roosevelt, he embraced eugenics.[69] In 1910, London published a story titled "The Unparalleled Invasion" in *McClure's Magazine*. A fantasy set in a future 1976, it tells a story of the West's recognition of China's enormous population and potential for world domination and preventing it with an "unparalleled invasion" of biological warfare that resulted in the complete annihilation of the Chinese people.[70]

London certainly had a deep effect on people of all classes, particularly in the San Francisco area. In February 1905, the *San Francisco Chronicle* stoked public fear, warning of a "raging torrent" of Japanese expected in California.[71] The California legislature called for the US Congress to limit Japanese immigration. Delegates from sixty-seven organizations in California, most of them labor unions, created the Asiatic Exclusion League, citing Japanese "low standard of civilization, living and wages." Branches proliferated, lobbying for exclusion and calling for boycotts. In 1906, the San Francisco Board of Education banned Japanese and Korean children, sending them to the "Oriental" School in Chinatown to join Chinese children who had been segregated there since 1885.[72]

WAR, OCCUPATION, COLONIZATION, AND FILIPINO AMERICANS

By the twenty-first century, there were four million citizens of Filipino descent living in the United States. Under the first three decades of US occupation and colonization of the Philippines, Filipinos were categorized as US nationals, the same status as Puerto Ricans, and there was no restriction on their entry to the United States. Not strictly immigrants or refugees, and not US citizens, Filipinos were colonial subjects. In 1910, only 406 Filipinos lived in the United States, most having arrived before the US invasion while Spain still held the Philippines as a colony. A decade later, in 1920, there were over 5,000 Filipinos in the US, and in 1930, 45,208. Filipinos were scattered in many states, the majority in California with 30,470, while there were 3,500 in Washington State, 2,000 in Illinois, over 1,000 in Oregon, and 1,000 in New York, some hundreds in Michigan, and smaller numbers in many other states.[73]

In 1930, Filipino workers comprised 80 percent of the asparagus workforce in the Sacramento Valley of California and the majority of lettuce workers in California's San Joaquin Valley. The workers suffered racial violence as early as 1926 in Stockton, California, and in 1928 in a central California town where young white men attacked Filipino workers. In the state of Washington, a group of white men forced some five hundred Filipino workers out of the Yakima Valley.[74] Historian Mae Ngai explains that the animosity of white people toward Filipinos was distinct from the ongoing Asian exclusion, first, because Orientalist characterizations didn't easily fit. Filipinos were Christians and spoke American English, wore Western clothes, and were fluent in US popular culture. It seemed that the discomfort white people felt reflected that seeming contradiction of familiarity but foreignness. She writes, "In a sense, the reaction of white Americans to the acculturation of Filipinos was similar to the unsettled response of nineteenth-century Americans to acculturated Native Americans." Then there were the sexual fears. Most Filipino workers, who were men, did not bring their families with them, although they sent home remittances; so being "womanless," they had relations with and married white as well as Native and Mexican women. Ngai quotes a sociologist of the time who said that Filipino men associating with white women "strained relations between the two races." He cited a white employer who said "he would have nothing against them if they did not display so much interest in American women."[75]

WAR AND JAPANESE AMERICANS

Neither the horrific atrocities committed by the Japanese military in China, Korea, and the Philippines, nor the attack on the US naval base in Hawai'i justified the actions taken by the Franklin Roosevelt administration, in concert with California attorney general Earl Warren. By 1940, two-thirds of the 120,000 Japanese Americans living on the West Coast, most in California, were American-born Nisei, that is, citizens of the United States. There were 158,000 Japanese living in the US colony of Hawai'i before it became a state, but the US military governor of the territory argued strongly against mass internment and won the day, so only 1,444 "suspect" Japanese were interned in Hawai'i.[76] Not so in white supremacist California, where Japanese Americans had little chance of escaping punishment after, as historian Richard Drinnon puts it, "decades of agitation against the 'yellow peril' by the Native Sons and Daughters of the Golden West, the California Joint Immigration Committee, the American Legion, and other champions of white supremacy, including the Hearst and the McClatchy newspapers, chambers of commerce, and agricultural, labor, and business organizations."[77]

Three days after the Pearl Harbor attack, FBI director J. Edgar Hoover reported that 1,291 Japanese—367 in the Hawaii colony, 924 in the United States—had been detained, along with 857 Germans and 147 Italians. Hoover, no flaming liberal, opined that mass internment of Japanese could not be justified on the basis of security.[78] The Germans and Italians who were detained had been under surveillance for some time and clearly had ties with the Nazi and Fascist regimes, but the nearly thirteen hundred detained Japanese Americans had no such complicity. They comprised the leadership of Japanese American communities—Buddhist priests, martial arts instructors, language teachers, members of theater companies, and editors of Japanese-language publications, as well as local political leaders.[79] In California, days after the Pearl Harbor attack, hundreds of Japanese American workers were fired and Japanese American businesses had few customers. In Los Angeles, twelve hundred Japanese American union workers in produce were laid off. The US Treasury Department closed down merchants in the wholesale markets.

Some of the fear and bigotry calmed down, with rehiring taking place, but would explode again with mass internment and war.[80]

Lieutenant General John L. DeWitt, head of the Western Defense Command in charge of California, disagreed with Hoover's assessment and insisted that all Japanese, including citizens from certain areas, should be relocated and interned away from the coast, saying he doubted Japanese loyalty. "A Jap is a Jap is a Jap," he said.[81] DeWitt pushed back at US attorney general Francis Biddle's argument that it was unconstitutional to forcibly relocate citizens en masse, and that "there were no reasons for mass evacuation." DeWitt insisted, "The Japanese race is an enemy race, . . . over 112,000 potential enemies, of Japanese extraction, are at large today." On February 19, 1941, President Franklin Roosevelt signed Executive Order 9066.[82] And as Roosevelt said of the December 7, 1941, attack on Pearl Harbor, February 19, 1941, was a day that will live in infamy. Not only were Japanese Americans removed from their homes, allowed to take only one suitcase each and deposited in military-guarded concentration camps, but so too were the Japanese living in the US colony of the Philippines. And so too were the Aleuts, the Indigenous people of the islands in the Bering Sea, off the coast of the US colony of Alaska. US authorities admitted that based on security, they had no suspicion of Aleuts, but they framed incarceration as being "for their own good." White US American settlers living on one of the Aleutian Islands were not evacuated or incarcerated. Nearly nine hundred Aleuts were forced onto ships and dropped off on the southeast Alaska mainland. The navy herded them into abandoned mining camps with no services.[83]

Presuming racial disloyalty, the US government removed 120,000 Japanese Americans, two-thirds of whom were citizens, from their homes on the Pacific coast and interned them in ten concentration camps.[84] Liberal Republican Earl Warren was California attorney general in 1941. Warren was born in California, the son of working-class union activists who had migrated from Scandinavia. Warren would go on to serve three terms as California governor and in 1953 became chief justice of the United States Supreme Court that handed down the school desegregation decision. Attorney General Warren argued that there was a reason for the difference in treatment of the Japanese in relation to the Germans and Italians: "We believe that when we are dealing with the Caucasian race we have methods that will test the loyalty of them. . . . But when we deal with the Japanese we are in an entirely different field and cannot form any opinion that we believe to be sound."[85] Warren initiated a mapping project to identify every parcel of Japanese American agricultural land, and under the guise of national security, all the farmland of Japanese Americans was confiscated, sold, and never returned to them, nor were they compensated for it.[86] The land, amounting to two hundred thousand acres, was transferred to new owners or renters, most of whom were naturalized European immigrants or white migrants from the Dust Bowl region. Japanese American truck farmers had produced 40 percent of all vegetables grown in the state, and nearly 100 percent of all tomatoes, celery, strawberries, and peppers. In his memoirs, Warren defended his central role in the internment, writing, "The atmosphere was so charged with anti-Japanese feeling that I do not recall a single public officer responsible for the security of the state who testified against a relocation proposal."[87] He did not apologize.

The War Relocation Authority (WRA) was the civilian agency under the Department of the Interior tasked with rounding up the detainees and managing the camps. New Deal Democrat Dillon S. Myer, lately in the US Department of Agriculture, was the director of the WRA. Myer and his crew perceived an opportunity to transform concentration camps into "planned communities" and "Americanizing projects, speed assimilation with self-government, schooling in English, work, and rehabilitative activities." Aware of the Nazi concentration camps, they believed their own project was "an ironic testimony to the value of American democracy." Historian Mae Ngai writes, "The greater irony, however, is that WRA's assimilationism led to the most disastrous and incendiary aspects of the internment experience—the loyalty questionnaire, segregation, and renunciation of [their Japanese] citizenship." WRA workers treated adult Japanese as children, infantilizing them, with the same mindset that prevailed in the US government's Indian boarding schools.[88]

Indeed, Dillon Myer's concentration camp experience led to his appointment as head of the Bureau of Indian Affairs in the Truman administration, 1950–1953. During his tenure he designed the federal government termination and relocation policy, which was projected to end treaty-based tribal sovereignty and dissolve the reservation land bases that had gained semi-autonomy with the New Deal legislation, the Indian Reorganization Act of 1934.[89]

The 1988 United States Congressional Civil Liberties Act granted "reparations" to the 82,219 still-living Japanese Americans who had been interned: the measly sum of twenty thousand dollars each, along with an apology.[90] The State of California Assembly apologized for California's role only in 2020, no compensation included.[91]

WAR AND KOREAN AMERICANS

The US war against Korea was ostensibly a United Nations intervention. The UN was only five years old in June 1950 and was dominated by the United States. It was made up of the five states that had won World War II—China, the Soviet Union, Britain, France, and the United States. The resolution demanded that North Korea cease crossing the Thirty-Eighth Parallel that had been established as its border with South Korea by the US military when it liberated the southern part of Korea from Japanese occupation, while the Red Army of the Soviet Union liberated the northern part, empowering the Korean resistance fighters and exiles who were communists. At the time of the UN Security Council's vote, Chiang Kai-shek still held the council seat for China, although he had retreated with his army to Taiwan (then called Formosa) following defeat by the communists, who were led by Mao Tse-Tung. The Soviet Union was boycotting the Security Council because of that.[92] Rather than going to Congress, President Harry Truman used the Security Council resolution to go to war.

Although the war was called a United Nations action, 90 percent of the military forces were US military personnel. Forty thousand of them were killed in action. Five million Koreans were killed, more than half of them civilians, 10 percent of Korea's prewar civilian population. Civilian casualties were higher in the Korean War than in World War II or the war in Vietnam. Massive numbers of Koreans were driven from their homes and became refugees. Refugees were constantly killed in US bombing raids of anything that moved. In the fifth month of the war, the US Air Force began burning and annihilating Korean towns and cities, with ground and naval operations also involved in the destruction, creating massive refugee flows.

As the US military tends to do in every war, based on its formation in the genocidal wars against Native Americans, it turned to total war, not distinguishing between civilian and military structures or people.[93] One of the many mass atrocities victimizing fleeing refugees was the 1950 No Gun Ri massacre, which was not revealed to the US public until 1999. The Associated Press (AP) issued a report using testimony of US Seventh Cavalry veterans and Korean survivors and gained access to documents that revealed US orders to fire on civilians and a three-day killing spree. Subsequent to the AP report, the army investigated and acknowledged the killings, but refused to apologize or pay reparations, describing the massacre as "an unfortunate tragedy inherent to war and not a deliberate killing." Later, the AP found other documents indicating that US commanders ordered soldiers to "shoot" and "fire on" civilians during the massacre. This exposure led the South Korean government to investigate, and they identified more than two hundred massive slaughters, mostly carried out by low-level air strafing. The number of dead from the No Gun Ri massacre is not known for certain, but North Korean journalists at the time reported some four hundred bodies in the area, including two hundred in one tunnel.[94] By mid-1951, whole swaths of North Korea were flattened, with people living in holes and caves, suffering infectious diseases and starvation and freezing in the very cold winters.[95]

By 2018, there were only 1.8 million Korean Americans in the United States, 99 percent from South Korea. Although Koreans make up a tiny percentage of the population, the United States is the site of the largest Korean-diaspora community in the world. Most live in the greater Los Angeles area, New York City, and Baltimore-Washington. Although there were a few thousand Koreans in the United States who arrived in the late nineteenth and early twentieth century, their numbers grew sharply after the 1965 immigration law removed restrictions on Asian immigration.[96] As in most brutal wars in which civilians are targeted and killed in large numbers, many orphans were left at the end of the US war in Korea. And, as in all US wars, the Christian missionaries poured in to exploit the trauma and destitution of the targeted population. US Americans have attempted to atone for the wreckage caused by their government and rushed to adopt orphans, adopting more than four thousand Korean children between 1955 and 1961. Some were "GI babies" with US military fathers. Twenty-nine percent of South Koreans were Christians, so Christian missions played a large role in facilitating the adoptions.[97]

US WAR IN VIETNAM

The fear and challenge of China have been the driving forces of US imperialism and wars, beginning in the 1840s with the wars to force US sovereignty on the North American continent and its peoples. Reaching the Pacific was the goal of the mid-nineteenth-century war against Mexico and annexation of California to open the door to the Pacific. By the mid-twentieth century, with the US at war in Korea—fundamentally a proxy war with newly Communist China—the United States considered China its number one enemy. With the 1953 stalemate and armistice, the Eisenhower administration believed that the real threat in Vietnam, as in Korea, was China. Ninety percent of the Chinese people who lived outside China lived in Southeast Asia.

After World War II, the US was paying 75 percent of the cost of French military operations in Vietnam. During 1954 and 1955, the US and China came close to a shooting war over two tiny islands, Mazu (Matsu) and Jimmen (Quemoy) off the coast of China.[98] These two obscure islands took center stage in the Kennedy-Nixon presidential race of 1960, Nixon urging war over the islands: "Now what do the Chinese Communists want? They don't want just Quemoy and Matsu, . . . they want the world."[99] John F. Kennedy was elected to the US Senate, representing Massachusetts, in 1952 at age thirty-five. Vietnam was not new to him when he was elected president in 1960. As a US senator, he was a booster of intervention. At a Washington, DC, luncheon meeting on the situation in

Vietnam in 1956, Kennedy, casting intervention as responsibility, said of Vietnam: "This is our offspring—we cannot abandon it, we cannot ignore its needs. And if it falls victim to any of the perils that threaten its existence—communism, political anarchy, poverty and the rest—then the United States, with some justification, will be held responsible, and our prestige in Asia will sink to a new low."[100]

In 1964, when the US military mobilized for war in Vietnam, only 603 Vietnamese people lived in the United States, and they were students, teachers, and diplomats. By the turn of the twenty-first century, there were some two million US citizens of Vietnamese descent, 40 percent living in California, nearly all of them among or descended from the half million war refugees.

Photographer Philip Jones Griffiths observed, "The Washington, D.C. memorial to the American war dead is 150 yards long; if a similar monument were built with the same density of names of the Vietnamese who died in it, it would be nine miles long."[101] The US war in Vietnam was a slaughterhouse. John F. Kennedy's use of "new frontier" to encapsulate his presidential campaign echoed debates about US history that had begun more than six decades earlier. Historian Frederick Jackson Turner had presented his history-making "frontier thesis" at the 1893 celebration of Columbus, claiming that the crisis of that era was the result of closing the frontier, and that a new frontier was needed to fill the ideological and spiritual vacuum created by the completion of settler colonialism of the continent. The frontier metaphor described Kennedy's plan for employing political power to make the world the new frontier of the United States, a new imperialism. Central to this vision was the obsession with communism, what Richard Slotkin calls "a *heroic* engagement in the 'long twilight struggle' " against communism, to which the nation was summoned, as Kennedy characterized it in his inaugural address. Soon after he took office, that struggle took the form of a counterinsurgency program in Vietnam. Slotkin writes, "Seven years after Kennedy's nomination, American troops would be describing Vietnam as 'Indian Country' and search-and-destroy missions as a game of 'Cowboys and Indians'; and Kennedy's ambassador to Vietnam would justify a massive military escalation by citing in metaphoric terms the necessity of moving the 'Indians' away from the 'fort' so that the 'settlers' could plant 'corn.' "[102] Another Indian war.

By 1966, returning soldiers were telling stories of witnessing or participating in massacres in Vietnam, and rumors circulated, but not until the documentation of a company of US soldiers murdering 504 villagers of My Lai—182 of them women, 17 of them pregnant, and 173 children, including 56 infants—on March 16, 1968, did the reality of the war come home. The killing stopped only when army helicopter pilot Hugh Thompson happened upon the site and landed between the soldiers and the terrified villagers trying to flee or hide, Thompson threatening to open fire on the killers. The army photographer assigned to the company photographed the carnage as it happened, and when the grisly photographs were published, there was no doubt as to the horror. There were no weapons in the village, not even the presence of young men of military age.[103] Those photographs made the attempted army coverup impossible, hard as the young major Colin Powell tried.

Lieutenant William Calley, who was the company commander, wrote in his memoir, *Body Count,* "We weren't in My Lai to kill human beings, really. We were there to kill ideology that is carried by—I don't know. Pawns, Blobs. Pieces of flesh. And I wasn't in My Lai to destroy intelligent men. I was there to destroy an intangible idea. To destroy communism. . . . I looked at communism as a southerner looks at a Negro, supposedly. It's evil. It's bad."[104] The only killer charged with crimes was Calley, a native of Columbus, Georgia. He was sentenced to life in prison, but after three days' detention, President Richard Nixon reduced his sentence to three years' house arrest. In 2009, he expressed remorse and apologized "for what happened that day in My Lai."[105]

VIETNAMESE REFUGEES

A week before the US was driven out of Vietnam on April 29, 1975, ten to fifteen thousand South Vietnamese allies, mostly military, and families were evacuated. Subsequently, 86,000 Vietnamese were airlifted out, among them over 3,300 infants and children in what was called Operation Babylift. One of the planes carrying infants and children exploded after takeoff, killing 138 passengers, 78 of them Vietnamese infants and children. A total of 110,000 Vietnamese were evacuated from Saigon.[106] Those evacuated made up only a small percentage of the South Vietnamese who had been allied with the United States. Between 1975 and 1978, thousands of others fled in boats. They landed on various islands and shores and were often refused entry in Malaysia, Hong Kong, and the Philippines. By mid-1979, there were 350,000 Vietnamese in refugee camps in Southeast Asia and Hong Kong. In all, some half million Vietnamese refugees were resettled around the United States.[107]

Yellow peril fears of the Vietnamese refugees followed the usual pattern of bigotry and discrimination, the most extreme publicized case taking place in the gulf area of Southeast Texas. In the late 1970s, around a hundred thousand Vietnamese refugees were resettled in Texas, mainly along the Gulf of Mexico, where they fished and shrimped. Immigration agents had asked Congress to scatter the refugees around the country to avoid what they called "ghettoism," that is, Vietnamese forming coherent communities and thereby not assimilating. This led to Vietnamese people being placed in states like Texas and Oklahoma that had small Asian populations or limited experience with Asians, but carried most of the bigotry embedded in US culture, which was exacerbated by regarding Vietnamese as the enemy.

Being excellent fishers and hard workers, the Vietnamese worked many more hours than the Anglo fishermen and lived more frugally, and they soon did well financially. Most of the refugees initially did not speak English and were Roman Catholics. They were surrounded by Anglo-Protestants and the virulently anti-Catholic, anti-immigrant Ku Klux Klan. By 1979, tensions were high and escalated over the next two years, with the Klan firebombing Vietnamese boats and houses and destroying fish traps, while the Vietnamese defended themselves with little help from law enforcement, which, at any rate, was friendly with the KKK if not members.

Many of the young Anglo fishers and shrimpers had served in Vietnam and regarded the Vietnamese as the enemy—"gooks," communists—that they believed the liberal Carter administration had rescued instead of helping the vets. They also thought that aid groups and the government were subsidizing the refugees, which was not the case. The late 1970s was a period of economic downturn and gas shortages, with fierce competition over the fishing grounds and cheaper imports driving many out of the industry. Rather than blaming the economy, the Anglo fishers and shrimpers scapegoated the Vietnamese.

On August 3, 1979, several Vietnamese boats were torched and a vacant Vietnamese house firebombed. Vietnamese and Anglo fishermen got into a brawl that ended with the shooting death of one of the Anglos. Two Vietnamese were tried for murder and acquitted on self-defense grounds. This made Anglos more resentful. One Anglo fisherman expressed a common sentiment saying, "There's too many of them, and there's not enough room for them and there's going to be lots of hard feelings if they don't get some of them out of here and teach the ones that they leave how to act and how to get along. I think they ought to be put on a reservation somewhere or in a compound to teach them our laws and our ways, the way we live, our courtesy as a people."[108]

On February 14, 1981, Anglo fishermen organized a rally that was attended by the Grand Dragon of the Texas Knights of the KKK, Louis Beam. More than a dozen uniformed men of the KKK's armed militia, the Texas Emergency Reserve, which boasted twenty-five hundred members, also attended. Beam threatened the federal government with action if they did not remove Vietnamese fishermen and shrimpers by May 15, the start of the shrimping season. Beam proceeded to demonstrate how to burn a boat, then invited the Anglo fishermen to join the Klan: "The Ku Klux Klan is more than willing to select out of the ranks of American fishermen some of your more hardy souls and send them through our training camps. And when you come out of that, they'll be ready for the Vietnamese."[109]

The following month, Beam led armed, hooded Klansmen and militia men to harass the Vietnamese fishermen with a "boat parade," stopping alongside Vietnamese communities to brandish their weapons, burning an effigy of a Vietnamese man being lynched. Civil rights attorney Morris Dees filed a federal lawsuit on behalf of the Vietnamese fishers against the Klan itself and Beam, plus other specific Klansmen. The case was assigned to the first African

American federal judge in Texas, Gabrielle Kirk McDonald. Beam demanded that the judge self-disqualify, referring to her as a "Negress" with prejudice against the Klan. Beam's demand was denied. At trial, Vietnamese fishers gave testimony to a courtroom packed with robed Klansmen. Judge McDonald issued a preliminary injunction on harassment of the Vietnamese. The shrimping season began the next day, with US marshals on the Vietnamese boats assigned to protect the fishers. The judge found in favor of the Vietnamese complaints. On June 9, 1982, the court issued a permanent injunction against the Klan's Texas Emergency Reserve and prohibited the Klan from having any military organization or training or parading in public with firearms.[110]

"SECRET" US WAR IN LAOS AND HMONG REFUGEES

Laos is a small landlocked and mountainous country bordered by China, Vietnam, Cambodia, and Myanmar (Burma). In 1960, it had a population of two million people. Like Vietnam and Cambodia, Laos had been colonized by France and won independence in 1953. The Kingdom of Laos was formed, but it was opposed by the communist Pathet Lao that had been successful, along with the Vietnamese communists, in defeating the French in their war to maintain occupation of Southeast Asia. The US Department of Defense promptly created an office to support and fully financed the Royal Lao Army against the Pathet Lao.

Laos was officially neutral during the US war in Vietnam, based on a neutrality agreement signed in 1962 by the United States, China, the Soviet Union, Vietnam, and ten other countries, forbidding signees from invading Laos or establishing military bases there. But the US ran a covert war in Laos for nine years, 1964–1973, called the "Secret War in Laos," which was secret to no one except the US public. During that time, the United States Air Force bombed nearly every inch of Laotian territory to annihilate the Pathet Lao, which they failed to do—the Pathet Lao took power in 1975, and Laos remains a socialist country. US planes dropped over two million tons of cluster bombs on the country, more bombs than all the ones dropped during World War II. No country has ever been bombed so heavily and for so long. Since the bombing ended, more than fifty thousand Lao civilians have been killed or maimed by the unexploded eight million US bombs left behind.[111]

By 1958, the US Central Intelligence Agency (CIA) had already covertly begun organizing the Hmong and other ethnic minority villagers in the Central Highlands of Laos into a proxy counterinsurgent force. The Hmong had one cash crop, opium, and the CIA became the main purchaser and distributor of the commodity. The Hmong's opium production for export was already well developed by the French military in the 1930s. The French promoted the opium industry all over Southeast Asia, but the Hmong territory in Laos became the most productive opium-growing area. Historian Alfred McCoy writes that it was the French that changed "the hill tribe economy from subsistence agriculture to cash-crop opium farming."[112]

Around 1958, the CIA took up the reins of the trade without missing a beat. The Hmong were the first to be drawn into the US mercenary warfare, which built up to all-out war against Vietnam, becoming entwined in counter-guerrilla operations and the drug trade. The local market itself included a million or so opium addicts when the CIA arrived. The CIA had the organization that was needed to move the opium from the mountains to urban markets. By the late 1960s, it served a global market in opium.[113]

The CIA recruited General Vang Pao in 1960 to be the commander of the CIA's secret Hmong army to destroy the Pathet Lao guerrillas in Laos, then to carry out counterinsurgency against the North Vietnamese army. Vang Pao had served in the French colonial military and became a major general in the Royal Lao Army after Laos became independent. Sixty percent of the Hmong male population joined the CIA's counterinsurgent Hmong army. The United States even operated a secret air force, Air America, which was the lifeblood of the CIA's Hmong counterinsurgency operation, transporting in personnel, food, and supplies to and from their remote bases and transporting out the opium.[114]

By 1975, nearly a quarter million Laotian civilians and military, a tenth of the total population, were dead. Twice as many were wounded. A full quarter of the population—750,000—had become refugees, including General Vang Pao himself. With the 1973 cease-fire agreement signed in Paris, some 120,000 Hmong became refugees in Laos, along with eighteen thousand Hmong soldiers. Around fifty thousand Hmong civilians had been killed or wounded in the war. Following the 1975 evacuation of US and South Vietnamese military personnel from Saigon, General Vang Pao and around twenty-five hundred Hmong military members and their families were airlifted to Thailand. Thousands more Hmong swarmed the air base but were left behind. They moved into Thai refugee camps that were established by the United Nations High Commissioner for Refugees (UNHCR) and began to be resettled, the first Hmong family resettled in Minnesota in November 1975. The largest resettlement came after the passage of the US Refugee Act of 1980. By the 2010 census, 260,000 Hmong had been resettled in communities across the United States, with 87,000 in California, 66,000 in Minnesota, 47,000 in Wisconsin, 10,000 in North Carolina, and under 10,000 scattered in Colorado, Georgia, Alaska, Oklahoma, and Oregon.[115]

Mai Der Vang, a second-generation Hmong writer raised in the United States, observed, "While a person can be evacuated from his war-torn country, he can never be evacuated from the trauma. . . . This war is my inheritance." Viet Thanh Nguyen points out that for Mai Der Vang and other Hmong Americans, "war, memory, and identity are inextricable because Hmong identity in the United Sates does not exist without war."[116] Some young and apparently healthy Hmong refugees go to sleep and never wake up, while their dark hair turns white overnight.[117]

US AIRSTRIKES IN CAMBODIA,
KILLING FIELDS, AND REFUGEES

In 1749, the Vietnamese conquered territory that included Cambodia. After many revolts against the occupation, Cambodia overthrew Vietnamese control in 1851. Thirty-six years later, the French absorbed Cambodia into their colonial Indochinese Union until Japan forced the French out and occupied Cambodia from 1941 to 1945. France returned but withdrew from Southeast Asia with their 1953 defeat in Vietnam. Norodom Sihanouk of the Cambodian royal family took power. With US war mobilization against North Vietnam on the horizon, Cambodia broke relations with South Vietnam in 1963. In March 1970, former prime minister General Lon Nol led a coup, overthrowing Sihanouk and the monarchy and establishing a republic. Two months later, the United States began its interminable bombing campaign in Cambodia, triggering a civil war between the Lon Nol government and the Khmer Rouge communist forces led by Pol Pot.

As the United States fled Southeast Asia in the spring of 1975, the Khmer Rouge formed an alliance with the exiled Sihanouk to capture the Cambodian capital, Phnom Penh, establishing the Kingdom of Cambodia headed by Prince Sihanouk. A year later the Khmer Rouge forced Sihanouk back into exile and established Democratic Kampuchea under Khmer Rouge dictatorship. The regime soon broke relations with the unified Socialist Republic of Vietnam. What followed was the Khmer Rouge's implementation of a death cult, forcing all professionals, teachers, intellectuals, and artists out of the capital into the countryside to work under starvation conditions, leaving two million dead. Thousands of others were slaughtered. In January 1979, the Vietnamese army intervened, capturing Phnom Penh and driving out the Khmer Rouge. Vietnamese occupation lasted until 1989. In 1992, a United Nations peacekeeping force monitored Cambodia, and free elections were held the following year, a constitution ratified restoring the monarchy, with Norodom Sihanouk returning to the throne. In 1997, a United Nations tribunal was established, which tried and convicted Khmer Rouge leaders. Pol Pot escaped by dying.[118]

Too often the brief but macabre and deadly Khmer Rouge terror reign over the Cambodian people is conceptualized in a vacuum, rather than acknowledging the central US role in terrorizing Cambodian civilians for four solid years of B-52 carpet bombings. Starting in 1965, the US had been bombing sites in Cambodia where they claimed Vietnam guerrillas had supply lines. Under the same international agreement that established Laotian neutrality, Cambodia also officially became a neutral country. In his 1979 book *Sideshow:*

Kissinger, Nixon, and the Destruction of Cambodia, British journalist William Shawcross placed blame directly on President Richard Nixon and his national security assistant Henry Kissinger for plunging Cambodia into the chaos that made possible the Khmer Rouge horrors that followed.[119] Genocide historian Ben Kiernan writes that the Khmer Rouge "would not have won power without U.S. economic and military destabilization of Cambodia. . . . It used the bombing's devastation and massacre of civilians as recruitment propaganda and as an excuse for its brutal, radical policies and its purge of moderate communists and Sihanoukists."[120] In his study of Henry Kissinger's role in the Nixon administration's acts of war, historian Greg Grandin cites the US bombings of Cambodia, spanning eight years, as driving the Cambodian peasantry to support the Khmer Rouge.[121]

Even after the Vietnamese drove out the Khmer Rouge regime of terror, the United States, along with Western Europe and China, continued to support them. Although the United States publicly condemned the Khmer Rouge, several presidential administrations, plus China and the US-dominated Association of South East Asian Nations (ASEAN), gave military support to the Khmer Rouge. During the Reagan administration, the US increased its covert aid to the Coalition Government of Democratic Kampuchea (CGDK) from four million to ten million dollars for its resistance to the Vietnam-aligned Cambodian government.[122] As a result of Chinese, US, and Western opposition to the Vietnamese intervention that overthrew the Khmer Rouge, the United States insisted that the disgraced and defeated Khmer Rouge, rather than the Cambodian Vietnam-aligned government, be allowed to hold Cambodia's United Nations seat until 1982. After 1982, the UN seat was filled by a Khmer Rouge–dominated coalition, CGDK, which it held until 1993. The United States did not recognize and open relations with unified Vietnam until 1995.[123] And, of course, the Clinton administration and subsequent ones did not even consider war reparations.

Trauma after trauma beset the Cambodian people, trauma that the refugees carried with them to the United States. Seven hundred thousand Cambodians were killed in US bombings and ground war. Viet Thanh Nguyen writes, "If we count what happened in a bomb-wrecked, politically destabilized Cambodia during the Khmer Rouge regime of 1975–1979 as the postscript to the war, the number of dead would be an additional two million, or close to one-third of the population."[124] Some 150,000 Cambodians were given refugee status in the United States, while another six thousand or so arrived as immigrants, and twenty-five hundred with humanitarian status. Besides Khmer Cambodians, there were also refugees from the Cham and Khmer Loeu ethnic communities. As with the Vietnamese and Hmong refugees, the Cambodians were purposely scattered around the country to promote cultural assimilation. The 2010 US census estimated that nearly three hundred thousand Cambodian Americans resided in California, Pennsylvania, and Massachusetts.[125]

"Among the refugees," Viet Thanh Nguyen writes, "some are the living dead."[126] Sixty-two to 92 percent of Cambodian refugees in the United States suffered post-traumatic stress disorder (PTSD). Some experienced an illness called hysterical blindness, during which the person cannot see, but there is no discernable medical cause. Nguyen asks, "What has traumatized, blinded, or killed these people? Memories."[127] Such extreme trauma reverberates intergenerationally. In the US wars in Southeast Asia, the United States carpet-bombing campaigns and planting of land mines left millions of tons of unexploded ordinance, killing or maiming hundreds each year.[128]

As in the aftermath of all US wars, Christian evangelicals of all stripes flock in to convert the vulnerable and traumatized people. Viet Thanh Nguyen, who immigrated as a child with his Vietnam War refugee family, writes, "When we remember the wars that forced people to flee, oftentimes into the embrace of their colonizer or invader, then we can see that the immigrant story, a staple of American culture, must actually be understood, in many cases, as a war story."[129] Indeed, as of 2020, the US had been at war against Asian peoples for 122 years, killing millions of civilians and creating internal and migrating refugees and immigrants, many to the United States.

The US Asian wars began with the invasion and occupation of the Philippines, 1898–1944. Since 1969, ten years after Philippine independence, the United States military has been involved in counterinsurgency in the Philippines against groups resistant to continued US domination, and with the post-9/11 "War on Terror," against the Muslim community. Robert Kaplan writes of the strategic importance of the Philippines for the United States, in terms of what he deems the real enemy, China: "Combatting Islamic terrorism in this region carried a secondary benefit for the United States: it positioned the U.S. for the future containment of nearby China."[130]

The war with Japan, 1941–1945, ended with the United States' use of its newly invented nuclear and hydrogen bombs, which killed and maimed hundreds of thousands of civilians in Hiroshima and Nagasaki, inaugurating the permanent threat of nuclear war and ramping up the military industrial complex. In a March 1947 address to Congress, President Harry Truman, who ordered the nuclear attacks on Japan, declared war on communism with the Truman Doctrine. Although preceding the communists coming to power in China by two years and targeting the perceived threat of communists coming to power in Greece, it guaranteed a foreign policy to counter communism in any country where is appeared: "The free peoples of the world look to us for support in maintaining their freedoms."[131] The end of Japanese occupation of Korea occasioned implementation of the Truman Doctrine with the 1950–1953 Korean War, hostilities with North Korea continuing in the twenty-first century. The US war in Vietnam began with a decade of counterinsurgency following the Vietnamese liberation movement's victory over the French military at the battle of Dien Bien Phu in 1954, then a virtual US declaration of war with the Gulf of Tonkin resolution and troop buildup in 1964.

US WARS IN WEST ASIA AND THE MIDDLE EAST

In 1990, the US mobilized for war against Iraq with the Gulf War of 1991, followed by military control and economic sanctions, becoming all-out war again in 2003, with an apparently permanent military presence. After decades of vilification, boycotts, and attempted assassinations of Muammar Gaddafi of Libya by five US administrations, the Obama administration destroyed that thriving country in 2011, leaving Gaddafi dead and mutilated. Soon after, the administration turned to a mostly covert and proxy war in Syria, with no end in sight. In 2019, Syrians accounted for the largest forcibly displaced population in the world at more than 13.4 million internal and external refugees out of a pre-2011 population of 21 million.[132] Although US wars, overt and covert, and arms sales are primarily responsible for the misery of these peoples, the US government accepts very few asylum seekers or immigrant applications from the war-torn countries. British journalist Patrick Cockburn observes, "The endless nature of these present-day conflicts has come to seem to be part of the natural order of things, but this is absolutely not the case." He points out that the Syrian government won the war there militarily by 2018, but the US and the West want to get rid of Assad, so they kept up the fighting, making Syrian civilians cannon fodder. Cockburn writes that "cynical calculations about denying the other side an outright victory kept the other wars going, regardless of the human cost."[133] In Yemen, where since 2015 the United States has fueled the war of its allies the Saudi Arabia and United Arab Emirates monarchies, 80 percent of the population is dependent on humanitarian aid for food and shelter and were on the brink of mass starvation, because the monarchies and the US blocked aid.[134]

US domination and military interventions in the Middle East, the Persian Gulf, and Afghanistan did not begin with President George W. Bush's terror wars in the twenty-first century. With only the United States among world powers having come out of World War II unscathed in the homeland and the beneficiary of wealth accumulation with the military-industrial complex that was built for the war, the Truman and Eisenhower administrations took up the banner of reconstructing the world order while managing the European colonies that were achieving or fighting for independence in Asia, Africa, and the Middle East. Edward Said wrote that, for the West, "everything to the east of an imaginary line drawn somewhere between Greece and Turkey was called the Orient," representing for the West "a special mentality, as in the phrase 'the Oriental mind,' and also a set of special cultural, political, and even racial characteristics (in such notions as the Oriental despot, Oriental sensuality, splendor, inscrutability)."[135]

By the end of World War I, the Western European states and the United States, squabbling among themselves, were in a colonial relationship with around 85 percent of the globe, whose peoples were struggling for independence, Arab peoples among them. Most of the former Ottoman-occupied peoples achieved independence from the 1930s to the 1970s. Starting in 1942, US ships, troops, and bases arrived in North Africa, Iran, and Saudi Arabia and have never left the Middle East since that time. In the beginning, it was about control of strategic oil reserves. In 1948, the state of Israel was established as a European and United States proxy in the mostly Muslim Middle East. As a settler state, its first order of business was to ethnically cleanse the lands within the newly UN-drawn boundaries of the indigenous Palestinian Arabs, undercutting longtime Palestinian national aspirations just coming out from under Ottoman, then British, colonization. Palestinian historian Rashid Khalidi aptly calls it "the hundred years' war on Palestine," which began with the Balfour Declaration supporting a homeland for Jews in Palestine.[136] In what Palestinians call the Nakba, meaning catastrophe, more than seven hundred thousand, about half their total population, were driven out of their homes by Israeli forces, becoming refugees. Hundreds of Palestinian villages were looted and destroyed between December 1947 and January 1949.[137] In 1967, in a six-day war, Israel captured the West Bank Palestinian area, which it has occupied since that time, inviting Jews in the diaspora to build settlements, which is illegal under international law. By the late 1970s, the United States became the central financial and military mainstay for Israel, the situation of the Palestinians worsening by the year.

The United Nations agency for Palestine refugees (UNRWA) provides services and operates camps. In 2020, there were some 5 million Palestine refugees eligible for UNRWA services. Nearly a third of registered Palestinian refugees, more than 1.5 million individuals, live in fifty-eight recognized refugee camps in Jordan, Lebanon, the Syrian Arab Republic, the Gaza Strip, and the West Bank, including East Jerusalem. UNRWA maintains schools and health-care centers. The majority of the 6 million people of Palestinian descent live in Jordan, Syria, and Lebanon, a total of 2.5 million, while 2 million Palestinians reside in their autonomous territories of the West Bank and beleaguered Gaza Strip. Approximately 750,000 Palestinians live in the state of Israel. There are some 200,000 Palestinian Americans.[138]

Following the Iranian revolution in 1979, Iran became the main target for the United States, increasingly involving Israel as a proxy. In 1953, the CIA, along with British intelligence agencies, staged a coup to overthrow the democratically elected president, Mohammad Mosaddegh, who had nationalized the oil industry, replacing him with the monarchal dictatorship of Shah Reza Pahlavi. The shah reprivatized the oil industry and, with the assistance of the CIA, created one of the world's most hideous secret surveillance and torture regimes, SAVAK.[139] Stephen Kinzer writes, "In 1953 the United States was still new to Iran. Many Iranians thought of Americans as friends, supporters of the fragile democracy they had spent half a century trying to build. It was Britain, not the United States, that they demonized as the colonialist oppressor."[140] This was a cruel awakening for former British and French colonies in the Persian Gulf region and the Middle East, knowing nothing about US imperialism, seduced by Hollywood westerns, war stories, and dramas of the everyday life of affluent white people.

The 1979 revolution that succeeded in overthrowing the shah was long in the making clandestinely but became public in early 1977 when journalists, intellectuals, lawyers, and political activists published a series of public letters criticizing the shah's dictatorship. This was followed later in the year by a ten-night poetry festival that attracted thousands of participants with lectures criticizing the government. Mass demonstrations in Tehran and other cities began a few months later. The protests grew in 1978, and at the end of that year, worker strikes and street demonstrations, with masses of women participating, paralyzed the country, shutting down the oil industry. The Carter administration arranged the departure of the shah in mid-January 1979, then did not interfere in the return of the conservative Ayatollah Khomeini. In a voter referendum, Iran became an Islamic republic on April 1, 1979. Iranian students stormed the US embassy in Tehran on November 4, 1979, and held diplomatic hostages for over a year, releasing them on January 20, 1981, after the inauguration of Ronald Reagan. The Carter administration cut off diplomatic relations with Iran and seized all Iranian assets in US banks. Four decades later, that non-relationship endures as does the US military threat to Iran.[141]

Acute anti-Muslim bigotry began with the hostage crisis. Four days after the hostages were taken, ABC television promptly began a nightly news program, *The Iran Crisis—America Held Hostage*, which pumped public anger. ABC newsman Ted Koppel became the face of the show when he began as anchor in March 1980, renaming it *Nightline*. Dark-skinned individuals misidentified as Iranians across the country were targets of attack; in the Southwest, gas stations put up signs informing that their employees were Mexicans, not Iranians, after one Mexican American employee was shot. Naveed Mansoori points out that "after the 1979 revolution, the figure of the Muslim attained an increasingly prominent role in US domestic and foreign policy. . . . In the so-called 'war on terror,' the Muslim serves as a foil against which the United States draws legitimacy to justify its military exploits in the Middle East. . . . The entanglements between anti-Muslim and anti-Black racism are tightly woven together in the concept of 'the riot.'"[142] By 1979, there were around 50,000 Iranian Americans, and more Iranians arrived in large numbers after the 1979 revolution. The 2000 US Census counted 385,488 Iranian Americans.[143]

As of 2020, the United States had been at war in Afghanistan, much of it covert, for forty years. In 1979, the Soviet Union responded to the neighboring and beleaguered Afghan communist government with support, sending troops in to fight the Mujahedeen guerrillas but giving up after a decade, triggering the collapse of the Soviet Union. Soon after the Soviet incursion, the Carter administration began a CIA covert war supporting the Mujahedeen that was continued and increased with the Reagan administration, cynically giving the Soviets "their own Vietnam," as Carter's fanatically anticommunist national security advisor Zbigniew Brzezinski put it in a memo to President Carter.[144] Hatred and animosity toward Russians as a component of the yellow peril was a fundamental aspect of the rabid anticommunism promoted by the US government and embraced nearly universally by the US population. Russiaphobia lessened during the 1990s, when Russia was in chaos due to US and Western European looting, but accelerated in the 2000s with the election of Vladimir Putin. During the 1980s fighting, more than five million Afghan civilians fled to Pakistan and three million to

Iran; even in 2020, Afghans made up the world's second largest refugee population.[145] When the Soviets left in 1989, the Mujahedeen groups battled one another for power, until the Taliban took Kabul in 1996, with the Mujahedeen groups retreating to the mountains, still supported by the CIA. Osama bin Laden, from a wealthy Yemeni family in Saudi Arabia, established Al Qaeda and became a player, leading to the September 11, 2001, terrorist attacks.

Although the United States' initial interest in dominating the Muslim Middle East and the Persian Gulf was control of the vast oil reserves, in the twenty-first century the US became self-sufficient in domestic petroleum reserves and one of the top exporters of oil and gas. It was no longer principally about oil; rather, it was about imperialism and intentionally creating chaos to maintain its dominance and large war budgets. US military interventions, starting with the 1991 Gulf War and coup attempts, some successful, led to hard-line international Muslim resistance with the founding of Al Qaeda in Afghanistan and the Sudan, spawning other Islamicist groups and spreading to the war zones created by the US invasions and occupations of Iraq and the US-led NATO war that destroyed Libya in 2011.[146]

One of the first acts of the Trump administration in early 2017 was to ban Muslim entrance into the United States. Trump signed an executive order that banned foreign nationals from seven predominately Muslim countries from visiting the country for ninety days, as well as suspending entry of all Syrian refugees indefinitely, and prohibited any other refugees from coming into the country for 120 days. Many family members of refugees and immigrants were stuck in transit at major airports. The American Civil Liberties Union immigration attorneys as well as other immigration attorneys and whole law firms crowded into international terminals of major airports to assist the stranded. Trump issued further bans, and in June 2018, the US Supreme Court upheld the ban. The ACLU's Immigrants' Rights Project stated, "This ruling will go down in history as one of the Supreme Court's great failures. It repeats the mistakes of the *Korematsu* decision upholding Japanese-American imprisonment and swallows wholesale government lawyers' flimsy national security excuse for the ban instead of taking seriously the president's own explanation for his action."[147] Upon assuming the presidency in 2021, Joe Biden rescinded the Muslim ban. But historian Elliot Young offers the reminder that in 2021, after nearly two decades, forty Muslim men were still caged in Guantanamo, with only two of them having been convicted.[148]

ASIA IMMIGRATION AFTER 1965

The Hart-Celler Act of 1965 raised the yearly US immigration numbers to 290,000, plus continuing as in the past the non-quota allowance of immediate family members of citizens immigrating. From the Eastern Hemisphere, spanning Europe, Asia, and Africa, 170,000 immigrants were allocated, with a hierarchy of preferences: 8 percent for family members and 20 percent for occupations, with a maximum of 20,000 per country. The Western Hemisphere quota was 120,000, without country- or occupation-specific requirements. The trade union lobby won a requirement that immigrants had to be certified by the US Department of Labor that there were not enough US workers "able, qualified, willing, and available" for the jobs the immigrant would seek. The Department of Labor listed particular professions that were in short supply for which an immigrant could enter without a specific job offer; this included doctors, nurses, and engineers.[149] The latter could and did amount to a brain drain from less developed countries; by 1972, 86 percent of the scientists and engineers and 90 percent of physicians and surgeons who immigrated to the United States were from poor countries.[150] In the wake of the powerful civil rights revolution led by African Americans, the Johnson administration made clear that the new immigration law, in abolishing national origins quotas, "repairs a very deep and painful flaw in the fabric of American justice. It corrects a cruel and enduring wrong in the conduct of the American Nation."[151] One consequence of the new immigration quotas, which included unrestricted family immigration, was a huge growth in Asian immigration. Between 1965 and 2000, the Asian American population grew from less than 1.2 million to nearly 11 million. Asians accounted for two-thirds of immigrant physicians.

In 1960, before the 1965 immigration act, there were only twelve thousand East Indian immigrants living in the United States. By 2015, there were 2.4 million, the second largest immigrant group after Mexicans, making up 6 percent of the 43.3 million foreign born. Forty-eight percent of South Asian Americans were professionals and business people, many in the electronics industry. Congress raised the immigration ceiling in 1990 by 35 percent in response to the 1980s' economic boom, and by the mid-1990s, annual immigration numbers were near a million.[152] Compared with both the immigrant and the native-born population, immigrants from India were more likely to be better educated and working in management positions with higher income. Nearly half obtained permanent residence status through employer sponsorship, while the remainder had immediate relatives in the US.[153]

Immigrants of East Indian descent did not migrate to the United States only from India. British colonialism's practice of forced labor and deportation was the South Asian indenture system. From the 1830s to 1920, more than two million subcontinent Indians were forcibly deported by Britain as indentured workers to labor in its far-flung colonies in Africa, the Caribbean, and the Pacific. With the British Empire's abolition of slavery in 1833, the system expanded, lasting into the 1920s, with indentured worker populations making up near majorities in some colonies and today's independent states—Malaya, Singapore, Burma, Trinidad, Jamaica, Suriname, Guyana, Mauritius, Fiji, South Africa, Uganda, Tanzania, and Kenya—with expulsions in the twentieth century in Uganda and Fiji and marginalization or repression in other states.[154] In 1972, the autocratic Uganda dictator Idi Amin expelled the sixty thousand longtime East Indian residents, most of them Ismaili Muslims, giving them only ninety days until departure. Their homes, businesses, farms, and all assets were seized.[155] Although most resettled in countries of the British Commonwealth, some—mostly professionals—immigrated to the United States.

In an attempt to detract from the continued oppression and exclusion of African Americans, the Nixon administration portrayed Asian Americans as the "model minority."[156] Historian Mae Ngai writes, "The model minority stereotype elides the existence of large numbers of working-class immigrants, undocumented workers, and refugees" reproducing "Asian Americans' foreignness," that could amount to a new version of "yellow peril" breeding new forms of discrimination.[157] Lisa Lowe notes a US national memory that haunts the characterization of Asian Americans, one that has persisted beyond the loosening of immigration restrictions and has been sustained by US wars in Asia, so that Asian Americans are seen as the perpetual immigrants, as the "foreigner-within," not actual citizens.[158] And although European othering of Asians long precedes the virulent and specific US anti-Asian discrimination and exclusion that began in the late nineteenth century, its particularity may stem from already-existing and deep-seated perception of Indians as the enemy. As Chickasaw scholar Jodi Byrd suggests, the supposedly scientific insistence that all Indigenous peoples of the entire Western Hemisphere migrated from Asia through the Bering Strait continents evokes yellow peril immigration of potential enemies.[159]

Wars and forced migrations have been the leitmotif of imperialism since Columbus landed on an island in the Caribbean. Even today, when the immigrant speaks of war as the origin of their Americanization, Viet Thanh Nguyen observes, many US Americans interpret that to mean the difficulties of being new to the country and the horrors of their original country:

> The mythical power of the immigrant story intoxicates. . . . While not all war stories involve immigrants, and while war stories do not scar all immigrants, a vast territory exists where war story and immigrant story overlap. Segregating immigrant story from war story cools the seething histories of strangers who carry troubling memories of American wars, creating in their place narratives filled with damage, wound, and identity. Readers and writers often imagine damage, wound, and identity as the results of cultural conflict, being torn between two worlds, rather than what they often are, the calamitous consequences of war, colonization, and exploitation conducted by foreign forces and domestic tyrants. The conventional immigrant story warms the heart, but the story of the immigrant as the collateral damage of American warfare warrants anger as much as tears.[160]

CHAPTER 8

THE BORDER

Donald Trump began his bid for the presidency in July 2015 by criminalizing Mexicans who attempt to migrate to the United States: "They're bringing drugs. They're bringing crime. They're rapists," which he repeated and expanded upon for the following sixteen months of stadium rallies, promising to build a wall across the entire border, and answered by chants of "Build that wall." However, the steady stream of undocumented families with children, as well as unaccompanied children, crowded at the border crossings seeking asylum, were not Mexican citizens, rather desperate families and children from Honduras, El Salvador, and Guatemala, refugees from dysfunctional governments, drug gang violence, and lack of employment, people running north for their lives and the lives of their children. They were refugees from the chaos and wreckage of the violent 1980s' US counterinsurgency wars and coups in their countries to destroy democratic left movements that were supported by majorities of those populations. But indeed, the refugees, mostly poor Mestizos from El Salvador and Honduras, along with a large number of Mayans from the Guatemalan highlands, were at the US-México border, a surge that began en masse in 2014 during the Obama administration.[1] A Fox News host, tapping into US Mexican-hating, erroneously said that the asylum seekers were from "three Mexican countries."[2] In the years leading up to Trump's campaign, the Mexican immigrant population in the United States shrank by three hundred thousand. By 2016, many more Mexicans in the US had returned to México than the numbers entering the United States, while detentions of undocumented Mexicans were at a forty-year low. México was no longer the top origin country among the most recent immigrants to the US.[3]

MEXICAN HATING

Thanks to his Mexican-hating top aide, Stephen Miller, Donald Trump was aware of the power of historical Mexican hating for attracting and building a white nationalist base.[4] Miller grew up in the 1990s in the affluent white west side of Santa Monica, an oceanside enclave in Los Angeles County. In the larger Los Angeles area, people of Mexican heritage numbered three and a half million out of the nine million population. During Miller's high school years, the Chicano youth organization MEChA (Movimiento Estudiantil Chicano de Aztlán) had an active presence, and he began nourishing a hatred for Mexicans and found mentors to educate him in white nationalist politics.[5] At Trump's stadium rallies, Miller's ideology reverberated as Trump conjured an "invasion" of "animals," raving about the dangers of the Salvadoran American Mara Salvatrucha—the MS-13 gang—whose members, none of whom are Mexican, comprise only 1 percent of all gang members in the entire United States.[6] Clearly, the 46 percent of voters who elected Donald Trump responded to Mexican hating with enthusiasm. With an instable two-thousand-mile border between México and the United States, and a half of US continental territory annexed from México, and with thirty-seven million Mexican Americans making up more than 60 percent of the entire Latino population in the United States and over 11 percent of the total US population, México and Mexicans loom large in the US political world of white supremacy and paranoia.[7]

Influential Harvard political science professor Samuel P. Huntington, who died in 2008, asserted, "The single most immediate and most serious challenge to America's traditional identity comes from the immense and continuing immigration from Latin America."[8] In a book, articles, and frequent public lectures and media interviews, Huntington specialized in demonizing Muslims and Mexicans—using the euphemism "Hispanic"—long before Donald Trump's 2015–2016 stadium speeches naming the same people as enemies and a danger to civilization. But Huntington was no vulgar politician, rather an esteemed Ivy League professor. He served in President Jimmy Carter's liberal administration, tasked with national security. Huntington believed that Latinos were unwilling to assimilate or even learn English, and that their affiliation with Roman Catholicism was a threat to the Protestant order. Huntington was a distinguished professor who is said to be the most quoted source for political science students.

On Sunday, August 3, 2019, Patrick Crusius, a twenty-one-year-old resident of suburban Dallas, Texas, drove 634 miles to the Walmart Supercenter in El Paso and with a WASR-10 rifle —a civilian version of the AK-47—shot and killed twenty-two people and injured twenty-three more, targeting Mexicans. Eight Mexican citizens were among the dead, while most of the others who were dead or injured were US citizens of Mexican descent. The self-identified Mexican-hating murderer wrote a manifesto that he posted on a white nationalist website more than an hour before he started shooting. The four-page manifesto is titled "The Inconvenient Truth," apparently referencing Al Gore's 2007 book and subsequent documentary film *An Inconvenient Truth*, which warned of catastrophic climate change. Under the cover of being concerned about the environment, blaming "Hispanic" immigrants for polluting and causing overpopulation in the US, he revealed his true motive: "This attack is a response to the Hispanic invasion of Texas. They are the instigators, not me. I am simply defending my country from cultural and ethnic replacement brought on by an invasion." This is what white nationalists claim to be a program of "white genocide." He also expressed fear that "Hispanic" voters would turn Texas into a Democratic Party–dominated state as well as making the United States a one-party country with the Democratic Party in power.[9]

As in California, Mexican Americans make up 38 percent of the population in Texas. Crusius appeared unaware that Texas, like California, had been a state of México populated entirely by Mexicans and Indigenous nations until the 1820s when Anglo slaver immigrants began invading, then took over and claimed Texas as an Anglo republic. Then, in 1846–1848, when the US invaded and took the northern half of México, Texas, with its storm-trooping Texas Rangers, became an ethnically cleansed state, reducing the Indigenous and Mexican peoples to minorities. Crusius's ignorance of or indifference to this fact reflects the infamous Texas public educational system in its teaching of state history.

The 2019 El Paso massacre was not the first mass shooting targeting Mexican Americans and Mexican citizens on the border. The July 18, 1984, massacre of Mexican Americans at a McDonald's in the border city of San Ysidro, California, was the largest mass shooting up to that time in the modern era of mass shootings in the United States, with twenty-two left dead, including the shooter, and nineteen wounded. One of the victims was pregnant, and another an eight-month-old baby. Nearly all were Mexican American or Mexican citizens visiting from Tijuana. The killer was a forty-one-year-old Anglo-American man armed with a shotgun and an Uzi. James Oliver Huberty, the shooter, was born and lived most of his life in Ohio. A serial failure at keeping a job or starting a business, he moved to Tijuana, then to San Ysidro a year before the massacre. Back in Ohio, he had been a survivalist hoarder, apparently not with an organized group; he had accumulated an arsenal and also hoarded food and other survival necessities, taking it all along in the move west. He believed government regulations caused his business failures, that international bankers controlled the Federal Reserve, and that communism was taking over, with economic collapse and nuclear war imminent. These were the Reagan years of deindustrialization, workplace shootings, and a widening wealth gap, as well as *Rambo* and burgeoning white power militias.[10]

San Ysidro is located up against the border inside the United States, directly across from Tijuana inside México. Residents of Mexican descent, mostly US citizens, comprise 90 percent of San Ysidro's population. At the time, the border crossing was open day and night to locals on both sides. San Diego is eighteen miles north of San Ysidro, but it took thirty-five minutes for police helicopters and a SWAT team to arrive at the crime scene. From the time the shooting began to when the shooter was gunned down was seventy-eight minutes, during which he fired some 245 rounds. Historian Roberto Hernández, a native of San Ysidro—the backyard of his childhood adjacent to the border—was five years old when the massacre took place, but he remembers the trauma vividly, because his family came close to being among the victims. He and his mother, grandmother, and sister had shopped for groceries and were headed to the McDonald's to buy ice cream for the kids when they recalled they had ice cream at home. The massacre had started by the time they arrived home.[11]

When US Americans talk with fear or hate about "Latinos" or "Hispanics," or that "there are too many of them," they are talking about Mexican Americans, not Cuban Americans or Argentine Americans. And the Mexican American population in the US at thirty-seven million does dwarf all other Latino groups, the second and third largest being Cuban Americans and Salvadoran Americans at over two million each. Importantly, unlike other Latin American nations, there is an ancient connection between Central México and the southeast and southwest, and beyond, of what is now the United States, with migrations, roads, and trade routes. The large Indigenous civilizations of what is now the US originated in central México centuries before the European invasions. In the Cherokee, Muskogee, and Puebloan migrations north, they carried the sacred corn food and the Green Corn Dance with them. The people who became the Nahuatl-speaking Mexica (Aztecs), ultimately ruling Central México, migrated from what is now the US Southwest to Central México, while their relatives who did not migrate, the Hopi people, still reside in the original homeland. The Nahuatl language of the Mexica people was widespread in New México when the Spanish over decades explored it, then invaded and occupied it in 1598.[12] Those centuries of migrations and exchanges prior to European colonization live in the memories and stories of the Indigenous peoples, north and south, who were cut off from one another with Spanish, then British and US colonialisms. Although not enunciated by the Mexican haters in the US, this affinity of north and south threatens the legitimacy of settler colonialism and the artificial border that the United States established and militarized but cannot control. Mexican hating is a form of Indian hating.[13]

"THE BORDER CROSSED US!"[14]

As narrated in chapter 4, the border between the United States and México was redrawn in 1848, at the end of the two-year violent US military invasion, occupation, and annexation of the northern half of México. Anglo intrusions began at the moment of México's independence from Spain following a decade of a massive war of independence. Anglo slavers from Missouri started purchasing land in the gulf and Río Grande area of the Mexican state of Tejas, then declared the independence of Texas as an Anglo republic. Anglo intruders in the New México state of México married into elite New Mexican families, setting the stage for US takeover. US citizens also settled in the Mexican state of California and took the side of the US when it invaded. Although the new border made by war was fixed, it was porous, with little restriction possible. However, Mexican Americans continued to experience settler and official violence in the United States for a half century before the mass migrations north began with the 1910 Mexican Revolution, when 10 percent of the Mexican population crossed the border to the US between 1911 and 1917.

Many people in the US are unaware that thousands of Mexican American men and women were lynched in the former Mexican territory, now the US Southwest, beginning with the gold rush in Northern California and increasingly in Arizona and New México.[15] Violence against Mexicans in Texas dates back to the US slaver settlers who came to dominate the southeast of the Mexican state of Tejas in the 1820s, following Mexican independence from Spain. But it was after the US war against México, annexing the northern half, with Anglo settlers pouring in, that lynching took off. Distinct from the lynching of African Americans, who mostly were individually hung in spectacles with large crowds, Mexican Americans were more often lynched in groups and only occasionally as spectacle. Historians William D. Carrigan and Clive Webb write,

There is little doubt that the unfamiliarity of most Anglos with Mexican culture, especially the Spanish language, made it difficult for them to conduct legal and extralegal investigations. Mobs seeking Mexicans accused of a crime often found it difficult to determine who among a group of Mexicans was guilty of an alleged transgression. Frustrated with the necessity of translation, unable to decide who was really "guilty," and fueled with racist feeling against persons of Mexican descent, Anglo mobs often chose to indiscriminately lynch whole groups of Mexicans.[16]

As Jean Guerrero writes in her biography of Stephen Miller, the abuse has never ended: "Anti-immigrant sentiments remained mainstream. . . . Slurs like 'wetbacks' and 'beaners' were common schoolyard taunts. The word 'Mexican' became an insult."[17] Most Mexicans and Mexican Americans felt pride in their heritage and resented that "Mexican" was pejorative. More affluent Mexican Americans preferred to be called Latin American or Spanish American, which suggested European heritage.[18] In 1929, prominent US citizens of Mexican descent founded the League of United Latin American Citizens (LULAC) and claimed whiteness: "As a matter of absolute record, it was the Latin American who first braved and tamed the Texas wilderness. They were the first white race to inhabit this vast empire of ours."[19] Many young Mexican Americans preferred to call themselves Hispanic or Latino or, in the twenty-first century, Latinx—in the words of Chicano historian Rodolfo F. Acuña, "anything but Mexican."[20]

THE MEXICAN REVOLUTION
AND US INTERVENTION, 1910–1917

Violence against Mexicans soared with great numbers of refugees arriving in the United States during the Mexican Revolution. During the 1913–1914 economic recession, the US immigration commissioner publicly lamented that Mexicans might demand public relief. That became and continues to be a common fear expressed about Mexican immigration. Historian Ricardo Romo wrote, "California nativists found immigrants a prime economic scapegoat." The *Los Angeles Times* warned that providing relief for "uninvited guests" could be costly. "During the period 1913–1918, a Brown hysteria fully as great as that aimed at Communists and other radicals elsewhere, was directed at Mexicans living in Los Angeles." Los Angeles

County supervisors requested the federal government to deport "*cholos* likely to become public charges."[21]

The Mexican Revolution overthrew the thirty-one-year authoritarian reign of Porfirio Díaz, who took power in México in 1877 in a successful military coup. Industrialization and destruction of the peasantry was his agenda, with the full participation of and investments by US corporations, allowing US railroad and mining companies to dominate. Being thrown off the land, the food self-sufficient, mostly Indigenous peasantry was crushed, left landless and starving. Both peasant and elite revolutionary movements developed over three decades and finally ousted Díaz in 1911 in a revolution that would last to 1917. In that period, some two million war refugees fled north across the border.

The Woodrow Wilson administration intervened militarily in the Mexican Revolution on two occasions. In 1914, US troops occupied the gulf port city of Veracruz for seven months. US warships arrived with 502 marines and 285 armed navy sailors who went ashore with orders to capture the customs house and telegraph offices, as well as the railroad terminal and power plant. Local authorities tried to arm the population to resist but lacked supplies for effective defense of the city. They were able to kill four US marines and wound twenty, which led to the US forces expanding the occupation from the port to the whole city. Street fighting ensued, but the US forces took control of the city with more than six thousand troops. The second US intervention came in March 1916, after revolutionary Pancho Villa's army, which was based at Agua Prieto across the border from Douglas, Arizona, had crossed the border three miles into the United States, burning the town of Columbus, New México. The US Army dispatched troops across the border deep into México to search for the elusive Villa and his army of peasants but failed to capture Villa. Wilson also deployed 130,000 national guardsmen and 30,000 troops along the border. Texas Rangers massed in the Lower Rio Grande Valley to patrol the borderlands and suppress revolutionary actions. Vigilantes and state officials acted in concert, using sheer force to enforce a color bar in the labor force and terrorizing Mexicans and Mexican Americans through beatings, torture, shootings, and mass decapitations. Thousands of Mexican

Americans were killed during La Matanza (the period of massacres), and in the Porvenir Massacre of 1919, fifteen men and boys were executed, their corpses left to rot.[22]

THE CONTINGENT STATUS OF MEXICAN WORKERS

The 1882 Chinese Exclusion Act was the first federal immigration law, marking the first time that a particular group was designated as "illegal."[23] Because of the exclusion, many Chinese immigrants entered the US through México, so the US further tightened restrictions at the border. The second law was the Immigration Act of 1917, extending exclusion to all Asians. That law targeting Asians also required an eight-dollar-per-person fee and a literacy test to enter the United States. The impact was immediate, reducing the number of legal immigrants at the border from 295,000 in 1917 to 111,000 in 1918.[24] The draconian 1924 Johnson-Reed National Origins Act limited the number of immigrants allowed entry into the United States through a national origins quota that provided visas to 2 percent of the total number of people of each nationality in the United States as of the 1890 national census. The total number of immigrants allowed entry under the law was 165,000. The total number admitted in 1924 was 162,000, of which 141,000 were from Northern and Western Europe.[25]

There were only 78,000 Mexicans counted in the 1890 US census, but the restrictive quotas did not apply, because a quota exception was made for workers from Western Hemisphere countries, which meant México, as immigration from the other Latin American countries was minimal. This exemption resulted from the political power of the business interests in the western states. The agricultural and mining industries were dependent on Mexican labor, which they preferred precisely because of the absence of the workers' bargaining power at the height of US labor wars. The Mexican workers, supporting large extended families and communities in México, worked cheap and withstood harsh working conditions to keep their jobs. Following the Mexican Revolution with the reform government in power, Mexican authorities attempted to persuade people to stay and work to rebuild war-torn México, but in reality, there were few jobs in México. The 1917 Mexican constitution guaranteed free movement but required work contracts in order to emigrate legally, which were nearly impossible to obtain, so the migrants' exit was usually undocumented, as was their entry into the United States, making them vulnerable to exploitation.[26]

The 1924 immigration law also created the US Border Patrol, housed in the Department of Labor, clearly targeting those crossing the US-México border, at the time seeking to bar the entrance of Chinese. Between 1900 and 1930, some seven hundred thousand Mexican migrants entered the US legally, while many others entered without documents. Most migrants worked seasonally and returned to their villages in México, which growers encouraged. As one California grower put it, after harvest "I will kick them out."[27] And that is exactly what happened on a large scale beginning in 1930. Agribusiness employers in the Southwest preferred Mexican seasonal migrant workers, because at the end of harvest, the workers were on their own, without pay or housing during the winter season. The migrants who chose to stay would relocate to cities where charities or local governments would provide relief during the periods there was no work. This shifted the expenses from employers to the public, which caused resentment, mostly toward the workers. But the caregivers also complained about the employers. The Colorado Catholic Charities director queried, "Why the citizens at large, the Community Chest, the churches, the tax-payers, should have to care for the employees of the sugar companies, the railroads, and mines, between seasons of labor, is not clear to the students of economics or justice."[28] This situation was dubbed the "Mexican problem," which came to encompass other racial resentments against Mexicans.[29]

One aspect of Anglo racism in the Southwest was not wanting their children to go to school with Mexican children. By 1928, segregation of Mexican American children in schools was widespread in California and Texas. In eight California counties, enrollment in sixty-four schools was 90 to 100 percent Mexican American, and in Texas, school boards created forty separate Mexican American schools. In 1930 in the San Diego County town of Lemon Grove, the local school board attempted to construct a segregated school for seventy-five Mexican and Mexican American elementary school children. The Mexican parents organized and took the school board to court and won. The Superior Court of San Diego County ruled that the move violated California state laws because ethnic Mexicans were considered white under the state's Education Code.[30]

This decision is often hailed as the first successful desegregation decision in the United States, preceding the 1954 *Brown v. Board of Education of Topeka*, the hallmark US Supreme Court decision ordering desegregation of all public schools. However, the Lemon Grove decision validated the US racial code that recognized only three "races": Black, white, and yellow. The 1848 Treaty of Guadalupe Hidalgo had guaranteed to Mexicans who remained within the United States after the new border was established "all the rights of citizens of the United States," including the right to vote, hold public office, own land, and testify in court—all the rights of white people. Elite former Mexican citizens were able to enter the Anglo social order. But many of those who were poor or owned little or no property, or who lived in socially segregated barrios, were sometimes classified by federal or state officials as Indian and denied white rights.[31] Yet there was no consistency or institutionalization of Mexicans racially; depending on the place and time, Mexicans were treated as white according to status and skin color.

The federal Census Bureau classified Mexicans as white up to 1930, when it responded to congressional pressure and started enumerating Mexicans as a separate racial group, "Mex," along with "Negro," "Indian," "Chinese," and "Japanese." Outside the Southern states, intermarriage was not illegal but often stigmatized. In many parts of the Midwest and even more in the Southwest, "Whites Only" signs barred Mexicans from public places such as theaters, dance halls, parks, swimming pools, beaches, beauty parlors and barber shops, bowling alleys, restaurants, and even cemeteries. Voter intimidation and workplace discrimination were common. None of these restrictions were sanctioned by law, as was the case for Black people under Jim Crow regimes. But in the Southwest, especially Texas, courts upheld the boundaries more often than they challenged them.[32] The Lemon Grove case was isolated as a local event and set no precedent affecting California or elsewhere; segregation of Mexican and Mexican American children continued in some places to the 1970s. While the Lemon Grove case was in process, forced "repatriation" of Mexicans and Mexican Americans was in full swing.

FROM MEXICAN "REPATRIATION" TO CONTRACT LABOR

The level of Anglo-Mexican hating in the West and Southwest skyrocketed with the onset of the Great Depression that followed the financial crash of 1929, and a twelve-year program of mass deportations ensued. As historian Mae Ngai writes, "As economic insecurities among Euro-Americans inflamed racial hostility toward Mexicans, efforts to deport and repatriate the latter to México grew," not distinguishing between documented immigrants, undocumented migrants, and US citizens of Mexican descent.[33]

Beyond the deportations carried out by the federal Immigration and Naturalization Service (INS), local and state authorities used every means at their disposal to expel Mexicans and Mexican Americans. California municipal governments passed laws restricting relief services and unemployment benefits. Los Angeles and many towns used police forces to block migrants from entering. In 1936, the Colorado governor imposed martial law in the southern counties, allowing officials of the Southern Colorado Military District to turn back Mexican workers trying to enter the state. In El Paso, Texas, Anglo locals demanded that the entry be closed during morning hours to prevent local commuters from the Mexican city of Juarez from walking across the bridge to go to their jobs in El Paso. And all over, local relief agencies gave lists of Mexicans to INS officials for deportation, including legal residents, with Anglos characterizing Mexican immigrants as lazy, dependent, diseased, illiterate, delinquent, and unwilling to assimilate. Sociologist Cybelle Fox observed that "the welfare office quite literally turned into an immigration bureau or became an extralegal arm of the Immigration Service," expelling those Mexicans who were documented or citizens, which the INS could not legally carry out.[34] Local authorities in the Southwest and Midwest forcibly deported some four hundred thousand Mexicans during the early 1930s.[35]

Between 1930 and 1934, dragnets scooped up people in workplaces, parks, and public squares, piling them onto trains headed south, often deep into México. There was abundant support for the mass deportations among Anglos and European immigrants, who were convinced that Mexicans were taking jobs that should be theirs. Social workers did not treat European immigrants living in the Midwest and Northeast in need of assistance as they treated Mexican immigrants.[36] Some two million individuals of Mexican descent were forced out of their homes, work, and communities, at least 1.2 million being naturalized US citizens or US born. Despite proposals, the US government has not apologized for the deportations, nor has any state except California. The California legislature passed the 2005 Apology Act for the 1930s Mexican Repatriation Program, which officially acknowledged "the unconstitutional removal and coerced emigration of United States citizens and legal residents of Mexican descent," and for the "fundamental violations of their basic civil liberties and constitutional rights committed during the period of illegal deportation and coerced emigration."[37] No reparations were attached to the words.

Due to pressure from Southwest agribusiness operators, in 1942, as it prepared for war with Japan, ramping up a war production industry, the United States signed the Mexican Farm Labor Agreement with México. It came to be known as the Bracero Program, the Spanish word *bracero* meaning man who worked with his arms, or manual laborer. The contract program lasted twenty-two years. When it was established, the US promoted it as a wartime emergency to prevent food shortages and high prices. The process began with US employers requesting a particular number of contract workers, then the US State Department could send the request to its Mexican counterpart who would then recruit the workers. The Mexican government was in charge of selecting the workers to be sent and approved only young and landless men whose labor was not needed in their communities, that is, the unemployed and landless. At the border, US-designated personnel met and transported the workers to the work sites. The workers' contracts specified that, in addition to free transportation to and from their work sites, they would receive wages similar to US farmworkers, along with decent living and working conditions. Ten percent of their earnings were to be withheld and deposited in a Mexican bank account to retrieve when they returned home. During the first five years of the program, 219,000 authorized workers participated, scattered over twenty-four states but the majority in California. A third were assigned to railroad companies.[38] None of the guarantees were adhered to in reality.

With the wartime emergency over, the Bracero Program lingered, although the congressional statutory basis for it had expired. In 1947, the Truman administration replaced the government contract system with direct employer recruitment of Mexican workers, assisted by the INS but without the processes required by the legislative program. In fact, the INS arranged legalization of unauthorized Mexican farmworkers. By 1950, the number "legalized" and "paroled" to employers was five times greater than the number recruited from México. The Korean war revived the employers' argument that labor shortages were imminent, and Congress passed a law that gave statutory legitimacy to the Bracero Program until its expiration in 1964. The government was again directly involved in recruitment.[39]

There was general consensus in the 1950s that Mexican contract labor was a government solution to economic and political issues, rather than what Mae Ngai calls "a form of imported colonialism." In 1951, President Harry Truman's Commission on Migratory Labor described seasonal Mexican labor migration as an invasion: "The magnitude of the wetback traffic has reached entirely new levels in the past 7 years. . . . In its newly achieved proportions, it is virtually an invasion."[40] But, the commission presented a rosy view that contract labor would bring order to the agricultural labor market and protect Mexican contract workers from abuse, especially endorsing a widespread belief that contract workers were the "legal successors to the illegal 'wetbacks.' "[41] On the contrary, as Ngai observes, imported contract labor had produced a low-wage regime outside the bounds of federal labor standards and workers' rights. Farm labor wages were 36.1 percent of manufacturing wages, a decline from 47.9 percent in 1946. This was the result of contract and undocumented workers having no legal standing.[42]

MIGRANT WORKERS ORGANIZING

Abuse of Mexican workers was rampant. During the Bracero Program, more undocumented workers entered than those under contract. There was no penalty for employers to hire the undocumented workers, and employers actually preferred them, as they were more vulnerable and could not make demands for higher pay or better conditions or try to form a union. They were criminalized as "illegal aliens." The employers could withhold wages, call the INS, or abuse the workers in any way, knowing they had no legal standing and had families in México dependent on them.[43] Contract workers were also exploited, and they began to organize in unions by 1960. They had a champion in Mexican American scholar and labor organizer Ernesto Galarza. Soon after he received a doctorate from Columbia University, Galarza began organizing Mexican workers in 1947, with a thirty-month strike against the huge DiGiorgio Corporation in the California Central Valley. Between 1948 and 1959, Galarza led the National Agricultural Workers Union in California in organizing more than twenty strikes and other actions, although he eschewed organizing undocumented workers. In 1959, the AFL-CIO contributed funds and assisted in organizing, which led to the 1960s and '70s strikes and boycott successes of the United Farm Workers.[44]

In the Pacific Northwest, living conditions were unsanitary or nonexistent. In 1943, in Grants Pass, Oregon, some five hundred Mexican contract workers became sick from food poisoning. Poor quality food persisted into 1945 until the Mexican government intervened. Lack of food, poor living conditions, discrimination, and exploitation led braceros to become active in strikes and to successfully negotiate their contract terms.[45] Mexican contract workers were discriminated against and exploited all over the Pacific Northwest, and they organized to improve conditions and wages in the work camps. During the first two years of the Bracero Program, the workers organized over twenty actions. They would load harvest sacks with rocks to increase their pay.[46] The workers timed their actions strategically, holding work stoppages at the height of harvest or in cold weather.[47] Workers were aware that their work was needed and that the employers would prefer negotiation over deporting them, especially at harvest time, because of the time and expense associated with the Bracero Program.[48]

After years of struggle and lobbying, finally Galarza and other union activists were able to bring the Bracero Program to an end in 1964. Up to that time, some 4.6 million contract workers' visas had been issued, with an average of around two hundred thousand a year. During the same period, the INS deported 5.5 million unauthorized Mexican workers, averaging around a half million a year, and then there was the 1954 "Operation Wetback."[49]

"ALL THEY WILL CALL YOU . . . DEPORTEE"

On February 3, 1948, the folk music artist Woody Guthrie penned a poem he titled "Los Gatos Plane Wreck," familiar to most people as the Pete Seeger song that was put to music by Martin Hoffman a decade later. Guthrie was unable to set it to music or record or perform the poem, as his mental health was declining from Huntington's disease. The haunting poem tells of the crash of an airplane on January 28, 1948, in Los Gatos Canyon, near the town of Coalinga, California, that was carrying twenty-eight undocumented Mexican farmworkers being deported to México during the Bracero Program. In news reports, the names of the four Anglo pilots and flight attendants were released, but the deportees were not named. Woody Guthrie gave them names he created—Juan, Rosalita, Jesus, Maria—decrying the dehumanization of calling them only deportees.

In 2010, award-winning poet and writer Tim Z. Hernandez, who grew up a child of Mexican farmworkers in the San Joaquin Valley of California, happened on an old news article about the tragic crash. He realized it was the event that Woody Guthrie had written a song about and that Pete Seeger had recorded, and he began listening to the many recordings of it, haunted by the song and the ghosts with no names. He was troubled that the deportees remained nameless and began researching, intent on finding out who these individuals were. Hernandez was able to identify all twenty-eight passengers and proceeded to search for the families of the deceased. He had found seven at the time his book *All They Will Call You* was published in 2017, and soon he found five more families as he continued to search. Hernandez also raised money, and with the cooperation of the Fresno, California diocese and Holy Cross Cemetery, they installed a memorial headstone listing the names of all the passengers. The bodies of the victims had been buried there in a mass grave, and the cemetery catalogue had listed each in the name column as "Mexican National."[50]

Tim Z. Hernandez's project reveals the longtime and continuing cruelty of US immigration policies at the border and of mass deportations. The twenty-eight deportees killed in the plane crash were among the estimated four hundred thousand deported mostly by trains in the preceding year. The US Justice Department took no responsibility for identifying the crash victims or compensating their families; rather, the department emitted a terse disclaimer: "No liability attaches to the government in connection with the Coalinga accident."[51] Deportations of Mexican workers took place constantly during the Bracero Program. Five years after the Los Gatos plane crash, one of the largest deportations in a two-year time span was carried out, with the official name "Operation Wetback." It had aspects of a showpiece intended to placate the Mexican-hating public and to give the appearance that the US government was successfully expelling Mexicans, while employers demanded more Mexican workers.

"OPERATION WETBACK"

The original idea for such an operation came from a dubious figure, Harlon B. Carter, the head of the US Border Patrol. His plan was to use the US military to round up and deport undocumented Mexicans. He titled it Operation Cloudburst and was able to get it to President Eisenhower, who considered it but turned it down due to the Posse Comitatus Act, which generally prohibits military use to enforce domestic law. Although Eisenhower didn't accept Carter's plan, it planted the idea that soon became "Operation Wetback," which Carter was appointed to lead on the border.

Carter was a convicted murderer before he became a border guard. He was born in 1931 in Laredo, Texas, where his father was a border guard. When he was seventeen, Carter shot and killed a Mexican American teenager, Ramón Casiano. Carter was angry that Casiano and some friends were talking outside his home, so when they left, he grabbed a shotgun and went after them, shooting Casiano in the chest. Carter was convicted of murder and sentenced to three years, but the sentence was overturned on a technicality, and he served less time.[52] Carter went on to graduate from the University of Texas and from law school at Emory University, then joined the US Border Patrol. He commanded the border patrol from 1950 to 1958, then directed the Immigration and Naturalization Service Southwest region until he retired in 1970. A member of the National Rifle Association, he joined its national board in 1951, then was NRA president from 1965 to 1967. He remained active and influential in NRA affairs. After retiring from the Border Patrol in 1970, Carter moved to eastern Washington State, bordering western Idaho, a region that was developing as a hub for the burgeoning white nationalist movement. There, Carter founded the Second Amendment Foundation in 1974, along with a lobbying arm, the Citizens Committee for the Right to Keep and Bear Arms. At the 1977 convention of the National Rifle Association, Carter and like-minded radicals were able to seize leadership in the NRA, with Carter serving as executive vice president until 1985. The post of executive vice president was the NRA's central operating position, and during Carter's eight-year tenure, membership tripled to three million and the annual budget grew hugely to $66 million. It was during this period that the NRA became the house of the Second Amendment and a white nationalist organization.[53]

With a Mexican-killing white nationalist in charge of the border and of "Operation Wetback," the Eisenhower administration installed a new commissioner general of the INS, Joseph M. Swing. Swing was a retired army general and former West Point classmate of Eisenhower. In May 1954, the US attorney general, Swing, and Harlon Carter issued a press release announcing "Operation Wetback." They executed their task aggressively, military style. Swing saw the undocumented Mexican workers' presence as "an actual invasion of the United States" and viewed the operation as an attack "upon the hordes of aliens facing us across the border." Carter told the *Los Angeles Times* that "an army of Border Patrol officers complete with jeeps, trucks, and seven aircraft" planned "all-out war to hurl . . . Mexican wetbacks back into México."[54] The highly publicized threats and rhetoric of military-like attacks spread panic throughout Mexican immigrant communities in the Southwestern states. Deportations had been climbing, from over ten thousand expulsions in 1942, when the Bracero Program began, to over nine hundred thousand in 1953. Swing and Carter were threatening many more, and the Border Patrol proceeded to convert public parks to concentration camps to hold a thousand or more people at a time.[55]

The operation was launched on June 10, 1954, with Border Patrol officers installing checkpoints across Southern California and western Arizona. During the days that followed, border guards apprehended around eleven thousand undocumented Mexicans, and by June 30, twenty-two thousand more. Then for several months, the Border Patrol forces swept through California, Arizona, Texas, Chicago, and the Mississippi Delta, raiding farms, restaurants, and Mexican communities. Everywhere the Border Patrol went, reporters thronged, broadcasting stories of roundups, detentions, and deportations.[56] The operation involved 750 INS officers, including Border Patrol and investigators; three hundred jeeps, cars, and buses; and seven airplanes.[57] Swing explained that "planes were used to locate wetbacks and to direct ground teams working in jeeps. Transport planes, trucks, and buses were used to convoy the arrested aliens to staging areas, and in order to discourage reentry, moved many far into the interior of México by train and ship." More than 30 percent of those deported were herded into hired cargo ships at Port Isabel, Texas, and shipped to Veracruz. A congressional investigation described one vessel, where a riot had taken place on board, as an "eighteenth century slave ship." Eighty-eight Mexican workers died of sunstroke in a roundup that was carried out in 112-degree heat. At Nuevo Laredo, on the Mexican side of the west end of the Texas border, a Mexican labor leader reported that the deportees were "brought in like cows" on trucks and unloaded fifteen miles down the highway from the border in the desert.[58]

By official government accounts, "Operation Wetback" apprehended three thousand undocumented workers a day and around
170,000 total during the first three months. In all, 801,069 Mexican migrants were reported to have been deported. In October 1954,
Swing declared that the operation had forced more than a million
Mexicans deep into México. However, historian Kelly Lytle Hernandez clarifies that although the treatment of the detained and
deported Mexican workers was brutal and hundreds of thousands
were deported, the actual number was likely closer to three hundred
thousand. "Operation Wetback" is often cited as the event that led
to mass deportations and more rigid border enforcement, but that
was not the case. Nor did it reduce the number of undocumented
Mexicans in the US, and it did not end unauthorized entry at the
border. Rather, after "Operation Wetback" ended, the Border Patrol deescalated, dispatching two-men patrols on foot or horseback.
Hernandez writes, "In other words, after General Swing declared
'conquest' at the border, he kept apprehensions low at the U.S.-
México border by changing patrol tactics."[59]

Miserable as it was for the Mexicans who were deported and the
communities affected, "Operation Wetback" was a cynical show for
the public, because agribusiness and mining giants demanded the
workers.

IMMIGRATION REFORM
AND THE UNITED FARM WORKERS

In the wake of the anti-racist civil rights movement, on October 3,
1965, President Lyndon Johnson signed the Hart-Celler Act in a
ceremony at the foot of the Statue of Liberty. He intoned that abolishing national quotas would "repair a very deep and painful flaw
in the fabric of American justice. It corrects a cruel and enduring
wrong in the conduct of the American Nation." He claimed that the
new law "says simply that from this day forth those wishing to immigrate to America shall be admitted on the basis of their skills and
their close relationship to those already here."[60] The law was lauded
by the liberal establishment, the *New York Times* editorializing that

it was a major reform that put all countries on an equal footing, removing race and Western European preference. Unmentioned in the president's speech and celebrations of the new immigration law was the quota on Western Hemisphere immigration of 120,000 annually. Immediately, more than a half million undocumented Mexican workers had no legal avenue to change their status, so were increasingly vilified as "illegal aliens." The law actually imposed quotas that had not existed before.

In the early 1960s, authorized Mexican migration comprised around two hundred thousand contract workers and thirty-five thousand regular admissions. Unsurprisingly, deportations of undocumented Mexicans increased by 40 percent in 1968, to 151,000.[61] Nicholas De Genova observes, "These enforcement proclivities and prerogatives, and the statistics they produce, have made an extraordinary contribution to the commonplace fallacy insinuating that Mexicans account for virtually all 'illegal aliens,' have served to stage the U.S.-México border as the theatre of an enforcement 'crisis,' and have rendered 'Mexican' as the distinctive national/racialized name for migrant 'illegality.' "[62] And it only got worse in 1976, when Congress amended the Hart-Celler Act, limiting México to twenty thousand immigrant visas annually and allowing only limited family reunification. In 1980, with the passage of the Refugee Act of 1980, the visa limit fell to 18,200. Between 1965 and 1986, there were twenty-eight million undocumented Mexican entries into the US and 23.4 million exits.[63]

This was the legal and policy setting in which the United Farm Workers (UFW) union was founded—first as the National Farm Workers Association (NFWA)—in 1962, by César Chávez and Dolores Huerta. Up until that time, both Chávez and Huerta, who were from middle-class Mexican American families, had been organizers with the Community Service Organization, founded by Fred Ross Sr. during the Depression era.[64] From the beginning in 1962, Chávez, like Galarza before him, lobbied for strict control of the US-México border, arguing that a mass of noncitizen and politically powerless workers would make it difficult to recruit US citizens to the union. They also viewed undocumented Mexican workers as strikebreakers. The UFW maintained that stance in its early years, even reporting undocumented workers to the immigration service. But by 1974, important Chicano support organizations were openly criticizing the stance, making newspaper headlines. It came to a crisis when Attorney General William B. Saxbe announced that the Justice Department would deport a million "illegal aliens" and claimed to have the full support of the UFW. The UFW backed off the stance, and Chávez wrote a letter, published in the *San Francisco Examiner*, denying Saxbe's claim, writing that "illegal aliens are doubly exploited, first because they are farm workers, and second because they are powerless to defend their own interests. . . . If there were no illegals being used to break our strikes, we could win those strikes overnight and then be in a position to improve the living and working conditions of all farm workers." But he promised that the United Farm Workers would support legalization for the undocumented, "our brothers and sisters." By the late 1970s, Chávez's views had changed, and he was advocating the legalization of undocumented immigrants and encouraged their inclusion in the union movement.[65]

The United Farm Workers' achievements in the 1960s went beyond any previous effort to bring dignity, safety, and fair pay to farmworkers in California, which by then was the bread basket of the world. In 1966, the UFW's collective bargaining agreement with growers was the first such agreement in the continental United States. The first union contracts required clothing to protect the workers from pesticides and banned pesticide spraying when workers were in the fields, plus banning DDT and other dangerous pesticides and requiring scheduled monitoring. Rest periods, hand-washing facilities, and clean drinking water were required in the fields. Union contracts replaced labor contractors with union hiring halls, guaranteeing workers' seniority rights and job security. A comprehensive health plan, a credit union, and pension plan were included in the contracts. The crippling short-handled hoe was abolished. State unemployment, disability, and workers' compensation were extended to farmworkers, as well as public assistance and amnesty rights. The contracts required regulation of the sanitary and safety conditions in farm labor camps, and banned discrimination in employment and sexual harassment of women farmworkers. The UFW also established in 1966 a nonprofit farmworkers service center separate from the union that operated three radio stations run by farmworkers and built single-family homes and rental complexes for low-income farmworkers and other rural residents.[66]

Since the US invasion and annexation of what is now the US Southwest, throughout a long history of discrimination, deportations, and hardships, the majority of Mexican people, whether citizens, immigrants, or undocumented, were vulnerable with little institutional support. They survived by developing communities of mutual assistance—cultural, economic, medical, education, legal. Mexican mutual aid societies began among those Mexican citizens living in the annexed states, as well as in México itself. As Mexicans entered the US in greater numbers after 1910, they brought mutual aid societies with them. Historian Julie Leininger Pycior observes that this mutual assistance continues in the twenty-first century at many levels.[67] One example is the sacrifices Mexican workers in the United States make in sending a part of their earnings back to their families and villages in México. Even during the 2020 pandemic, such remittances actually increased. In August 2020, they amounted to $3.57 billion, baffling US economists who predicted an extreme decrease, underestimating the strength of the human networks between Mexican migrants in the US and their families and communities back home.[68] Mexican Americans built organizations and institutions that benefited all migrants, immigrants, and refugees, such as the National Network for Immigrant and Refugee Rights (NNIRR), the National Council of the Raza, and many others.[69]

FROM REAGAN'S 1986
IMMIGRATION REFORM TO NAFTA

At the end of the US wars in Southeast Asia in 1975, along with a perceived energy crisis, a right-wing backlash paralleled a disappearance of not only anti-war and anti-imperialist protests on campuses and on the streets but also the media, which turned away from covering continuing protests for women's and gay rights and racial justice. At the same time, right-wing nationalists developed think tanks and strategy for reversing the gains of the civil rights, women's, and

LGBTQ movements, gaining traction with the burgeoning conservative evangelical movement's opposition to women's reproductive rights. These social developments resulted in the rise of Ronald Reagan and the Republican Party's "Southern strategy" of blatant white supremacy and demonization of unions, combined with exporting production for cheap labor, resulting in deindustrialization.

Unsurprisingly, a new wave of anti-Mexican panic broke out that resulted in the Immigration Reform and Control Act of 1986 (IRCA), authored by Wyoming Republican senator Alan Simpson and Representative Pete Rodino, Democrat of New Jersey.[70] Mexican American civil rights groups, along with immigration advocates, lobbied for and won a form of amnesty that allowed access to legalization for nearly three million undocumented immigrants, the majority being Mexican. Organized labor lobbied for employer sanctions, so that in the legislation any employer with more than three workers was required to check and verify immigrant status of their employees and was subject to fines for hiring undocumented workers. The Immigration and Naturalization Service budget was increased by 50 percent, and the Labor Department's by nearly that amount for the purpose of document verification and work-site inspections.

These requirements were easy for employers to circumvent, and INS inspections were a farce. The most egregious part of the legislation was the ramping up of border control, consuming 90 percent of the INS budget, while only 10 percent was designated for workplace verification and employer sanctions. With increasingly harsh interdiction, undocumented workers were not able to continue their seasonal migrations and had to stay living in the shadows, with the threat of deportation and no return possible. New immigration laws were enacted during the Clinton administration under the guise of welfare reform. The Illegal Immigration Reform and Immigrant Responsibility Act (IIRIRA) gave the Border Patrol the power to admit, detain, and deport without judicial review any person arriving at the nation's border, which applied also to refugees and asylum seekers.[71]

The North American Free Trade Agreement (NAFTA), which created a trading bloc between the United States, Canada, and México, went into effect during the Clinton administration on January 1, 1994. On that New Year's Day, the world woke to find televised images of an army of around three thousand masked Tzeltzal Mayans, armed with a few old rifles, the rest mostly symbolic wooden ones, occupying six municipalities in the Mexican state of Chiapas, including San Cristóbal de las Casas. The EZLN—Zapatista Army of National Liberation—had formed in 1983 and organized the Mayan villages clandestinely for a decade. They had come out of hiding to protest, on behalf of all Indigenous peoples and small farmers of México, the NAFTA measure that changed Article 27 of the 1918 Mexican constitution to allow the influx of cheap corn from the US commercial corn industry, which would destroy the self-sufficient livelihood of small farmers, who were mostly Indigenous.[72] NAFTA soon wiped out subsistent farmers and commercial operators in México as they could not compete with the cheap, GMO-modified corn from Iowa that was mainly producing ethanol and animal feed.[73]

The negotiations that produced NAFTA began in the first Reagan administration, continued with George H. W. Bush's administration, and was sealed a year after Bill Clinton took office. Important elements of the Democratic Party's constituents opposed NAFTA, including the AFL-CIO, the Congressional Black Caucus, and environmentalists. Historian Greg Grandin writes, "Clinton was Reagan's greatest achievement. He carried forward the Republican agenda. . . . NAFTA, though, represents the clearest and most consequential throughline."[74] NAFTA allowed unrestricted passage of goods and investments over the border but did not grant the same to workers, who were not even mentioned in the agreement. With farmers in every part of México thrown off the land, undocumented migration from deep within southern México soared. Grandin writes, "Rapid militarization of the border . . . took place exactly at the moment NAFTA went into effect. . . . The Clinton administration knew that NAFTA would lead to a spike in undocumented migration, and planned accordingly. It significantly increased the budget and staff of the border patrol, supplied it with ever more technologically advanced equipment. . . . A substantial length of what the administration didn't want to admit was a wall was built." The wall forced desperate migrants to take extremely dangerous routes, the Border Patrol in 1998 reporting nearly seven thousand known deaths, the estimate a fraction of the actual toll.[75]

POST 9/11 IMMIGRATION

In the wake of NAFTA, which opened the border to trade, three harsh laws were enacted in 1996. The Illegal Immigration Reform and Immigrant Responsibility Act gave the Border Patrol authority to admit, detain, and deport any arrival at the border without judicial review, and included refugees and asylum seekers as well. The Personal Responsibility and Work Opportunity Reconciliation Act was primarily a part of the Clinton welfare reform, but it also included immigrant provisions.[76] The Antiterrorism and Effective Death Penalty Act required mandatory detention of noncitizens awaiting a decision as to whether they were deportable and indefinite detention of noncitizens ordered removed to countries that would not accept them. INS detention increased from 8,500 in 1996 to nearly 16,000 in 1998.[77] It also severely restricted "the constitutional rights and judicial resources traditionally afforded to legal resident aliens," as it authorized local police to enforce immigration laws.[78] And that was five years before the "War on Terror" was declared.

On October 26, 2001, President George W. Bush signed the USA Patriot Act that enveloped all immigrants, tightening border controls. It allowed the monitoring of all private communications that originated in a foreign country and authorized the blocking of all suspected terrorists from entering the country and the deportation of anyone suspected of terrorism who lived in the US, even with valid documents. The following spring the Enhanced Border Security and Visa Entry Reform Act was signed, and President Bush ordered the INS to share all its "alien" data with the State Department. It also funded the hiring of 1,600 additional INS agents. In November 2002, the Department of Homeland Security was established, which unified twenty-two federal departments and agencies, including the INS, the name of which was changed to Immigration and Customs Enforcement (ICE). The 2005 Real ID Act established federal information standards for all state drivers' licenses and ID cards; it changed visa limits for temporary workers, tightened laws of asylum and the deportation of terrorists, and funded the construction of a fourteen-mile border wall across San Diego County in California. ICE undertook Operation Frontline in 2004–2005, to deport undocumented immigrants who were considered national security threats. ICE sweeps during the Bush administration netted 8.3 million "voluntary returns." Undocumented Mexican immigrants who were caught in the sweeps were transported to the border without fingerprinting or paperwork. There were two million formal deportations during the period.[79]

In late 2005, Congress passed the Border Protection, Antiterrorism, and Illegal Immigration Control Act of 2005 (H.R. 4437), a bill that required more stringent employment verification and sought funding for a seven-hundred-mile border fence. But most onerous were proposed penalties for entering the country without documents, including a ten-year minimum sentence for entry with forged documentation and the criminalization of anyone who helped undocumented immigrants, even by providing water and food or teaching English. Immigrants arrested for drunk driving were to be deported. All undocumented entries were classified as aggravated felonies subject to extended detention. In March 2006, a half million people protested the legislation in Chicago, and a few days later a million protested in Los Angeles, along with many other cities across the country. A powerful movement emerged, bringing together immigrant and labor organizations with religious and civil rights leaders and legal aid and immigrant rights advocates. They organized the National Day of Action for Immigrant Social Justice in April 2006, with marches and rallies in over sixty cities. This led to the May Day 2006, "A Day Without an Immigrant" rally, which brought out massive crowds, primarily Mexican workers.[80]

During Barack Obama's two-term presidency, deportations increased with his "zero tolerance" policy, with 2.1 million "voluntary" returns and three million removals, earning him the nickname "Deporter in Chief." His justification was to demonstrate that the US-México border was secure in order to push Congress to enact comprehensive immigration reform, which never happened.[81] Many Mexicans had returned home during the 2008 recession and few were entering the US. Before the recession, the undocumented Mexican population was approximately 6.9 million, and by 2015 it had decreased to 5.6 million.[82] When Donald Trump began his campaign for the presidency, warning of masses of Mexicans entering the US illegally, they were actually leaving. The "Dream Act," which would allow undocumented immigrants who were brought as children to the US a path to citizenship, began circulating in Congress in 2001 and through both the Bush and Obama administrations. With no action from Congress, in 2012 President Obama introduced the Deferred Action for Childhood Arrivals (DACA) program, which stopped the deportation of immigrants who fit certain criteria. If applicants would graduate from a community college, or study two years toward a four-year university degree, or serve in the military for two years, they could be granted permanent resident status. In 2017, the Trump administration rescinded the program. New versions of the Dream Act circulated in Congress without resolution, while an impressive movement of DACA applicants organized, garnering considerable public support.[83] On his first day in office, President Joe Biden reinstated the DACA program.[84]

THE CHICANO MOVEMENT

Student activism in the 1960s opened a dynamic new front in the defense of Mexican Americans. At the height of the successes of the United Farm Workers movement in the 1960s, with the increasing participation of a generation of Mexican American students along with the example of the Black Power movement, the Puerto Rican independence movement, and the American Indian Movement, the Chicano movement and identity surged in 1968 and quickly spread throughout the Southwest and the entire country. Chicano students founded the Movimiento Estudiantil Chicano de Aztlán (MEChA). In 1968, Chicanos formed CASA, the Centros de Acción Social Autónomos, which counted several thousand dues-paying members in the Los Angeles area who, along with many volunteers and activists, provided some sixty thousand undocumented people with legal aid as well as food and shelter. They also developed links with the Left in México. Their newspaper, *Sin Fronteras* (Without Borders), was widely distributed.[85] CASA was also a training ground for union organizers, immigration lawyers, and future political leaders in California.[86] Also in 1968, the first

Chicano studies program was established at the University of California, Los Angeles as a research and publication center and later became a full academic department, the UCLA César E. Chávez Department of Chicana/o and Central American Studies. Under various names, university programs and departments were established all over the Southwest.[87] The extraordinary 1970 anti-war march in Los Angeles, the Chicano Moratorium, led by the Chicano organization Brown Berets and which drew thirty thousand participants, was described by historian Lorena Oropeza as "one of the largest assemblages of Mexican Americans ever."[88]

The idea of Chicano/a was embraced enthusiastically by Mexican American public school students and barrio youth. Many young people from Central American immigrant families joined the Chicano movement in California. Embedded in the new moniker was a particular mindset. Most who identified as Chicanos were born in the United States, and either did not speak Spanish or spoke very little. Many Mexican parents, in an attempt to protect their children, had not encouraged them to learn Spanish. These young people rejected earlier generations' attempts to assimilate and be accepted as white.[89] Instead, they proudly embraced their mestizo ancestry and promoted the Spanish language. They called for community control of institutions and self-determination, indeed revolution. They identified with the working class and poor people, the farmworkers movement, and with Emiliano Zapata and the women soldiers of the Mexican Revolution.

Chicanos identified the greater Southwest—Aztlán—as their homeland, as was discussed in chapter 4. They adopted Aztec iconography, dances, and ceremonies and did not specify territorial rights. The inchoate idea of a Southwest homeland took dubious form with the establishment of the August 29 Movement (ATM), founded in 1974. The organization held that Chicanos constituted an oppressed nation that had been annexed by the United States and had the right to independence.[90] Four years after its founding, ATM merged with the Asian American organization Wor Kuen and formed the League of Revolutionary Struggle (LRS), which lasted until 1990. Part of the LRS joined the Freedom Road Socialist Organization (FRSO) in 1994. The FRSO split but continues to exist and endorses the Chicano nation claim in the Southwest, including "the right to self-determination, up to and including independence from the United States."[91] The majority of FRSO members formed a new organization, Liberation Road, which does not claim Indigenous territories although their program states, "The Chicano-Mexicano people in the Southwest and California are an oppressed nation."[92] The territory that some Chicanos claim for the Chicano nation overlaps the ancient homelands and contemporary federal reservations of the Navajo, Apache, Ute, and Pueblo Nations. This is similar to but distinct from the Hispano self-indigenization discussed in chapter 4.

During the first few years of Chicano formation of organizations and leadership in Colorado, Texas, and Southern California, the movement did not deal primarily with immigration or border issues, but they did strongly support the farmworkers' movement and attempt to organize unions.[93] That changed with the increase in undocumented immigration countered by Anglo nativism and INS repression. In the late 1970s, Chicano activists were inspired by and supported the Sandinistas (FSLN) in Nicaragua, and some Chicanos volunteered during the insurgency that led to the 1979 victory.[94] They also supported the revolutionary movements in Guatemala and El Salvador and the war refugees who were turned away at the border and forced to enter illegally.

US INVASIONS, OCCUPATIONS, WARS, AND COVERT OPERATIONS IN CENTRAL AMERICA

The ignorant Fox News host who identified El Salvador, Honduras, and Guatemala as "three Mexican countries" was unintentionally not that far off. The Mayan nation extends south from Yucatan, Chiapas, and Quintana Roo in México across borders to Guatemala and Honduras, while many of the Nahua-speaking farmers of central México migrated as far as western El Salvador, Honduras, and Nicaragua long before the European invasions. These states are specific and particular with varied historical trajectories, linked, however, since their independence from Spain by an intruder in common, the United States.

Before there were the independent states of El Salvador, Guatemala, Honduras, and Nicaragua, there was the Federal Republic of Central America that also included Costa Rica and what is now the southern Mexican state of Chiapas. Panama was not a part of Central America but rather was a province of Colombia. When the US determined that the interoceanic canal should go through the Panama province, the Republic of Colombia refused, so the US incited a secessionist movement and recognized Panama as an independent state in November 1903. The Central American Republic, with its capital in Guatemala City, existed from 1823 to 1841. In December 1823, President James Monroe, in the annual message to Congress, included what came to be known as the Monroe Doctrine, which officially established US intentions to dominate the newly independent Central and South American nations, stating "that the American continents . . . are henceforth not to be considered as subjects for future colonization by any European powers."[95] Since independence, the United States has never allowed Central Americans to pursue their own destiny. With its foothold of British Honduras (now Belize) as a colony and indirect economic control of eastern Honduras and Nicaragua (the Mosquitia), British imperialism, through unequal trade in Central America after its independence, paved the way for US economic dominance and military interventions. The Federal Republic of Central America did not survive British imperialism, and the small separate states, governed by elites of two warring parties and reliant on mono-agribusiness—bananas and coffee—owned by foreign companies, were too weak to defend their countries from the predatory Great Britain and United States.[96]

In 1849, the gold rush brought hordes of gold seekers from Nicaragua's Caribbean coast to the Pacific and north to San Francisco, a scheme established by the US shipping and railroad tycoon Cornelius Vanderbilt. Already, the US aspired to dig an interoceanic canal through Nicaragua, and this was the possible route.[97] Under the guise of protecting US lives and interests during political disturbances, in March 1853, US Marines landed on the Caribbean coast of Nicaragua for two days, and in July 1854, US naval forces bombed and burned San Juan del Norte on the Nicaraguan coast over a period of nearly a week.[98] US pro-expansionist

William Walker, under the banner of manifest destiny, believed Central America was destined to be the key to global trade and should be annexed by the United States. In April 1855, Walker and fifty-seven mercenaries (called *filibusters* at the time) sailed from San Francisco to Nicaragua to support one side in an ongoing civil war, but within a few months the mercenaries seized control of the country with a plan to make it a white settler country, introducing slavery, with Walker as president. President Franklin Pierce recognized the regime as legitimate. The other Central American countries combined their armies, with support from South American states as well, and forced Walker out in May 1857, executing him in a firing squad.[99] Although Walker's plan failed, it was a dress rehearsal for longer official US occupations and military interventions. After sending troops to eastern Nicaragua for varying lengths of time in 1894, 1896, 1898, 1899, 1907, and 1910, the US occupied Nicaragua from 1912 to 1933, leaving once the first Somoza family dictatorship was installed and ruled for more than four decades. During the same time frame, the US invaded and occupied Haiti from 1914 to 1934, with a reign of torture, murder, and forced labor that left some fifteen thousand Haitians dead. In 1954, the US Central Intelligence Agency recruited, trained, armed, and financed a mercenary army to overthrow the democratically elected president of Guatemala, Jacobo Árbenz.[100]

The 1980s Reagan administration enacted its campaign to overthrow the popular 1979 Nicaragua revolution, which had ousted the US-backed dictator Anastasio Somoza. The leftist Sandinista National Liberation Front (FSLN) established democratic institutions that had not existed in Nicaraguan history since its independence from Spain, implementing democratic socialism, a mixed economy, land distribution to landless peasants, and widespread literacy, while the US mounted a brutal counterrevolution.[101] The Contra war, using neighboring Honduras as a base, turned that impoverished country into a stationary US battleship overrun with armed militias and right-wing evangelicals from the United States to assist the Contras.[102] In order to illegally transport arms to the Contras, the CIA collaborated with the drug kingpin of Honduras that owned an airline, its flights returning from the US with arms. In El Salvador, an armed socialist movement (FMLN) was attempting to take political power and was met with US-backed counterinsurgency and death squads.[103] In Guatemala, the US supported a repressive military dictatorship against a resistance that had been fighting for nearly three decades to restore democracy since the US overthrew their democratic government to protect the United Fruit Company.[104] With resistance suppressed, the Sandinistas voted out of power, and the collapse of the Soviet Union removing the motive of anticommunism for intervention, the US abandoned war-torn Central America and turned to invading Iraq in 1991. The body count from Reagan's wars in Central America was horrendous, with sixty-five thousand dead in El Salvador, fifty thousand in Nicaragua, and more than two hundred thousand in Guatemala, the majority rural Mayans.

Between 1981 and 1990, some one million refugees from El Salvador and Guatemala crossed the México-US border, fleeing the violence in their countries. By 1982, some two hundred thousand to three hundred thousand refugees from El Salvador—a country of only five million people—and tens of thousands of Guatemalans had fled to the US. Under the 1980 Refugee Act and international law, they had the right to asylum, but the migrants' applications were turned down, while there was no limit on those claiming asylum from socialist Cuba and Nicaragua, or the European socialist states.[105] The Reagan administration categorized the refugees as "economic migrants," maintaining that the Salvadoran and Guatemalan governments had not violated their human rights. The administration only increased deportation. Of more than six thousand asylum petitions in 1981, 154 were considered and only two granted, while a thousand were deported. By 1986, around fifty thousand people had been forced to return, and some did not survive the military regimes in their home countries.[106]

Consequently, approval rates for asylum were less than 3 percent in 1984, while in the same year approval rates for Iranians was 60 percent and 40 percent for Afghans fleeing the Soviet military intervention. The Salvadoran and Guatemalan refugees were detained at the border and herded into crowded detention centers, then pressured to agree to "voluntary return" to their countries. Thousands were deported without having legal counsel. With pressure from US support groups, in 1983, eighty-nine members of Congress requested that the attorney general and the Department of State grant "extended voluntary departure" to Salvadorans who had fled the war, but their request was denied, the Reagan administration stating that such a grant would be a "magnet" for more undocumented Salvadorans. In the late 1980s, the Democratic-controlled House of Representatives passed bills to suspend deportations, but none passed the Senate.[107] A coalition of dozens of local, regional, and national civil society organizations, along with both Catholic and Protestant religious figures and parishioners, opposed the US interventions in Central America with marches, petitions, delegations, and lobbying Congress. Thousands more provided assistance and sanctuary to the refugees arriving in the United States.

In 1980, a network of religious congregations formed the Sanctuary Movement, starting in Tucson, Arizona, on the border. At its height in the mid-1980s, over 150 congregations openly defied the government and publicly sponsored and supported undocumented Salvadoran and Guatemalan refugee families. Another thousand local Christian and Jewish congregations endorsed sanctuary. The movement coordinated with the many activists in México to smuggle refugees across the border, providing legal and humanitarian assistance to the refugees. The Department of Justice initiated criminal prosecution against two Texas activists in 1984, which ended in one conviction and one acquittal. A more serious seventy-one-count criminal conspiracy federal indictment was made against sixteen US and México religious activists in 1985. A volunteer team of criminal defense attorneys took on the cases, with much publicity exposing the Reagan administration's treatment of the refugees. All those defendants were convicted, but none received jail time. It was a boon to the movement, as the number of congregations involved in sanctuary increased, and no more indictments were forthcoming.[108]

In a speech to the nation about Central America in May 1984, President Reagan used scare rhetoric invoking invasion, saying that "San Salvador is closer to Houston, Texas, than Houston is to Washington D.C."[109] Coordinated with the speech was the launch of a Hollywood fantasy, *Red Dawn*, that had the Nicaraguan and Cuban armies successfully invading and occupying the United

States, of course on behalf of the Soviet Union, and imposing communism.[110] General Alexander Haig, Reagan's former secretary of state, sat on the board of directors of MGM, which produced the film, and it premiered in the White House.[111] *Red Dawn* fit the Reagan era of "Rambo" blockbusters. Hate and anticommunism were highly profitable.[112]

CENTRAL AMERICAN REFUGEES OF WAR, STARVATION, AND VIOLENCE

Between 2011 and 2016, the number of people from El Salvador, Honduras, and Guatemala who sought refuge in surrounding countries increased by 2,259 percent, and by the end of 2019, an estimated 539,500 people would be displaced from those countries. In 2018 alone, 49,000 children and adolescents in El Salvador dropped out of school, and in Guatemala and Honduras, there were over two million children out of school. Gang warfare had made those countries into the most dangerous places on earth, with high rates of brutal homicides, extortion, and rape, but most disturbing was the aggressive recruitment of young boys into gangs. This was the main reason that parents gave for sending their children to the US border. The United Nations refugee agency (UNHCR), based in Geneva, responded with personnel on the ground, but UNHCR can set up and administer refugee camps only with the invitation of a government.[113]

The US government assumed no responsibility for the damage wrought, nor were US people and the media interested in Central America after the bang-bang and headlines ceased. Then, in 2014, two years into President Barack Obama's second term, 68,541 unaccompanied children from Honduras, El Salvador, and Guatemala were detained at the US border with México.[114] For many of the Salvadoran children, reunification with their parents who had fled to the United States was the objective. Honduras was the murder capital of the world, and the violence was the push factor for Honduran families sending their children north. Guatemalan Mayan families living in the most extreme poverty in the rural areas could not feed their children and risked sending them north. The Reagan administration had used Honduras as a military base of operations for the Contra war while tolerating drug trafficking and militarily assisted the El Salvador government's slaughter of peasants and the Guatemalan military genocide against the Quiche Mayan people, which left them impoverished and displaced. By definition of law and ethics, these unaccompanied children at the border constituted a severe refugee crisis, but they were treated as an alien invasion while elected officials called for massive deportations. The chickens had come home to roost, but few US citizens, journalists, or politicians seemed to remember that the situation was a predictable consequence of US policies and actions that led to a humanitarian crisis, violence, drug gangs, and chaos in Central America, now visible on the US border.

A third of the children were from Honduras. Certainly, state violence had been rampant in Honduras during and after the US Contra war was staged there, as was the growth of drug cartels, which had been tied to the US military presence. But change had been palpable when President Manuel Zelaya took office in January 2006. As an heir of a wealthy provincial family in the logging, timber, and cattle businesses, Zelaya was a member of the small Honduran elite. He ran for offices in his home province in the 1980s as a member of the Liberal Party, which was not liberal in the sense the term invokes in the US but rather was a party of free-trade capitalism. Zelaya campaigned for the presidency promising to fight crime and the drug cartels, but once in office he turned to measures to improve rural food production and the environment, initiating reforestation projects. He began moving away from his party's center-right position and looked to Venezuelan president Hugo Chávez for assistance in dealing with Honduras's extreme poverty. In 2008, Zelaya took Honduras into the ALBA group. This Bolivarian Alternative for the Americas had been formed in 2004 by Venezuela and Cuba. When Honduras joined in 2008, there were seven other member states, and soon after, five other Latin American countries joined. The following year, President Zelaya organized a referendum that would have allowed revision of the constitution to change presidential terms from one term to two. But on June 28, 2009, the day the referendum was to take place, the military, led by Honduran officers who had been trained at the US' infamous School of the Americas, forced Zelaya out of office and out of the country, quickly installing the conservative leader of the National Congress.[115]

International opposition was immediate and forceful; the United Nations condemned the coup, and the Organization of American States (OAS) suspended Honduras's membership and established the Honduras Truth and Reconciliation Commission to investigate, finding that it was an illegal coup. The United States, being the principal source of funding for the OAS, wields sway in the organization, which is based in Washington, DC. The Obama administration, which had taken office only months before, publicly worked through diplomatic channels for months to reverse the coup. But behind closed doors in Washington, a parallel, personal diplomacy was going in another direction, which culminated in official recognition of the coup government. Lanny Davis, former special counsel to President Bill Clinton and a Clinton family friend, played a pivotal role as the lobbyist for the Honduran business leaders who backed the coup.[116]

In a 2014 article, Hillary Clinton bragged that she had used her role as secretary of state to assure that Zelaya would not be reinstated. She wrote, "In the subsequent days I spoke with my counterparts around the hemisphere. . . . We strategized on a plan to restore order in Honduras and ensure that free and fair elections could be held quickly and legitimately, which would render the question of Zelaya moot."[117] The Obama administration provided military support and police training to the post-coup government, made up of pro-coup loyalists, which constructed a horrendous human rights crisis as drug cartels flourished. Government violence against activists, especially Indigenous and Black communities and environmentalists, was symbolized in its complicity in the murder of environmental activist Berta Isabel Caceres Flores and was responsible for the massive emigration of children in 2014, continuing thereafter.[118]

One stark fact stood out in the 2014 situation at the border: not a single one of the children was from Nicaragua, one of the poorest countries in the hemisphere, which also had been left in shambles by the eight-year Contra war. There were several factors that explain why Nicaraguans were not fleeing or sending their children out of the country. The refugees from the other Central America countries were fleeing violence—some of the highest homicide rates in the world—with instable or corrupt governments and organized drug gangs dominating the streets. At the time the Central American children appeared at the border in 2014, Nicaragua had little gang activity and minimal drug trafficking, logging the lowest homicide rate in Latin America with 8.7 per 100,000 inhabitants, down from 17.4 in 2006 when the Sandinista party returned to power, sixteen years after they had been ousted in the 1989 election. In 2014, neighboring Costa Rica, the most affluent Central American country, had a higher homicide rate than Nicaragua, with 10.3 homicides per 100,000 inhabitants. Honduras had the highest murder rate in the world with ninety-two homicides per 100,000 inhabitants, while El Salvador rated sixty-eight and Guatemala thirty-nine. The United Nations Development Program (UNDP) 2014 report on the region classified Nicaragua as "atypical."[119] Although the majority of Nicaraguans were poor and rural, land distributions to the peasantry in the 1980s endured, and the government supported small farmers and agricultural cooperatives, creating universal food self-sufficiency, as well as community health care, especially preventive care. In 2018, Nicaragua ranked second in Latin America and the Caribbean (after Venezuela) in reducing the gap between rich and poor, the poverty level reaching a low 7.6 percent in 2013 (the US poverty rate was 11.8).[120] The Trump administration's secretary of state, John Bolton, branded Nicaragua, along with Cuba and Venezuela, as a "troika of tyranny," and the US government imposed severe economic sanctions on Nicaragua while fomenting violence there in 2018. The Nicaraguan economy was set back and the future of possible Nicaraguan emigration is not clear, although there were few Nicaraguans in the caravans of Central Americans that arrived at the border in 2018.[121]

UNACCOMPANIED CHILDREN AND CHILD SEPARATION

Although the Trump administration practices in 2018 and 2019 appeared to be unprecedented in terms of harsh detention of unauthorized immigrants and refugees and family separation, it had long been a practice in the sordid history of US immigration practices, particularly with people of color. Unlike past administrations, President Trump and his twisted assistant Stephen Miller trumpeted their intentions and practices with glee. But it was George W. Bush's administration that first separated asylum-seeking parents from their children. They opened the notorious T. Don Hutto Center in Texas where children were separated from parents and abused by staff. Only an ACLU lawsuit put a stop to it. The Obama administration used harsh measures against immigrants and asylum seekers and deported record numbers, housing unaccompanied children at military bases and incarcerated mothers with small children in camps, and on occasion tried to put children in solitary confinement to punish their mothers for going on hunger strikes. However, the administration mostly detained parents and children together.[122]

In November 2017, Department of Homeland Security officials in California gathered four Central American families into a room together. When one of the asylum seekers from El Salvador protested that his twelve-year-old son was handcuffed, a DHS officer told him, "You don't have any rights here." DHS proceeded to separate the children of the four families. The families had documents proving the family relationships and had presented themselves at the border as asylum seekers fleeing persecution in their own countries. In this way, the Trump administration quietly tested family separation of asylum seekers in 2017, then in 2018 launched and implemented a policy of separating thousands of families, with the stated goal of severely punishing the asylum seekers and deterring others from attempting to seek asylum for fear of losing their children. Some eight thousand families were separated, children, even infants, taken away and housed in makeshift structures, many enclosed in cages.[123]

The 1948 international Convention on the Prevention and Punishment of Genocide states that a government "forcibly transferring children of the group to another group" is an act of genocide.[124] This was one of the arguments made in the United States Senate to not adhere to the treaty until 1988, given the century-long practice of separating Native children from their families and the seven decades of chattel slavery, when slavers could separate children from their families at will in the manner of other property. In May 2018, the five US immigration attorneys along the border, three of them appointed by Trump, were reported to have expressed concern when they received Attorney General Jeff Sessions's order to prosecute all undocumented immigrants, even if it meant separating children from their parents. "We need to take away children," Sessions told the prosecutors, adding that if the parents cared about their kids, they would not bring them, and that there would be no amnesty to people with kids. After two government lawyers had refused to prosecute two cases because the children were infants, Rod J. Rosenstein, the deputy attorney general at the time, told the prosecutors that it did not matter how young the children were.[125]

By the middle of 2018, the US was holding nearly thirteen thousand children in border detention centers, ten times as many as in 2017.[126] The 2018 horror show of family separations elicited massive negative publicity and outrage from citizens and organizations all over the country, many of whom rushed to the border to protest. Lawsuits and court decisions ensued. But in the end, the administration found ways to continue separating children, maintaining that children were being taken because their parents were neglectful or a danger to their children.[127]

The American Civil Liberties Union (ACLU), which had been tasked by the courts to locate the parents, reported that around two-thirds of the parents who had been separated from their children were deported to their countries of origin in Central America with the children left behind. Some 1,030 children were removed from their parents. The ACLU had found the parents of 485 of the children, but the parents of more than six hundred of the children had not been found. In the rush of summary deportations, the destinations of the deported parents were not recorded. Paola Luisi, the director of Families Belong Together, a coalition of 250 groups, said, "The Trump administration ripped hundreds of children away from their parents, lied about it, then lost track of them as they departed into danger. That's par for the course for a sadistic immigration system."[128]

THE BORDER DIVIDES INDIGENOUS COMMUNITIES

The border itself has been transformed into a forbidding wall, whether or not an eventual structure will be in place. Harsha Walia writes, "A long arc of dirty colonial coups, capitalist trade agreements extracting land and labor, climate change, and enforced oppression is the primary driver of displacement from México and Central America. Migration is a predictable consequence of these displacements, yet today the US is fortifying its border against the very people impacted by its own policies."[129]

For the Indigenous peoples, whose homelands span the 1848 border between México and the United States, the border itself is static invasion. The barriers and walls that have been constructed, and the ones being planned, cut through their living rooms and fields. The territories of thirty-six US federally recognized tribes, including the Kumeyaay, Cocopah, Quechan, Tohono O'odham, Yaqui, Tigua, and Kickapoo, straddle the two-thousand-mile border. Tens of thousands of Native people live near the border in the Mexican states of Baja California, Sonora, and Chihuahua and are not recognized as Indigenous by US authorities. They cross the border into the US for their kin's cultural events and sacred sites, to attend burials and visit family. Like other "nonresident aliens," they are required to pass through the rigid security checkpoints where they are subject to interrogation and delay, often rejection. The kind of border wall being planned by the US government would make their visitations much more difficult, if not impossible.

The Tohono O'odham Nation, whose homeland straddles the border in Arizona, has fought the government's plans for a border wall. Through hard-fought law over many years, Tohono O'odham citizens who reside in México are eligible to receive educational and medical services in Tohono O'odham facilities inside the US. Before the border terror panic of the twenty-first century, Tohono O'odham people in México would simply drive or even walk directly across their land cut by the border, but after 9/11 and the militarized security measures, they have to drive long distances to official ports of entry, where they are inspected and delayed. One Tohono O'odham rancher on the US side said he has to travel several miles to draw water from a well that is a hundred yards away from his house but inside México. In 2019, three Tohono O'odham villages in Sonora, México, were cut off from their nearest food supply; although it was nearby, it was in the US. All the Indigenous nations whose territories were divided by the imposition of the 1848 border experience similar problems. International agreements that the US government is party to, including the 2007 United Nations Declaration on the Rights of Indigenous Peoples, confirm Indigenous peoples' rights to draw on cultural and natural resources across international borders. Several US laws also confirm such rights. United States law also requires that federally recognized tribal nations on the US-México border must be consulted in federal border-enforcement planning. Yaqui elder and activist José Matus, who died in 2017, lived in Yaqui territory north of the border. He said, "Our relatives are all considered aliens. They're not aliens. . . . They're indigenous to this land. We've been here since time immemorial."[130]

The border has long been a nightmare for people, both migrants and Indigenous residents, but the walls and barriers that have been constructed and proposed also cut through one of the most diverse and biologically rich regions of North America. The border region is home to species whose survival depends on an ecosystem stretching from well into the United States to México, with more than fifteen hundred plants and animal species, ninety-three of them listed by the International Union for Conservation and Nature as critically endangered, endangered, or vulnerable. The wall affects not only habitats but also the flow of food, protection, and even mating partners. An extended network of national parks, archaeological monuments, and wilderness and nature reserves straddles the border, protecting wildlife habitat and cultural resources on both sides. The US Fish and Wildlife Service warned that an impermeable barrier and bright light at night will destroy many endangered species.[131]

Joseph Nevins writes, "The Border, *strictusenso*, is a state-sanctioned system of violence: Physical, environmental, economic, and cultural."[132] What is to be done about this open sore that causes so much suffering and death? Mostly, the horror is invisible to people across the United States, even those who work for social change. The outrage generated by media coverage of the 2018 detentions of children and turning away thousands of asylum seekers, victims of US wars, receded while the atrocities continued. Ideally, the Mexican government could take the United States to the International Court of Justice (World Court) and question the very legitimacy of the border. The US would boycott the proceedings, and México would win by default. For the Mexican government to launch such a challenge would require a mass movement in México itself, as well as in the United States. But change has to start somewhere, and with the massive uprising demanding defunding or even abolishing the police in the summer of 2020, there were calls to abolish ICE (US Immigration and Customs Enforcement). As Mexican immigration historian Alexandra Délano Alonso writes, abolishing ICE would include shutting down detention centers and ending deportations, breaking the cycle of violence and lack of accountability "embedded in immigration enforcement and incarceration." Délano Alonso acknowledges that the project of dismantling ICE can't be left to the will of the government; rather it will require reimagining society's vision of justice and "a reckoning with the racial and economic injustice built into the 'nation of immigrants' from its very origins." The words "illegal" and "immigration" must be decoupled in our public and private conversations.[133]

CONCLUSION

The United States has never been "a nation of immigrants." It has always been a settler state with a core of descendants from the original colonial settlers, that is, primarily Anglo-Saxons, Scots Irish, and German. The vortex of settler colonialism sucked immigrants through a kind of seasoning process of Americanization, not as rigid and organized as the "seasoning" of Africans, which rendered them into human commodities, but effective nevertheless.

In the 1960s, US historians were having to adjust the historical narrative of the white republic and progress in response to Black civil rights demands for a reckoning about racism. But in the process of those adjustments and reforms, the settler state was never a subject of debate. Mahmood Mamdani writes, "If America's greatest social successes have been registered on the frontier of race, the same cannot be said of the frontier of colonialism. If the race question marks the cutting edge of American reform the native question highlights the limits of that reform. The thrust of American struggles has been to deracialize but not to decolonize. A deracialized America still remains a settler society and a settler state."[1] Attempts to "include" Native peoples as victims of racism further camouflages settler colonialism and constitutes a type of social genocide. The US polity has been trying to rid itself of Indigenous nations since first settlement. Four hundred years later, multiculturalism is the mechanism for avoiding acknowledgment of settler colonialism. Mamdani correctly observes that the very existence of Indigenous nations "constitutes a claim on land and therefore a critique of settler sovereignty and an obstacle to the settler economy."[2]

Multiculturalism was the response to civil rights demands, which required revision of the US history narrative. For this scheme to work—and affirm US historical progress—Indigenous nations and communities had to be left out of the picture or somehow woven into the story.[3] As territorially and treaty-based peoples in North America, they do not fit the grid of multiculturalism but were included by transforming them into an inchoate, oppressed racial group, while oppressed Mexican Americans and colonized Puerto Ricans were dissolved into another such group, variously called "Hispanic" or "Latino," and more recently "Latinx." The multicultural approach emphasized the "contributions" of oppressed groups and immigrants to the United States' presumed greatness. Indigenous peoples were thus credited with contributing corn, beans, buckskin, log cabins, parkas, maple syrup, canoes, hundreds of place names, ecology, Thanksgiving, and even contributing to the US Constitution the concepts of democracy and federalism.

This idea of the gift-giving Indian helping to establish and enrich the development of the United States is a screen that obscures the fact that the very existence of the country is a result of the looting of an entire continent and its resources, reducing the Indigenous population, and forcibly relocating and incarcerating them in reservations. The fundamental unresolved issues of Indigenous lands, treaties, and sovereignty could not but scuttle the premises of multiculturalism for Native Americans. Multiculturalism persisted into the neoliberal twenty-first century, culminating in widespread "diversity" training, the coining of a new term, "people of color," and the production of *Hamilton*, which not only erased the Indigenous peoples and African slavery but also turned the white founding fathers, who authored a Constitution that recognized only white people as citizens, into brown and Black men.

The Black Power and women's liberation movements of the 1960s gave birth to "identity politics," which saw the coalescence of Mexican American youth as Chicanos, Native American Red Power, and a trans-Asian Pacific American identity. A generation that came to adulthood in the 1960s who could not speak Chinese or Spanish, as their immigrant parents felt it might hold their children back, embraced bilingualism. European immigrants or second-generation US Americans, whose parents and grandparents had strived so hard to be considered white, saw the cultural power of whiteness diminishing and began to hyphenate their identity as Polish-American, Italian-American, Irish-American, while white Appalachians and

New Mexico Hispano settlers claimed indigeneity. Instead of the melting pot that erased ethnic heritage, there was talk of patchwork quilts and threads, multiculturalism and diversity.

Immigration at the turn of the millennium looked different from past immigration in that Asia was the major region of origin rather than Latin America, at 41 percent of all immigrants, with 38.9 percent from Latin America, primarily México. Between 2000 and 2017, the top three countries of origin were China, India, and Pakistan, followed by the Philippines. Most importantly, nearly half of the new immigrants were college graduates, many with advanced degrees. They were not heading only to Silicon Valley or other high-tech industrial centers, nor were they, as had immigrants in the past, settling mainly in the large coastal cities. Rather, they could be found in the Deep South, the Great Plains, the intermountain West, and Appalachia. In North Dakota, where immigrants represented about 4 percent of residents, immigrant numbers increased by 87 percent after 2010, while West Virginia and South Dakota increased in foreign-born residents by a third, and Kentucky and Tennessee by over one-fifth.[4] And many of these immigrants, some of whom were refugees, others undocumented, came not only from South, West, and East Asia but also from African and Arab countries, the Caribbean, and Central and South America. Like the Chinese and Mexican immigrants before them, they experienced racialization, thereby lacking a key element of settler colonialism: potential whiteness. They or their children could become thoroughly Americanized but still remain contingent, even the son of a Kenyan who was twice elected president but whose citizenship was questioned by a substantial part of the population, including by the US president who followed him.[5]

The trend of "third world" immigration began with the 1965 immigration law but accelerated with the Western nations' retreat from funding and supporting decolonization and nation building, which accelerated debt, austerity, and famine, and in the case of the US, fronting and arming counterinsurgencies to prevent authentic self-determination, making the countries of origin unlivable. Suketu Mehta immigrated with his family from Mumbai, India, at age fourteen. A prize-winning author and associate professor of journalism at New York University, he observes in his book *This Land Is Our Land: An Immigrant's Manifesto* that "they are here because you were there." He corrects the idea that immigrants clamor to leave their homelands to pursue the American Dream. "When migrants move, it's not out of idle fancy, or because they hate their homelands, or to plunder the countries they come to, or even (most often) to strike it rich. They move—as my grandfather knew—because the accumulated burdens of history have rendered their homelands less and less habitable." Mehta questions the presumed US reader to consider how frequently the US military has gone over its southern border or into the Caribbean or Southeast Asia, going over the borders of Iraq or Afghanistan. "The United States has not acted lawfully with other nations, including the Native American nations on its soil, through most of the nineteenth and twentieth centuries. How can it now expect the human victims of that enormous illegality to obey the laws of the United States and stay home or wait thirty years for a visa to rejoin their families?"[6]

Mehta proposes that the United States (and other Western countries) pay reparations: "If the rich countries don't want the poor countries to migrate, then there's another solution. Pay them what they're owed. Pay the costs of colonialism, of the wars you imposed on them, of the inequality you've built into the world order, and the carbon you've put into the atmosphere. Settle the account, and the creditors will have no reason to come to your house. Reparations or migration: choose."[7] Mehta points out that migrants, as we have seen with Mexican and Philippine migrants, send back to their home countries some $600 billion in remittances every year, amounting to four times more than all the Western foreign aid and a hundred times more than the amount of all debt relief.[8] In addition to the ruin wrought by European colonization and US wars and interventions, plus extreme economic inequality, Mehta sees catastrophic climate change as a source of mass migrations in the twenty-first century, displacing far more people than were displaced at the end of World War II. By 2050, up to 30 percent of the planet's surface could be unlivable desert, forcing a billion and a half people into migration. In Bangladesh alone, twenty million people could be forced out due to rising sea levels, and by the end of the century, the lands of 650 million people could be underwater. Obviously, rich countries will be increasingly a destination for desperate migrants and need to plan to provide assistance, not build walls or increase mass deportations.[9]

Mehta's manifesto is deeply researched and insightful and should be a refreshing rejoinder to the American Dream and bootstrap stories that many immigrants, and more Anglo settlers, are asked to tell themselves. But Mehta does characterize the United States as "a nation of immigrants" that does not live up to that aspiration.[10] Although he is critical of US imperialism and immigration policies, Mehta does not acknowledge settler colonialism and the immigrant's role in perpetuating it. The Native is mentioned as an oppressed demographic, but otherwise is invisible. Jodi Byrd writes, "As metropolitan multiculturalism and dominant postcolonialism promise the United States as postracial asylum for the world, the diminishing returns of that asylum meet exactly at the point where diaspora collides with settler colonialism."[11]

Moroccan Muslim immigrant Laila Lalami, a prize-winning novelist and writer and a university professor, aptly titled her 2020 nonfiction book *Conditional Citizens: On Belonging in America.*[12] She was born in Rabat, Morocco, was educated in Morocco, Great Britain, and the United States, married a US citizen, and was naturalized in 2000. Lalami relates that she had no trouble with the citizenship test, because before she came to the United States, she had taken courses on US history, had studied its literature, and had become acquainted with the culture. She discovered quickly on arrival in the United States that the US people she met knew nothing of her country's history or culture, although they exhibited the racist caricatures of Arabs and Muslims. As an immigrant, a woman, an Arab, and a Muslim, Lalami was made to feel like a "conditional citizen."[13] That feeling escalated with the Al Qaeda attacks on the World Trade Center and the Pentagon on September 11, 2001, because the nineteen airplane hijackers were all Muslim, all but one from the US-allied country, Saudi Arabia. The US revenge war in Afghanistan was framed as anti-Muslim, as was the 2003 invasion of Iraq, where, in fact, there was little hard-line Islam and no terror attacks by Iraqis. As that heated anti-Muslim period abated somewhat,

Lalami was disturbed by the citizen birthright rhetoric that began with the presidency of Barack Obama, who was the target of the "birther" craze, claiming that Obama was a secret Muslim actually born in Kenya, making him ineligible for the presidency. The instigator of this false charge, real-estate mogul Donald Trump, ascended to the presidency in 2017 largely on birtherism and his attacks on Muslim and Mexican immigrants. As one of his first acts as president, he banned visitors and immigrants from some Muslim-majority countries by executive order.[14] In a chapter titled "Assimilation," Lalami insightfully discusses the US nineteenth-century programs to erase the languages, cultures, and social relations practiced by Indigenous peoples, citing the mandatory boarding schools that took Native children from their families and communities. She is alert to that process of Americanization being demanded of immigrants to the US as well. While making common cause between immigrants, especially immigrants of color, and Native Americans, she does not interrogate the role of immigrants in perpetuating settler colonialism.[15] Lisa Lowe writes that "the affirmation or the desire for freedom is so inhabited by the forgetting of its condition of possibility that every narrative articulation of freedom is haunted by its burial, by the violence of forgetting."[16] The instability caused by the conditionality of citizenship that Lalami expresses is a barrier to the immigrant's ability to see the role they may play in normalizing settler colonialism.

Most immigration scholars, who are also often activists in support of immigrants, are reluctant to go beyond reforming the system rather than deconstructing the history of US immigration and settler colonialism as a framework. This is understandable, with so many refugees and immigrants being pushed out of their homelands and the US restrictions and deportations. With the intricately constructed Americanization process developed in the second half of the nineteenth century, along with the constitutional ambiguity of citizenship requirements, those who immigrate to the United States are practically required to embrace the settler perspective or their right to citizenship is doubted. However, many diaspora humanities scholars and writers in the United States ignore the risk and contribute to the discourse on US settler colonialism, and even more so, those in Canada, where the settler-colonial situation is similar, historically and in the government's policies.[17]

Dean Itsuji Saranillio writes that migration does not equal colonialism necessarily; migration to a settler-colonial state is fraught because Native land and resources "are under political, ecological, and spiritual contestation," which means that immigrant communities can duplicate a colonial system initiated by white settlers. "This is particularly so since the avenues laid out for success and empowerment are paved over native lands and sovereignty."[18] Saranillio is referencing Hawaii, where the Native Hawaiian (Kanaka Maoli) population is 10 percent, and Asians, primarily Japanese and Filipino, make up the majority at nearly 40 percent, while the US settler population is just under 30 percent. Although the United States occupied Hawai'i and overthrew its constitutional monarchy as a prelude to the invasion and occupation of the Philippines, Guam, and other Pacific islands in the late nineteenth century, the US Congress long considered Hawai'i to be unqualified for statehood, because it was "Asiatic," which was the reason that none of the Pacific territories the US held were considered for statehood. But the resident US citizen settlers in Hawai'i, who had been uninvited businessmen and missionaries even before the US occupation, desired statehood and lobbied hard for it.

These wealthy US businessmen settlers operated vast sugar and pineapple plantations in Hawai'i and recruited migrant agricultural workers from Japan and the Philippines, who then came to make up a large part of the foreign residents, outnumbering the indigenous Kanaka Maoli. Saranillio detects the hidden motive for US support of Hawai'i statehood:

> In the 1940s and 1950s, when decolonization was transforming an international order and criticism of Western imperialism was the dominant international sentiment, Cold Warrior ideologues realized that Hawaii's multiracial population had ideological value in winning the "hearts and minds" of newly decolonized nations. . . . The US liberal multicultural discourse—articulated through a multicultural "nation of immigrants" narration—helped achieve seemingly permanent

control of Hawaii through statehood while creating a multi-cultural image of the United States that facilitated US ambitions for global hegemony.[19]

Hawai'i became a state in 1959, despite the fact that as an island subjected to Western colonization, it was eligible for independence under international law. In 1946, Hawai'i was deemed a non-self-governing territory and placed on the UN List of Non-Self-Governing Territories, but it was unilaterally removed from that list in 1959 when the US government reported to the UN that Hawai'i had achieved self-government. The same applied to Alaska. The Kanaka Maoli of Hawai'i, Alaskan Inuit, American Indians, and their allies continue to pursue independence.[20]

Asian American scholar Iyko Day challenges a binary theory of settler colonialism regarding non-European immigration. "While scholarship on the settler-Indigenous dialectic has been tremendously valuable, it often falls short of clarifying the role that non-white migration plays within such a framework or how it intersects with other aspects of white supremacy." Day rightly objects to the settler status collapsing all migrants into a group of "occupiers."[21] Chickasaw scholar Jodi Byrd extends the term *arrivant*, which refers to enslaved Africans transported against their will, to refugees and immigrants forced out of their homelands; that is, "those people forced into the Americas through the violence of European and Anglo-American colonialism and imperialism around the globe."[22]

But the migrant forced into migration to the United States or other states structured on settler colonialism—Canada, New Zealand, Australia, Israel—is susceptible, as Saranillio points out, to the ideology of settler colonialism, which in the United States is imprinted in the content of patriotism, Americanism. Without consciousness of and resistance to this pull, the migrant can passively contribute to the continued settler-colonial order. The desire to relieve the non-European migrant or descendants of enslaved Africans from responsibility is understandable but not sustainable if the settler-colonial foundation is to be eradicated, that is, the decolonization of the entire apparatus of the settler state. What would that entail? US social movement organizer Clare Bayard likely captured the dilemma for most non-Indigenous activists in the United States, saying, "The difficulty that a lot of non-Native people have in imagining what unsettling would look like in this country is that it's not seen as a political possibility. We can't even imagine what that would look like—how do we do that?"[23] Lack of imagination also indicates lack of commitment for figuring it out.

These questions took a sharp turn in a debate between Indigenous and migrant scholars in Canada and mirror the contradictions that exist in the United States as well as Canada. In 2005, Indigenous Mi'kmaq scholar Bonita Lawrence and scholar of anti-racism Enakshi Dua, both professors at York University in Toronto, published a provocative essay, "Decolonizing Antiracism," in which they argued that anti-racist scholarship had systematically ignored the situation of Indigenous peoples and thereby was complicit with the settler-colonial agenda.[24] Their argument also reflected criticisms that Indigenous scholars and activists have of anti-racist scholarship in the US. In response, anti-racist postcolonial Canadian scholars Nandita Sharma and Cynthia Wright, in an essay titled "Decolonizing Resistance, Challenging Colonial States," argued that attempts to reclaim Native sovereignty could strengthen exclusion and discrimination against non-Western immigrants.[25] Lawrence and Dua identified five areas that international critical race and postcolonial theory have failed to address. First, Native presence is erased; second, theories of Atlantic diasporic identities do not take into account the fact that they are settling on Native lands; third, histories of colonization are erased through emphasis on writings on slavery; fourth, decolonization politics are equated with anti-racist politics; and fifth, theories critical of nationalism contribute to ongoing delegitimizing of Indigenous nationhood.[26] Regarding Sharma and Wright's views, Jodi Byrd is critical, writing, "In arguing against indigenous claims to land, sovereignty, and nation, they suggest that autochthony stands in the face of global capitalism and migration . . . as xenophobic elitism that traffics as neoliberal hatred of foreigners."[27] Perhaps these starkly opposing arguments contributed to a dialog among diasporic migrant scholars and activists in Canada, as well as the United States, although less so.

In the early 2000s, a new immigrant organization made up of immigrants and refugees and their allies, No One Is Illegal (NOII), was founded in Canada, with chapters in Vancouver, Toronto, Montreal, Ottawa, and Halifax.[28] Its initial goals, similar to other immigrant organizations, was to assist immigrants, particularly the undocumented. Within a few years, Indigenous groups and representatives, especially in Vancouver, pressed NOII to include Indigenous sovereignty issues, and the organization responded so that Indigenous rights became a central focus. This is reflected in Harsha Walia's 2013 book, *Undoing Border Imperialism.*[29] Walia, herself from an Asian Indian immigrant family, had formed the Vancouver chapter of NOII. In 2012, she wrote, "A growing number of social movements are recognizing that Indigenous self-determination must become the foundation for all our broader social justice mobilizing. . . . We have to be cautious not to replicate the Canadian state's assimilationist model of liberal pluralism, forcing Indigenous identities to fit within our existing groups and narratives. The inherent right to traditional lands and to self-determination is expressed collectively and should not be subsumed within the discourse of individual or human rights."[30]

The claim that the United States is "a nation of immigrants" is the benevolent version of US nationalism. The ugly, predominant underside is the panic of enemy invasion. Echoing Alexander Hamilton, the judge in the case of the Chinese Exclusion Act of 1882 justified exclusion, writing that if the government of the United States considers "the presence of foreigners of a different race in this country . . . to be dangerous to its peace and security, their exclusion is not to be stayed because at the time there are no actual hostilities with the nation of which the foreigners are subject. The existence of war would render the necessity of the proceeding only more obvious and pressing."[31] Rendering migrants as proxies for foreign troops dates back to the founders of the US and the Alien and Sedition Acts. Immigration historian Mae Ngai sees the character of US nationalism as the driver of its fear of immigrants: "Americans want to believe that immigration into the United States proves the universality of the nation's liberal democratic principles; we resist examining the role that American world power has played in the global structures of migration. We like to believe that our immigration policy is generous, but we also resent the demands made upon us by others and we think we owe outsiders nothing."[32]

The US is under the illusion it is surrounded by enemies, must strike first, savagely, with preemptive action, even war. Historian Walter Hixson writes of the "boomerang of savagery," arguing that "the history of American settler colonialism, and the indiscriminate violence that it entailed, burrowed into US national identity and foreign relations."[33] As Native nations resisted encroachment, starting with the first English settlement in 1607, the traumatized settlers hardened the mythology of providential destiny, fueling indiscriminate carnage, which was even more hideous in the Plymouth and Massachusetts Bay Colonies, escalating exponentially until total conquest was complete in 1900. Hixson writes, "Americans thus internalized a propensity for traumatic, righteous violence, and a quest for total security, which came to characterize a series of future conflicts. Violence against Indians, replete with demonizing colonial discourse and indiscriminate killing, established a foundation for virulent national campaigns against external enemies across the sweep of American history."[34]

This is the chief characteristic of US nationalism, similar to other settler states, such as Australia, New Zealand, Canada, Northern Ireland, and twentieth-century copycat settler states—Israel and the now-defunct Afrikaner apartheid regime in South Africa. But only the United States became an unparalleled capitalist state and military machine, so unlike those other states, whose damage, damaging as it is, remains mostly local or regional while the United States rules the seas that are overheating, with the earth and the future of humanity itself at stake.

Immigrants and refugees from US wars, including Mexicans from the war that created the southern border, have an important role to play if there is to be change. Viet Thanh Nguyen observes that "identity politics" is treated as a slur, something to be avoided. It appears to be the one thing that many on the left and the solid right agree on. Nguyen writes, "To have no identity at all is the privilege of whiteness, which is the identity that pretends not to have an identity, that denies how it is tied to capitalism, to race, and to war."[35] He calls on minorities to dissent from the terms that a regime of whiteness offers: "They must call forth anger and rage, demand solidarity and revolution, critique whiteness, domination, power, and all the faces of the war machine," and in particular for Southeast Asians, insist that "the war that defines them in America is not only their war, but a war made by white people, a war that is not an aberration but a manifestation of a war machine that would prefer refugees to think of their stories as immigrant stories. . . . We must also tell the war stories that made ghosts and made us ghosts, the war stories that brought us here."[36]

This book is a call for all those who have gone through the immigrant or refugee experience or are descendants of immigrants to acknowledge settler colonialism and the Americanization process that sucks them into complicity with white supremacy and erasure of the Indigenous peoples. It's a call too for descendants of original settlers to understand and reject settler colonialism and the romanticizing of original white settlers who were instrumentalized to reproduce white supremacy and white nationalism. It's a call for those who work tirelessly for workers' rights and working class solidarity to recognize that it's not only racism that divides the working class but also the effects of settler colonialism. It limits workers' identification as even being working class and worker solidarity in the US and with other workers of the world. The Eurocentric model of a proletarian revolution challenging, much less overcoming, the US fiscal-military capitalist and imperialist state has not and will not work. A revolutionary working class must be able to acknowledge its enemy and eschew not only capitalism but also colonialism and imperialism.

Given the long history of the US demand for unquestioning patriotism and the contingency of citizenship that immigrants experience, there is a deep fear of appearing unpatriotic. Not only immigrants but also descendants of enslaved Africans experience the contingency. When the San Francisco 49ers quarterback Colin

Kaepernick kneeled during the national anthem to protest racism and police brutality, he felt it necessary to declare his patriotism following the game: "I'm not anti-American. I love America."[37] Despite his expressed patriotism, Kaepernick was ousted from professional football, and his former fans burned their Kaepernick jerseys during the national anthem. US president Donald Trump said that a player who kneeled during the anthem was a "son of a bitch."[38] James Baldwin felt obligated in his *Notes of a Native Son* to declare his patriotism: "I love America more than any other country in this world, and, exactly for this reason, I insist on the right to criticize her perpetually."[39] Not expressing patriotism can be deadly. Black Panthers who boldly told the truth about the United States were imprisoned and killed by police. The world-famous opera star Paul Robeson, who was Black and openly leftist, was driven out of the country and his career. American Indian Movement activist Leonard Peltier was imprisoned for life for the death of two FBI agents, a crime he did not commit. Jobs and careers can be crushed. Running for public office is out of the question.

US leftists have long compensated for their critiques of US capitalism and imperialism by waving the flag or celebrating Tom Paine. At the end of World War II, the US Communist Party was at its height of respectability, having been the driver of the success of New Deal reforms and workers' rights. But their usefulness had run its course, and communists and other leftists were subjected to prosecution and fired from jobs; even tenured university professors were ousted and civil service workers purged. To punctuate the terror, the government executed Julius and Ethel Rosenberg in a very public burning. Even after the firing of all federal civil servants and private sector employees suspected of being Reds and cleaning out Hollywood, FBI agents appeared at their homes or new places of employment, if they found work, followed them in unmarked cars, and made their lives and that of their children miserable.

Perhaps that is one reason so few US historians are willing to risk their careers by writing US history objectively. Even Howard Zinn's 1980 book, *A People's History of the United States*, remains eschewed by most professional historians, and in September 2020, the book was publicly condemned by President Donald Trump, who introduced an initiative to require the teaching of patriotic history: "The left-wing rioting and mayhem are the direct result of decades of left-wing indoctrination in our schools. It's gone on far too long. Our children are instructed from propaganda tracts, like those of Howard Zinn, that try to make students ashamed of their own history."[40]

Perhaps most important of all, this book is a call to acknowledge settler colonialism and to put away the myth that the United States is "a nation of immigrants." As Mamdani insists, the US autobiography must be rewritten. This is a project that cannot be left to professional US historians. It will require that all oppressed people and educators take history into their own hands. They must dissect that history, rewrite and disseminate it. The United States will not decolonize until it is forced to do so. And unless colonization and imperialism are understood to be inherent in the very founding and all US institutions, we cannot begin to dismantle the fiscal-military state.

ACKNOWLEDGMENTS

Although this is a book of several years' gestation, I wrote it during the 2020 pandemic, while massive demonstrations for racial justice were pumping me with energy and hope and an extremely conflictive national election took place. Writing that focused on unjust immigration policies took on added resonance with farmworkers, meat packing workers, and delivery workers, many undocumented or with precarious status, risking their lives to feed over three hundred million people. Racial capitalism and white supremacy are major themes of the book, their continuance vividly displayed by white nationalist and presidential threats against the Black Lives Matter demonstrators. Writing on the fundamental injustice of the US Constitution, highlighting the role of Alexander Hamilton, took on added meaning during the electoral process, which ended in a Trump-led white nationalist mob seizing the Capitol building during the final congressional certification of the electoral votes.

I thank my longtime editor, Gayatri Patnaik, for her support and editorial skills, working under difficult conditions. Her enthusiasm for the project and for my approach kept me going. And many thanks to the talented staff at Beacon Press, including Maya Fernandez, Helene Atwan, Susan Lumenello, Sanj Kharbanda, Carol Chu, Christian Coleman, Caitlin Meyer, Alyssa Hassan, and Ruthie Block.

Under the disturbing and stressful circumstances of 2020, friends and colleagues were generous in responding when I asked for feedback on what I was writing. I am grateful to Jordon Camp and Christina Heatherton for organizing a remote workshop to read and critique an early draft of the book. I thank Alexandra Délano Alonso, Manu Karaka, and Nick Estes for participating and making useful suggestions. These brilliant scholars were also teaching courses remotely at their respective institutions, plus having important research, writing, and activist work of their own. Irish studies historians Patrick Higgins and Matthew Horton generously read and critiqued chapter 5 on Irish refugees and immigrants. Labor activist and author Bill Fletcher Jr. provided important insights on enslaved and indentured labor. Thanks to poet and writer Ishmael Reed for making his one-act play on Lin-Manuel Miranda's musical *Hamilton* available to me before it was published and for his deep critique of Miranda's opportunistic production.

Thanks to my friends in the San Francisco Bay Area who were always available to visit, providing much-needed emotional and intellectual support and conversations, and who came by my place for socially distanced visits outside, bringing me books, treats, and groceries: Anne Weills, Tina Gerhardt, Steve Hiatt, Diana Block, and Claude Marks. Thanks to the Zoom, phone, email, social media conversations, and interviews that never failed to fortify, inspire, and motivate me, with Sherman Alexie, Yousuf Al-Bulushi, Chude Allen, Graham Lee Brewer, Lili Callarman, Roisin Davis, Nick Estes, Breanne Fahs, Johanna Fernandez, Bill Gallegos, Dina Gilio-Whitaker, Kalen Goodluck, Lena Herzog, David Hogg, Josh Hunt, Rachel Jackson, Walter Johnson, Julie Leavitt, Mahmood Mamdani, Nils McCune, Hilary Moore, Hanki Ortiz, Raho Oritz, Raoul Peck, Kathy Power, Margaret Randall, Dan Siegel, Diane Tomhave, James Tracy, Devra Weber, Unitarian Universalists, and the National Council of Elders.

Above all, thanks to my beautiful artist daughter Michelle Callarman for daily text or phone conversations and support and weekly grocery runs along with visits outside, inspiring me with her admirable work ethic and calm, creating amazing works of art.

NOTES

INTRODUCTION

1. Safia Samee Ali, "U.S. Citizenship and Immigration Services Drops 'Nation of Immigrants' from Mission Statement," NBC News, February 22, 2018, https://www.nbcnews.com/politics/immigration/u-s-citizenship-immigration-services-drops-nation-immigrants-mission-statement-n850501.
2. US Citizenship and Immigration Services website, https://www.uscis.gov/aboutus.
3. Biden-Harris Campaign, "The Biden Plan for Securing Our Values as a Nation of Immigrants," 2020, https://joebiden.com/immigration.
4. *NBC Nightly News*, January 11, 2018, available at https://www.youtube.com/watch?v=HcMFmoTCdcU.
5. Michael D. Shear and Julie Hirschfeld, "Stoking Fears, Trump Defied Bureaucracy to Advance Immigration Agenda," *New York Times,* December 23, 2017.
6. "Donald Trump Presidential Announcement Speech: US Became Dumping Ground/China/México," YouTube, June 18, 2015, https://youtu.be/-VQy82BhCGM.
7. "Fact Checking Donald Trump's Immigration Comments," CNN, July 2, 2015, https://youtu.be/BhbOEduvA9U.
8. Osha Gray Davidson, producer, "Reparations," *The American Project,* season 1.
9. BuzzFeed, "A Nation of Immigrants," March 2, 2017, video, https://www.youtube.com/watch?v=vUeLvBFjFlM.
10. "Transcript: Mitt Romney's Acceptance Speech," August 30, 2012, National Public Radio, https://www.npr.org/2012/08/30/160357612/transcript-mitt-romneys-acceptance-speech.
11. Barack Obama, "We Are a Nation of Immigrants," CNN, March 31, 2016, https://www.youtube.com/watch?v=TAeU6pBT70E.
12. Hillary Clinton, "We Are a Nation of Immigrants," Associated Press Archive, November 16, 2016, https://youtu.be/UTYbEAx_Qto; Tim Kaine, "We're a Nation of Immigrants," NBC News, October 4, 2016, https://www.youtube.com/watch?v=moQztB9tDlA.

13. John F. Kennedy, *A Nation of Immigrants* (1958; repr., New York: Harper Perennial Modern Classics, 2018). This is the most recent of dozens of editions of the book, following its first printing in 1958.

14. Kennedy, *A Nation of Immigrants*, 2–3.

15. Erwin Chemerinsky, "Chemerinsky: Predicting the Supreme Court in 2021 May Be Dangerous and Futile," *ABA Journal*, December 18, 2020, https://www.abajournal.com/columns/article/chemerinsky-predicting -scotus-in-2021-may-be-dangerous-and-futile.

16. See Roxanne Dunbar-Ortiz, *Loaded: A Disarming History of the Second Amendment* (San Francisco: City Lights, 2019).

17. Andrew Macdonald (pseudonym for William Pierce), *The Turner Diaries* (Mountain City, TN: Cosmotheist Books, 2018); see Brad Whitsel, "*The Turner Diaries* and Cosmotheism: William Pierce's Theology," in *Nova Religio: The Journal of Alternative and Emergent Religions* 1, no. 2 (April 1998): 183–97.

18. Barack Obama, "Remarks by the President at 'Hamilton at the White House,'" White House, Office of the Press Secretary, March 14, 2016, https://obamawhitehouse.archives.gov/the-press-office/2016/03/14 /remarks-president-hamilton-white-house.

19. Walter Johnson, *River of Dark Dreams: Slavery and Empire in the Cotton Kingdom* (Cambridge, MA: Belknap Press of Harvard University Press, 2013), 252–53.

20. See Noel Ignatiev, *How the Irish Became White* (New York: Routledge, 1995).

21. Mahmood Mamdani, "Settler Colonialism: Then and Now," *Critical Inquiry* 41, no. 3 (2015): 607.

CHAPTER 1: ALEXANDER HAMILTON

1. *Hamilton: An American Musical*, music and lyrics by Lin-Manuel Miranda, dir. Thomas Kail; hist. consultant Ron Chernow.

2. Michel-Rolph Trouillot, *Silencing the Past: Power and the Production of History* (Boston: Beacon Press, 1995), 17–18.

3. Ron Chernow, *Alexander Hamilton* (New York: Penguin, 2004).

4. Ron Chernow, *Washington: A Life* (New York: Penguin, 2010); Chernow, *House of Morgan: An American Banking Dynasty and the Rise of Modern Finance* (New York: Macmillan, 1990); Chernow, *The Life of John D. Rockefeller, Sr.* (New York: Random House, 1998).

5. Nancy Isenberg, "'Make 'Em Laugh': Why History Cannot Be Reduced to Song and Dance," *Journal of the Early Republic* 37, no. 2 (Summer 2017): 299.

6. Isenberg, "'Make 'Em Laugh,'" 302.

7. Joanne Freeman, "How Hamilton Uses History," *Slate*, November 11, 2015, https://slate.com/culture/2015/11/how-lin-manuel-miranda-used -real-history-in-writing-hamilton.html.

8. See Wendell Bird, *Criminal Dissent: Prosecutions Under the Alien and Sedition Acts of 1798* (Cambridge, MA: Harvard University Press, 2020).

9. James Morton Smith, "Alexander Hamilton, the Alien Law, and Seditious Libels," *Review of Politics* 16, no. 3 (July 1954): 305–6.

10. Hamilton to Pickering, June 7, 1798, *Pickering Papers*, Massachusetts Historical Society, XXII, 196, quoted in Smith, "Alexander Hamilton, the Alien Law, and Seditious Libels," 306–7.

11. Smith, "Alexander Hamilton, the Alien Law, and Seditious Libels," 307.

12. Douglas M. Bradburn, " 'True Americans' and 'Hordes of Foreigners': Nationalism, Ethnicity and the Problem of Citizenship in the United States, 1789–1800," *Historical Reflections / Réflexions Historiques* 29, no. 1 (2003): 3–4, 24.

13. Nancy Isenberg, "Liberals Love Alexander Hamilton. But Aaron Burr Was a Real Progressive Hero," *Washington Post*, March 30, 2016, https:// www.washingtonpost.com/posteverything/wp/2016/03/30/liberals -love-alexander-hamilton-but-aaron-burr-was-a-real-progressive-hero.

14. Ishmael Reed, *The Haunting of Lin-Manuel Miranda* (New York: Archway Editions, 2020).

15. Ishmael Reed, "When You Mess with Creation Myths, the Knives Come Out," *Counterpunch*, September 13, 2019.

16. Ishmael Reed, " 'Hamilton: The Musical': Black Actors Dress Up Like Slave Traders . . . and It's Not Halloween," *Counterpunch,* August 21, 2015, http://www.counterpunch.org/2015/08/21/hamilton-the-musical -black-actors-dress-up-like-slave-tradersand-its-not-halloween.

17. Annette Gordon-Reed, "Hamilton: The Musical; Blacks and the Founding Fathers," National Council on Public History, April 6, 2016, http://ncph.org/history-at-work/hamilton-the-musical-blacks-and-the -founding-fathers.

18. Lyra D. Monteiro, "Race-Conscious Casting and the Erasure of the Black Past in Lin-Manuel Miranda's Hamilton," *Public Historian* 38, no. 1 (February 2016): 95, https://www.academia.edu/21739155 /RaceConscious_Casting_and_the_Erasure_of_the_Black_Past_in _Lin-Manuel_Mirandas_Hamilton.

19. Sarah Churchwell, " 'The Lehman Trilogy' and Wall Street's Debt to Slavery," *New York Review of Books,* July 11, 2019, https://www .nybooks.com/daily/2019/06/11/the-lehman-trilogy-and-wall-streets -debt-to-slavery.

20. Jennifer Schuessler, "Alexander Hamilton, Enslaver? New Research Says Yes," *New York Times*, November 9, 2020, https://www.nytimes .com/2020/11/09/arts/alexander-hamilton-enslaver-research.html.

21. Mary Esch, "New Research Paper Claims Abolitionist Owned Slaves," *San Francisco Chronicle*, November 12, 2020, https://www.pressreader .com/usa/san-francisco-chronicle/20201112/281616717897567.

22. Michelle DuRoss, "Somewhere in Between: Alexander Hamilton and Slavery," *Early America Review* 9, no. 4 (2010): 1–8, https://www .varsitytutors.com/earlyamerica/early-america-review/volume-15 /hamilton-and-slavery.

23. Chernow, *Alexander Hamilton*, 121.

24. Richard Brookhiser, *Alexander Hamilton: American* (New York: Free Press, 1999), 175–76.

25. DuRoss, "Somewhere in Between," 2–3.

26. Phil Magness, "Alexander Hamilton's Exaggerated Abolitionism," History News Network, July 2020, https://historynewsnetwork.org /blog/153639.

27. Monteiro, "Race-Conscious Casting and the Erasure of the Black Past in Lin-Manuel Miranda's Hamilton," 97.

28. Kathryn Lurie, "Playing the Man Who Shot Hamilton," *Wall Street Journal*, August 6, 2015, https://www.wsj.com/articles/playing-the-man -who-shot-hamilton-1438896589.

29. Monteiro, "Race-Conscious Casting and the Erasure of the Black Past in Lin-Manuel Miranda's Hamilton," 97. In the 1940s, psychologists Kenneth and Mamie Clark designed and conducted a series of experiments known colloquially as "the doll tests" to study the psychological effects of segregation on African American children. Drs. Clark used four dolls, identical except for color, to test children's racial perceptions. Their subjects, children from age three to seven, were asked to identify both the race of the dolls and which color of doll they preferred. A majority of the children preferred the white doll and assigned positive characteristics to it. The Clarks concluded that "prejudice, discrimination, and segregation" created a feeling of inferiority among African American children and damaged their self-esteem. https://www.naacpldf.org/ldf-celebrates-60th -anniversary-brown-v-board-education/significance-doll-test.

30. Lin-Manuel Miranda and Jeremy McCarter, *Hamilton: The Revolution* (New York: Grand Central, 2016), 33.

31. Max M. Edling, *A Revolution in Favor of Government: Origins of the U.S. Constitution and the Making of the American State* (New York: Oxford University Press, 2003), 47–49, 227.

32. Stephen S. Cohen and J. Bradford DeLong, *Concrete Economics: The Hamilton Approach to Economic Growth and Policy* (Cambridge, MA: Harvard Business Review Press, 2016).

33. Edling, *A Revolution in Favor of Government*, 47–49, 227.

34. Edling, *A Revolution in Favor of Government*, 140.

35. Gregory Ablavsky, "The Savage Constitution," *Duke Law Journal* 63, no. 5 (February 2014): 999–1000, https://www.researchgate.net /publication/256051346_The_Savage_Constitution. See Jeffrey Ostler, " 'Just and Lawful War' as Genocidal War in the (United States) North-

west Ordinance and Northwest Territory, 1787–1832," *Journal of Genocide Research* 18, no. 1 (2016): 1–20, https://www.tandfonline.com/doi /abs/10.1080/14623528.2016.1120460. Also see Jeffrey Ostler, *Surviving Genocide: Native Nations and the United States from the American Revolution to Bleeding Kansas* (New Haven, CT: Yale University Press, 2019).

36. Ablavsky, "The Savage Constitution," 1007.

37. Alan Singer, "The Twisted History of Domestic Military Intervention," History News Network, July 2020, https://historynewsnetwork.org /article/176068.

38. See John Grenier, *The First Way of War: American War Making on the Frontier* (New York: Cambridge University Press, 2005), 5.

39. Ablavsky, "The Savage Constitution," 1078–79, 1082.

40. Ablavsky, "The Savage Constitution," 1050.

41. Ablavsky, "The Savage Constitution," 1050.

42. Ablavsky, "The Savage Constitution," 1083, 1085. The 2003 US Justice Department's Office of Legal Counsel assistant US attorney general penned the infamous "Torture Memo," creating the term "illegal combatant" based on the precedent of the US Supreme Court 1873 decision in *Modoc Indian Prisoners.*

43. William Hogeland, "Inventing Alexander Hamilton: The Troubling Embrace of the Founder of American Finance," *Boston Review*, November 1, 2007, http://www.bostonreview.net/hogeland-inventing-alexander -hamilton. Hogeland wrote of the Whiskey rebels: "Contrary to what many historians suggest, the Whiskey Rebellion can't be understood as a last gasp of anti-federalism. After all, the rebels weren't against taxes. In most cases, they weren't against the federal government: indeed, many were veterans who had fought to install that government in the first place. What they wanted was 'equal taxation'—i.e., progressive taxes that would impose a lesser burden on the poor." See William Hogeland, *The Whiskey Rebellion: George Washington, Alexander Hamilton, and the Frontier Rebels Who Challenged America's Newfound Sovereignty* (New York: Scribner's, 2006).

44. Robert Sullivan, "The Hamilton Cult," *Harper's Magazine*, October 2016, https://harpers.org/archive/2016/10/the-hamilton-cult/2.

45. "President's General," The Society of the Cincinnati, https://www .societyofthecincinnati.org/about/history/presidents_general.

CHAPTER 2: SETTLER COLONIALISM

1. Patrick Wolfe, "Settler Colonialism and the Elimination of the Native," *Journal of Genocide Research* 8, no. 4 (2006): 387–409. See also Patrick Wolfe, *Settler Colonialism and the Transformation of Anthropology: The Politics and Poetics of an Ethnographic Event* (New York: Continuum, 1998). In addition to the late Australian anthropologist Patrick

Wolfe's groundbreaking work on settler colonialism in Australia, New Zealand, and North America, two historians have published important books in this growing field. Australian historian Lorenzo Veracini is the author of *Israel and Settler Society* (New York: Pluto Press, 2006); *Settler Colonialism: A Theoretical Overview* (New York: Palgrave, 2010); and *The Settler Colonial Present* (New York: Palgrave, 2013). He is also the founder and managing editor of the scholarly journal *Settler Colonial Studies*. Veracini's work is global and comparative, as is Wolfe's. US historian Walter L. Hixson's book *American Settler Colonialism: A History* (New York: Palgrave, 2013) focuses on the United States, as does German historian of Anglo-American history Julius Wilm in *Settlers as Conquerors: Free Land Policy in Antebellum America* (Stuttgart: Franz Steiner Verlag, 2018). For the views of Native and Latino Studies scholars, see Alyosha Goldstein, ed., *Formations of United States Colonialism* (Durham, NC: Duke University Press, 2014).

2. Howard Lamar, *The Far Southwest, 1846–1912* (New Haven, CT: Yale University Press, 1966), 7–10.

3. David Reynolds, *America, Empire of Liberty* (New York: Penguin, 2010), xvii, 304, 458.

4. Wolfe, "Settler Colonialism and the Elimination of the Native."

5. Henry George, 1839–1897, was a US economist and journalist whose 1879 book *Progress and Poverty* sold millions of copies worldwide and was a longtime best seller in the United States. George argued that individuals should own the value they produce themselves, but that the value derived from land and natural resources should belong equally to all, that is, the socialization of land and natural resources rents.

6. See Wilm, *Settlers as Conquerors*.

7. Donald Harman Akenson, "The Great European Migration and Indigenous Populations," in *Irish and Scottish Encounters with Indigenous Peoples*, ed. Graeme Morton and David A. Wilson (Montreal: McGill-Queen's University Press, 2013), 22–48. See also Michael Witgen, "A Nation of Settlers: The Early American Republic and the Colonization of the Northwest Territory," *William & Mary Quarterly* 76, no. 3 (2019): 391–98, muse.jhu.edu/article/730611.

8. Mahmood Mamdani, *Neither Settler nor Native: The Making and Unmaking of Permanent Minorities* (Cambridge, MA: Harvard University Press, 2020), 98; see also James Q. Whitman, *Hitler's American Model: The United States and the Making of Nazi Race Law* (Princeton, NJ: Princeton University Press, 2017); Carroll P. Kakel III, *The American West and the Nazi East: A Comparative and Interpretive Perspective* (New York: Palgrave Macmillan, 2013); Robert Miller, "Nazi Germany and American Indians," *Indian Country Today*, August 14, 2019, https://indiancountrytoday.com/opinion/nazi-germany-and-american-indians-Uhao7e3luUCaeLq1nJP5-Q.

9. See Paul Wallace Gates, *History of Public Land Law Development* (New York: Arno Press, 1979).

10. Richard White, *"It's Your Misfortune and None of My Own": A New History of the American West* (Norman: University of Oklahoma Press, 1991), 139.

11. Victor Westphall, *The Public Domain in New Mexico, 1854–1891* (Albuquerque: University of New Mexico Press, 1965), 43.

12. See Manu Karuka, *Empire's Tracks: Indigenous Nations, Chinese Workers, and the Transcontinental Railroad* (Berkeley: University of California Press, 2019); Richard White, *Railroaded: The Transcontinentals and the Making of Modern America* (New York: W. W. Norton, 2011).

13. Raphael Lemkin, *Axis Rule in Occupied Europe: Laws of Occupation, Analysis of Government, Proposals for Redress* (Clark, NJ: Lawbook Exchange, 2008).

14. William L. Patterson, ed., *We Charge Genocide: The Historic Petition to the United Nations for Relief from a Crime of the United States Government Against the Negro People*, Civil Rights Congress, January 1, 1951, https://www.blackpast.org/global-african-history/primary -documents-global-african-history/we-charge-genocide-historic -petition-united-nations-relief-crime-united-states-government-against.

15. Convention on the Prevention and Punishment of the Crime of Genocide, Adopted by the General Assembly of the UN, December 9, 1948, https:// treaties.un.org/doc/publication/unts/volume%2078/volume-78-i-1021 -english.pdf.

16. Patterson, ed., *We Charge Genocide,* https://www.blackpast.org /global-african-history/primary-documents-global-african-history /we-charge-genocide-historic-petition-united-nations-relief-crime -united-states-government-against.

17. "Genocide Hearings Underway in Cambodia's War Crimes Tribunal," Deutsche Welle, August 29, 2015, http://www.dw.com/en/genocide -hearings-underway-in-cambodias-war-crimes-tribunal/a-18699601.

18. "Capt. Richard H. Pratt on the Education of Native Americans," *Official Report of the Nineteenth Annual Conference of Charities and Correction*, 1892, 46–59, http://carlisleindian.dickinson.edu/sites/all/files /docs-resources/CIS-Resources_PrattSpeechExcerptShort.pdf.

19. April 17, 1873, quoted in John F. Marszalek, *Sherman: A Soldier's Passion for Order* (New York: Free Press, 1992), 379.

20. See Jeffrey Ostler, " 'Just and Lawful War' as Genocidal War in the (United States) Northwest Ordinance and Northwest Territory, 1787– 1832," *Journal of Genocide Research* 18, no. 1 (2016): 1–20; Ostler, *Surviving Genocide*. Also see Witgen, "A Nation of Settlers: The Early American Republic and the Colonization of the Northwest Territory."

21. Robert J. Miller, "The International Law of Colonialism: A Comparative Analysis," in "Symposium of International Law in Indigenous Affairs:

The Doctrine of Discovery, the United Nations, and the Organization of American States," special issue, *Lewis and Clark Law Review* 15, no. 4 (Winter 2011): 847–922. See also Vine Deloria Jr., *Of Utmost Good Faith* (San Francisco: Straight Arrow Books, 1971), 6–39; Steven T. Newcomb, *Pagans in the Promised Land: Decoding the Doctrine of Christian Discovery* (Golden, CO: Fulcrum, 2008).

22. Johnson v. McIntosh, 21 U.S. (8 Wheaton), 543, 1823, p. 573.

23. Robert A. Williams Jr., *The American Indian in Western Legal Thought: The Discourses of Conquest* (New York: Oxford University Press, 1990), 233–86.

24. Harvey D. Rosenthal, "Indian Claims and the American Conscience: A Brief History of the Indian Claims Commission," in *Irredeemable America: The Indians' Estate and Land Claims*, ed. Imre Sutton (Albuquerque: New Mexico University Press, 1985), 36.

25. See chapter 6 for discussion of the US cult of Columbus as original founder of the United States.

26. See Alex Trimble Young, "The Settler Unchained: Constituent Power and Settler Violence," *Social Text* 124, vol. 33, no. 3 (September 2015): 4, https://read.dukeupress.edu/social-text/article-abstract/33/3%20(124)/1/33827/The-Settler-UnchainedConstituent-Power-and-Settler.

27. "Barack Obama's Inaugural Address," transcript, *New York Times*, January 20, 2009.

28. Alyosha Goldstein, "Where the Nation Takes Place: Proprietary Regimes, Antistatism, and U.S. Settler Colonialism," *South Atlantic Quarterly* 107, no. 4 (2008): 835.

29. Stephen Pearson, "'The Last Bastion of Colonialism': Appalachian Settler Colonialism and Self-Indigenization," *American Indian Culture and Research Journal* 37, no. 2 (2013): 165–84.

30. See Philip J. Deloria, *Playing Indian* (New Haven, CT: Yale University Press, 1999).

31. See David S. Reynolds, *Walking Giant: America in the Age of Jackson* (New York: Harper, 2008), and David S. Reynolds, *Walt Whitman's America: A Cultural Biography* (New York: Vintage, 1995).

32. Carl Degler, *Out of Our Past: The Forces That Shaped Modern America* (New York: Harper, 1959), 511.

33. Richard Slotkin, *Regeneration Through Violence: The Mythology of the American Frontier, 1600–1860* (Middletown, CT: Wesleyan University Press, 1973), 42.

34. Slotkin, *Regeneration Through Violence*, 394–95.

35. William Hogeland, *Autumn of the Black Snake: The Creation of the U.S. Army and the Invasion That Opened the West* (New York: Farrar, Straus & Giroux, 2017), 19–44.

36. Stephen Pearson created the term "self-indigenization" to describe the process in this perceptive article, "'The Last Bastion of Colonialism':

Appalachian Settler Colonialism and Self-Indigenization," *American Indian Culture and Research Journal* 37, no. 2 (2013): 165–84; Eve Tuck and K. Wayne Yang, "Decolonization Is Not a Metaphor," *Decolonization: Indigeneity, Education and Society* 1, no. 1 (2012): 9, https://clas .osu.edu/sites/clas.osu.edu/files/Tuck%20and%20Yang%202012%20 Decolonization%20is%20not%20a%20metaphor.pdf.

37. Steven Stoll, *Ramp Hollow: The Ordeal of Appalachia* (New York: Hill & Wang, 2017), 27.

38. See E. P. Thompson, *The Making of the English Working Class* (New York: Pantheon, 1963).

39. Nina Silber, *The Romance of Reunion: Northerners and the South, 1865–1900* (Chapel Hill: University of North Carolina Press, 1997), 14–39.

40. Pablo Gonzalez Casanova, "Internal Colonialism and National Development," *Studies in Comparative International Development* 1, no. 4 (1964): 27–37; *Democracy in México* (first published in Spanish in 1965; New York: Oxford University Press, 1972).

41. See Jodi Byrd, *The Transit of Empire: Indigenous Critiques of Colonialism* (Minneapolis: University of Minnesota Press, 2011), 117–46.

42. Harry M. Caudill, *Night Comes to the Cumberlands: A Biography of a Depressed Region* (Boston: Little, Brown, 1963).

43. Harry Caudill, "Misdeal in Appalachia," *Dissent* 14 (1967): 719.

44. Pearson, " 'The Last Bastion of Colonialism': Appalachian Settler Colonialism and Self-Indigenization," 169.

45. Pearson, " 'The Last Bastion of Colonialism': Appalachian Settler Colonialism and Self-Indigenization," 165.

46. Pearson, " 'The Last Bastion of Colonialism': Appalachian Settler Colonialism and Self-Indigenization," 168.

47. Helen Lewis, ed., *Colonialism in Modern America: The Appalachian Case* (Boone, NC: Appalachian Consortium Press, 1978).

48. Pearson, " 'The Last Bastion of Colonialism': Appalachian Settler Colonialism and Self-Indigenization," 170–71; Helen Lewis and Edward Knipe, "The Colonialism Model: The Appalachian Case," in Lewis et al., *Colonialism in Modern America*.

49. Edward Guinan, "Ashes to Ashes, Dust to Dust," in *Redemption Denied: An Appalachian Reader*, ed. Edward Guinan (Washington, DC: Appalachian Documentation, 1978), 10.

50. Quoted in Silas House and Jason Howard, *Something's Rising: Appalachians Fighting Mountaintop Removal* (Lexington: University of Kentucky Press, 2011), 144.

51. David Whisnant, "Ethnicity and the Recovery of Regional Identity in Appalachia: Thoughts upon Entering the Zone of Occult Instability," *Soundings* 56 (1973): 134.

52. Rodger Cunningham, "The Green Side of Life: Appalachian Magic as a Site of Resistance," *Appalachian Heritage* 38, no. 2 (2010): 60.

53. Pearson, " 'The Last Bastion of Colonialism': Appalachian Settler Colonialism and Self-Indigenization," 172.

54. Razib Khan, "The Scots-Irish as Indigenous People," *Discover*, July 22, 2012, https://www.discovermagazine.com/mind/the-scots-irish-as-indigenous-people.

55. J. D. Vance, *Hillbilly Elegy: A Memoir of a Family and Culture in Crisis* (New York: HarperCollins, 2016).

56. James Webb, *Born Fighting: How the Scots-Irish Shaped America* (New York: Broadway, 2005).

57. Vance, *Hillbilly Elegy*, 2–3.

58. Vance, *Hillbilly Elegy*, 3–4.

59. Anthony Harkins and Meredith McCarroll, eds., *Appalachian Reckoning to Hillbilly Elegy* (Morgantown: West Virginia University Press, 2019).

60. T. R. C. Hutton, "Hillbilly Elitism," in Harkins and McCarroll, *Appalachian Reckoning to Hillbilly Elegy*, 28.

61. Lisa R. Pruitt, "What Hillbilly Elegy Reveals About Race in Twenty-First-Century America," in Harkins and McCarroll, *Appalachian Reckoning to Hillbilly Elegy*, 109.

62. Ellen Wayland-Smith, "The Mythic Whiteness of the Hillbilly," *Boston Review*, November 20, 2020, http://bostonreview.net/arts-society/ellen-wayland-smith-mythic-whiteness-hillbilly.

63. For another example of settler-colonial self-indigenization in New Mexico, see chapter 5.

64. Peter Walker, *Sagebrush Collaboration: How Harney County Defeated the Takeover of the Malheur Wildlife Refuge* (Corvallis: Oregon State University Press, 2018), 2–3; Jacqueline Keeler, *Standoff: Standing Rock, the Bundy Movement, and the American Story of Sacred Lands* (Salt Lake City, UT: Torrey House Press, 2021); see also Alyosha Goldstein, "By Force of Expectation: Colonization, Public Lands, and the Property Relation," *UCLA Law Review* 65, 2018; online symposium, https://www.academia.edu/36047291/_By_Force_of_Expectation_Colonization_Public_Lands_and_the_Property_Relation.

65. Walker, *Sagebrush Collaboration*, 92–97.

66. Joshua F. J. Inwood and Anne Bonds, "Property and Whiteness: The Oregon Standoff and the Contradictions of the U.S. Settler State," *Space and Polity* 21, no. 3 (2017): 1, https://www.tandfonline.com/doi/full/10.1080/13562576.2017.1373425.

67. Inwood and Bonds, "Property and Whiteness," 12.

68. Walker, *Sagebrush Collaboration*, 45.

69. Ted Koppel, "Guns, a Family Affair," *CBS Sunday Morning*, March 13, 2016, http://www.cbsnews.com/ news/guns-a-family-affair.

70. Transcript: "Face to Face with Alan Simpson," CBS News, February 23, 2012, http://www.cbsnews.com/news/transcript-face-to-face-with-alan-simpson.

71 Witgen, "A Nation of Settlers," 398.

72. Mahmood Mamdani, "Settler Colonialism: Then and Now," *Critical Inquiry* 41, no. 3 (Spring 2015): 602–3, https://www.jstor.org /stable/10.1086/680088. This text is a revised version of the Edward Said Lecture, Princeton University, December 6, 2012, https://mediacentral .princeton.edu/media/Settler+ColonialismA+Then+and+Now%2C +Mahmood+Mamdani/0_crzrp53l.

73. Mamdani, *Neither Settler nor Native*, 20–21.

74. Lorenzo Veracini, *Settler Colonialism: A Theoretical Overview* (New York: Palgrave Macmillan, 2010), 3.

CHAPTER 3: ARRIVANTS

1. Edward Kamau Brathwaite, *The Arrivants: A New World Trilogy— Rights of Passage/Islands/Masks* (New York: Oxford University Press, 1988). For discussion of the term, see Byrd, *The Transit of Empire*, 58–59, 91, 92.

2. Ibram X. Kendi, *Stamped from the Beginning: The Definitive History of Racist Ideas in America* (New York: Bold Type Books, 2016), 23.

3. Papal Bull Dum Diversas, June 18, 1452, https://doctrineofdiscovery.org /dum-diversas.

4. Trouillot, *Silencing the Past*, 17.

5. See Andrés Reséndez, *The Other Slavery: The Uncovered Story of Indian Enslavement in America* (New York: Mariner Books, 2016).

6. The 1619 Project, *New York Times Magazine*, 2019, dir. Nikole Hannah-Jones, https://www.nytimes.com/interactive/2019/08/14/magazine/1619 -america-slavery.html.

7. Michael Grossberg and Christopher Tomlins, eds., *The Cambridge History of Law in America*, vol. 1 (Cambridge, UK: Cambridge University Press), 260.

8. Sally E. Hadden, *Slave Patrols: Law and Violence in Virginia and the Carolinas* (Cambridge, MA: Harvard University Press, 2001).

9. Horton, "Working Against Racism from White Subject Positions," 165.

10. See Magnus Mörner, *Race Mixture in the History of Latin America* (New York: Little Brown, 1967). On the origins of race and racism, see Sven Lindqvist, *"Exterminate All the Brutes": One Man's Odyssey into the Heart of Darkness and the Origins of European Genocide* (New York: New Press, 1992), 122–41.

11. Robin D. G. Kelley, "The Rest of Us: Rethinking Settler and Native," *American Quarterly* 69, no. 2 (June 2017): 268–69.

12. Cedric J. Robinson, *Black Marxism: The Making of the Black Radical Tradition* (1983; repr., Chapel Hill: University of North Carolina Press, 2000), 121–22.

13. Trouillot, *Silencing the Past*, 17–20.

14. Fara Dabhoiwala, "Speech and Slavery in the West Indies," *New*

York Review of Books, August 20, 2020. Dabhoiwala reviews three books: Miles Ogborn, *The Freedom of Speech: Talk and Slavery in the Anglo-Caribbean World* (Chicago: University of Chicago Press, 2019); Vincent Brown, *Tacky's Revolt: The Story of an Atlantic Slave War* (Cambridge, MA: Harvard University Press, 2020); and Tom Zoellner, *Island on Fire: The Revolt That Ended Slavery in the British Empire* (Cambridge, MA: Harvard University Press, 2020), https://www.nybooks.com/articles/2020/08/20/speech-slavery-west-indies.

15. Dabhoiwala, "Speech and Slavery in the West Indies."

16. See Brown, *Tacky's Revolt: The Story of an Atlantic Slave War.*

17. Kathryn L. MacKay, "Selected Statistics on Slavery in the United States," 1860 census, Weber State University, https://faculty.weber.edu/kmackay/selected_statistics_on_slavery_i.htm.

18. Stefano Massini, *The Lehman Trilogy*, 2013, adapted and condensed by Sam Mendes, opened off Broadway in 2019 and opened on Broadway in March 2020, but was shown digitally during the pandemic.

19. Sarah Churchwell, " 'The Lehman Trilogy' and Wall Street's Debt to Slavery," *New York Review of Books*, July 11, 2019, https://www.nybooks.com/daily/2019/06/11/the-lehman-trilogy-and-wall-streets-debt-to-slavery.

20. See Johnson, *River of Dark Dreams.*

21. Churchwell, " 'The Lehman Trilogy' and Wall Street's Debt to Slavery."

22. David Brion Davis, "The Slave Trade and the Jews," *New York Review of Books*, December 22, 1994, https://www.nybooks.com/articles/1994/12/22/the-slave-trade-and-the-jews.

23. MacKay, "Selected Statistics on Slavery in the United States."

24. Eric Williams, *Capitalism and Slavery* (1944; repr., Chapel Hill: University of North Carolina Press, 1994).

25. Cedric J. Robinson, *On Racial Capitalism, Black Internationalism, and Cultures of Resistance* (London: Pluto Press, 2019). Several subsequent books have expanded and deepened the study of the rise of capitalism in the United States as located in the Mississippi Valley cotton industry: Johnson, *River of Dark Dreams*; Calvin Schermerhorn, *The Business of Slavery and the Rise of American Capitalism, 1815–1860* (New Haven, CT: Yale University Press, 2015); and Edward Baptist, *The Half Has Never Been Told: Slavery and the Making of American Capitalism* (New York: Basic Books, 2016).

26. W. E. B. Du Bois, *The Suppression of the African Slave Trade to the United States* (1896; repr, New York: Oxford University Press, 2014), 98.

27. Johnson, *River of Dark Dreams*, 28, 32.

28 Johnson, *River of Dark Dreams*, 10.

29. Johnson, *River of Dark Dreams*, 41–42.

30. Hadden, *Slave Patrols*, 2.

31. Hadden, *Slave Patrols*, 25–28.

32. Hadden, *Slave Patrols*, 32–35.
33. From Edward Cantwell's 1860 judicial hornbook, *The Practice at Law in North Carolina*, quoted in Hadden, *Slave Patrols*, 105.
34. Johnson, *River of Dark Dreams*, 222–23, 234–35.
35. Johnson, *River of Dark Dreams*, 198–202.
36. Johnson, *River of Dark Dreams*, 204–5.
37. Phillip W. Magnes, *Colonization After Emancipation: Lincoln and the Movement for Black Resettlement* (Columbia: University of Missouri Press, 2018).
38. Walter Johnson, "The Racial Origins of American Sovereignty," *Raritan: A Quarterly Review* 31, no. 3 (Winter 2012), https:// raritanquarterly.rutgers.edu/issue-index/all-volumes-issues/volume-31 /volume-31-number-3.
39. See Martha S. Jones, *Birthright Citizens: A History of Race and Rights in Antebellum America* (New York: Cambridge University Press, 2019).
40. Michelle Alexander, *The New Jim Crow: Mass Incarceration in the Age of Colorblindness* (New York: New Press, 2012), 31; Ruffin v. Commonwealth 62 VA 790 (1871). See also Ava DuVernay, *13th*, documentary film, 2016, available for viewing at https://www.netflix.com/title /80091741.
41. Richard Rothstein, *The Color of Law: A Forgotten History of How Our Government Segregated America* (New York: Liveright, 2017), 155.
42. See Boyd Cothran, *Remembering the Modoc War: Redemptive Violence and the Making of American Innocence* (Chapel Hill: University of North Carolina Press, 2014). Also see Benjamin Madley, *An American Genocide: The United States and the California Indian Catastrophe, 1846–1873* (New Haven, CT: Yale University Press, 2016).
43. Malcolm Harris, "The Future of the United States," a review essay of Ned Sublette and Constance Sublette, *The American Slave Coast*, in *Pacific Standard Magazine*, January 26, 2016, https://psmag.com /a-future-history-of-the-united-states-2965a114f8ee#.6t82shj6j.
44. Hadden, *Slave Patrols*, 216.
45. See Bill Fletcher Jr., "Race Is About More Than Discrimination: Racial Capitalism, the Settler State, and the Challenges Facing Organized Labor in the United States," *Monthly Review* 72, no. 3 (July 2020), https://monthlyreviewarchives.org/index.php/mr/article/view/MR-072-03 -2020-07_3.
46. Mike Davis, *City of Quartz: Excavating the Future of Los Angeles* (New York: Vintage Books, 1990), chap. 4. Davis doesn't make the slave patrol connection but is the best source on the LAPD during Parker's reign. For the export of this kind of racist police training to states supported or often imposed by the US, see Jeremy Kuzmarov, *Modernizing Repression: Police Training and Nation-Building in the American Century* (Amherst: University of Massachusetts Press, 2012).

47. See Elizabeth Hinton, *From the War on Poverty to the War on Crime: The Making of Mass Incarceration in America* (Cambridge, MA: Harvard University Press, 2017).

48. See Max Felker-Kantor, *Policing Los Angeles: Race, Resistance, and the Rise of the LAPD* (Chapel Hill: University of North Carolina Press, 2018).

49. Bureau of Justice Statistics, Office of Justice Programs. See Angela Y. Davis, *Are Prisons Obsolete?* (New York: Seven Stories Press, 2003). On mass incarceration, see Alexander, *The New Jim Crow*; Jordan T. Camp, *Incarcerating the Crisis: Freedom Struggles and the Rise of the Neoliberal State* (Berkeley: University of California Press, 2016); Dan Berger, *The Struggle Within: Prisons, Political Prisoners, and Mass Movements in the United States* (Oakland, CA: PM Press, 2014); James Kilgore, *Understanding Mass Incarceration: A People's Guide to the Key Civil Rights Struggle of Our Time* (New York: New Press, 2015).

50. Ruth Wilson Gilmore, *Golden Gulag: Prisons, Surplus, Crisis, and Opposition in Globalizing California* (Berkeley: University of California Press, 2007), 7–12.

51. Ruth Wilson Gilmore, foreword to Dan Berger, *The Struggle Within: Prisons, Political Prisoners, and Mass Movements in the United States* (Oakland, CA: PM Press, 2014), vii–viii.

52. Alex S. Vitale, *The End of Policing* (New York: Verso, 2017), 4. On policing, see also Angela J. Davis, ed., *Policing the Black Man: Arrest, Prosecution, and Imprisonment* (New York: Vintage, 2018); see also Jordan T. Camp and Christina Heatherton, eds., *Policing the Planet: Why the Policing Crisis Led to Black Lives Matter* (New York: Verso, 2013). With contributions from #BlackLivesMatter cofounder Patrisse Cullors, Ferguson activist and law professor Justin Hansford, director of New York–based Communities United for Police Reform Joo-Hyun Kang, poet Martín Espada, and journalist Anjali Kamat, as well as articles from leading scholars Ruth Wilson Gilmore, Robin D. G. Kelley, Naomi Murakawa, Vijay Prashad, and more, *Policing the Planet* describes ongoing struggles from New York to Baltimore to Los Angeles, London, San Juan, and San Salvador.

53. Prison Policy Initiative, June 2020, https://www.prisonpolicy.org/blog/2020/06/05/policekillings.

54. See Ronald F. Jacobs, *Race, Media, and the Crisis of Civil Society: From the Watts Riots to Rodney King* (New York: Cambridge University Press, 2000).

55. See Angela Y. Davis, *Freedom Is a Constant Struggle: Ferguson, Palestine, and the Foundations of a Movement* (New York: Haymarket Books, 2016).

56. Radley Balko, *Rise of the Warrior Cop: The Militarization of America's Police Forces* (New York: Public Affairs, 2014), 253–54.

57. Alisha Haridasani Gupta, "Since 2015: 48 Black Women Were Killed by the Police. And Only 2 Charges," *New York Times*, September 24, 2020,

https://www.nytimes.com/2020/09/24/us/breonna-taylor-grand-jury-black-women.html. See Andrea J. Ritchie, *Invisible No More: Police Violence Against Black Women and Women of Color* (Boston: Beacon Press, 2017).

58. See Alicia Garza, *The Purpose of Power: How We Come Together When We Fall Apart* (New York: One World, 2020); Patrisse Khan-Cullors and asha bandele, *When They Call You a Terrorist: A Black Lives Matter Memoir* (New York: St. Martin's Griffin, 2020). For a history of Black movements with women's leadership that led to the founding of Black Lives Matter, see Barbara Ransby, *Making All Black Lives Matter: Reimagining Freedom in the Twenty-First Century* (Berkeley: University of California Press, 2018). Also see Jordan T. Camp and Christina Heatherton, eds., *Policing the Planet: Why the Policy Crisis Led to Black Lives Matter* (New York: Verso, 2016).

59. Keeanga-Yamahtta Taylor, ed., *How We Get Free: Black Feminism and the Combahee River Collective* (New York: Haymarket Books, 2017).

60. Mohamed Abdulkadir Ali, "Trey's Rage: An African's Education in Being Black in America," *New York Review of Books*, June 20, 2020, https://www.nybooks.com/daily/2020/06/18/treys-rage-an-africans-education-in-being-black-in-america.

61. Ali, "Trey's Rage."

62. Ali, "Trey's Rage."

63. Ali, "Trey's Rage."

64. Ali, "Trey's Rage."

65. Ali, "Trey's Rage."

66. With the months' long protests of police killing African Americans, a reckoning with anti-Black racism emerged. Sydney Trent, "Young Asians and Latinos Push Their Parents to Acknowledge Racism Among Protests," *Washington Post*, June 22, 2020, https://www.washingtonpost.com/local/young-asians-and-latinos-push-their-parents-to-acknowledge-racism-amid-protests/2020/06/21/97daa5f2-b193-11ea-856d-5054296735e5_story.html.

67. Edwidge Danticat, "So Brutal a Death," *New Yorker*, June 22, 2020, https://www.newyorker.com/contributors/edwidge-danticat.

68. Ryan Fontanilla, "Immigration Enforcement and the Afterlife of the Slave Ship," *Boston Review*, February 11, 2021, https://bostonreview.net/race/ryan-fontanilla-immigration-enforcement-and-afterlife-slave-ship.

69. Suketu Mehta, *This Land Is Our Land: An Immigrant's Manifesto* (New York: Farrar, Straus & Giroux, 2019), 10.

70. "Declaration," World Conference against Racism, Racial Discrimination, Xenophobia and Related Intolerance, Durban, South Africa, *United Nations Documents* (August 31–September 8, 2001), 6, https://www.un.org/WCAR/durban.pdf.

71. Trouillot, *Silencing the Past*, 146–47.

72. Trouillot, *Silencing the Past*, 150.

73. Trouillot, *Silencing the Past*, 153–54.

CHAPTER 4: CONTINENTAL IMPERIALISM

1. For a concise overall narrative of the US war against Mexico and the colonization of Texas, New Mexico, Arizona, and California, see Rodolfo F. Acuña, *Occupied America: A History of Chicanos*, 5th ed. (New York: Pearson Longman, 2002), 42–148.

2. Greg Grandin, *The End of the Myth: From the Frontier to the Border Wall in the Mind of America* (New York: Metropolitan Books, 2019), 152.

3. Frederick Jackson Turner, *International Monthly*, December 1901; Frederick Jackson Turner, "The Significance of the Frontier in American History," presented at the meeting of the American Historical Association in Chicago, July 12, 1893, during the World's Fair Columbian Exposition, a celebration of the onset of European colonialism and the transatlantic slave trade, http://nationalhumanitiescenter.org/pds/gilded/empire/text1/turner.pdf.

4. Lamar, *The Far Southwest*, 7–10. See chapter 2 for the Northwest Ordinance.

5. R. O. Ulibarri, "American Interest in the Spanish Mexican Southwest, 1803–1848" (PhD diss., University of Utah, 1963), 261.

6. See Robert W. Tucker and David C. Hendrickson, *Empire of Liberty: The Statecraft of Thomas Jefferson* (New York: Oxford University Press, 1992).

7. Walter Johnson, *The Broken Heart of America: St. Louis and the Violent History of the United States* (New York: Basic Books, 2020), 13–40. See also Daniel K. Richter, *Facing East from Indian Country: A Native History of Early America* (Cambridge, MA: Harvard University Press, 2001).

8. Elliot Coues, *The Expeditions of Zebulon Montgomery Pike*, 3 vols. (New York: Francis P. Harper, 1895).

9. President James Monroe, *Transcript of Monroe Doctrine*, 7th Annual Message to Congress, December 2, 1823, https://www.ourdocuments.gov/doc.php?flash=false&doc=23&page=transcript.

10. Quoted in Joseph Nevins, *Operation Gatekeeper: The Rise of the "Illegal Alien" and the Making of the U.S.-México Boundary* (New York: Routledge, 2002), 15.

11. Andrew A. Lipscomb, ed., *The Writings of Thomas Jefferson* (Washington, DC: Thomas Jefferson Memorial Association, 1903), 296.

12. Gary Clayton Anderson, *The Conquest of Texas: Ethnic Cleansing in the Promised Land, 1830–1875* (Norman: University of Oklahoma Press, 2005), 7. See also Doug J. Swanson, *Cult of Glory: The Bold and Brutal History of the Texas Rangers* (New York: Viking, 2020).

13. Anderson, *The Conquest of Texas*, 3–6.

14. Howard Zinn, *A People's History of the United States: 1492–Present* (New York: HarperCollins, 1980), 149–50. Zinn's chapter 8, "We Take Nothing by Conquest, Thank God," on the invasion, occupation, and annexation of half of México is an excellent analysis and summary.

15. Captain Lemuel Ford of the First Dragoons, United States Army, wrote the comment in his diary in reference to a group of comancheros he met on the Plains. Quoted in Charles Kenner, A *History of New México-Plains Indian Relations* (Norman: University of Oklahoma Press, 1969), 83.
16. Waddy Thompson, *Recollections of México* (New York: Wiley and Putnam, 1836), 72.
17. Lamar, *The Far Southwest*, 63.
18. William I. Parish, *The Charles Ilfeld Company: A Study of the Rise and Decline of Mercantile Capitalism in New México* (Cambridge, MA: Harvard University Press, 1961), 4.
19. Walter Johnson, *The Broken Heart of America: St. Louis and the Violent History of the United States* (New York: Basic Books, 2020), 5–6.
20. Parish, *The Charles Ilfeld Company*, 3.
21. Lamar, *The Far Southwest*, 42–47.
22. H. Bailey Carroll and J. Vallasana Haggard, eds. and trans., *Three New México Chronicles incl. The Exposicion of Don Pedro Bautista Pino, 1812; The Ojeada of Lic. Antonio Barreiro, 1832; and Don Agustin de Escudero* (Albuquerque: Quivira Society, 1942), 39.
23. David Weber, *Los Extranjeros: Selected Documents from the Mexican Side of the Santa Fé Trail, 1825–1828* (Santa Fé: Stagecoach Press, 1967), 22; Report on Foreigners by Antonio Narbonne, Santa Fé, February 1, 1826.
24. Max L. Moorhead, *New Mexico's Royal Road: Trade and Travel on the Chihuahua Trail* (Norman: University of Oklahoma Press, 1958), 76.
25. Johnson, *The Broken Heart of America*, 50. Following the seizure of northern México, in 1853–1854, Frémont again traveled to the Rockies in search of a gap that might allow the building of a transcontinental railroad along the thirty-eighth parallel, from St. Louis to San Francisco.
26. Hampton Sides, *Blood and Thunder: An Epic of the American West* (New York: Random House, 2006), 92–101. See also Tom Chaffin, *Pathfinder: John Charles Frémont and the Course of American Empire* (New York: Hill & Wang, 2002).
27. See chapter 5 , pp. 132–34, for the Irish immigrants' role in the war.
28. Stephen A. Carney and Center of Military History, *The Occupation of México, May 1846–July 1848*, The U.S. Army Campaigns of the Mexican American War (Washington, DC: US Army Center of Military History, 2005), https://history.army.mil/html/books/073/73-3/CMH_Pub_73-3 .pdf. For further reading on the US war against México, see Paul Foos, *A Short, Offhand, Killing Affair: Soldiers and Social Conflict During the Mexican-American War* (Chapel Hill: University of North Carolina Press, 2002); John Pinheiro, *Missionaries of Republicanism: A Religious History of the Mexican-American War* (New York: Oxford University Press, 2014); Danny Sjursen, "The Tortured Legacy of the Mexican-American War," Future of Freedom Foundation, June 2020, https://www.fff.org

/explore-freedom/article/the-tortured-legacy-of-the-mexican-american
-war-part-1-by-danny-sjursen.

29. Carney and Center of Military History, *The Occupation of México*, 12.

30. See Swanson, *Cult of Glory*.

31. See Gabrielle M. Neufeld Santelli and Charles R. Smith, eds., *Marines in the Mexican War*, Occasional Papers series (Washington, DC: History and Museums Division Headquarters, US Marine Corps, 1991), iii, https://www.usmcu.edu/Portals/218/Marines%20In%20The%20 Mexican%20War.pdf?ver=2018-10-29-143813-560. This does not cover in depth Marines activities that took place in California and western México. For that, see Charles R. Smith, ed., *The Journals of Marine Second Lieutenant Henry Bulls Watson, 1845–1848* (Washington, DC: History and Museums Division Headquarters, US Marine Corps, 1990). Being from North Carolina, Watson joined the Confederacy in the Civil War, https://www.marines.mil/Portals/1/Publications/THE%20 JOURNALS%20OF%20MARINE%20SECOND%20LIEUTENANT %20HENRY%20BULLS%20WATSON%201845-1848%20%20PCN %2019000400000_1.pdf.

32. See John H. Coatsworth, *Growth Against Development: The Economic Impact of Railroads in Porfirian México* (De Kalb: Northern Illinois University Press, 1981); Juan Mora-Torres, *The Making of the Mexican Border: The State, Capitalism, and Society in Nuevo León, 1848–1910* (Austin: University of Texas Press, 2001).

33. Mora-Torres, *The Making of the Mexican Border*, 11, 37.

34. George Sanchez, *Becoming Mexican American: Ethnicity, Culture, and Identity in Chicano Los Angeles, 1900–1945* (New York: Oxford University Press, 1993), 51.

35. Alexandra Délano Alonso, *México and Its Diaspora in the United States: Policies of Emigration Since 1848* (New York: Cambridge University Press, 2011), 60–61. Chapter 8 deals with twentieth-century Mexican migrant workers and the border today.

36. Treaty of Guadalupe Hidalgo, 1848, transcript, https://www.ourdocuments .gov/doc.php?flash=false&doc=26&page=transcript.

37. Alejandro Murguía, *The Medicine of Memory: A Mexican Clan in California* (Austin: University of Texas, 2002), 40–41.

38. Robert F. Heizer, *The Destruction of California Indians: A Collection of Documents from the Period 1847 to 1865 in Which Are Described Some of the Things That Happened to Some of the Indians of California* (1976; repr. Lincoln: University of Nebraska Press, 1993); Sherburne F. Cook, *The Population of the California Indians, 1769–1970* (Berkeley: University of California Press, 1976); Benjamin Madley, *An American Genocide: The United States and the California Indian Catastrophe, 1846–1873* (New Haven, CT: Yale University Press, 2017).

39. See Boyd Cothran, *Remembering the Modoc War: Redemptive Violence*

and the Making of American Innocence (Chapel Hill: University of North
Carolina Press, 2017).

40. Ralph Emerson Twitchell, "The Conquest of New México," in *New
México Past and Present*, ed. Richard Ellis (Albuquerque: University of
New México Press, 1971), 119; Marc Simmons, *The Little Lion of the
Southwest: A Life of Manuel Antonio Chaves* (Chicago: Swallow Press,
1973), 70, 101–2, 165.

41. Carlton F. W. Larson, "Treason, the Death Penalty, and American
Identity," History News Network, October 2020.

42. Lawrence R. Murphy, "The United States Army in Taos, 1847–1852,"
New México Historical Review 47 (January 1972): 33–34.

43. Lamar, *The Far Southwest*, 33, 73, 83–171, 198.

44. Tom Deignan, *Irish America*, February/March 2008, https://irishamerica
.com/2008/02/the-irish-in-california. See chapter 6 for a discussion of the
Knights of Columbus and the Columbus cult.

45. The Capitol Museum, https://capitolmuseum.ca.gov/the-museum
/junipero-serra.

46. "Christopher Columbus Statue Removed from California Capitol,"
ABC10, July 7, 2020.

47. For Navajo history, see Jennifer Nez Denetdale, *Reclaiming Diné History:
The Legacies of Navajo Chief Manuelito and Juanita* (Tucson: University
of Arizona Press, 2007).

48. White, Koch, Kelly & McCarthy, *Land Title Study: Technical Report*
(Santa Fé: State Planning Office, 1971), 29.

49. Herbert O. Brayer, *Pueblo Indian Land Grants of the "Rio Abajo"
New México* (Albuquerque: University of New México Press, 1939), 26;
William F. Stone, *Report on the Court of Private Land Claims: Minutes
of the New México Bar Association Eighteenth Annual Session* (Santa Fé:
New México Bar Association, 1904).

50. *"United States v. Sandoval,"* U.S. Reports, vol. 231, p. 28 (1913). See
M. S. Heaston, "Whiskey Regulation and Indian Land Titles in New
México Territory, 1851–1861," *Journal of the West* 10 (1971): 474–83;
also Frank D. Reeve, "Federal Indian Policy in New México, 1858–1880,"
New México Historical Review 12 (July 1937): 218–19; 13 (January 1938):
14–62; 13 (April 1938): 146–91; 13 (July 1938): 261–313.

51. "An Act to Quiet Title to Lands Within Pueblo Indian Land Grants,"
U.S. Statutes 43 (1924): 636; Brayer, *Pueblo Indian Land Grants of the
"Rio Abajo" New México*, 31.

52. Felix Cohen, *Handbook of Federal Indian Law* (1942; reprint ed.,
Albuquerque: University of New México Press, 1972), 393.

53. Allan Harper, Andrew Cordova, and Kalervo Oberg, *Man and Resources
in the Middle Río Grande Valley* (Albuquerque: University of New México Press, 1943), 29–30, 35, 40–42, 51–52.

54. Charles Loomis, "Wartime Migration from the Rural Spanish American

Villages of Northern New México," *Rural Sociology* 7 (December 1942): 384–95. For an overview, see David Correia, *Properties of Violence: Law and Land Grant Struggle in Northern New México* (Athens: University of Georgia Press, 2013), 84–119.

55. Clark Knowlton, "Land Grant Problems Among the State's Spanish Americans," *Albuquerque Journal* (December 30, 1979): B4. The region has been described as "a kind of Afghanistan of North America."

56. Lorena Oropeza, "Becoming Indo-Hispano: Reies López Tijerina and the New Mexican Land Grant Movement," in Goldstein, *Formations of United States Colonialism*, 180.

57. Patricia Bell Blawis, *Tijerina and the Land Grants* (New York: International Publishers, 1971), 80–98; Lorena Oropeza, *The King of Adobe: Reies López Tijerina, Los Prophet of the Chicano Movement* (Chapel Hill: University of North Carolina Press, 2019); Correia, *Properties of Violence*.

58. Richard Allen Nielson, "American Indian Land Claims," *University of Florida Law Review*, 25 (Winter 1972): 321, 323; William F. Deverell, "The Return of Blue Lake to the Taos Pueblo," *Princeton University Library Chronicle* 49, no. 1 (Autumn 1987): 56–73: https://www.jstor.org/stable/26404208?seq=1#metadata_info_tab_contents; Taos Pueblo official website: https://taospueblo.com/blue-lake.

59. From the statement of James E. Snead, president, Santa Fe Wildlife and Conservation Association; "Taos Indians—Blue Lake," hearings before the Subcommittee on Indian Affairs of the Committee on Interior and Insular Affairs, US Senate, Nineteenth Congress, Second Session, September 19–20, 1968, in Primitive Law—United States Congressional Documents, vol. 9, part 1 (Washington, DC: US Government Printing Office, 1968), p. 216.

60. For senators' arguments against the return of Blue Lake to Taos, see "Pueblo de Taos Indians Cultural and Ceremonial Shrine Protection Act of 1970," Proceedings and Debates of the Ninety-First Congress, Second Session, December 2, 1970, *United States of America Congressional Record*, vol. 116, part 29 (Washington, DC: US Government Printing Office, 1970), pp. 39, 587, 29, 589–90, 39, 594–97.

61. Nielson, "American Indian Land Claims," 324.

62. US General Accounting Office (GAO), Treaty of Guadalupe Hidalgo: Definition and List of Community Land Grants in New México, Exposure Draft (2001) Report No. GAO-01-330. Download at http://www.gao.gov/assets/gao-01-951.pdf. US General Accounting Office (GAO), Treaty of Guadalupe Hidalgo: Findings and Possible Options Regarding Long-standing Community Land Grant Claims in New México (2004) Report No. GAO-04-59. Download at http://www.gao.gov/assets/gao-04-59.pdf.

63. US General Accounting Office (GAO), Treaty of Guadalupe Hidalgo:

Findings and Possible Options Regarding Longstanding Community Land Grant Claims in New México (2004) Report No. GAO-04-59, 12–13.

64. H.R. 6365 (115th): Treaty of Guadalupe-Hidalgo Land Claims Act of 2018, https://www.govtrack.us/congress/bills/115/hr6365.

65. Oropeza, "Becoming Indo-Hispano," 182.

66. Laura Gómez, *Manifest Destinies: The Making of the Mexican American Race* (New York: New York University Press, 2018), 49–50.

67. John M. Nieto-Phillips, *The Language of Blood: The Making of Spanish-American Identity in New México, 1880s–1930s* (Albuquerque: University of New México Press, 2008).

68. Gwen Aviles, "Racist, Brutal Past or Hispanic History? Latinos Clash over Spanish Colonial Statues," *NBC News Online*, July 5, 2020, https://www.nbcnews.com/news/latino/racist-brutal-past-or-hispanic-history-latinos-clash-over-spanish-n1232412.

69. Pueblo leaders have long objected to the celebrations of Spanish colonization. See Joe S. Sando, *The Pueblo Indians* (San Francisco: Indian Historian Press, 1976), 129.

70. See Michael V. Wilcox, *The Pueblo Revolt and the Mythology of Conquest: An Indigenous Archaeology of Contact* (Berkeley: University of California Press, 2009).

71. James Brooke, "In New México, Hispanic Pride Clashes with Indian Anger," *New York Times*, February 8, 1998.

72. George Hammond and Agapito Rey, *Don Juan Oñate and the Founding of New México* (Albuquerque: Historical Society of New México, 1927), 463, 477.

73. Hammond and Rey, *Don Juan Oñate and the Founding of New México*, 818.

74. H.R. 6365 (115th): Treaty of Guadalupe-Hidalgo Land Claims Act of 2018.

75. Marc Simmons, *The Last Conquistador: Juan de Oñate and the Settling of the Far Southwest* (Norman: University of Oklahoma Press, 1991), 123–46.

76. Michael Trujillo, "Oñate's Foot: Remembering and Dismembering in Northern New México," *Aztlán: A Journal of Chicano Studies* 33, no. 2 (Fall 2008): 106, https://www.academia.edu/231413/Onates_Foot_Remembering_and_Dismembering_in_Northern_New_México.

77. See Kim TallBear, *Native American DNA: Tribal Belonging and the False Promise of Genetic Science* (Minneapolis: University of Minnesota Press, 2013).

78. Maurus Chino email to the author, June 23, 2006; see James W. Loewen, "The Footless Statue," in *Lies Across America: What Our Historic Sites Get Wrong* (New York: New Press, 1999), 119–22.

79. Published in the South-West Organizing Project newsletter, *Voces Unidas* 8, no. 1 (May 1998).

80. *Surviving Columbus*, PBS, 1992, https://www.pbs.org/video/surviving
-columbus-h5sfei.

81. Hammond and Rey, *Don Juan Oñate and the Founding of New México*,
395.

82. Jack Forbes, *Aztecas del Norte: The Chicanos of Aztlán* (New York:
Fawcett Books, 1973); see also Jack Forbes, "Analco: Birthplace of the
Chicano," *El Grito del Norte* 4, nos. 11–12 (December 6, 1971): 17.
A 1999 interview with Forbes expanding on the concept of "Aztlán" can
be read online at http://www.insearchofaztlan.com/forbes.html.

83. See Juan Gómez-Quiñones, *Roots of Chicano Politics, 1600–1940*
(Albuquerque: University of New México, 1994).

84. For an excellent history of the American Indian Movement, see Nick
Estes, *Our History Is the Future: Standing Rock Versus the Dakota
Access Pipeline, and the Long Tradition of Indigenous Resistance*
(New York: Verso, 2019), 169–86.

85. Rudolfo Anaya, *Bless Me, Ultima* (New York: Warner Books, 1994).

86. A famous docudrama made in the 1950s, *Salt of the Earth*, was a reenactment of a successful strike in 1952 by Mexican migrants in a zinc
mine in Grant County, New México, the actors being the strikers playing
themselves. In the midst of the 1950s "red scare," the filmmakers were
blacklisted in Hollywood, and the film was not screened until the 1960s:
https://www.youtube.com/watch?v=5Dt2PKU4yLg.

87. Ken Flynn, "Views Differ on Statue's Renaming," *El Paso Times*,
November 12, 2003, http://www.nmhcpl.com/Onatestatue.htm. When
the Spanish were driven out during the Pueblo Revolution in 1680, some
2,000 people, 317 who were Pueblos loyal to the Spanish, were allowed to
leave New México and were removed to El Paso. The exiled Pueblos established a new village there, and the Tigua Indian Reservation still exists.

88. "From the Mother City," *Albuquerque Journal*, April 22, 2006.

89. *Albuquerque Journal*, May 2, 2006.

90. The Red Nation: https://therednation.org.

91. Matthew Reisen and Elise Kaplan, "City Removes Oñate Statue After
Monday's Violence," *Albuquerque Journal*, June 16, 2020, https://www
.abqjournal.com/1467018/city-removes-onate-statue-after-protest
-shooting-ex-two-councilors-others-questions-apds-response.html.

92. Lewis, *Colonialism in Modern America*.

93. Levi Romero, "Introduction," *Querencia: Reflections on the New México
Homeland*, ed. Vanessa Fonseca-Chávez, Levi Romero, and Spencer R.
Herrera (Albuquerque: University of New México Press, 2020), 1; Juan
Estevan Arellano, *Taos: Where Two Cultures Met Four Hundred Years
Ago* (Seattle: Grantmakers in the Arts, 2007).

94. For further discussion of Aztlán, see chapter 8.

95. Jake Kosek, *Understories: The Political Life of Forests in Northern
New México* (Durham, NC: Duke University Press, 2006), 139.

96. Rudolfo Anaya, "Foreword," in Fonseca-Chávez, Romero, and Herrera, *Querencia*, xvii.

97. Aviles, "Racist, Brutal Past or Hispanic History?"

98. Russell Contreras, "Hispanic Activist Wants Chicano Studies Classes Censored," Associated Press, July 22, 2020.

99. "From the Mother City," *Albuquerque Journal*, April 22, 2006.

100. *Albuquerque Journal*, May 2, 2006.

101. The Red Nation, https://therednation.org.

102. Reisen and Kaplan, "City Removes Oñate Statue After Monday's Violence."

103. Lewis, *Colonialism in Modern America*.

104. Levi Romero, introduction, in Fonseca-Chávez, Romero, and Herrera, *Querencia*, 1; Arellano, *Taos*.

105. Kosek, *Understories*, 139.

106. Rudolfo Anaya, foreword, Fonseca-Chávez, Romero, and Herrera, *Querencia*, xvii.

107. Aviles, "Racist, Brutal Past or Hispanic History?"

108. Contreras, "Hispanic Activist Wants Chicano Studies Classes Censored."

CHAPTER 5: IRISH SETTLING

1. Ron Formisano, *Boston Against Busing: Race, Class, and Ethnicity in the 1960s and 1970s* (Chapel Hill: University of North Carolina Press, 2004), 1.

2. Formisano, *Boston Against Busing*, 1–2, 111–12.

3. Robbie McVeigh and Bill Rolston, *Anois ar theacht an tsamhraidh: Ireland, Colonialism and the Unfinished Revolution* (Belfast: Beyond the Pale Books, 2021), 67–100.

4. Cedric J. Robinson, *Black Marxism: The Making of the Black Radical Tradition* (1983; repr., Chapel Hill: University of North Carolina Press, 2000), 38; McVeigh and Rolston, *Anois ar theacht an tsamhraidh*, 101–35.

5. Gustave de Beaumont, *Ireland: Social, Political, and Religious* (1839; repr., Cambridge, MA: Belknap Press of Harvard University Press, 2006), 128.

6. De Beaumont, *Ireland: Social, Political, and Religious*, 5.

7. William H. McNeill, "The Introduction of the Potato into Ireland," *Journal of Modern History* 21, no. 3 (1949): 218–21.

8. See Ireland's Great Hunger Institute, Quinnipiac University, Hamden, CT, https://www.qu.edu/on-campus/institutes-centers/irelands-great-hunger-institute.html.

9. The UN Convention on the Prevention and Punishment of the Crime of Genocide of 1948 is not retroactive as law, so Britain cannot be held responsible under the covenant. However, the terms of the convention

clearly fit the conditions that led to the Irish famine under Article II[c]: "Deliberately inflicting on the group conditions of life calculated to bring about its physical destruction in whole or in part," https://www.un.org /en/genocideprevention/documents/atrocity-crimes/Doc.1_Convention %20on%20the%20Prevention%20and%20Punishment%20of%20 the%20Crime%20of%20Genocide.pdf.

10. "An Irishman's Diary," *Irish Times,* November 11, 2020, https://www .irishtimes.com/opinion/an-irishman-s-diary-1.370003. See Charles E. Trevelyan, *The Irish Crisis* (1848; repr., London: Kessinger, 2010).

11. Robert Knox, *The Races of Men: A Philosophical Enquiry into the Influence of Race over the Destinies of Nations* (1862; repr. Gloucester, UK: Franklin Classics, 2018), 379.

12. Letter of May 23, 1856, from *Selected Correspondence, 1846–95,* quoted in Nicholas Mansergh, *The Irish Question, 1840–1921* (London: George Allen & Unwin, 1965), 88–89.

13. Mark Holan, "The History of the Boycott Shows a Real Cancel Culture," History News Network, August 2, 2020, https://historynewsnetwork.org /article/176682.

14. Samuel Clark, *Social Origins of the Irish Land War* (Princeton, NJ: Princeton University Press, 1979, 2016), 298.

15. Patrick Higgins, "Ireland, America and Settler-Colonialism," video lecture, *Irish Socialist Republicans,* YouTube, June 23, 2020, https://www .youtube.com/watch?v=HvMJxu70500. See Brian Kelly, "Gathering Antipathy: Irish Immigrants and Race in America's Age of Emancipation," in *Rethinking the Irish Diaspora: After the Gathering (Migration, Diasporas and Citizenship),* ed. Johanne Devlin Trew and Michael Pierse (New York: Palgrave Macmillan, 2018), 157–86.

16. Cecil Rhodes, 1895, in Immanuel Ness and Zak Cope, eds., *The Palgrave Encyclopedia of Imperialism and Anti-Imperialism* (London: Palgrave Macmillan UK, 2015), 1052.

17. Walter Johnson, *The Broken Heart of America: St. Louis and the Violent History of the United States* (New York: Basic Books, 2021), 110.

18. Kevin Kenny, *The American Irish: A History* (New York: Routledge, 2016), 45–46.

19. See John Killen, *The Famine Decade, Contemporary Accounts 1841–1851* (Newfoundland, UK: Blackstaff, 1995).

20. Kerby A. Miller, *Emigrants and Exiles: Ireland and the Irish Exodus to North America* (New York: Oxford University Press, 1988), 4–7.

21. Curtis L. Perry Jr., *Apes and Angels: The Irishman in Victorian Caricature* (Washington, DC: Smithsonian Institution Press, 1997).

22. David R. Roediger, *The Wages of Whiteness: Race and the Making of the American Working Class* (London: Verso, 1991), 133.

23. Tom Riley, "The Orphan Trains," *Irish America,* April/May 2014, https://irishamerica.com/2014/03/the-orphan-trains.

24. Linda Gordon, *The Great Arizona Orphan Abduction* (Cambridge, MA: Harvard University Press, 2001), 1–19.

25. Ignatiev, *How the Irish Became White.*

26. Donald Yacovone, "Review Work, *How the Irish Became White* by Noel Ignatiev," *New England Quarterly* 69, no. 4 (December 1996): 667–69, https://www.jstor.org/stable/366567.

27. Mary Mullen, "How the Irish Became Settlers: Metaphors of Indigeneity and the Erasure of Indigenous Peoples," *New Hibernia Review/Iris Éireannach NUA* 20, no. 3 (Autumn 2016): 83, https://www.academia.edu/29096569/How_the_Irish_Became_Settlers_Metaphors_of_Indigeneity_and_the_Erasure_of_Indigenous_Peoples?email_work_card=view-paper.

28. The 1882 founding and role of the Catholic organization the Knights of Columbus is discussed in chapter 6.

29. Correspondence with Irish studies scholar Matthew Horton, September 5, 2020.

30. David R. Roediger, *Towards the Abolition of Whiteness: Essays on Race, Politics, and Working Class History* (New York: Verso, 1994), 65.

31. James Truslow Adams, *The Epic of America* (New York: Little, Brown, 1931).

32. Jonas Clark, "In Search of the American Dream," *Atlantic*, June 2007, https://www.theatlantic.com/magazine/archive/2007/06/in-search-of-the-american-dream/305921.

33. W. E. B. Du Bois, *Black Reconstruction in America, 1860–1880* (1935; repr., New York: Free Press, 1998), 700.

34. Patricia J. Ferreira, "Frederic Douglass and the 1846 Dublin Edition of His Narrative," *New Hibernia Review* 5, no. 1 (Spring 2001): 53–67, https://muse.jhu.edu/article/23965/pdf.

35. Ignatiev, *How the Irish Became White*, iii.

36. Roediger, *The Wages of Whiteness*, 141.

37. Bryan Patrick McGovern, "Andrew Jackson and the Protestant Irish of Philadelphia: Early Nineteenth-Century Sectarianism," *Pennsylvania History: A Journal of Mid-Atlantic Studies* 87, no. 2 (2020): 313–37, www.jstor.org/stable/10.5325/pennhistory.87.2.0313.

38. Lorraine Boissoneault, "How the 19th-Century Know Nothing Party Reshaped American Politics," *Smithsonian Magazine*, January 26, 2017, https://www.smithsonianmag.com/history/immigrants-conspiracies-and-secret-society-launched-american-nativism-180961915.

39. Higgins, "Ireland, America and Settler-Colonialism."

40. Robert Miller, *Shamrock and Sword: The Saint Patrick's Battalion in the U.S.-Mexican War* (Norman: University of Oklahoma Press, 1989), 120.

41. Michael Hogan, *The Irish Soldiers of México* (Guadalajara: Intercambio Press, 2011), 192. For further reading on the San Patricio Brigade, see Marc Cramer, "The Fighting Irish of Mexico," *Americas* 48, 1996, 20;

Edward S. Wallace, "The Battalion of St. Patrick in the Mexican War," *Military Affairs* 14 (1950): 84–91; Peter Guardino, "Gender, Soldiering, and Citizenship in the Mexican-American War of 1846–1848," *American History Review* (2014): 119; Enrique Krauze, "The Ugly Legacy of the Mexican-American War," *Foreign Affairs* 92 (2013): 155–63; Frederick Wertz, "St. Patrick's Battalion: What Caused Them to Turn on the U.S. and Fight for Mexico?," *Irish Central*, February 29, 2020, https://www.irishcentral.com/roots/history/st-patricks-battalion-mexico?fbclid=IwAR3z2U3EMumE-s-e-qvIi9hgDnMkIsDDwjhsSKoMWJy5Mx JAIoL4T8S3xtM.

42. Johnson, *The Broken Heart of America*, 69

43. Hogan, *The Irish Soldiers of México*, 15, 54.

44. Johnson, *The Broken Heart of America*, 66–68.

45. Foos, *A Short, Offhand, Killing Affair*, 107–8.

46. Brian Kelly, "Gathering Antipathy: Irish Immigrants and Race in America's Age of Emancipation," in *Rethinking the Irish Diaspora: Migration, Diasporas and Citizenship*, ed. J. Devlin Trew and M. Pierse (Basingstoke: Palgrave Macmillan, 2018), 157, https://doi.org/10.1007/978-3-319-40784-5_77.

47. Author's correspondence with Matthew Horton, September 2020.

48. List of New York police commissioners as of 2020, https://en.wikipedia.org/wiki/New_York_City_Police_Commissioner?fbclid=IwAR3P_dQoi-z4111u6735g8L9JAGNOqXjKCa9oLwPvHhNN_mwDJbHwdkY_EE.

49. Livia Gershon, "How Stereotypes of the Irish Evolved from 'Criminals' to Cops," *History*, June 10, 2019, https://www.history.com/news/how-stereotypes-of-the-irish-evolved-from-criminals-to-cops.

50. Gary Potter, *The History of Policing in the United States*, part 1, https://plsonline.eku.edu/insidelook/history-policing-united-states-part-1.

51. Marian Betancourt, "The Fading of the Green at NYPD," *Irish America*, August/September 2003, https://irishamerica.com/2003/08/the-fading-of-the-green-at-nypd.

52. James R. Barrett, *The Irish Way: Becoming American in the Multiethnic City* (New York: Penguin Books, 2013), 31.

53. Higgins, "Ireland, America and Settler-Colonialism."

54. See David Paul Kuhn, *The Hardhat Riot: Nixon, New York City, and the Dawn of the White Working-Class Revolution* (New York: Oxford University Press, 2020), 76, 232.

55. Angela Serratore, "The 'Hard Hat Riot' of 1970 Pitted Construction Workers Against Anti-War Protestors," *Smithsonian Magazine*, May 8, 2020, https://www.smithsonianmag.com/history/hard-hat-riot-1970-pitted-construction-workers-against-anti-war-protestors-180974831. See also the original *New York Times* report the day after: Homer Bigart, "War Foes Here Attacked by Construction Workers," *New York Times*,

May 9, 1970, https://www.nytimes.com/1970/05/09/archives/war-foes
-here-attacked-by-construction-workers-city-hall-is-stormed.html.

56. Kuhn, *The Hardhat Riot*, 250.

57. Emanuel Perlmutter, "Head of Building Trades Unions Here Says
Response Favors Friday's Action," *New York Times*, May 12, 1970.

58. Mike Davis, *Prisoners of the American Dream: Politics and Economy
in the History of the US Working Class* (New York: Verso Books, 1986),
21–22.

59. Davis, *Prisoners of the American Dream*, 22–23.

60. See Daniel Walker Howe, *What Hath God Wrought: The Transformation of America 1815–1848* (New York: Oxford University Press, 2007);
Slotkin, *Regeneration Through Violence*, 313–508.

61. Davis, *Prisoners of the American Dream*, 23.

62. Roediger, *The Wages of Whiteness*, 151.

63. Davis, *Prisoners of the American Dream*, 26.

64. Davis, *Prisoners of the American Dream*, 27–28.

65. Bill Fletcher Jr., "Race Is About More Than Discrimination: Racial
Capitalism, the Settler State, and the Challenges Facing Organized Labor
in the United States," *Monthly Review* 72 no. 3 (July 2020): 24–25.

66. David Doyle, "The Irish and American Labour, 1880–1920," in *Saothar* 1,
no. 1 (May 1, 1975): 43–44, https://www.jstor.org/stable/23194162.

67. Mullen, "How the Irish Became Settlers," 83–85.

68. Luke Gibbons, "Race Against Time: Racial Discourse and Irish History,"
in *Transformations in Irish Culture* (Cork: Cork University Press, 1996),
154, 155.

69. Mullen, "How the Irish Became Settlers," 86.

70. See Kennedy, *A Nation of Immigrants*, chap. 1, p. 3.

71. Mullen, "How the Irish Became Settlers," 86.

72. "Letters from America No. IX," *Nation*, June 24, 1843, 9.

73. Author's correspondence with Irish studies scholar Patrick Higgins,
August 24, 2020.

74. Mullen, "How the Irish Became Settlers," 87–88; Thomas D'Arcy McGee,
*A History of the Irish Settlers in North America: From the Earliest Period
to the Census of 1850* (Boston: American Celt Office, 1851), 20, 22.

75. Mullen, "How the Irish Became Settlers," 88.

76. "Anglo-Saxon Ideas," *Nation*, June 13, 1856, 9.

77. "The 'Saturday Review' on Ireland," *Irish People* 1, no. 3 (December 12,
1863): 41.

78. Mullen, "How the Irish Became Settlers," 91.

79. See David Lloyd, "Black Irish, Irish Whiteness and Atlantic State
Formation," in *The Black and Green Atlantic: Cross-Currents of the
African and Irish Diasporas*, ed. Peter D. O'Neill and David Lloyd,
(New York: Palgrave Macmillan, 2009), 18. See also Patrick Higgins,
"Ireland, America and Settler-Colonialism," *Irish Socialist Republicans*,

YouTube, June 23, 2020, https://www.youtube.com/watch?v=HvM
Jxu70500.

80. Mark Rifkin, "Making Peoples into Populations: The Racial Limits of
Tribal Sovereignty," in *Theorizing Native Studies*, ed. Audra Simpson
and Andrea Smith (Durham, NC: Duke University Press, 2014), 155.

81. Higgins, "Ireland, America and Settler-Colonialism."

82. Liam Hogan, " 'Irish Slaves': The Convenient Myth," openDemocracy, January 14, 2015, https://www.opendemocracy.net/en/beyond
-trafficking-and-slavery/irish-slaves-convenient-myth. For a compilation
of Hogan's work, see "All of My Work on the 'Irish Slaves' Meme (2015-
'20)," *Medium*, March 12, 2017, https://medium.com/@Limerick1914
/all-of-my-work-on-the-irish-slaves-meme-2015-16-4965e445802a and
https://medium.com/@Limerick1914/the-imagery-of-the-irish-slaves
-myth-dissected-143e70aa6e74. See also David M. Perry, "No, the Irish
Were Not Slaves Too," *Pacific Standard*, March 15, 2018, https://psmag
.com.amp/social-justice/the-irish-were-not-slaves.

83. Brian Kelly, " 'Irish Slaves': Debunking the Myth," *Rebel*, July 2,
2020, http://www.rebelnews.ie/2020/07/02/irish-slaves-debunking
-myth. See also Brian Kelly, "Ireland and Slavery: Debating the
'Irish Slaves Myth,' " *Counterpunch*, August 6, 2020, https://www
.counterpunch.org/2020/08/06/ireland-and-slavery-debating-the
-irish-slaves-myth.

84. Liam Hogan, "How the African Victims of the Zong Massacre Were
Replaced with 'Irish Slaves,' " https://medium.com/@Limerick1914
/how-the-african-victims-of-the-zong-massacre-were-replaced-with
-irish-slaves-2574dac1fc55. See further documentation by Liam Hogan:
"Exaggeration and the Appropriation of the Torture of Enslaved Africans
in the 'Irish Slaves' Meme," *Medium*, 2015, https://medium.com
/@Limerick1914/we-had-it-worse-eebe705c41a; " 'Irish Slaves': The
Convenient Myth," openDemocracy, 2015, https://www.opendemocracy
.net/en/beyond-trafficking-and-slavery/irish-slaves-convenient-myth;
"Sinn Féin Not Allowing Facts Derail Good 'Irish Slaves' Yarn," *Irish
Times*, May 11, 2016, https://www.irishtimes.com/news/politics/sinn
-f%C3%A9in-not-allowing-facts-derail-good-irish-slaves-yarn-1.2644397;
"Two Years of the 'Irish Slaves' Myth: Racism, Reductionism and the
Tradition of Diminishing the Transatlantic Slave Trade," openDemocracy,
2016, https://www.opendemocracy.net/beyondslavery/liam-hogan
/two-years-of-irish-slaves-myth-racism-reductionism-and-tradition-of
-diminis; "When History Goes Bad," *Rabble*, 2017, http://www.rabble
.ie/2016/02/04/when-history-goes-bad; "The Founder of Irish Central
Attempts to Whitewash Their Influential Role in Spreading Ahistorical
'Irish Slaves' Propaganda," *Medium*, 2017, https://medium.com
/@Limerick1914/niall-odowd-whitewashes-history-by-denying-the-role
-irish-central-continue-to-play-spreading-b602522a11f8; "Reviewing the

Fallout from an Influential but Fatally Flawed Work of Popular History About 'White Slaves,'" *Medium*, June 2017, https://medium.com /@Limerick1914/reviewing-the-fallout-from-an-influential-but-fatally -flawed-work-of-popular-history-about-white-be6cfc37069b.

85. Matthew W. Horton, "Working Against Racism from White Subject Positions: White Anti-Racism, New Abolitionism and Intersectional Anti-White Irish Diasporic Nationalism" (PhD diss., University of California, Berkeley, 2019), 28–29.

86. Horton, "Working Against Racism from White Subject Positions," 195.

87. Tom Hayden, *Irish on the Inside: In Search of the Soul of Irish America* (New York: Verso Books, 2001), 6, 10, 285. For an in-depth critique of Hayden's views and practices regarding the Irish question, see Horton, "Working Against Racism from White Subject Positions," 191–204.

88. See Timothy J. White, "The Impact of British Colonialism on Irish Catholicism and National Identity: Repression, Reemergence, and Divergence," *Études d'histoire et de civilization* 35, no. 1 (2010): 21–37, https://journals.openedition.org/etudesirlandaises/1743?fbclid =IwAR372TduB-fwB_eCwREo1EWHmscOeehLK3A1ORMqsxYfubVE _wHoqaBxd-Q.

89. Trouillot, *Silencing the Past*, 123.

CHAPTER 6: AMERICANIZING COLUMBUS

1. Mamdani, *Neither Settler nor Native*, 1–2.

2. Trouillot, *Silencing the Past*, 114.

3. Andrew Glass, "President Harrison Urges Americans to Mark Columbus Day, Oct. 12, 1892," *Politico*, October 12, 2016, https://www.politico .com/story/2016/10/president-harrison-urges-americans-to-mark -columbus-day-oct-12-1892-229293.

4. Claudia L. Bushman, *America Discovers Columbus: How an Italian Explorer Became an American Hero* (Lebanon, NH: University Press of New England, 1992).

5. George R. Stewart, *Names on the Land: A Historical Account of Place-Naming in the United States* (New York: New York Review of Books, 2008), 169–73, 233, 302.

6. Brian Handwerk, "Why Christopher Columbus Was the Perfect Icon for a New Nation Looking for a Hero," *Smithsonian Magazine*, October 9, 2015, https://www.smithsonianmag.com/history/why-christopher-columbus -was-perfect-icon-new-nation-looking-hero-180956887/#:~:text=As%20 Columbia%20University%20historian%20Claudia,15%2C000%20years %20before%20Columbus%20arrived.

7. Bushman, *America Discovers Columbus*.

8. David Vine, "Stop Calling Him 'Columbus': How Anglicizing Cristóbal Colón's Name Celebrates Colonial Conquest and Genocide," *Medium*, October 12, 2020, https://medium.com/@vine_58154/stop-calling-him

-columbus-how-anglicizing-cristobal-colons-name-celebrates-colonial
-conquest-3828c9a5e2ba.

9. Ronald Takaki, *Iron Cages: Race and Culture in 19th-Century America*
   (New York: Oxford University Press, 2000), 155.
10. Joan M. Marter, *The Grove Encyclopedia of American Arts* (New York:
    Oxford University Press, 2011), 144.
11. Trouillot, *Silencing the Past*, 123.
12. Christopher J. Kauffman, "Columbus and Columbianism and the
    Knights of Columbus, 1882–1900," *American Catholic Studies* 118,
    no. 4 (2007): 93–95, https://www.jstor.org/stable/44195574. See also
    Christopher J. Kauffman, *Faith and Fraternalism: The History of the
    Knights of Columbus, 1882–1982* (New York: Harper & Row, 1982).
13. Thomas J. Schlereth, "Columbia, Columbus, and Columbianism,"
    Journal of American History 79, no. 3 (December 1992): 957–58.
14. "Beatification," *San Francisco Chronicle*, November 2, 2020.
15. Kauffman, "Columbus and Columbianism and the Knights of Columbus,
    1882–1900," 94.
16. Trouillot, *Silencing the Past*, 123.
17. Schlereth, "Columbia, Columbus, and Columbianism," 955.
18. John Joseph Flinn, ed., *Official Guide to the World's Columbian
    Exposition* (Chicago: Columbian Guide, 1893), 7–8.
19. Richard Slotkin, *Gunfighter Nation: The Myth of the Frontier in
    Twentieth-Century America* (New York: Macmillan, 1992), 63.
20. Schlereth, "Columbia, Columbus, and Columbianism," 960.
21. Kevin M. Kruse, *One Nation Under God: How Corporate America
    Invented Christian America* (New York: Basic Books, 2015), 104.
22. Schlereth, "Columbia, Columbus, and Columbianism," 965.
23. Trouillot, *Silencing the Past*, 134.
24. US Congress, House Committee on Immigration and Naturalization
    (62d, 2d session: 1911–1912). See "Immigration to the United States,
    1789–1930" collection, Widener Library, Harvard University, https://
    curiosity.lib.harvard.edu/immigration-to-the-united-states-1789-1930
    /catalog/39-990041277670203941.
25. Rudolph J. Vecoli, "Prelates and Peasants: Italian Immigrants and the
    Catholic Church," *Journal of Social History* 2, no. 3 (Spring 1969):
    232, https://doi.org/10.1353/jsh/2.3.217.
26. Trouillot, *Silencing the Past*, 134.
27. Danielle Battisti, *Whom We Shall Welcome: Italian Americans and
    Immigration Reform, 1945–1965* (New York: Fordham University
    Press, 2019). See also Thomas A. Guglielmo, *White on Arrival: Italians,
    Race, Color, and Power in Chicago, 1890–1945* (New York: Oxford
    University Press, 2003).
28. Matthew Frye Jacobson, *Whiteness of a Different Color: European Immi-*

grants and the Alchemy of Race (Cambridge, MA: Harvard University Press, 1999), 8.

29. Quoted in David R. Roediger, *Working Toward Whiteness: How America's Immigrants Became White; The Strange Journey from Ellis Island to the Suburbs* (2005; repr., New York: Basic Books, 2018), 3.

30. James Baldwin, "On Being White . . . and Other Lies," *Essence*, April 1984, 90–92.

31. James Baldwin, "The Price of the Ticket," in *The Price of the Ticket: Collected Nonfiction, 1948–1985* (New York: St. Martin's Press, 1985), xiv; see Roediger, *Working Toward Whiteness*.

32. Baldwin, "On Being White . . . and Other Lies," 90.

33. See Alexander Saxton, *The Rise and Fall of the White Republic: Class Politics and Mass Culture in Nineteenth Century America* (New York: Verso Press, 2003).

34. Christine Grimaldi, "The Paesano of Shame: Trump's Italian American Consiglieres," *Los Angeles Review of Books*, November 2, 2020.

35. John Mack Faragher, Mari Jo Buhle, Daniel Czitrom, and Susan H. Armitage, *Out of Many: A History of the American People* (Saddle River, NJ: Prentice Hall, 2000), 623–30.

36. Johnson, *The Broken Heart of America*, 114–15.

37. See Roxanne Dunbar-Ortiz, *Roots of Resistance: A History of Land Tenure in New Mexico* (1980; repr., Norman: University of Oklahoma Press, 2007), 111.

38. Steven R. Weisman, *The Chosen Wars: How Judaism Became an American Religion* (New York: Simon & Schuster, 2018), xxiii.

39. Neal Gabler, *An Empire of Their Own: How the Jews Invented Hollywood* (New York: Anchor Books, 1989).

40. Will Herberg, "Jewish Labor Movement in the United States: Early Years to World War I," *Industrial and Labor Relations Review* 5, no. 4 (1952): 501–23, www.jstor.org/stable/2519135.

41. Julian E. Zelizer, "Trump Needs to Demilitarize His Rhetoric," *Atlantic*, October 29, 2018, https://www.theatlantic.com/ideas/archive/2018/10/americas-long-history-anti-semitism/574234.

42. After the Pittsburgh massacre, President Donald Trump advised synagogues to hire guards armed with assault rifles. Zelizer, "Trump Needs to Demilitarize His Rhetoric."

43. See Karen Brodkin, *How Jews Became White Folks and What That Says About Race in America* (Piscataway, NJ: Rutgers University Press, 2000).

44. Statue of Liberty, National Monument New York, National Park Service, https://www.nps.gov/stli/learn/historyculture/colossus.htm.

45. Barry Moreno, *The Statue of Liberty Encyclopedia* (New York: Simon & Schuster, 2000), 71.

46. "Postponing Bartholdi's Statue Until There Is Liberty for Colored As Well," *Cleveland Gazette*, November 27, 1886, 2.

47. Paul Auster, "NYC = USA," *Collected Prose: Autobiographical Writings, True Stories, Critical Essays, Prefaces, and Collaborations with Artists* (New York: Picador, 2019), 508.

48. See James R. Barrett, "Americanization from the Bottom Up: Immigration and the Remaking of the Working Class in the United States, 1880–1930," *Journal of American History* 79, no. 3 (1992): 996–1020. www.jstor.org /stable/2080796.

49. Theodore Roosevelt, "Americanism," *Fear God and Take Your Own Part* (1916; repr., New York: George H. Doran, 2016), 154–56. For a critique of the speech, see Horton, "Working Against Racism from White Subject Positions," 177–78.

50. H. W. Brands, *TR: The Last Romantic* (New York: Basic Books, 1997), 126.

51. Slotkin, *Gunfighter Nation*, 37.

52. Slotkin, *Gunfighter Nation*, 42.

53. Slotkin, *Gunfighter Nation*, 41–42.

54. Nancy Isenberg, *White Trash: The 400-Year Untold History of Class in America* (New York: Viking, 2016), 190.

55. Quoted in Slotkin, *Gunfighter Nation*, 201.

56. E. O. Wilson, *Sociobiology: The New Synthesis* (Cambridge MA: Harvard University Press, 1975); see also Richard J. Herrnstein and Charles Murray, *The Bell Curve: Intelligence and Class Structure in American Life* (New York: Free Press, 1996); James Q. Wilson and Richard J. Herrnstein, *Crime and Human Nature: The Definitive Study of the Causes of Crime* (New York: Free Press, 1998); Charles Murray, *Coming Apart: The State of White America, 1960–2010* (New York: Crown Forum, 2012); Charles Murray, *Human Diversity: The Biology of Gender, Race, and Class* (New York: Twelve, 2020).

57. Slotkin, *Gunfighter Nation*, 201–2; Isenberg, *White Trash*, 174–205.

58. *Buck v. Bell*, 274 U.S. 200, 1927; Edward J. Larson, "Belated Progress: The Enactment of Eugenic Legislation in Georgia," *Journal of the History of Medicine and Allied Sciences* 46, no. 1 (1991): 44–64. See also T. G. Dyer, *Theodore Roosevelt and the Idea of Race* (Baton Rouge: Louisiana University Press, 1992).

59. Whitman, *Hitler's American Model*; Kakel, *The American West and the Nazi East*; Robert Miller, "Nazi Germany and American Indians," *Indian Country Today*, August 14, 2019, https://indiancountrytoday.com /opinion/nazi-germany-and-american-indians-Uha07e3luUCaeLq1nJP5-Q.

60. William Appleman Williams, *Empire as a Way of Life: An Essay on the Causes and Character of America's Present Predicament Along with a Few Thoughts About an Alternative* (New York: Oxford University Press, 1980), 73–76, 102–10.

61. Robert Kaplan, *Imperial Grunts: The American Military on the Ground* (New York: Random House, 2005), 138. Also see Richard Immerman, *Empire for Liberty: A History of American Imperialism from Benjamin Franklin to Paul Wolfowitz* (Princeton, NJ: Princeton University Press, 2010).

62. For the resistance movement and US counterinsurgency war, see Leon Wolff, *Little Brown Brother: America's Forgotten Bid for Empire Which Cost 250,000 Lives* (New York: Longmans, Green, 1961).

63. Kaplan, *Imperial Grunts*, 138.

64. Mililani B. Trask, "Hawai'i and the United Nations," *Cultural Survival*, March 2000, https://www.culturalsurvival.org/publications/cultural-survival-quarterly/hawaii-and-united-nations.

65. Theodore Roosevelt, "The Expansion of the White Races," address at the Methodist Episcopal Church, Washington, DC, January 18, 1909, in "Two Essays by Theodore Roosevelt," *Modern American Poetry* (English Department, University of Illinois, 1909, http://www.english.illinois.edu/maps/poets/a_f/espada/roosevelt.htm. See also *The Works of Theodore Roosevelt*, memorial ed., *North American Review* 15, 1890.

66. Arthur Lennig, "Myth and Fact: The Reception of 'The Birth of a Nation,'" *Film History* 16, no. 2 (2004): 117–41.

67. Dick Lehr, "The Racist Legacy of Woodrow Wilson," *Atlantic*, November 27, 2015, https://www.theatlantic.com/politics/archive/2015/11/wilson-legacy-racism/417549.

68. See Elaine Frantz Parsons, *Ku-Klux: The Birth of the Klan During Reconstruction* (Chapel Hill: University of North Carolina Press, 2015).

69. See Nancy MacLean, *Behind the Mask of Chivalry: The Making of the Second Ku Klux Klan* (New York: Oxford University Press, 1995); Linda Gordon, *The Second Coming of the KKK: The Ku Klux Klan of the 1920s and the American Political Tradition* (New York: Liveright, 2017), 21–23; Charles C. Alexander, *The Ku Klux Klan in the Southwest* (1965; repr., Norman: University of Oklahoma Press, 1995); Kathleen Blee, *Women of the Klan: Racism and Gender in the 1920s* (Berkeley: University of California Press, 1992).

70. Gordon, *The Second Coming of the KKK*, 2–4.

71. Gordon, *The Second Coming of the KKK*, 26–27.

72. Devra Anne Weber, "'Different Plans': Indigenous Pasts, the Partido Liberal Mexicano, and Questions About Reframing Binational Social Movements of the 20th Century" (unpublished research paper, May 26, 2015), 10–16; Juan Gomez-Quiñones, *Sembradores: Ricardo Flores Magon y el Partido Liberal Mexicano; A Eulogy and Critique* (Los Angeles: Aztlan Publications, Chicano Studies Center, University of California, Los Angeles, 1973).

73. Espionage Act of 1917, June 15, 1917, Sixty-Fifth Congress, Session I. Chapters 29, 30, 1917, p. 217. The original Espionage Act remains in

effect, https://www.digitalhistory.uh.edu/disp_textbook.cfm?smtid
=3&psid=3904.

74. Roxanne Dunbar-Ortiz and John Womack Jr., "Dreams of Revolution:
Oklahoma, 1917," *Monthly Review* 62, no. 6 (November 2010): 387–409,
https://monthlyreview.org/2010/11/01/dreams-of-revolution-oklahoma
-1917. See also William Cunningham, *The Green Corn Rebellion*
(1936; repr., Norman: University of Oklahoma, 2010); Richard Grant,
"When the Socialist Revolution Came to Oklahoma—and Was Crushed,"
Smithsonian Magazine, October 2019, https://www.smithsonianmag
.com/history/socialist-revolution-oklahoma-crushed-green-corn-rebellion
-180973073.

75. Zinn, *A People's History of the United States*, 372–73.

76. Zinn, *A People's History of the United States*, 372–73.

77. Zinn, *A People's History of the United States*, 366–68.

78. Dillingham-Hardwick Act, US 40 Statute 1012, Ch. 186, October 16, 1918.

79. "Haywood in Russia as Sentence Begins," *New York Times*, April 22,
1921, 14.

80. David S. Foglesong, *America's Secret War Against Bolshevism: U.S.
Intervention in the Russian Civil War, 1917–1920* (Chapel Hill: University of North Carolina Press, 2014), 4–5.

81. Joseph S. Roucek, "The Image of the Slave in U.S. History and in Immigration Policy," *American Journal of Economics and Sociology* 28, no. 1
(January 1969): 29–48.

82. Rothstein, *The Color of Law*, 228n2; see also David Nasaw, *The Last
Million: Europe's Displaced Persons from World War to Cold War*
(New York: Penguin, 2020).

CHAPTER 7: "YELLOW PERIL"

1. Anne Anlin Cheng, "What This Wave of Anti-Asian Violence Reveals
About America," *New York Times*, February 21, 2021, https://www
.nytimes.com/2021/02/21/opinion/anti-asian-violence.html.

2. Iyko Day, "The Yellow Plague and Romantic Anticapitalism," *Monthly
Review*, (July–August 2020): 64–65.

3. Marie Myung-Ok Lee, " 'Wuhan Coronavirus' and the Racist Art of
Naming a Virus," *Salon*, February 7, 2020, https://www.salon.com/2020
/02/06/the-racist-art-of-naming-a-virus.

4. For a critique of the move, see John Ford, "The Pivot to Asia Was
Obama's Biggest Mistake," *The Diplomat*, January 21, 2017, https://
thediplomat.com/2017/01/the-pivot-to-asia-was-obamas-biggest-mistake.

5. Eric Westervelt, "Anger and Fear as Asian American Seniors Targeted in
Bay Area Attacks," National Public Radio, February 12, 2021, https://
www.npr.org/2021/02/12/966940217/anger-and-fear-as-asian-american
-seniors-targeted-in-bay-area-attacks.

6. "Comparing United States and China by Economy," *Statistical Times,* August 2, 2019, http://statisticstimes.com/economy/united-states-vs-china -economy.php#:~:text=United%20States%20and%20China%20are,PPP %20terms%2C%20respectively%20in%202019; Danny Haiphong, "American Exceptionalism Won't Save the U.S. Empire from Itself, or Stop China's Rise," *Black Agenda Report,* November 4, 2020, https:// www.blackagendareport.com/american-exceptionalism-wont-save-us -empire-itself-or-stop-chinas-rise.

7. Gary Y. Okihiro, *Margins and Mainstreams: Asians in American History and Culture* (Seattle: University of Washington Press, 2014), 119–20.

8. Okihiro, *Margins and Mainstreams,* 120.

9. Leung Wing-Fai, "Perceptions of the East—Yellow Peril: An Archive of Anti-Asian Fear," *Irish Times,* August 31, 2020; John Kuo Wei Tchen and Dylan Yeats, *Yellow Peril! An Archive of Anti-Asian Fear* (London: Verso Books, 2014).

10. Oswald Spengler, *The Decline of the West: Form and Actuality* vol. 1, (1918; repr., CreateSpace Independent Publishing Platform, 2014); Oswald Spengler, *The Decline of the West: Perspectives of World-History,* vol. 2 (1922; repr., London: Forgotten Books, February 9, 2017).

11. Karl August Wittfogel, *Oriental Despotism: A Comparative Study of Total Power* (New Haven, CT: Yale University Press, 1957).

12. Edward Said, *Orientalism* (New York: Pantheon, 1978), 2–3.

13. Said, *Orientalism,* 7.

14. Edward Said, *Culture and Imperialism* (New York: Vintage Books, 1993), 9.

15. Wendy Rouse, "Jiu-Jitsuing Uncle Sam: The Unmanly Art of Jiu-Jitsu and the Yellow Peril Threat in the Progressive Era United States," *Pacific Historical Review* (October 2015): 448–50.

16. Daniel M. Bays, *A New History of Christianity in China* (Oxford: John Wiley & Sons, 2012), 4–40.

17. Bays, *A New History of Christianity in China,* 41–65.

18. *The Opening to China Part 1: The First Opium War, the United States, and the Treaty of Wangxia, 1839–1844* (Washington, DC: US Government, Office of the Historian), https://history.state.gov/milestones/1830 -1860/china-1.

19. Isabella Jackson, "Who Ran the Treaty Ports? A Study of the Shanghai Municipal Council," in *Treaty Ports in Modern China: Law, Land and Power,* ed. Robert Bickers and Isabella Jackson (New York: Routledge, 2016), 43–60.

20. Yuan Ding, with Roland Hsu, "Overseas Remittances of Chinese Laborers in North America," in *The Chinese and the Iron Road: Building the Transcontinental Railroad,* ed. Gordon Chang (Palo Alto, CA: Stanford University Press, 2019), 76–89.

21. For an in-depth study of racial capitalism and labor in California, see Stacey L. Smith, *Freedom's Frontier: California and the Struggle over*

Unfree Labor, Emancipation, and Reconstruction (Chapel Hill: University of North Carolina Press, 2013).

22. Ronald Takaki, *Strangers from a Different Shore* (1989; repr., New York: Back Bay Books, 1998), 79–80.

23. Leland Stanford, inaugural address, January 10, 1862, Governor's Gallery, https://governors.library.ca.gov/addresses/08-Stanford.html.

24. "Timeline of Chinese Immigration to the United States," Digital Archive, Bancroft Library, University of California, Berkeley, https://bancroft .berkeley.edu/collections/chinese-immigration-to-the-united-states-1884 -1944/timeline.html, accessed February 23, 2021.

25. See Karuka, *Empire's Tracks*.

26. Gordon H. Chang, Shelley Fisher Fishkin, and Hilton Obenzinger, introduction to Chang, *The Chinese and the Iron Road*, 1–2.

27. Quoted in Ronald Takaki, *A Different Mirror: A History of Multicultural America* (1993; repr., New York: Back Bay Books, 2008), 181.

28. Takaki, *A Different Mirror*, 181.

29. Karuka, *Empire's Tracks*, 85.

30. Gordon Chang, *Ghosts of Gold Mountain: The Epic Story of the Chinese Who Built the Transcontinental Railroad* (New York: Mariner, 2020), 555; Chang, *The Chinese and the Iron Road*, 2919; see also Johnson, *The Broken Heart of America*, 50–51.

31. Karuka, *Empire's Tracks*, 82. Karuka's work is one of the few that study in depth the centrality of Indigenous lands taken in order to build the railroad, affecting particularly the Paiute, Lakota, Pawnee, and Cheyenne nations. See also Hsinya Huang, "Tracking Memory: Encounters Between Chinese Railroad Workers and Native Americans," in Chang, *The Chinese and the Iron Road*, 179–94.

32. Rouse, "Jiu-Jitsuing Uncle Sam," 451–52.

33. Erika Lee, "The 'Yellow Peril' and Asian Exclusion in the Americas," *Pacific Historical Review* 76, no. 4, 538. See also Watt Stewart, *Chinese Bondage in Peru: A History of the Chinese Coolie in Peru, 1849–1874* (Durham, NC: Duke University Press, 1951).

34. Lee, "The 'Yellow Peril' and Asian Exclusion in the Americas," 541–42.

35. Lee, "The 'Yellow Peril' and Asian Exclusion in the Americas," 547.

36. Lee, "The 'Yellow Peril' and Asian Exclusion in the Americas," 554–55.

37. Bird, *Criminal Dissent*, 37.

38. Chinese Exclusion Act of 1882 text, https://www.ourdocuments.gov/doc .php?flash=true&doc=47&page=transcript; https://en.wikipedia.org/wiki /Chinese_Exclusion_Act. See Andrew Gyory, *Closing the Gate: Race, Politics, and the Chinese Exclusion Act* (Chapel Hill: University of North Carolina Press, 1998), 3–16.

39. Mae M. Ngai, *Impossible Subjects: Illegal Aliens and the Making of Modern America* (Princeton, NJ: Princeton University Press, 2014), 17–18.

40. US Congress, 1925 [1924], p. 159 (as determined by "country of birth"); US Congress 1925 [1924], p. 160). See Ngai, *Impossible Subjects*, 21–55.

41. Quoted in Matthew Frye Jacobson, *Whiteness of a Different Color: European Immigrants and the Alchemy of Race* (Cambridge, MA: Harvard University Press, 1999), 90.

42. "The Immigration Act of 1924 (Johnson-Reed Act) (Washington, DC: US Department of State, Office of the Historian).

43. Padma Rangaswamy, *Namaste America: Indian Immigrants in an American Metropolis* (State College: Pennsylvania State University Press, 2000); Takaki, *Strangers from a Different Shore*, 62–64, 295–300; Joan M. Jensen, *Passage from India: Asian Indian Immigrants in North America* (New Haven, CT: Yale University Press, 1988).

44. Stanford Lyman, *Postmodernism and a Sociology of the Absurd: Absurd and Other Essays on the "Nouvelle Vague" in American Social Science* (Little Rock: University of Arkansas Press, 1997), 143–45.

45. Mamdani, *Neither Settler nor Native*, 106.

46. Whitman, *Hitler's American Model*, 27, 29, 34–72, 122–32.

47. John Swinton, "The New Issue: The Chinese-American Question," *New York Tribune*, June 30, 1870; John Kuo Wei Tchen, *New York Before Chinatown: Orientalism and the Shaping of American Culture, 1776–1882* (Baltimore: Johns Hopkins University Press, 2001), 188–89.

48. Swinton, "The New Issue: The Chinese-American Question," 189.

49. Gary M. Fink, ed., *Biographical Dictionary of American Labor Leaders* (Westport, CT: Greenwood Press, 1974), 346–47.

50. Jacobson, *Whiteness of a Different Color*, 5.

51. Rouse, "Jiu-Jitsuing Uncle Sam," 452; Gyory, *Closing the Gate*, 109–35.

52. Stephanie S. Pinceti, *Transforming California: A Political History of Land Use and Development* (Baltimore: Johns Hopkins University Press, 2003), 23; Gary Kamiya, "S.F. Had Its Own Divisive, Trump-Like Demagogue," *San Francisco Chronicle*, February 20, 2021, https://www.sfchronicle.com/chronicle_vault/article/S-F-had-its-own-demagogue-who-capitalized-on-15963251.php.

53. Quoted in Gyory, *Closing the Gate*, 112.

54. Quoted in Viscount James Bryce, *The American Commonwealth* (New York: Macmillan, 1889), 385–408, http://www.sfmuseum.org/hist9/brycenotes.html. The Canadian Parliament passed the Chinese Immigration Act in 1923, also known as the Chinese Exclusion Act.

55. Aviva Chomsky, *"They Take Our Jobs!" and 20 Other Myths About Immigration* (Boston: Beacon Press, 2007), 3.

56. Chomsky, *"They Take Our Jobs!" and 20 Other Myths about Immigration*, 7, 9, 10.

57. Chomsky, *"They Take Our Jobs!" and 20 Other Myths about Immigration*, 31.

58. Chomsky, *"They Take Our Jobs!" and 20 Other Myths about Immigration*, 32.

59. Peter Kwong, *Forbidden Workers: Illegal Chinese Immigrants and American Labor* (New York: New Press, 1997), 147.

60. Alexander Saxton, *The Indispensable Enemy: Labor and the Anti-Chinese Movement in California* (Berkeley: University of California Press, 1995), 1.

61. Bill Fletcher Jr., "Race Is About More Than Discrimination: Racial Capitalism, the Settler State, and the Challenges Facing Organized Labor in the United States," *Monthly Review* 72, no. 3 (July 2020): 25, https://monthlyreviewarchives.org/index.php/mr/article/view/MR-072-03-2020-07_3.

62. Fletcher, "Race Is About More Than Discrimination," 25.

63. Fletcher, "Race Is About More Than Discrimination," 25.

64. Kevin Starr, *Americans and the California Dream, 1850–1915* (New York: Oxford University Press, 1973), 214.

65. Paul Hampton, *Jack London, Socialist*, Workers' Liberty, August 13, 2008, https://www.workersliberty.org/blogs/2019-02-25/jack-london-socialist. See *The Radical Jack London: Writings on War and Revolution*, ed. Jonah Raskin (Berkley: University of California Press, 2008).

66. Jack London, "How I Became a Socialist," in *War of the Classes* (New York: Macmillan, 1905), http://london.sonoma.edu/Writings/WarOfTheClasses/socialist.html.

67. Raskin, *The Radical Jack London*, 4–5.

68. Starr, *Americans and the California Dream*, 251.

69. Thomas C. Leonard, *Illiberal Reformers: Race, Eugenics, and American Economics in the Progressive Era* (Princeton, NJ: Princeton University Press, 2016), 114.

70. John N. Swift, "Jack London's 'The Unparalleled Invasion': Germ Warfare, Eugenics, and Cultural Hygiene," *American Literary Realism* 35, no. 1 (2002): 59, www.jstor.org/stable/27747084.

71. "Japanese Invasion the Problem of the Hour for the United States," *San Francisco Chronicle*, February 23, 1905.

72. Rouse, "Jiu-Jitsuing Uncle Sam," 452–53. See also Roger Daniels, *The Politics of Prejudice: The Anti-Japanese Movement in California and the Struggle for Japanese Exclusion* (Berkeley: University of California Press, 1962), 1, 6–7; Roger Daniels, *Guarding the Golden Door: American Immigration Policy and Immigrants Since 1882* (New York: Hill & Wang, 2004), 40–41; for the anti-Japanese movement in Hawai'i, see Gary Okihiro, *Can Fires: The Anti-Japanese Movement in Hawaii, 1865–1945* (Philadelphia: Temple University Press, 1991).

73. Takaki, *Strangers from a Different Shore*, 315.

74. Ngai, *Impossible Subjects*, 104–5.

75. Ngai, *Impossible Subjects*, 109–11.

76. Takaki, *A Different Mirror*, 342–43.

77. Richard Drinnon, *Keeper of the Concentration Camps: Dillon S. Myer and American Racism* (Berkeley: University of California Press, 1987), 33.

78. Takaki, *A Different Mirror*, 343.

79. Ngai, *Impossible Subjects*, 176.

80. Scott Kurashige, *The Shifting Grounds of Race: Black and Japanese Americans in the Making of Multiethnic Los Angeles* (Princeton, NJ: Princeton University Press, 2010), 109–10.

81. Roger Daniels, *Concentration Camps USA: Japanese Americans and World War II* (New York, 1971), 45–46.

82. Takaki, *A Different Mirror*, 343–44.

83. Daniel Immerwahr, *How to Hide an Empire: A History of the Greater United States* (New York: Farrar, Straus & Giroux, 2019), 181–82.

84. Ngai, *Impossible Subjects*, 176.

85. Ngai, *Impossible Subjects*, 176.

86. Sumi K. Cho, "Redeeming Whiteness in the Shadow of Internment: Earl Warren, Brown, and a Theory of Racial Redemption," *Third World Law Journal* 19, no. 1 (1998): 91–103, http://lawdigitalcommons.bc.edu/twlj /vol19/iss1/6.

87. Cho, "Redeeming Whiteness in the Shadow of Internment," 130.

88. Ngai, *Impossible Subjects*, 178–79.

89. Drinnon, *Keeper of the Concentration Camps*, 233–48. The government provocation of termination gave rise to what became a powerful Red Power movement that reversed termination in 1974. See Daniel M. Cobb, *Native Activism in Cold War America: The Struggle for Sovereignty* (Lawrence: University Press of Kansas, 2008).

90. Civil Liberties Act of 1988 Public Law 100–383, title 1, August 10, 1988.

91. Laurel Wamsley and Colin Dwyer, "California Lawmakers Apologize for U.S. Internment of Japanese Americans," National Public Radio, February 20, 2020, https://www.npr.org/2020/02/20/807428171/california -lawmakers-expected-to-apologize-for-u-s-internment-of-japanese-americ.

92. Roy E. Appleman, *South to the Naktong, North to the Yalu: United States Army in the Korean War* (Washington, DC: Center of Military History, US Army, 1992), 7–49.

93. Sahr Conway-Lanz, *Collateral Damage: Americans, Noncombatant Immunity, and Atrocity After World War II* (New York: Routledge, 2006), 83–84. For the formation of the US Army in "Indian Wars," see Grenier, *The First Way of War*.

94. Conway-Lanz, *Collateral Damage*, 96–97.

95. Conway-Lanz, *Collateral Damage*, 149.

96. Ngai, *Impossible Subjects*, 262; Allison O'Connor and Jeanne Batalova, "Korean Immigrants in the United States," Migration Policy Institute, April 10, 2019, https://www.migrationpolicy.org/article/korean -immigrants-united-states-2017#English.

97. Arissa Oh, "A New Kind of Missionary Work: Christians, Christian

Americanists, and the Adoption of Korean GI Babies, 1955–1961,"
Women's Studies Quarterly (2005): 161.

98. Ngai, *Impossible Subjects*, 208.

99. "October 13, 1960 Debate Transcript: The Third Kennedy-Nixon
Presidential Debate," Commission on Presidential Debates, October 13,
1960, https://www.debates.org/voter-education/debate-transcripts
/october-13–1960-debate-transcript.

100. Quoted in Viet Thanh Nguyen, *Nothing Ever Dies: Vietnam and the
Memory of War* (Cambridge, MA: Harvard University Press, 2016), 125.

101. Quoted in Nguyen, *Nothing Ever Dies*, 66.

102. Slotkin, *Gunfighter Nation*, 1–2; Michael Bilton and Kevin Sim, *Four
Hours in My Lai* (New York: Viking, 1992), 365–66.

103. Bilton and Sim, *Four Hours in My Lai*, 102–62.

104. Quoted in Bilton and Sim, *Four Hours in My Lai*, 372.

105. "Calley Apologizes for Role in My Lai Massacre," NBC News.com,
August 21, 2009, http://www.nbcnews.com/id/32514139/ns/us_news
-military/t/calley-apologizes-role-my-lai-massacre/#.X2kpE5NKiN8.

106. Takaki, *Strangers from a Different Shore*, 449.

107. Larry Clinton Thompson, *Refugee Workers in the Indochina Exodus*
(Jefferson, NC: MacFarland, 2010), 150–52, 164–65.

108. Andrew Chin, "The KKK and Vietnamese Fishermen," *Legal Thinking
for the 21st Century Economy*, University of North Carolina School
of Law, undated blog post, http://www.unclaw.com/chin/scholarship
/fishermen.htm, accessed February 23, 2021.

109. Chin, "The KKK and Vietnamese Fishermen."

110. Chin, "The KKK and Vietnamese Fishermen."

111. Chin, "The KKK and Vietnamese Fishermen."

112. Alfred W. McCoy, *The Politics of Heroin: CIA Complicity in the Global
Drug Trade*, rev. ed. (Chicago: Lawrence Hill Books, 2003), 119–21.

113. McCoy, *The Politics of Heroin*, 130, 146. McCoy writes that the CIA
was also working concurrently with the Afghan opium farmers that had
developed under British imperialism.

114. Jessica Pearce Rotondi, "Why Laos Has Been Bombed More Than Any
Other Country," *History*, December 5, 2019, https://www.history.com
/news/laos-most-bombed-country-vietnam-war.

115. Hmong Timeline, Minnesota Historical Society, https://www.mnhs
.org/hmong/hmong-timeline. For the operation of the UNHCR camps
in Thailand, see William Shawcross, *The Quality of Mercy: Cambodia,
Holocaust and Modern Conscience* (New York: Simon & Schuster, 1984).

116. Quoted in Nguyen, *Nothing Ever Dies*, 281.

117. Nguyen, *Nothing Ever Dies*, 234.

118. "Genocide Hearings Underway in Cambodia's War Crimes Tribunal,"
Deutsche Welle, August 29, 2015, https://www.dw.com/en/genocide
-hearings-underway-in-cambodias-war-crimes-tribunal/a-18699601.

119. William Shawcross, *Sideshow: Kissinger, Nixon, and the Destruction of Cambodia*, rev. ed. (New York: Cooper Square Press, 2002), 92–100, 106–12.

120. Ben Kiernan, *The Pol Pot Regime: Race, Power, and Genocide in Cambodia Under the Khmer Rouge, 1975–1979* (New Haven, CT: Yale University Press, 2008), 16–19.

121. Greg Grandin, *Kissinger's Shadow: The Long Reach of America's Most Controversial Statesman* (New York: Henry Holt , 2015), 179–80.

122. Michael Haas, *Cambodia, Pol Pot, and the United States: The Faustian Pact* (Santa Barbara, CA: ABC-CLIO, 1991).

123. Dinah PoKempner, *Cambodia at War* (New York: Human Rights Watch, 1995).

124. Nguyen, *Nothing Ever Dies*, 7.

125. Carl L. Bankston III, "Cambodian Americans," in *Gale Encyclopedia of Multicultural America*, vol. 1, ed. Thomas Riggs (Detroit: Gale Research, 2014), 381–93. See also Sucheng Chan, "Cambodians in the United States: Refugees, Immigrants, American Ethnic Minority," *Oxford Research Encyclopedia of American History*, 2015, https:// oxfordre.com/americanhistory/view/10.1093/acrefore/9780199329175 .001.0001/acrefore-9780199329175-e-317.

126. Nguyen, *Nothing Ever Dies*, 234.

127. Nguyen, *Nothing Ever Dies*, 234.

128. "War Legacy Issues in Southeast Asia: Unexploded Ordnance," Congressional Research Service, June 3, 2019, https://fas.org/sgp/crs /weapons/R45749.pdf.

129. Nguyen, *Nothing Ever Dies*, 220.

130. Robert D. Kaplan, *Imperial Grunts: The American Military on the Ground* (New York: Random House, 2005), 134. See US Embassy in the Philippines, "U.S. and Philippine Special Forces Train to Counter Insurgency," February 27, 2020, https://ph.usembassy.gov/us-and -philippine-special-forces-train-to-counter-insurgency.

131. "Truman Doctrine: President Harry S. Truman's Address Before a Joint Session of Congress, March 12, 1947," Avalon Project, Yale Law School, Lillian Goldman Law Library, https://avalon.law.yale.edu/20th_century /trudoc.asp.

132. "Refugee Statistics," UN High Commissioner for Refugees, December 2019, https://www.unrefugees.org/refugee-facts/statistics.

133. Patrick Cockburn, "America's War on Terror Is the True Cause of Europe's Refugee Crisis," *Counterpunch*, September 15, 2020, https:// www.counterpunch.org/2020/09/15/americas-war-on-terror-is-the -true-cause-of-europes-refugee-crisis. See also Alexander Betts, "Analyzing the New EU Asylum Policy," *Amanpour & Co.*, PBS, September 24, 2020, http://www.pbs.org/wnet/amanpour-and-company /video/analyzing-the-new-eu-asylum-policy.

134. Nima Elbagir, "A Crisis Made in Yemen," *Democracy Now*, September 17, 2020, https://www.democracynow.org/2020/9/17/yemen_crisis_us_uae _saudi_arabia.

135. Edward W. Said, *The Question of Palestine* (New York: Vintage, 1992), 3.

136. Rashid Khalidi, *The Hundred Years' War on Palestine: A History of Settler Colonialism and Resistance, 1917–2017* (New York: Metropolitan Books, 2020).

137. Khalidi, *The Hundred Years' War on Palestine*, 55–95.

138. UNRWA, "Palestine Refugees," UN Relief and Works Agency for Palestine Refugees in the Near East, https://www.unrwa.org/palestine -refugees; Ken Kurson, "Palestinian Americans," *Countries and Their Cultures*, https://www.everyculture.com/multi/Pa-Sp/Palestinian -Americans.html.

139. Mark J. Gasiorowski, "The 1953 Coup d'État in Iran," *International Journal of Middle East Studies* 19, no. 3 (1987): 261–86, www.jstor.org /stable/163655. See also Bethany Allen-Ebrahimian, "64 Years Later, CIA Finally Releases Details of Iranian Coup," *Foreign Policy*, June 20, 2017, https://foreignpolicy.com/2017/06/20/64-years-later-cia-finally-releases -details-of-iranian-coup-iran-tehran-oil.

140. Stephen Kinzer, *All the Shah's Men: An American Coup and the Roots of Middle East Terror* (Hoboken, NJ: John Wiley, 2008), 2.

141. See Nikki R. Keddie, *Modern Iran: Roots and Results of Revolution* (New Haven, CT: Yale University Press, 2003).

142. Naveed Mansoori, "Covering Race and Rebellion," *Jadaliyya*, September 4, 2019, https://www.jadaliyya.com/Details/39945.

143. "Iranian Americans: Immigration and Assimilation," Public Affairs Alliance of Iranian Americans (PAAIA), Washington, DC, April 2014, 2–3.

144. Richard Immerman, "Brezenski [sic] Memoranda to Carter on Soviet Intervention in Afghanistan, December 26, 1979," Temple University website, https://sites.temple.edu/immerman/brezenski-memoranda-to -carter-on-soviet-intervention-in-afghanistan.

145. "A Timeline of Key Events in Afghanistan's 40 Years of Wars," Associated Press, February 29, 2020, https://apnews.com/article/7011b50 86a21f7f57c3cb218947742b2.

146. Jeremy Kuzmarov, *Obama's Unending Wars: Fronting the Foreign Policy of the Permanent Warfare State* (Atlanta: Clarity Press, 2019), 118–42.

147. "Timeline of the Muslim Ban," American Civil Liberties Union (ACLU), Washington, DC, https://www.aclu-wa.org/pages/timeline-muslim-ban.

148. Elliot Young, "Immigrant Families Are the Second Casualty of War," History News Network, February 14, 2021, https://historynewsnetwork .org/article/179135.

149. Ngai, *Impossible Subjects*, 258–59.

150. Ngai, *Impossible Subjects*, 260.

151. Quoted in Ngai, *Impossible Subjects*, 259.

152. Ngai, *Impossible Subjects*, 262, 265.

153. Jie Zong and Jeanne Batalova, *Indian Immigrants in the United States* (Washington, DC: Migration Policy Institute, August 31, 2017), https://www.migrationpolicy.org/article/indian-immigrants-united-states-2015.

154. Dahini Jeyathurai, "The State of Statelessness," South Asian American Digital Archive, January 21, 2012. See Gaiutra Bahadur, *Coolie Woman: The Odyssey of Indenture* (Chicago: University of Chicago Press, 2014).

155. Jan Jeimert Jorgensen, *Uganda: A Modern History* (Oxfordshire, UK: Taylor & Francis, 1981).

156. See Jack Forbes, *Native Americans and Nixon: Presidential Politics and Minority Self-Determination, 1969–72* (Los Angeles: American Indian Studies Center, 1981). Historian Jack Forbes documents and analyzes the process President Richard Nixon and his advisers took in an attempt to discredit the Black civil rights movement by elevating a "model minority," first considering Native Americans for that role. That backfired when, in November 1972, Native activists formed a cross-country caravan that ended in Washington, DC, and their takeover of the Bureau of Indian Affairs building, renaming it Native American Embassy.

157. Ngai, *Impossible Subjects*, 267.

158. Lisa Lowe, *Immigrant Acts: On Asian American Cultural Politics* (Durham, NC: Duke University Press, 1996), 174–77.

159. Jodi Byrd, *The Transit of Empire: Indigenous Critiques of Colonialism* (Minneapolis: University of Minnesota Press, 2011), 51–52.

160. Nguyen, *Nothing Ever Dies*, 220.

CHAPTER 8: THE BORDER

1. Dan Restrepo and Ann Garcia, "The Surge of Unaccompanied Children from Central America," Center for American Progress, July 24, 2014, https://www.americanprogress.org/issues/immigration/reports/2014/07/24/94396/the-surge-of-unaccompanied-children-from-central-america-root-causes-and-policy-solutions.

2. Barbie Latza Nadeau, "Fox Refers to El Salvador, Guatemala and Honduras as 'Three Mexican Countries,'" *Daily Beast*, May 31, 2019.

3. Jeffrey S. Passel and D'Vera Cohn, "Overall Number of U.S. Unauthorized Immigrants Holds Steady Since 2009," Pew Research Center, September 20, 2016.

4. Brendan O'Connor, *Blood-Red Lines: How Nativism Fuels the Right* (New York: Haymarket Books, 2021), 55–57, 68–69, 71.

5. Jean Guerrero, *Hatemonger: Stephen Miller, Donald Trump, and the White Nationalist Agenda* (New York: William Morrow, 2020), 56–59; see also Victor Hanson Davis, *Mexifornia: A State of Becoming* (New York: Encounter Books, 2007).

6. Guerrero, *Hatemonger*, 4. See also Roberto Lovato, *Unforgetting: A*

Memoir of Family, Migration, Gangs, and Revolution in the Americas (New York: Harper Collins, 2020).

7. See Richard Hofstadter, *The Paranoid Style in American Politics* (1964; repr., New York: Vintage Books, 2008).

8. Samuel P. Huntington, "The Hispanic Challenge," *Foreign Policy*, October 28, 2009, https://foreignpolicy.com/2009/10/28/the-hispanic -challenge. See also Samuel P. Huntington, *Who Are We? The Challenges to America's National Identity* (New York: Simon & Schuster, 2005).

9. Text of Patrick Crusius, "Manifesto: The Inconvenient Truth," *Grabancijas*, May 8, 2019, https://grabancijas.com/patrick-crusius -manifesto-the-inconvenient-truth; Adam Elmahrek, Melissa Etehad, and Matthew Ormseth, "Suspect in El Paso Massacre 'Didn't Hold Anything Back' in Police Interrogation," *Los Angeles Times*, August 4, 2019, https://www.latimes.com/world-nation/story/2019-08-03/what-we -know-about-patrick-crusius-el-paso-rampage.

10. "San Ysidro Massacre," *San Diego Union-Tribune*, July 19, 1984, www.sandiegouniontribune.com/sdut-san-ysidro-massacre-1984jul19 -story.html. See also Dunbar-Ortiz, *Loaded*, 35.

11. Roberto D. Hernández, *Coloniality of the US/Mexico Border: Power, Violence, and the Decolonial Imperative* (Tucson: University of Arizona Press, 2018), 112–13.

12. See Roxanne Dunbar-Ortiz, *An Indigenous Peoples' History of the United States* (Boston: Beacon Press, 2014), 15–31.

13. See Hernández, *Coloniality of the US/México Border*, 154–80.

14. "The border crossed us!" is a Chicano affirmation. See Rodolfo F. Acuña, *Anything But Mexican: Chicanos in Contemporary Los Angeles* (New York: Verso Books, 1996), 109–38.

15. Ronald E. Hall, "They Lynched Mexican-Americans Too: A Question of Anglo Colorism," *Hispanic Journal of Behavioral Sciences*, January 20, 2020; Matthew Wills, "The Untold History of Lynching in the American West," *JSTOR Daily*, March 26, 2019, https://daily.jstor.org/the-untold -history-of-lynching-in-the-american-west.

16. William D. Carrigan and Clive Webb, *Forgotten Dead: Mob Violence Against Mexicans in the United States, 1848–1928* (New York: Oxford University Press, 2017), 77–78.

17. Guerrero, *Hatemonger*, 16.

18. See Ian Haney López, "White Latinos," *Harvard Latino Law Review* 6, 2003, 1–7.

19. Ngai, *Impossible Subjects*, 74.

20. Acuña, *Anything But Mexican*.

21. Ricardo Romo, *East Los Angeles: History of a Barrio* (Austin: University of Texas Press, 1933), 90–91; quoted in Acuña, *Anything But Mexican*, 110.

22. Harsha Walia, *Border and Rule: Global Migration, Capitalism, and the Rise of Racist Nationalism* (New York: Haymarket Books, 2021), 33.

23. See "Texas-México Center," Southern Methodist University, Dedman College of Humanities and Sciences, https://www.smu.edu/Dedman /Research/Institutes-and-Centers/Texas-México/About/Timeline.

24. Immigration Act of 1917, 39 Stat. 874; see "Immigration Act of 1917 (Barred Zone Act)," Immigration History, https://immigrationhistory.org /item/1917-barred-zone-act.

25. US Congress, 1925 [1924], p. 159 (as determined by "country of birth"); US Congress 1925 [1924], p. 160. See Ngai, *Impossible Subjects*, 21–55.

26. Ramón A. Gutiérrez, "Mexican Immigration to the United States," *Oxford Research Encyclopedia: American History*, July 2019, 7, https:// oxfordre.com/americanhistory/view/10.1093/acrefore/9780199329175 .001.0001/acrefore-9780199329175-e-146#:~:text=The%20Mexican %20immigrant%20population%20of,1920%3B%20and%20641%2 C000%20in%201930.

27. Gutiérrez, "Mexican Immigration to the United States," 7.

28. Quoted in Cybelle Fox, *Three Worlds of Relief: Race, Immigration, and the American Welfare State from the Progressive Era to the New Deal* (Princeton, NJ: Princeton University Press, 2012), 41.

29. Gutiérrez, "Mexican Immigration to the United States," 8.

30. Robert R. Alvarez Jr., "The Lemon Grove Incident," *Journal of San Diego History* 32, no. 2 (Spring 1986), https://sandiegohistory.org/journal/1986 /april/lemongrove.

31. Tomas Almaguer, *Racial Fault Lines: The Historical Origins of White Supremacy in California* (Berkeley: University of California Press, 1994), 57.

32. Cybelle Fox and Thomas A. Guglielmo, "Defining America's Racial Boundaries: Blacks, Mexicans, and European Immigrants, 1890–1945," *American Journal of Sociology* 118, no. 2 (September 2012): 353, 356, 358, 361, https://www.jstor.org/stable/10.1086/666383?seq=3#metadata _info_tab_contents; US Bureau of the Census, 1933, 27.

33. Ngai, *Impossible Subjects*, 71.

34. Fox, *Three Worlds of Relief*, 124.

35. Fox, *Three Worlds of Relief*, 72.

36. Gutiérrez, "Mexican Immigration to the United States," 8–9.

37. California SB670, Dunn Mexican Repatriation Program of the 1930s, 2–5. See Gutiérrez, "Mexican Immigration to the United States," 9.

38. Kitty Calavila, *Inside the State: The Bracero Program, Immigration, and the INS* (New Orleans: Quid Pro Books, 2010), 18–21; see also Justin Akers Chacón and Mike Davis, *No One Is Illegal: Fighting Racism and State Violence on the U.S.-México Border*, 2nd ed. (New York: Haymarket Books, 2018), 139–48.

39. Calavila, *Inside the State*, 2–3.

40. President's Commission on Migratory Labor, 1951, 69; see Robert S. Robinson, "Taking the Fair Deal to the Fields: Truman's Commission on Migratory Labor, Public Law 78, and the Bracero Program, 1950–1952,"

Agricultural History 84, no. 3 (2010): 381–402, http://www.jstor.org /stable/27868998.

41. Ngai, *Impossible Subjects*, 139.

42. Ngai, *Impossible Subjects*, 139.

43. Gutiérrez, "Mexican Immigration to the United States," 11; see also Chacón and Davis, *No One Is Illegal*, 191–96.

44. Calavila, *Inside the State*, 133–35; see also Ernesto Galarza, *Merchants of Labor: The Mexican Bracero Story; An Account of the Managed Migration of Mexican Farm Workers in California, 1942–1960* (Santa Barbara, CA: McNally & Loftin, 1964).

45. Erasmo Gamboa, "Mexican Migration into Washington State: A History, 1940–1950," *Pacific Northwest Quarterly* 72, no. 3 (1981): 125. See also Erasmo Gamboa, "Braceros in the Pacific Northwest: Laborers on the Domestic Front, 1942–1947," *Pacific Historical Review* 56, no. 3 (1987): 378–98, www.jstor.org/stable/3638664.

46. Mario Jimenez Sifuentez, *Of Forests and Fields: Mexican Labor in the Pacific Northwest* (New Brunswick, NJ: Rutgers University Press, 2016), 25.

47. Erasmo Gamboa, *Mexican Labor and World War II: Braceros in the Pacific Northwest, 1942–1947* (Seattle: University of Washington Press, 1990), 85.

48. Sifuentez, *Of Forests and Fields*, 28–29.

49. Gutiérrez, "Mexican Immigration to the United States," 11.

50. Tim Z. Hernandez, *All They Will Call You* (Tucson: University of Arizona Press, 2017), 204.

51. Hernandez, *All They Will Call You*, 177.

52. Kelly Lytle Hernandez, "Largest Deportation Campaign in US History Is No Match for Trump's Plan," *The Conversation*, March 8, 2017, https:// theconversation.com/largest-deportation-campaign-in-us-history-is-no -match-for-trumps-plan-73651. See also Kelly Lytle Hernández, *Migra! A History of the U.S. Border Patrol* (Berkeley: University of California Press, 2010).

53. Bruce Lambert, "Harlon B. Carter, Longtime Head of Rifle Association, Dies at 78," *New York Times*, November 22, 1991, https://www.nytimes .com/1991/11/22/us/harlon-b-carter-longtime-head-of-rifle-association -dies-at-78.html. See Mark Ames, "From 'Operation Wetback' to New-town: Tracing the Hick Fascism of the NRA," *Pando*, December 17, 2012, www.nsfwcorp.com/dispatch/newtown; Joel Achenbach, Scott Higham, and Sari Horwitz, "How NRA's True Believers Converted a Marksmanship Group into a Mighty Gun Lobby," *Washington Post*, January 12, 2013, www. washingtonpost.com/politics/how-nras-true - believers-converted-a-marksmanship-group-into-a-mighty-gun-lobby /2013/01/12/51c62288-59b9-11e2-88d0-c4cf65c3ad15_story.html. See also Dunbar-Ortiz, *Loaded*.

54. Hernandez, "Largest Deportation Campaign in US History Is No Match for Trump's Plan."

55. Hernandez, "Largest Deportation Campaign in US History Is No Match for Trump's Plan." See also Matt Ballinger, "From the Archives: How the Times Covered Mass Deportations in the Eisenhower Era," *Los Angeles Times*, 2020, https://documents.latimes.com/eisenhower-era-deportations.

56. Hernandez, "Largest Deportation Campaign in US History Is No Match for Trump's Plan."

57. Ngai, *Impossible Subjects*, 155.

58. Ngai, *Impossible Subjects*, 157.

59. Hernandez, "Largest Deportation Campaign in US History Is No Match for Trump's Plan."

60. Quoted in Ngai, *Impossible Subjects*, 259.

61. Ngai, *Impossible Subjects*, 260–61.

62. Nicholas P. De Genova, "Migrant 'Illegality' and Deportability in Everyday Life," *Annual Review of Anthropology* 31, 2002, 436, www.jstor.org/stable/4132887.

63. Gutiérrez, "Mexican Immigration to the United States," 13.

64. Gabriel Thompson, "Fred Ross," Zinn Education Project, 2013, https://www.zinnedproject.org/materials/ross-fred.

65. David Gutiérrez, *Walls and Mirrors: Mexican Americans, Mexican Immigrants, and the Politics of Ethnicity* (Berkeley: University of California Press, 1995), 197–98. See also Miriam Pawel, *The Crusades of Cesar Chavez: A Biography* (New York: Bloomsbury Press, 2014); Frank Bardacke, *Trampling Out the Vintage: Cesar Chavez and the Two Souls of the United Farm Workers* (New York: Verso Books, 2012).

66. Pawel, *The Crusades of Cesar Chavez*, 197–213.

67. Julie Leininger Pycior, *Democratic Renewal and the Mutual Aid Legacy of US Mexicans* (College Station: Texas A&M Press, 2014); Alexandra Délano Alonso, *México and Its Diaspora in the United States: Policies of Emigration Since 1848* (New York: Cambridge University Press, 2011), 74–76; Juan Gómez-Quiñones, "Notes on an Interpretation of the Relations Between the Mexican Community in the U.S. and México," in *Mexican-U.S. Relations: Conflict and Convergence*, ed. Carlos Vasquez and Manuel Garcia y Griego (Los Angeles: Chicano Studies Research Center Publications, 1983), 417–39.

68. Chronicle News Service, "Remittances Increase Despite Virus Travails," *San Francisco Chronicle*, October 6, 2020, A6, https://www.pressreader.com/usa/san-francisco-chronicle/20201006/281651077565696.

69. National Network for Immigrant and Refugee Rights, http://www.nnirr.org/drupal.

70. Gutiérrez, "Mexican Immigration to the United States," 14.

71. Gutiérrez, "Mexican Immigration to the United States," 14–15; see Nevins, *Operation Gatekeeper*, 67–70.

72. For a history of the EZLN, see Gloria Muñoz Ramírez, *The Fire and the Word: A History of the Zapatista Movement* (San Francisco: City Lights, 2008); Hilary Klein, *Compañeras: Zapatista Women's Stories* (New York: Seven Stories Press, 2015).

73. See Acuña, *Anything But Mexican*, 231–49.

74. Grandin, *The End of the Myth*, 233–35.

75. Grandin, *The End of the Myth*, 244–45.

76. Gutiérrez, "Mexican Immigration to the United States," 15.

77. "Analysis of Immigration Detention Policies," American Civil Liberties Union, Washington, DC, https://www.aclu.org/other/analysis -immigration-detention-policies.

78. Lisa C. Solbakken, "The Anti-Terrorism and Effective Death Penalty Act: Anti-Immigration Legislation Veiled in an Anti-Terrorism Pretext," *Brooklyn Law Review* 63, no. 4 (1997): 1382.

79. Gutiérrez, "Mexican Immigration to the United States," 17–18.

80. Gutiérrez, "Mexican Immigration to the United States," 19.

81. Gutiérrez, "Mexican Immigration to the United States," 18.

82. Jeffrey S. Passel and D'Vera Cohn, "As Mexican Share Declined, U.S. Unauthorized Immigrant Population Fell in 2015 Below Recession Level," Pew Research Center, June 12, 2019.

83. "Deferred Action for Childhood Arrivals (DACA)," Howard University School of Law, Washington, DC, https://library.law.howard.edu /civilrightshistory/immigration/daca.

84. The White House, "Preserving and Fortifying Deferred Action for Childhood Arrivals (DACA)," *Presidential Actions*, January 20, 2021, https://www.whitehouse.gov/briefing-room/presidential-actions /2021/01/20/preserving-and-fortifying-deferred-action-for-childhood -arrivals-daca.

85. Mike Davis and Jon Wiener, *Set the Night on Fire: L.A. in the Sixties* (New York: Verso Books, 2020), 572–73.

86. Rodolfo Acuña, *Occupied America: A History of Chicanos* (New York: Pearson Longman, 2002), 343; see also Hernández, *Coloniality of the US/ Mexico Border*, 169–71.

87. Acuña, *Occupied America*, 312, 315–21, 329, 347, 350–400.

88. Lorena Oropeza, *Raza Si, Guerra No: Chicano Protest and Patriotism During the Viet Nam War Era* (Berkeley: University of California Press, 2005), 155; see also George Mariscal, *Aztlán and Viet Nam: Chicano and Chicana Experiences of the War* (Berkeley: University of California Press, 1999).

89. For an excellent analysis of the US demand for assimilation, see Catherine S. Ramírez, *Assimilation: An Alternative History* (Berkeley: University of California Press, 2020).

90. Elly Lary and Anne Lewis, "Interview with Bill Gallegos," *Monthly Review*, October 1, 2015, https://monthlyreview.org/2002/07/01/a-view-from-new

-mexico/; Elizabeth (Betita) Martínez, *A View from New Mexico: Recollections of the Movimiento Left,*" *Monthly Review,* July 1, 2002, https://monthlyreview.org/2002/07/01/a-view-from-new-mexico.

91. "National Oppression, National Liberation and Socialist Revolution," Freedom Road Socialist Organization, adopted in 2004, https://frso.org/main-documents/statement-on-national-oppression-national-liberation-and-socialist-revolution.

92. Liberation Road, "Unity Statement on Racism, National Oppression, Self-Determination, and Strategy for U.S. Socialism," https://roadtoliberation.org/unity-statement-on-national-oppression, accessed May 20, 2021.

93. Davis and Wiener, *Set the Night on Fire,* 539–40.

94. See Alejandro Murguía, *Southern Front* (San Francisco: Bilingual Press/Editorial Bilingue, 1990).

95. President James Monroe, Transcript of Monroe Doctrine, 7th Annual Message to Congress, December 2, 1823, https://www.ourdocuments.gov/doc.php?flash=false&doc=23&page=transcript.

96. Robert A. Naylor, "The British Role in Central America Prior to the Clayton-Bulwer Treaty of 1850," *Hispanic American Historical Review* 40, no. 3 (1960): 361–82, www.jstor.org/stable/2509955.

97. Jonathan D. Del Buono, "The Business of Empire: American Capitalists, the Nicaraguan Canal, and the Monroe Doctrine, 1849–1858" (master's thesis, University of Montana, 2017), https://scholarworks.umt.edu/etd/10951.

98. Brian Loveman, "US Foreign Policy Toward Latin America in the 19th Century," *Oxford Research Encyclopedias: Latin American History,* July 2016.

99. Michel Gobat, "The Invention of Latin America: A Transnational History of Anti-Imperialism, Democracy, and Race," *American Historical Review* 118, no. 5 (December 2013): 1345–75, 1364. The author notes that South American support for the Central American war against Walker was highly unusual, as similar forms of transnational solidarity do not seem to have marked other anti-imperial struggles of the era. See also Johnson, *River of Dark Dreams,* 367–94.

100. Marc Becker, *History of U.S. Interventions in Latin America,* 2011, https://www.yachana.org/teaching/resources/interventions.html.

101. See Holly Sklar, *Washington's War on Nicaragua* (Boston: South End Press, 1999); Roxanne Dunbar-Ortiz, *Blood on the Border: A Memoir of the Contra War* (Norman: University of Oklahoma Press, 2016).

102. "Case Concerning the Military and Paramilitary Activities in and Against Nicaragua (Nicaragua v. United States of America)," http://www.icj-cij.org/en/case/70. See also Abram Chayes, "Nicaragua, the United States, and the World Court," *Columbia Law Review* 85, no. 7 (November 1985): 1445–82.

103. See Carolyn Forché, *What You Have Heard Is True: A Memoir of*

Witness and Resistance (New York: Penguin Books, 2020); see also Mark Danner, *The Massacre at El Mozote* (New York: Vintage Books, 1994).

104. See Beatriz Manz, *Paradise in Ashes: A Guatemalan Journey of Courage, Terror, and Hope* (Berkeley: University of California Press, 2005); see also Brennan Grayson and Dave Tynes, *Sanctuary Matters: The Betrayal of Cincinnati's New Immigrants* (Cincinnati: Interfaith Workers Center, 2020), 21–22.

105. Paul A. Kramer, "Sanctuary Unmasked: The First Time Los Angeles (Sort of) Became a City of Refuge," *Los Angeles Review of Books*, October 25, 2020, https://lareviewofbooks.org/article/sanctuary -unmasked-the-first-time-los-angeles-sort-of-became-a-city-of-refuge.

106. Kramer, "Sanctuary Unmasked."

107. Susan Gzesh, "Central Americans and Asylum Policy in the Reagan Era," Migration Policy Institute, Washington DC, April 1, 2006, https://www.migrationpolicy.org/article/central-americans-and-asylum -policy-reagan-era#:~:text=It%20is%20estimated%20that%20 between,entering%20the%20United%20States%20clandestinely .&text=However%2C%20thousands%20were%20also%20detained ,near%20the%20México%2DU.S.%20border.

108. Brian D'Haeseleer, Charles F. Hewlett, Jeremy Kuzmarov, John Marciano, Robert Peace, and Virginia S. Williams, "Central America Wars, 1980s," *United States Foreign Policy: History and Resource Guide*, http://peacehistory-usfp.org/central-america-wars/#:~:text=Between %201981%20and%201990%2C%20an,and%20entered%20the%20 United%20States.

109. Ronald Reagan, "Central America Is of Great Importance to the United States," speech, *Washington Post*, May 10, 1984, https://www .washingtonpost.com/archive/politics/1984/05/10/central-america-is-of -great-importance-to-the-united-states/c3d60464-205b-45f4-bd03 -b5164363df37.

110. Preview of *Red Dawn*, https://www.youtube.com/watch?v=mRTzUH mx9ZA.

111. Elisabeth Bumiller, "Alexander Haig, Returning Fire," *Washington Post*, June 24, 1984.

112. Rita Beamish, "Moviemakers, Government Say 'Rambo,' 'Rock' Just Show Biz, Not Propaganda," *Associated Press News*, February 9, 1986, https://apnews.com/article/246c33a4e9b5dcafoe318aa9dddee009.

113. "Central America Refugee Crisis," UN High Commissioner for Refugees, 2019, https://www.unrefugees.org/emergencies/central-america.

114. Hayyoun Park, "Children at the Border," *New York Times*, October 21, 2014, https://www.nytimes.com/interactive/2014/07/15/us/questions -about-the-border-kids.html.

115. Clayton M. Cunha Fiho, André Luiz Coelho, and Fidel I. Pérez Flores, "A Right-to-Left Policy Switch? An Analysis of the Honduran Case

Under Manuel Zelaya," *International Political Science Review* 34, no. 5 (2013): 519–42.

116. "Debate on Honduras: Former Clinton Lawyer Lanny Davis, Lobbyist for Honduras Business Leaders vs. NYU Historian Greg Grandin," *Democracy Now*, August 7, 2009.

117. Mark Weisbrot, "Hard Choices: Hillary Clinton Admits Role in Honduran Coup Aftermath," *Al Jazeera America*, September 29, 2014, http://america.aljazeera.com/opinions/2014/9/hillary-clinton-honduraslatinamericaforeignpolicy.html. See also Dana Frank, "Hopeless in Honduras? The Election and the Future of Tegucigalpa," *Foreign Affairs*, November 22, 2013.

118. Jake Johnston, "How Pentagon Officials May Have Encouraged a 2009 Coup in Honduras," *The Intercept*, August 29, 2017; Jeremy Kuzmarov, "Obama Administration Report Card on Foreign Policy," *Huffington Post*, December 12, 2017.

119. *Human Development Report 2014* (New York: United Nations Development Program [UNDP], 2014), http://hdr.undp.org/sites/default/files/hdr14-summary-en.pdf.

120. Gloria Carrión, "The Political Economy of Domestic Resource Mobilization in Nicaragua: Changing State-Citizen Relations and Social Development," UN Research Institute for Social Development (UNRISD), 2019.

121. Yorlis Gabriela Luna, "The Other Nicaragua, Empire and Resistance," Council on Hemispheric Affairs (COHA), Washington, DC, October 2, 2019, https://www.coha.org/the-other-nicaragua-empire-and-resistance.

122. Laura Briggs, *Taking Children: A History of American Terror* (Berkeley: University of California Press, 2020), 3–4, https://www.amazon.com/Taking-Children-History-American-Terror/dp/0520343670.

123. Amnesty International, *USA: "You Don't Have Any Rights Here"* (London: Amnesty International, 2018), 6–7, https://www.amnesty.org/download/Documents/AMR5191012018ENGLISH.PDF.

124. Convention on the Prevention and Punishment of the Crime of Genocide, adopted by the General Assembly of the UN, December 9, 1948, https://treaties.un.org/doc/publication/unts/volume%2078/volume-78-i-1021-english.pdf.

125. Michael D. Shear, Katie Benner, and Michael S. Schmidt, "'We Need to Take Away Children,' No Matter How Young, Justice Dept. Officials Said," *New York Times*, October 8, 2020, https://www.nytimes.com/2020/10/06/us/politics/family-separation-border-immigration-jeff-sessions-rod-rosenstein.html.

126. Caitlin Dickerson, "Detention of Migrant Children Has Skyrocketed to Highest Levels Ever," *New York Times*, September 12, 2018, https://www.nytimes.com/2018/09/12/us/migrant-children-detention.html.

127. Briggs, *Taking Children*, 7–8; Walia, *Border and Rule*, 36–37.

128. Ed Pilkington, "Parents of 545 Children Still Not Found Three Years

After Trump Separation Policy," *Guardian*, October 21, 2020, https://www.theguardian.com/us-news/2020/oct/21/trump-separation-policy-545-children-parents-still-not-found.

129. Walia, *Border and Rule*, 3.

130. Christina Leza, "For Native Americans, US-México Border Is an 'Imaginary Line,'" *The Conversation*, March 19, 2019; see map at https://decolonialatlas.wordpress.com/2017/03/21/the-border-la-frontera. See also "Tribal Governance," National Congress of American Indians, Washington, DC, http://www.ncai.org/policy-issues/tribal-governance. For extensive discussion of Trump's obsession with a border wall, see Julie Hirschfeld Davis and Michael D. Shear, *Border Wars: Inside Trump's Assault on Immigration* (New York: Simon & Schuster, 2019).

131. Alejandro Prieto, "Wall of the Wild: Animals on the U.S.-Mexico Border —in Pictures," *Guardian*, October 26, 2020, https://www.theguardian.com/environment/gallery/2020/oct/26/wall-of-the-wild-animals-on-the-us-mexico-border-in-pictures-aoe.

132. Nevins, *Operation Gatekeeper*, x.

133. Alexandra Délano Alonso, "Abolish ICE. For a Start," *New York Times*, December 3, 2020.

CONCLUSION

1. Mamdani, "Settler Colonialism: Then and Now," 607.

2. Mamdani, *Neither Settler nor Native*, 95.

3. Mamdani, *Neither Settler nor Native*, xxix, xx.

4. William H. Frey, "21st Century Immigration Favors Asians and College Grads as the US Foreign-Born Share Rises," *The Avenue*, Brookings, September 24, 2018, https://www.brookings.edu/blog/the-avenue/2018/09/24/21st-century-immigration-favors-asians-and-college-grads-as-the-us-foreign-born-share-rises. For insight into the reception of non-European immigrants in the Midwest, read the 1989 fiction account *Jasmine* by the South Asian immigrant author Bharati Mukherjee.

5. Alana Abramson, "How Donald Trump Perpetuated the 'Birther' Movement for Years," ABC News, September 16, 2016, https://abcnews.go.com/Politics/donald-trump-perpetuated-birther-movement-years/story?id=42138176.

6. Suketu Mehta, *This Land Is Our Land: An Immigrant's Manifesto* (New York: Farrar, Straus & Giroux, 2019), 61.

7. Mehta, *This Land Is Our Land*, 208.

8. Mehta, *This Land Is Our Land*, 212.

9. Mehta, *This Land Is Our Land*, 101–4.

10. Mehta, *This Land Is Our Land*, 128.

11. Byrd, *The Transit of Empire*, xix.

12. Laila Lalami, *Conditional Citizens: On Belonging in America* (New York: Pantheon, 2020).

13. Lalami, *Conditional Citizens*, 5–6.
14. Lalami, *Conditional Citizens*, 9–22.
15. Lalami, *Conditional Citizens*, 72–92.
16. Lisa Lowe, "The Intimacies of Four Continents," in *Haunted by Empire: Geographies of Intimacy in North American History*, ed. Ann Laura Stoler (Durham, NC: Duke University Press, 2006), 207.
17. See Sonia Chatterjee, "Immigration, Anti-Racism, and Indigenous Self-Determination: Towards a Comprehensive Analysis of the Contemporary Settler Colonial," *Social Identities: Journal for the Study of Race, Nation and Culture* 25, no. 5 (2019): 644–61.
18. Dean Itsuji Saranillio, "Why Asian Settler Colonialism Matters: A Thought Piece on Critiques, Debates, and Indigenous Difference," *Settler Colonial Studies* 3, no. 3–4 (2013): 280, https://www.academia.edu/4691386/Why_Asian_Settler_Colonialism_Matters_a_Thought_Piece_on_Critiques_Debates_and_Indigenous_Difference.
19. Saranillio, "Why Asian Settler Colonialism Matters," 281.
20. Ramon Lopez-Reyes, "The Re-Inscription of Hawaii on the United Nations' List of Non-Self-Governing Territories," *Peace Research* 28, no. 3 (August 1996): 71, https://www.jstor.org/stable/23607288?seq=1; Mililani B. Trask, "Hawai'i and the United Nations," *Cultural Survival Quarterly Magazine* (March 2000), https://www.culturalsurvival.org/publications/cultural-survival-quarterly/hawaii-and-united-nations.
21. Iyko Day, *Alien Capital: Asian Racialization and the Logic of Settler Colonial Capitalism* (Durham, NC: Duke University Press, 2016), 19–20.
22. Byrd, *The Transit of Empire*, xix.
23. Craig Fortier, *Unsettling the Commons: Social Movements Within, Against, and Beyond Settler Colonialism* (Winnipeg: ARP Books, 2017), 32.
24. Bonita Lawrence and Enakshi Dua, "Decolonizing Antiracism," *Social Justice* 32, no. 4 (2005): 120–43, https://www.jstor.org/stable/29768340.
25. Nandita Sharma and Cynthia Wright, "Decolonizing Resistance, Challenging Colonial States," *Social Justice* 35, no. 3 (2008–9): 120–38.
26. Sharma and Wright, "Decolonizing Resistance, Challenging Colonial States," 127–28.
27. Sharma and Wright, "Decolonizing Resistance, Challenging Colonial States," 204; see also Craig Fortier, "No One Is Illegal, Canada Is Illegal! Negotiating the Relationships Between Settler Colonialism and Border Imperialism Through Political Slogans," *Decolonization: Indigeneity, Education and Society* (September 21, 2015), https://decolonization.wordpress.com/2015/09/21/no-one-is-illegal-canada-is-illegal-negotiating-the-relationships-between-settler-colonialism-and-border-imperialism-through-political-slogans.
28. "No One Is Illegal," rabble.ca, https://rabble.ca/toolkit/rabblepedia/no-one-illegal.
29. Harsha Walia, *Undoing Border Imperialism* (Oakland: AK Press, 2013).

30. Harsha Walia, "Decolonizing Together: Moving Beyond a Politics of Solidarity Toward a Practice of Decolonization," in *The Winter We Danced: Voices from the Past, the Future, and the Idle No More Movement*, ed. Kino-nda-niimi Collective (Winnipeg: Arbeiter Ring, 2014), 44–51, http://www.wrongkindofgreen.org/2013/08/13/decolonizing-together -moving-beyond-a-politics-of-solidarity-toward-a-practice-of -decolonization.

31. Fong Yue Ting v. United States, 149 U.S., p. 706; quoted in Ngai, *Impossible Subjects*, 11.

32. Fong Yue Ting v. United States, 149 U.S., p. 706.

33. Hixson, *American Settler Colonialism*, 197–98.

34. Hixson, *American Settler Colonialism*, 197–98.

35. Nguyen, *Nothing Ever Dies*, 221.

36. Nguyen, *Nothing Ever Dies*, 222.

37. Josh Peter, "Colin Kaepernick: I'm Not Anti-American, Will Donate $1 Million," *USA Today Sports*, September 1, 2016.

38. Theodore R. Johnson, "The Challenge of Black Patriotism," *New York Times Magazine*, November 18, 2020, https://www.nytimes.com/2020 /11/18/magazine/black-voters-election-patriotism.html.

39. James Baldwin, *Notes of a Native Son* (Boston: Beacon Press, 1955).

40. Donald J. Trump, "Remarks by President Trump at the White House Conference on American History," National Archives Museum, Washington, DC, September 17, 2020, https://www.whitehouse.gov /briefings-statements/remarks-president-trump-white-house-conference -american-history.

INDEX